RIFLEMEN
FORM

RIFLEMEN FORM

A Study of the Rifle Volunteer Movement

1859-1908

by

Ian F. W. Beckett

Pen & Sword
MILITARY

First published in Great Britain in 1982 by The Ogilby Trusts
Published in this format in 2007 by
PEN & SWORD MILITARY
an imprint of
Pen & Sword Books Ltd
47 Church Street
Barnsley
South Yorkshire
S70 2AS

ISBN 978 1 84415 612 2

A CIP catalogue record for this book is
available from the British Library

Printed and bound in Great Britain
By CPI UK

Pen & Sword Books Ltd incorporates the Imprints of
Pen & Sword Aviation, Pen & Sword Maritime, Pen & Sword Military,
Wharncliffe Local History, Pen & Sword Select,
Pen & Sword Military Classics and Leo Cooper.

For a complete list of Pen & Sword titles please contact:
PEN & SWORD BOOKS LIMITED
47 Church Street, Barnsley, South Yorkshire, S70 2AS, England
E-mail: enquiries@pen-and-sword.co.uk
Website: www.pen-and-sword.co.uk

For My Parents

THE OGILBY TRUSTS

The Army Museums Ogilby Trust was founded by the late Colonel R. J. L. Ogilby, D.S.O., D.L., in 1954 with the principal object of encouraging, equipping, caring for and maintaining existing Army and Regimental Museums. Since its formation the Trust has helped Regimental and other military Museums in a number of ways. As well as providing finance to enable them to purchase historical items of particular Regimental interest for the improvement of Regimental Collections, the Trust has itself purchased items of military and historical importance, and it has provided an advisory service which is available to Museum Trustees and Curators.

The Trust had also endeavoured to foster interest in regimental and military tradition by sponsoring the publication of certain printed works and catalogues. A number of copies of each book sponsored in this way have been distributed free of charge by the Trust to existing Army and Regimental Museums so as to provide them with authoritative works of reference. In addition, by making such books available to the general public, the Trust has endeavoured to stimulate and encourage interest in regimental and military tradition.

The Robert Ogilby Trust was founded in 1964 with aims similar to the Army Museums Ogilby Trust, but with wider powers of publication. This book has been produced by collaboration between the two Trusts.

The Trusts have their offices at Connaught Barracks, Duke of Connaught Road, Aldershot.

ACKNOWLEDGEMENTS

Quotations from Crown-copyright records in the Public Record Office and Greater London Record Office (Middlesex Records) appear by permission of Her Majesty's Stationery Office. Quotations from Post Office Records appear by courtesy of Post Office Records.

I am indebted to the following for permission to quote from private records:

The Marquess of Salisbury (Salisbury Papers, Hatfield House, Herts); Earl Kitchener (Kitchener/Marker Papers, British Museum); Lord Egremont (Petworth House Archives, West Sussex R.O.); Lady Barttelot and Major Sir Brian Barttelot, Bt. (Barttelot Papers, West Sussex R.O.); Sir Ralph Verney, Bt. (Verney/Calvert Papers, Claydon House); Sir Francis Hill (Hill 12th Deposit, Lincoln R.O.); Mrs J Burden (Dickinson Family Papers, Somerset R.O.); Mrs N Y Troyte-Bullock (Troyte-Bullock of Zeals House Papers, Wilts R.O.); E. S. Curwen, Esq. (Curwen Family Papers, Cumbria R.O.); Philip Haynes, Esq. (Hollingbourne, Kent); Messrs Heath and Blenkinsop (muster roll, Warwick R.O.); Messrs Mole, Metters and Forster (Mole. Metters and Forster deposit, Surrey R.O.); Mrs Wade-Gery (Wade-Gery Papers, Beds R.O.).

I wish to thank the following for making available papers in their care and for permission to quote:

The British Library Board (British Museum Dept. of Manuscripts); the Guildhall Library; the National Trust (Hughenden Papers); the Bodleian Library; the Army Museums Ogilby Trust (Spenser Wilkinson Papers); the National Army Museum; the Ministry of Defence Library (Central and Army) formerly the War Office Library; Guildford Muniments Room; Guildford Museum; Surrey Archaeological Society; Manchester Central Library; East Sussex County Library (Wolseley Papers, Hove); Archives and Local History Department, London Borough of Lewisham Library; and Castle Morpeth Borough Council (papers in Northumberland R.O.).

I especially wish to thank the following for their help in consulting regimental and local archives:

Lt.-Col. D. V. W. Wakely (Dorset Military Museum); the late Lt.-Col. E. A. T. Boggis (Wiltshire Regimental Museum); P. Douglas Niekirk, Esq. and David Colquhoun, Esq. (London Scottish Regimental Library); K. J. Collins, Esq. (Queen's Own Royal West Kent Regimental Museum); and W. W. Slade, Esq. (Gillingham Local History Society Museum, Gillingham, Dorset).

This book could not have been written without the courtesy and co-operation of the staffs of the County Record Offices and I wish to thank the following for their help and permission to quote from records in their possession:

Bedfordshire; Berkshire; Buckinghamshire; Cornwall; Cumbria; Devon; Dorset; Durham; Essex; Gwent; Greater London (Middlesex); Hampshire; Kent; Lancashire; Lincolnshire; Northamptonshire; Northumberland; Oxfordshire; Somerset; Staffordshire; Surrey; West Sussex; Warwickshire; and Wiltshire.

In particular, my thanks go to my old friends of the Buckinghamshire Record Office; the staff of the National Register of Archives for their initial help in tracing many collections and to the staffs of the Library of the Royal United Services Institute for Defence Studies, the Ministry of Defence Library (Central and Army), the University of Salford Library, the Open University Library, and the Library of the Royal Military Academy, Sandhurst.

My personal thanks for helpful advice and criticism go to members of the Institute of Historical Research military seminar, before whom parts of the original thesis were read, and to Mr Brian Bond and Dr Michael Dockrill of King's College, University of London, who acted as supervisors to the original thesis. Valuable advice has also been rendered by Professor Donald Read of the University of Kent; Professor Paul Smith, then of the University of London; Professor Harold Perkin of the University of Lancaster (chapter V); and my colleagues in the Department of War Studies and International Affairs at Sandhurst. Especial thanks go to Dr John Gooch of the University of Lancaster, who suggested the original research and assisted its progress and revision for publication in innumerable ways; Mr Arthur Taylor of Aylesbury Grammar School, who set me on the trail of the Auxiliary Forces many years ago; and to Miss Joan Cooper of the University of Salford, who valiantly undertook to type portions of the manuscript from the almost illegible scrawl (even when typed) with which she was presented. None of these, of course, can be held responsible for any errors that remain.

The author also gratefully acknowledges his thanks to Colonel P. S. Newton, Major J. M. A. Tamplin and Major A. F. Flatow of the Army Museums Ogilby Trust and to all the Trustees of the Robert Ogilby Trust, in particular Major S. G. P. Ward, for enabling this work to appear in print. Additional financial assistance has also been generously given towards publication by grants from the late Miss Isobel Thornley's Bequest to the University of London and the British Academy's Special Fund in Support of Academic Publications.

My greatest debt, however, goes to my wife and especially to my parents for their support over so many years. To the latter this book is gratefully dedicated.

ABBREVIATIONS USED IN THE TEXT

A.A.G.	Assistant Adjutant General
A.B.	Administrative Battalion
A.C.	Army Council
A.G.	Adjutant General
A.V.	Artillery Volunteers
C.G.S.	Chief of the General Staff
C. in C.	Commander-in-Chief
C.I.V.	City Imperial Volunteers
D.A.A.G.	Deputy Assistant Adjutant General
D.A.F.	Director of Auxiliary Forces
D.A.G.	Deputy Adjutant General
D.M.I.	Director of Military Intelligence
D.M.O.	Director of Military Operations
D.M.T.	Director of Military Training
D.N.I.	Director of Naval Intelligence
E.V.	Engineer Volunteers
I.G.A.F.	Inspector General of Auxiliary Forces
I.G.R.F.	Inspector General of Reserve Forces
I.Y.	Imperial Yeomanry
L.H.V.	Light Horse Volunteers
L.R.B.	London Rifle Brigade
M.G.O.	Master General of Ordnance
M.R.V.	Mounted Rifle Volunteers
Q.E.R.B.	Queen's Edinburgh Rifle Brigade
Q.M.G.	Quartermaster General
R.V.C.	Rifle Volunteer Corps
V.B.	Volunteer Battalion

ABBREVIATIONS USED IN FOOTNOTES

A.D.	Army Debates
A.Q.	Army Quarterly
B.M. Add.Mss.	British Museum Additional Manuscripts
B.P.P.	British Parliamentary Papers
E.H.R.	English Historical Review
G.L.R.O. (M).	Greater London Record Office (Middlesex Records)
H.J.	Historical Journal
I.N.M.M.	Illustrated Naval and Military Magazine
J.B.S.	Journal of British Studies
J.R.U.S.I.	Journal of the Royal United Services Institute
J.S.A.H.R.	Journal of the Society for Army Historical Research

L.B.	Liverpool Bulletin
L.S.R.G.	London Scottish Regimental Gazette
N.A.M.	National Army Museum
P.R.O.	Public Record Office
Q.O.G.	Queen's Own Gazette
	(Royal West Kent Regiment)
R.O.	Record Office
U.S.M.	Colborn's United Service Magazine
V.S.	Victorian Studies
V.S.G.	Volunteer Service Gazette
W.O. Lib.	War Office Library

CONTENTS

LIST OF TABLES

LIST OF ILLUSTRATIONS

Photographic acknowledgements

Army Museums Ogilby Trust — 1, top right; 2; 3, top and bottom; 4; 5; 6; 7 (with G. Archer Parfitt); 8.

Major A. F. Flatlow — 1, top left, bottom left, bottom right; 3, middle.

National Army Museum — 3, bottom.

INTRODUCTION

> I verily believe when the history of the present time comes to be written in future years, the historian will record the formation of the Volunteers as one of the most remarkable events in the century — an event quite as remarkable as the Battle of Waterloo.[1]

So spoke Lt.-Gen. Sir Garnet Wolseley to an audience of Volunteers at Derby on 2 February 1881. The official organ of the Volunteer Movement, the *Volunteer Service Gazette*, readily agreed with Wolseley for the journal displayed a great sense of history and an unshakable belief that 'some day or other, the historian will be moved to inquire into the phenomena connected with this great armed body . . .'[2] As a result the *Volunteer Service Gazette* urged units to compile adequate records to assist the historian of the future before memories faded. Records, in any case, were theoretically required to be kept by the provisions of Section 23 paragraph 44 of the Volunteer Act of 1863.[3]

Unfortunately, most Volunteer units took little care of their records and those unit histories which were produced are, without exception, antiquarian in approach and take little note of the wider military, social and political issues which affected the Volunteer Force as a whole between 1859 and 1908. Only five general histories of the Volunteer Movement have ever been published, the last in 1909, and all have their limitations. Two, those by G.B.L. Woodburne and James Walter were published in 1881 to commemorate the twenty-first anniversary of the formation of the Volunteer Force.[4] Woodburne was, in many ways, a highly perceptive writer and well aware of wider issues but, of course, his narrative finished in 1881 and Walter, who raised the 4th Lancs. Artillery Brigade in 1859, was seemingly more concerned with recording general historical anec-

1

dotes of doubtful accuracy and little relevance than with the history of the Volunteers. Robert Potter Berry, a former Lieutenant in the 6th West Yorks R.V.C., published his study of the Volunteer Force in general and of Huddersfield Volunteers in particular from 1794 onwards in 1903.[5] Although usefully recording the successive changes in Volunteer Regulations, Berry was more interested in the case for conscription than deeper analysis of the Volunteer Movement. Cecil Sebag Montefiore's history of the Volunteer Movement from earliest times, published in 1908, finished in 1860. The last general history, published by Major-General Sir James Grierson in 1909, was mainly concerned with uniforms of the Scottish Volunteers and merely gave a brief résumé of Volunteer Regulations based on Berry.[6] The centenary of the Volunteer Force in 1959 produced some more regimental histories but, from the point of view of the historian, these were no better than those published before 1914.

Fortunately, documentary evidence has survived in sufficient quantities to make a modern reassessment of the Volunteer Movement possible, although this evidence is widely scattered among official, regimental, local and private repositories. In 1975 a modern study was published concentrating largely on the social aspects of the Volunteer Movement.[7] However, as the author freely admitted in his introduction, he could take no more than a 'sample' of the local material available. This inevitably tends to distort the overall picture of the Volunteer Movement and this present work seeks to utilise a much wider range of primary source material. It is offered in the belief that much more remains to be said of the social composition of the Volunteer Movement and, equally, much more of their role as a Parliamentary pressure group and in national defence in Victorian England.

Thus it is hoped that the Movement, largely forgotten for over sixty years, can now be seen in its proper perspective within the structure of Victorian and Edwardian social, political and military affairs from its formation in 1859 to its absorption in the Territorial Force in 1908. The Volunteer Movement was, as Wolseley implied, remarkable in many ways and its history, as the *Volunteer Service Gazette* always supposed it would be, is 'worth writing', not least because it is long overdue.

[1] *Volunteer Service Gazette* 12.2.81, p 230-2

[2] *VSG* 8.11.84, p 22

[3] *VSG* 30.8.79, p 721-2 'Volunteer Records; 17.10.85, p 858, 'Contributions to Volunteer History'.

[4] G.B.L. Woodburne, *The Story of Our Volunteers* (London 1881); James Walter, *The Volunteer Force: History and Manual* (London 1881).

[5] Robert Potter Berry, *A History of the Formation and Development of Volunteer Infantry* (London and Huddersfield 1903).

[6] Cecil Sebag Montefiore, *A History of the Volunteer Force: From Earliest Times to the Year 1860* (London 1908); Maj. Gen. Sir James Grierson, *Records of the Scottish Volunteer Force, 1859-1908* (London 1909).

[7] H. Cunningham, *The Volunteer Force* (London 1975).

CHAPTER I

THE ORIGINS OF THE VOLUNTEER MOVEMENT
1845-1859

"Cannot we see them? — impatiently waiting,
    Hundreds of thousands, all hungry for spoil,
Breathing out slaughter, and bitterly hating
    Britain and all that is born of her soil!
Jesuit priests and praetorian legions
    Clamour like hounds to be loosed on the prey,
Eager to devastate Protestant regions,
    And to take vengeance for Waterloo day!"

'Arm', Martin Tupper, 1852.

5

The natural temptation for both the British public and British politicians, after so traumatic an experience as the twenty years continuous struggle against Revolutionary and Napoleonic France, was to descend once more into a lethargic belief in the adequacy of the Royal Navy to meet the requirements of domestic and colonial defence. The resentment of a large standing Army, owing much to traditional but vaguely perceived threats to political liberties and public morals was sufficiently instilled in English folk-lore to reassert itself almost before the more immediate memories of the wars had dimmed. Thus military expenditure was considerably reduced; the large numbers of wartime auxiliaries disbanded; the ballot for the Militia suspended in 1816 and even the politically reliable Yeomanry cut back in 1827. From an estimated 220,000 Regulars in 1816, the Army had been reduced by 1841 to 94,571 men,[1] a nucleus of fighting men with a bare minimum of supporting services and scattered in piecemeal colonial garrisons to escape further reduction. Nor was there public interest in the actual condition of the Navy other than the complacent faith in its superiority. It was however, precisely that superiority which was most vulnerable to the technological advances in the first few decades of the Nineteenth Century.

It is the object of this chapter to outline the factors which contributed to the marked decline in British defence capabilities; to indicate why British society was so peculiarly susceptible to the resulting phenomena of the invasion panic and to explain how a popular rather than a military response to the problem, in the form of a revival of the Volunteer Movement, came to be accepted by the politicians in 1859.

Crisis and Response

The constant factor underlying what Richard Cobden termed the 'Three Panics' of 1846-47, 1851-52 and, finally, 1858-59 was the often exaggerated but nonetheless real progress of France towards the construction of the world's first ironclad fleet. The weaker of two possible naval opponents naturally has the greater interest in new possibilities of naval warfare, whilst the nominally superior power prefers the existing *status quo* by which that superiority is maintained. The simultaneous developments of steam power, the screw propellor, rifled ordnance and armour plate made the concept of a sea-going armoured fleet a feasible possibility by the 1840's.[2] The frequent clashes of Anglo-French interests in these years, such as the Mehemet Ali crisis of 1839-41, the more obscure Pritchard affair on Tahiti in 1841 and the Spanish Marriages in 1846 were disquietening. In particular, the publication in May 1844 of a pamphlet by the Prince de Joinville, son of King Louis Philippe, which forcibly argued the possibilities of the application of steam power to naval warfare and the announcement in 1846 of a naval building programme of 93 million francs seemed indications of likely French intentions.

Added impetus for French naval expansion came from the enthusiastic interest and support of Louis Napoleon Bonaparte whose *coup d'état* of December 1851 once more raised the spectre of Napoleonic ambitions. It is not entirely clear what Napoleon III hoped to gain from indulging in a massive naval programme announced in August 1855 which was virtually beyond French financial and technological capabilities. It could indeed be argued that the long term advantage of any naval arms 'race' would lie with Britain but to contemporary statesmen Napolean III's character and intentions remained largely enigmatic.[3] The effectiveness of shell projectiles upon wooden ships, spectacularly demonstrated during the Crimean War by the destruction of the Turkish Fleet at Sinope in November 1853 and again by the damage inflicted on the Allied Fleets before Sebastopol in November 1854, underlined the almost revolutionary changes in naval warfare. The advantage of any new military or naval weapon lies in the unpredictability of its ultimate application under battle conditions. In face of the possibilities inherent in a rapidly changing military and naval environment, it was no longer possible in the 1840's and 1850's to be entirely certain of the outcome of a future naval war between Britain and France.

Soldiers have frequently been charged with an unresponsive attitude towards technological changes in military science but, in the 1840's and 1850's, leading British soldiers such as the Duke of Wellington and the Inspector General of Fortifications, Sir John Fox Burgoyne, did recognise the dangers which French naval expansion might pose for British defence. Their forecasts of the probable course and effects of a French invasion were so universally pessimistic that, were they to become public knowledge, they could only add to the fears of the more informed sections of the public increasingly aware of French naval preparations. Successive memoranda by Wellington and Burgoyne between 1844 and 1846 urged adequate means for the defence of Great Britain in the event of the British Fleet temporarily losing command of the Channel which alone could make a French landing possible. Both assumed such a venture would prove popular in France. Both recognised that a war, even short of complete disaster, would cost Britain dear in terms of wealth, property, possible European allies and international status. Neither doubted that once a successful landing has been made, there was little in the way of available troops or adequate fortifications to prevent the fall of London. Wellington's letter to Burgoyne of 4 January 1848, containing such emotive phrases as 'we are not safe for a week after the declaration of war', once leaked to the press, was sufficient to lead to the first of the 'panics'.[4] Though such 'panics' were of short duration, the military viewpoint as expressed by Burgoyne remained a constant.

Burgoyne, who circulated more warnings of the dire consequences of neglecting Britain's defences in May 1850, was not alone in playing this 'Cassandra' role. Another soldier, Sir Francis Head, compared the French Army of over 400,000 Regulars and 2 million Garde Nationale with the 120,000 Regulars of the British Army, of whom barely 37,000 were stationed in Britain itself. Although differing from Burgoyne in their assessment of the problem, in that they believed Napoleon III could not risk invasion for fear of giving too much power to his generals, both Sir Charles and Sir William Napier believed invasion possible.[5] Britain's military position continued to decline, the Crimean War not only exposing major deficiences but taxing resources sufficiently to require the dispatch of Militia battalions to the Mediterranean and the enrolment of a foreign legion of Germans and Italians. Burgoyne's minimum level of forces compatible with the prevailing conditions of Europe was made a nonsense during the Indian Mutiny when the Army was reduced to a mere 14 battalions in Britain.[6] Such a combination of constants in the 1840's and 1850's as naval developments, military deficiences and suspicion of France did little to enhance confidence within a society peculiarly susceptible to the phenomena of the 'invasion panic'.

The two decades of the 1840's and 1850's presented at the very least an uncertain face to the most casual of Victorian observers. Britain had hardly emerged from the implied threat of Chartism and social chaos and was only just beginning to move towards an appearance of increased economic prosperity. There was a great admiration for science, progress and achievement but at the same time modern technology as epitomised by French steam power could pose a serious threat to that very progress. Thus the reaction to the series of seeming threats posed by successive French régimes can be seen in almost psychological terms. There was, in many ways, a more militant attitude developing towards such threats. How far this is attributable to the influence on the middle class of the methods of entreprenurial enterprise detected by Professor Perkin is difficult to assess. Nevertheless, there was a perceptible swing away from the overt pacifism of Cobden and the Manchester School for whom peaceful competition in trade was vastly prefereable to war. This can be traced in the almost Darwinian terms in which the outbreak of the Crimean

War was viewed within British society; in the growth of the 'cult' of the Christian Hero arising principally from the Indian Mutiny and the electoral defeat of both Cobden and Bright in 1857.[7] For all the efforts of such leaders of the peace movement as Cobden, Bright and Peto, considerable suspicions were aroused in England at Louis Napoleon's seizure of power in December 1851. A pacifist pamphleteer such as Richard Barrett could claim that there need be no concern 'about the nephew who is minus the military genius of his uncle' but for the majority there was a feeling that 'there was a possibility rather than a probablity of the Empire not being peace' (sic).[8]

To a large extent the fears were engendered by Louis Napoleon's own pandering to his uncle's memory which had contributed to his victory in the 1848 presidential election. However, the chief responsibility for the continuing anxieties of the 1850's must lie with the national press. French works on invasion were frequently translated in English military journals and there was a constant stream of invasion literature in England of varying quality and credibility.[9] The shocks of the Crimean War and the Indian Mutiny were vividly reported virtually for the first time. Indeed it was these two wars that virtually created the new popular press. A leading influence in the presentation of defence issues to the public was *The Times* which, Professor Vincent has suggested, advocated a national policy to preserve its own monopoly in that the paper duties which worked to the benefit of the paper would be relinquished if a peacetime rate of expenditure was restored.[10] It was *The Times* and other newspapers which gave widespread publicity in the 1850's to the many individuals who were increasingly pressing for the establishment of Volunteer corps as a solution to British military weakness. This 'popular' solution was not one shared by either leading soldiers or politicians.

It is apparent that no serving soldier in a position of responsibility seriously contemplated the revival of the Volunteer Movement as the answer to the threat of invasion. The solution of Wellington and Burgoyne lay in an increase of fortifications around London, an increase in stores available, a re-organisation of the Militia and, most important of all, a rapid augmentation of regular troops permanently stationed in Britain. Estimates of the numbers required varied from 100,000 men advocated by Wellington in 1845 to Burgoyne's original call for 30,000 Regulars independent of Irish requirements and capable of expansion in emergencies to a force of 60,000 men. By 1856 Burgoyne had amended his calculations to a minimum requirement of 80,000 infantry, roughly twice the numbers currently available for field service in Britain. Both he and Wellington shared a common distrust of any useful contribution likely to be made by an unorganised rising of the general population against invading troops even if they outnumbered the invaders by as much as ten to one. For Burgoyne the value of such an undisciplined mob was illusory, a *levée en masse* likely to be 'peculiarly feeble'.[11]

The Napier Brothers did not share the view that irregulars were entirely unsuited to British requirements. Sir Charles Napier, in calling for the establishment of defensive forces on an adequate and workable basis in February 1852, advocated the use of volunteers in desultory operations on an enemy flank or rear using ditches, banks and woods for cover. He considered that: 'If the Militia are called out and Volunteer corps formed I think we are safe enough; not otherwise.'[12] Sir William Napier, as a former Lieutenant Governor of Guernsey, was perhaps more sensitive than most to a French threat and had submitted plans for a defence of the Channel Isles to Wellington in 1847. He had little hope of defending Ireland and, like Burgoyne, feared United States intervention in Canada. William Napier considered that it was impossible to defend London completely and therefore a force of 20-40,000 Regulars should be held in flanking camps around the capital so that they were capable of continuing the battle if London fell. The defence of London must rest with Volunteer corps and the citizens fighting, if necessary, in the streets.[13]

Burgoyne's reaction to the discussions on Volunteer corps and to those formed in the early 1850's was only a slight modification of his earlier outlook. He attacked what he termed the 'fallacies' that irregulars could operate successfully in the closed country of the South East which favoured attack rather than defence. In any case guerillas were at their most successful only when an Army had dispersed in occupation. He considered that Militia units required several annual trainings to fit them to work alongside Regular troops and then only if the Regulars were in at least equal proportions. But the chief objection of Burgoyne and many other officers was that the type of gentlemanly Volunteer corps envisaged in the 1850's, with shooting seen as a substitute for any other requirement, would prove unequal to the discipline and hardship of a campaign. A role was seen for Volunteers under strict Regular supervision in local defence around ports and to ward off marauding raids for which no Regular troops could be spared. Burgoyne hoped that the range of the modern rifle would keep the Volunteers out of close quarters with an enemy. The Duke of Cambridge, Commander-in-Chief from 1855 to 1895, was equally opposed to Volunteer corps of whom he spoke in 1857 in terms of a 'very dangerous rabble' and 'unmanageable bodies that would ruin our Army'.[14] Such sentiments were conceived in a spirit of

11

narrow professionalism rather than as a comment upon the social class of likely Volunteers. The marked military conservatism of the Regular Army and its resistance to change was a consistent feature of its later relationship with the Volunteers which will be examined more fully in a later chapter. Suffice to say here that if the view of Burgoyne and the Duke of Cambridge was not shared by all soldiers, it was the opinion of those who mattered.

Nor did the Volunteers enter over much into the calculations of successive governments. Though not always as unsympathetic to the civilian and military pressures as they appeared, most politicians based their solutions to the invasion threat on the 'Old Constitutional Force', the Militia.

In the face of Wellington's warnings, Peel had declined to act due to Britain's poor financial position, the possible repercussions of British military preparations in France and from a desire not to call attention to Britain's weakness. This latter view was not shared by Palmerston who had made an emotive speech in June 1845 on the way in which steam power had bridged the traditional barrier of the Channel.[15] It was thought that the continuation of peace would be better served by a steady and unpublicised augmentation of defensive preparations. It might also be said that the revival of the Militia ballot as considered by Sidney Herbert and Sir James Graham in August 1845 was hardly likely to prove popular in either the country or the House of Commons.[16] Lord John Russell's Local Militia plan, announced to the House of Commons on 18 February 1848, was certainly unpopular when financed by a proposed increase in income tax from 7d. to 1s. in the pound.[17] The measure had a distinctly dampening effect on the first invasion panic but in any case, on 22 February 1848 revolution broke out in Paris. King Louis Philippe abdicated on 24 February and on 28 February Russell withdrew the measure. Russell was able to revive the Militia issue only in February 1852 when agitation was at a height following Louis Napoleon's *coup d'état*. Yet this Bill too failed on its second reading and the Government resigned in the face of predictable opposition from Radical M.P.'s and from Palmerston who not only considered the measure inadequate but was seeking 'tit for tat' for his dismissal from the Foreign Office.[18] Lord Derby's government brought in a Militia Bill to raise 80,000 militiamen by voluntary enlistment and 3,000 additional Regulars in April 1852. There was again opposition from the pacifists such as Cobden, Lord Dudley Stuart, Jacob Bell and Elihu Burritt and over 800 petitions were presented against the Bill but the Royal Assent was given on 30 June 1852.[19]

The outgoing Russell ministry had not been favourable to

Volunteers and Russell himself had intended to incorporate existing units into his Local Militia scheme. Palmerston in 1847 had considered that local defence corps might prove useful around major cities but shared the military viewpoint that corps composed of attornies, tradesmen and shopkeepers could not be expected to quit their homes to take the field.[20] Criticisms of the Russell ministry by the Earl of Ellenborough in the Lords and by Sir George de Lacy Evans in the Commons were based on the fear that the refusal to accept offers of Volunteer corps in such a cold and ungracious manner would have a harmful effect on the exertions of individuals.[21] The attitude of the new Derby government was that such corps should only be accepted on condition that their arms and equipment conformed to Government patterns. However, no more offers could be accepted until the Militia proposals had been considered in the House of Commons for Volunteers might well be exempted from the provisions of any such bill.[22] The fear that Volunteer corps would escape the ballot was undoubtedly the reason behind Spencer Walpole's refusal to accept more offers. William Napier, however, considered that the Government was afraid to arm Volunteers in case they demanded 'an extension of reform'.[23] Little more was heard in political circles until 1858. In March 1855 Palmerston dismissed Volunteers as too costly, of no real military value in inland areas and unfitted by habit, occupation and constitution to meet the hardship of campaigns. In 1857 Lord Panmure, in considering the Duke of Cambridge's strictures on the pressure for Volunteer corps, agreed that Volunteers were utterly useless and a greater danger to friend than foe.[24] Nevertheless, the demand for the creation of Volunteer corps continued to be made throughout the 1850's and it is necessary to determine both the origins and nature of the offers emanating from the public.

A lively controversy arose in the closing months of 1860, most notably in the correspondence columns of the *Volunteer Service Gazette*, over who had the best claim to be considered the most likely originator of the Volunteer Movement. Many of the most prominent enthusiasts in 1859 had not previously advocated the establishment of Volunteer corps and made no claim. Equally, there were many who sought the distinction and it was not uncommon for journals or authors to support particular claimants.[25] In September 1861 Sir Duncan MacDougall, who had himself played some part in the early years, published a detailed investigation into the conflicting claims. He concluded that no single man could claim to have originated the Movement.[26] Volunteers were, of course, hardly a novel concept in England and in fact one corps had apparently survived, or rather

13

claimed to have survived, from the post-Napoleonic Wars reduction — the Royal Victoria Rifle Club claiming a connection with the Duke of Cumberland's Sharpshooters of 1794. There were also many examples of existing volunteer organisations of one kind or another in the United States, Canada, India, New Zealand, Australia and Switzerland. Many British officers had experience of leading irregular units in such conflicts as the Carlist Wars in Spain, the Maori Wars and in the Indian Mutiny.[27] However, contemporaries generally recognised three men as the chief protagonists for the honour of reviving the idea of Volunteers in England — Hans Busk, Alfred Richards and Nathaniel Bousfield.

It is worth looking in some detail at the activities of these three. Hans Busk claimed that he had first called for the establishment of Volunteer corps in 1837 whilst an undergraduate at Trinity College, Cambridge. A barrister and former High Sheriff of Radnor, Busk was a prolific writer on subjects as diverse as naval affairs and cookery. In 1858 he was instrumental in rejuvenating the Victoria Rifles, formerly the Royal Victoria Rifle Club and now reduced to only 35 effective members. He also claimed to have travelled 11,600 miles in 1858 and 1859 and to have delivered 147 lectures alone between March 1858 and August 1861 to propagate the Movement. His claim was supported by the *Volunteer Service Gazette*, of which he was briefly editor in December 1860, but he played no part in any subsequent developments.[28]

Alfred Richards was, like Busk, trained in the law and also an astute self-propagandist. Editor successively of the *Mirror of the Times*, *British Army Despatches* and the *Daily Telegraph and Courier*, Richards contributed a large number of articles on the need for Volunteer corps to various journals and, between December 1853 and April 1859, some 17 leading articles to the *Morning Advertiser*. Busk was apt to make capital of the connection of this particular organ, of which Richards was editor from 1870-6, with the drink interest. Richards retaliated with the claim that Busk was merely an alarmist in the years before 1859.[29] Richards failed to form a Temple Rifle Club in 1852 but in 1855 became secretary of the so-called National and Constitutional Defence Association of whose role much was made in 1859.

Nathaniel Bousfield, who had the distinction of being the first commissioned officer of the infant Volunteer Force in 1859, was a Liverpool cotton broker who attempted to form a corps with 20 fellow gentlemen in 1852. This offer being declined, Bousfield founded from the earlier nucleus the Liverpool Drill Club in 1855 with 120 'young fellows' drawn from the cotton trade and drilling twice weekly in his warehouse. A further offer was declined in 1857 despite support from leading Liverpool politicians and Sir Duncan MacDougall, who placed the Royal Lancashire Militia Artillery barracks at Bousfield's disposal.[30]

There were many lesser propagandists at work during the 1850's such as A.W. Playfair, H. Culling, John Kinloch and Hugh Miller of the *Edinburgh Witness*. A Birmingham barrack master, Captain J.E. Acklom, staked his claim to be a founder of the Movemment on his March 1859 pamphlet entitled *Ready! Or England for Ever Safe from the Invader*.[31] Better known enthusiasts were Lord Tennyson and Martin Tupper. Tupper, author of the highly popular *Proverbial Philosophy* published in 1838, supported Richards' claim but had himself written some prophetic lines entitled 'A Stirring Song for Patriots in the Year 1860' as early as 1845. A stream of patriotic poems and songs followed in the *Morning Star* and *Daily News*, among the better known of which were 'Arm' in 1852 and 'National Defences' in 1856. Tupper failed to form a corps in Surrey in 1852 and again in 1854 but was a firm supporter in 1859 and the Volunteer Force adopted as its motto the title of another Tupper poem, 'Defence not Defiance'.[32] Many considered Tupper an unofficial poet laureate but Tennyson himself had published verses such as 'Britons, guard your Own' and 'Hands all round' in the *Examiner* in 1852. At first many thought Tupper was the author of the famous poem 'The War' which appeared in *The Times* of 9 May 1859 but it was the work of Tennyson. Some even went as far as to claim that this poem had played the major role in the establishment of the Volunteers, a claim best summed up in Acklom's acid remark: 'As well say that Sebastopol fell because 'Cheer, Boys, Cheer' was versified!'[33]

Certain conclusions can be drawn about the activities of the Volunteer advocates before 1859. It is clear that, other than presenting the public at large with an alternative solution to increasing the Regular Army or reviving the Militia ballot, the progress of the Volunteer Movement met with a singular lack of success between 1851 and 1858. The offers to form Volunteer corps, which numbered 15 in January and February 1852 and 22 between 1853 and 1854, though showing common characteristics, were from widely scattered areas of the country and each case was treated very much on its merits by successive Governments.[34] Thus after Louis Napoleon's coup in December 1851, offers were accepted by Sir George Grey at Cheltenham and Hull and from the Sports Club, Hanover Park, Peckham. At Bridport Henry Templer, a solicitor, convened a meeting on 20 March 1852 which passed resolutions calling for a Volunteer corps 'to protect that part of the coast between Portland and the River Exe'. The new Home Secretary, Spencer Walpole, was less enthusiastic than his predecessor informing Templer that there was 'no immediate necessity' for Volunteer corps. However, on 26 March Walpole did accept an offer resulting from a meeting at the Exeter Athenaeum on the danger to the Devon coast.[35] This resulted in the formation of the premier Volunteer corps in the country apart from the ancient Honourable Artillery Company — the Exeter and South Devon corps.

These offers were without exception from essentially upper middle class elements of society led by professional men such as Bousfield and the trio trained in the legal profession of Busk, Richards and Templer. Instrumental in founding the Exeter corps were Dr (later Sir) John Bucknill, the Superintendent of the Exminster Lunatic Asylum, and Denis Moore, Exeter's Town Clerk. The object of such Corps was to accommodate those unable to join the Militia and for whom there was no place in the Regular Army such as gentlemen, professional men, merchants, tradesmen and 'other respectable inhabitants of their respective districts'.[36] This was reflected in the expensive nature of such early corps. The Peckham club, later the nucleus of the 1st Surrey R.V.C., had an initial outlay of £14 on uniform and £6 on a rifle while the estimated cost of uniform and equipment in the Exeter corps in 1857 was 12 guineas.[37] There was an idea that such corps could free the Regular Army to serve abroad and when the campaign for Volunteer corps drew new inspiration from the Indian Mutiny there were even suggestions that Volunteers could be sent to India to cruise up the Indus and Ganges in armed boats. One correspondent also suggested a role in aid of the civil power as in Torquay the mere threat of assembling the Exeter corps had prevented a bread riot without the necessity of calling upon the Militia to restore order.[38] But such arguments singlarly failed to impress either soldiers or politicians. At the close of 1857 there seemed very little chance indeed that Volunteer corps would ever be accepted as a permanent addition to the defensive forces of the country. What changed the attitude of the politicians was the so-called 'third panic' of 1858-9.

The Third Panic and the Government

The immediate cause of the 'third panic' was the repercussions in France of the bomb plot attempt upon the life of Napoleon III by the Italian refugee, Orsini, on 14 January 1858. Orsini had close connections with fellow refugees in London and his bomb had allegedly been made in Birmingham. To such observers as Ralph Earle, who sent regular reports back to Disraeli, the resulting agitation in France against England appeared genuine rather than a ministerial ploy.[39] The most inflammatory reactions came from the French Army whose addresses to the Emperor congratulating him on his escape began appearing in the official government organ, *Moniteur*, from 19 January onwards. Of the 170 or so addresses published, comparatively few spoke of following 'wild beasts' to their dens or demanding 'an account from the land of impunity where are the haunts of the monsters who are sheltered under its laws'. However, their publication implied at least tacit government approval and the hostile inclinations of many French soldiers formerly well disposed towards England were verified by Colonel Claremont's mission to France on behalf of the Foreign Secretary, Cowley, in August 1858.[40]

Palmerston's attempt to placate the French by introducing a Conspiracy to Murder Bill making it a felony rather than a misdemeanour to plot murder abroad from England was widely regarded on both sides of the Channel as meeting insult with concession. The bill was defeated on its second reading and Palmerston resigned. The new Conservative ministry of Lord Derby was far more inclined to review military and naval arrangements in view of continuing rumours of French hostility. It must be said that some of the information reaching London was of highly suspect quality. Nevertheless, the Queen and Prince Albert were both strongly inclined to suspicion when they visited Cherbourg in August 1858 and viewed the extent of French fortifications erected since their visit of the previous year.[41] The preparations of the Derby ministry were also conducted against a background of rising tension in Europe where Napoleon III, committed to intervention in Italy by the meeting with Cavour at Plombières in July 1858, moved towards war with Austria-Hungary. Peace efforts failed and on 3 April 1859 war was declared by an Austro-Hungarian Empire unable to maintain its army at full mobilisation any longer without action.

The immediate thoughts of the Derby ministry on defence did not, however, include Volunteer corps. Despite the reservations of the Chancellor of the Exchequer, Disraeli, the Cabinet agreed on 18 January 1859 to increase naval expenditure. On 25 January the First Lord, Sir John Pakington, announced not only an increase in screw line of battle ships but also the construction of two ironclads to maintain naval superiority over France. The Secretary of State for War, General Jonathan Peel, was equally concerned with the military situation. On 7 May 1858, he established a secret Home Defence Committee under the chairmanship of the Duke of Cambridge to consider the best means of repelling any invasion, the number of troops available, their fitness for service and the use of irregular levies.

The Committee reported on 25 May 1858 that the total numbers of Regulars and existing auxiliary troops available totalled 153,285 men. Many of those detailed for garrisons were unfit for their duties and after deducting young recruits, battalions under training, depot troops and inexperienced men the total effective strength for the field shrunk to a bare 42,000 men. Tentative plans were put forward for the defence of London but it was concluded that its fall 'could not be prevented by the present very inadequate number of troops in the country'.[42] The Committee recommended an urgent increase in Regular troops and provision for fitting the Militia for Channel Isles defence. Any general enrolment of irregular levies in the interior was once more rejected on the grounds that they could never be available for combined operations with Regulars, would hamper Militia arrangements, absorb valuable military resources needed elsewhere, add to expense and produce the greatest confusion. These conclusions were reinforced by another memorandum from Burgoyne in June 1858. This argued that the Regular Army would require at least six months' training to face continental troops and at least two-thirds of the Militia was either inexperienced or unlikely to answer a call. As for irregulars, they would be slaughtered just as British troops could be expected to dispel a riot with minimum effort.[43]

Peel had also instituted on 8 July 1858 a Royal Commission on the Militia. The Commission, which was chaired by the Duke of Richmond, was charged with examining the organisation, government and direction of the Militia. Its elaborate recommendations, produced in April 1859, were designed to enable the Militia to become more efficient for military purposes on the occasion of any emergency. It was now considered that the Militia would prove equal to its duties although its actual duties were never defined in the report. The only two Regular Army witnesses took the opportunity to deliver some more well directed blows at the possible use of Volunteers. The Adjutant General, Lt.-General Sir George Wetherall, dismissed Volunteers as incapable of discipline and a bad substitute for the Militia. The Inspector General of Musketry, Major-General Hay, foresaw a role for the Militia on the flanks and rear of an enemy which had normally been defined as a possible area where Volunteers might prove useful. Much the same views would be presented by both Burgoyne and the Duke of Cambridge to the Select Committee on Military Organisation which also began its work whilst Peel was Secretary of State. This latter investigation was primarily concerned with the effects of administrative changes wrought in 1855 after the Crimean debacle. Its recommendations were not in fact published until June 1860 and were, moreover, not strictly relevant to the Volunteer Movement.

Nevertheless the evidence presented by various Regular witnesses, which will be discussed in a later chapter, was clearly intended to pour grave doubts on the value of the infant Volunteer Force.[44]

Although general military opinion was unfavourable to the formation of Volunteers in response to the growing tensions in Europe, there appeared to be increasing demands from the public. On 16 April 1859 Alfred Richards covened a public meeting of the National and Constitutional Defence Association at St Martin's Hall, Long Acre. The Hall was only a third full on a cold evening and the main speaker, Admiral Sir Charles Napier, M.P., arrived an hour late. Speakers urged that Britain's defences be placed in a condition to ensure that the country was not embroiled in a continental war. Resolutions were passed calling for a memorial to the Queen and petition to Parliament urging the maintenance of the Fleet, an increase in the Militia and the enrolment of Volunteer corps. Richards himself was chiefly concerned that the impending general election, due on 30 April, and a result of the Derby ministry's defeat on electoral reform, would take precedence over the issue of national defence.[45]

The Long Acre meeting initiated an increasingly hysterical press campaign for the creation of Volunteer corps notably in the editorial and correspondence columns of *The Times*, whose articles were widely reproduced elsewhere. It was argued that the Regular Army could not be increased without a corresponding increase in taxation whereas the formation of Volunteer Corps would not only provide support for the Regulars but instil and indoctrinate the country at large with military knowledge. The revival in the use of arms would also have a tendency to prevent the recurrence of invasion panics every few years. The concept of these Volunteer corps was much as in 1852 with men of wealth and leisure who could afford the time and money to drill. It was concluded that a grave responsibility would fall on any government which neglected to encourage the popular spirit and the unexploited mine of Volunteers resources.[46] There were also indications of growing support outside London. A public meeting had been held in Bristol as early as February and on 28 April MacDougall and Bousfield renewed their application to form a Liverpool corps.[47] The campaign culminated on 9 May 1859 with the publication of Tennyson's poem in *The Times* mirroring the mood of many with its suspicion of Napoleon III and calls for preparation for eventualities and to lay reform issues to one side.

The Government response to the growing pressure was a circular on 12 May 1859 authorising Lords Lieutenant to raise Volunteer corps under the Yeomanry and Volunteer Consolidation Act of 1804. *The Times* welcomed the circular with its promise of a second line of defence for the country. If only one man in ten would learn the use of the rifle then England would be safe and Europe respect her shores.[48] Relief was also expressed by men soon to become leading influences in the Volunteer Movement. Lord Elcho's heart gave a 'leap of joy' at the opportunity of remedying the defenceless state of the country, a view echoed in Cornwall by Sir Richard Rawlinson Vyvyan.[49] But why had the government's attitude towards the Volunteers changed?

It is clear that Peel and his colleagues did not fear invasion and indeed he later claimed that the acceptance of the Volunteers was solely in response to popular opinion.[50] Electoral considerations can be discounted as the main election had been concluded and Derby's ministry returned with a slightly increased number of seats though it remained in the minority. The Government had, however, to make at least some concession to popular pressure especially as it owed its assumption of power in 1858 to anti-Gallic feelings. The public at large would not favour an increase in the standing Army with its attendant increase in taxation. In any case, naval expenditure was already high. Peel, speaking to the Select Committee on Military Organisation on 1 August 1859, said that the Government could not have asked Parliament for men they could not get. He also repudiated the idea that the country could have supported a standing Army of 200,000 men on the lines suggested by Burgoyne. However, it was advisable to have men available in an emergency by utilising the Militia or other means.[51] It would seem then that Peel himself was not altgether opposed to Volunteer corps which was the only real alternative to the Militia.

The problem with the Militia was that the ballot would prove possibly even more unpopular than an increase in the Army and it could cause large scale disruption of both agricultural and industrial labour forces. The ballot was to remain, in the eyes of politicians, tantamount to political suicide. Elcho, looking back in 1898 when deeply involved in ballot agitation, was particularly critical of what he regarded as lack of courage on the part of Peel and his colleagues in enforcing the ballot in 1859. The full embodiment of the Militia as it existed on a voluntary basis would prove costly and in the light of the most recent military advice to Peel it would probably prove more profitable to spend money on the Regulars than on the Militia. Indeed, in the East Riding only 250 out of 900 Militiamen had turned out for the annual training.[52]

Despite equal, if not stronger, military objections to the formation of Volunteer corps, the Volunteers had the over-riding advantage of satisfying public opinion at absolutely no cost to the Government. Steps would be taken but they would be taken by the people themselves for these were to be self-supporting units. Those capable of supplying their own arms and equipment were unlikely to be those liable to join either the Militia or the Regular Army, thus there would be no disruption of normal recruiting. There was no longer any real fear of entrusting the 'people' with arms and, in any case, no Government arms would be issued and only the wealthy could afford to buy their own weapons. There was no reason to believe that the novelty and enthusiasm would not quickly wear off as danger receded and the whole concept would thus prove of little cost to the Government in the future.

The lack of interest in the actual terms of Volunteer employment is apparent in the 12 May circular, which was no more than a selection from the provisions of the 1804 Act. Volunteers were to take the oath of allegiance and be liable to serve on actual or apprehended invasion. In return for the rather empty reward of exemption from the ballot, the Volunteer must participate in at least eight drills in four months or twenty-four drills in a year. There was the power to resign on 14 days' notice except on active service, the Volunteer being subject to military law only when under arms. Lords Lieutenant were made responsible for general administration such as the commissioning of officers and supervision of uniforms while the Secretary of State remained responsible for establishments. All arms, equipment, ammunition and expenses were to be borne by the men themselves with property invested in the Commanding Officer and subscriptions and disciplinary fines recoverable under the bye laws of the units before Magistrates. But the circular did not actually define the purpose of the new Volunteer corps. The Duke of Cambridge had recommended that administration should rest with the Lords Lieutenant, that officers should be responsible for their men, that all must take the oath of allegiance and that arms must be of government pattern. Above all, they must be disciplined though drills should not interfere with civil occupations unnecessarily. It was left, however, to the Prince Consort to define some purpose for men who were dependent upon 'temporary enthusiasm, and the temporary agreement among themselves of individuals, who may probably change soon after their first formation, and who can transfer neither their original enthusiasm nor their mutual agreement'.[53]

Prince Albert was conscious of the need for discipline and the possible dangers to internal security in peace and to the Army in war if that condition remained unfulfilled. His 'Instructions to Lords Lieutenant' were submitted to Peel on 20 May, approved by the Cabinet on 23 May and issued to Lords Lieutenant on 25 May 1859. This second circular was a considerable improvement on the first but

21

did not reveal any copious concessions on the part of the Government. It did, however, outline a purpose for the Movement 'to induce those classes to come forward as Volunteers who do not, under our present system, enter either the Regular Army or the Militia'.[54] Drill was not to interfere with any private avocations and was to teach the use of the rifle in leisure hours as the first priority. Some basic drill lessons to be learned were outlined but it was not intended that there should be any more than small bodies of Volunteers to avoid the necessity of more complicated instruction. The military role of the new corps was also defined — Volunteer corps would operate in closed country using their skill with the rifle, reliance on their comrades and local topographical knowledge 'to hang with the most telling effect upon the flanks and communications of a hostile Army'. There was also provision for artillery batteries on the coast, formed by men less fitted by health or family commitments to serve in the field, and for boat sections in ports. The Government was now prepared to issue ammunition from Government stores at cost price but, as *The Times* noted, this was hardly a liberal gesture.[55]

The ambivalent attitude of the Derby ministry to the Volunteers, once public opinion had been satisfied, was particularly marked in the question of arms and ammunition. There was strong feeling in Cornwall that the Government refusal to issue arms would severely hamper the progress of the Movement. The Lord Lieutenant, Lord Vivian, appealed to the Secretary of State on 16 May 1859, a gesture reinforced by resolutions at a county meeting at Bodmin two days later. But Peel in a cryptically short reply indicated that there could be no deviation from the terms of the first circular. Peel later stated, rather significantly, that the Government had intended a drilled but unarmed population with arms available in an emergency.[56] Arms in his view could not be issued to Volunteers over whom the Government had little control and who might disappear after expending valuable ammunition. It was clear that Peel thought the Volunteers must go their own way without Government interference. Lord Derby, on the other hand, claimed that the small arms supply did not warrant the disposal of large numbers of rifles to the Volunteers.[57]

The inescapable conclusion, from both the circulars and the refusal to issue arms, is that the Government had found in the Volunteers a convenient means of escaping both unpopularity and expense.

It was at this point that other events intervened. The new Liberal coalition effected at Willis' Rooms on 6 June 1859 brought down the Derby ministry on a motion of confidence on 10 June. The new ministry headed by Palmerston was a curious blend of former rivals and not generally welcomed by military men, who discovered too many ministers tainted with the administrative failures of the Crimea.[58] Notwithstanding, Sidney Herbert, who now became Secretary of State, and Earl de Grey and Ripon, his Under-Secretary, made a significant contribution to the permanency of the Volunteer Movement. On 1 July 1859 it was announced that the new Government intended to issue 25 Long Enfield rifles per 100 Volunteers on condition that the corps undertook to provide a safe range, secure custody for the arms, a set of approved rules and made themselves subject to periodic military inspection. Instructors were to be provided at the expense of the corps from the staffs of the disembodied Militia and a modified musketry course at Hythe was to be opened to Volunteers at their own expense. Artillery units were to be given free ammunition and access to guns for practise. Both Herbert and de Grey and Ripon expressed the wish to encourage the Volunteers to become something of more tangible military value than mere rifle clubs and recognised the value of imbuing the middle class with military interests. In reply to an address for further concessions on arms and ammunition on 5 July 1859, Herbert deprecated the withholding of arms until an emergency when without practise few men would be capable of using them. He denied that the Volunteers would be used as an excuse to reduce the Regular Army.[59] More important, he also spoke of the need for equity in dealings between Government and Volunteers for, in return for aid, the Government could exact influence on the Movement. It was precisely the virtual independence of the Volunteer Movement that Herbert hoped to control. He was perhaps a little jealous of the possible effects of the Volunteers upon the Militia which he himself had always preferred as giving better security for Government aid than a Volunteer on 14 days' notice to quit.[60] The Volunteer Movement could not be ignored and the issue of arms could give the Government a lever over the Volunteers which Peel's refusal and *laissez faire* attitude could not. Some Volunteers did resent this government intrusion. The Lord Lieutenant of Surrey, Viscount Lovelace, writing to the secretary of the Reigate corps in August 1859, hoped that the Government would not force arms upon units that did not want them and spend public money 'of which there is not too much'. He concluded that 'the Pall Mall men cannot dispense with our acceptance of them'.[61]

On 13 July Herbert issued a circular confirming the arrangements and the conditions attached to them. An accompanying memorandum dealt with formation, organisation, establishment and instruction. It outlined once more the provisions for use:

> In all cases of actual invasion or appearance of any enemy in force on the coast of Great Britain, or of rebellion or insurrection arising or

23

existing within the same, or the appearance of any enemy in force on the coast, or during any invasion, but not otherwise, the services of the Volunteer Force will extend to any part of Great Britain.[62]

To be accepted a Corps required a safe range of 200 yards, a place of custody for arms, approved rules, a uniform approved by the Lord Lieutenant. Establishment was fixed at one Captain, one Lieutenant and one Ensign for a company which would consist of 60-100 effectives but a subdivision could be formed with one Lieutenant, an Ensign and not less than 30 men. Honorary and supernumerary members were authorised and the circular also laid down the equipment to be provided by each man. Precedence was by formation date, by county and by corps. Details were given for the use of Militia instructors, the Hythe course and a manual priced 6d. recommended for perusal. This manual, *Drill and Rifle Instruction for Volunteer Rifle Corps*, the work of Colonel D. Lysons, became popularly known from the colour of its cover as the 'Green Book'.

To indicate the sort of rules that would be approved by the Secretary of State, Herbert established a War Office Rules Committee which reported on the 10 August 1859. Its members were chosen from those prominent in the infant Volunteer Force: Lord Ranelagh (South Middlesex), Earl Spencer (Althorp Rifles), Major Clifford (Victoria Rifles), J.H. Orde (Yarmouth), Wilbraham Taylor (Middlesex and Barnet Rifles), Captain Moore (Exeter and South Devon Rifles), W. Hyett (Gloucester and Stroud), Montagu Hicks (London Rifle Brigade), R. Blackburne (Edinburgh), Adam Gladstone (5th Lancs. R.V.C.), Henry Templer (Bridport) and W. Laird (Birkenhead).[63] Their recommendations were widely accepted and copied with minor variations throughout the country where the response to the May circulars already displayed infinite local and regional variations.

The Third Panic and the Local Community

The Times spoke on 25 June 1859 of 'an impulse, an influence, an instinct perhaps' sweeping the country in the wake of the government circulars. But is it in fact possible to find common themes at local level in the summer and autumn of 1859? Did the provinces reflect the views of *The Times*? An answer might lie in the contemporary accounts of public meetings held throughout the country in the months following the circulars.

Suspicion of French ambition was certainly an underlying theme at most local meetings although it is noticeable that views expressed at local level tended to be at a lower key than those expressed in either Parliament or the renewed spate of invasion literature. Lords Ellenborough, Brougham, Howden and Lyndhurst were singularly unimpressed by the Government's belief in the persistence of the Anglo-French alliance when they spoke in the House of Lords in July 1859. In particular, both Howden and Lyndhurst believed that invasion would prove popular in France. In the Commons Horsman made a memorable 'panic' speech and Sir Lewis Palk talked darkly of French ships taking soundings off the English coast.[64]

In the provinces this theme was reflected by such as Sir John Coleridge at Ottery in Deveon speaking of the popularity of an invasion in France.[65] On 19 May the Rev. T.V. Fosbery told the meeting at Reading:

> It is impossible to disguise from ourselves, when we see an Imperial autocrat swaying the destinies of the French nation, that the tide of affairs may turn at any moment, and an invasion may be attempted upon our little island home when we least expect it . . .[66]

In the north of England there seems to have been a deeper fear of invasion and W.E. Duncombe, M.P., recorded heavy recruiting in North Yorkshire from anxiety. At a meeting at Ulverston in Furness in December 1859, T. Ainsworth showed an equally anxious reaction:

> What is to prevent a French corvette from sailing up to Barrow and taking possession of the harbour and railway? Perhaps the last friendly and English message by telegraph the Ulverstonians would have from Furness Abbey would be that the French had taken possession of the hotel, that they were drinking all the light wines, that our friend Mr Ramsden was dangling by the neck to the Station lamp post and in a very short time Ulverston was to be sacked and pillaged..[67]

A more common view was that expressed by Archdeacon Bickersteth at Aylesbury on 22 December 1859: 'When we compare our naval and military position with that of France, we cannot feel satisfied that in one of the political changes which may take place amongst that restless people, there should not arise a desire to invade these our happy shores.'[68]

The most widely held view in these public meetings was that it would be better to be prepared and indeed the concept of 'arm for peace' became the motto of the 36th Middlesex R.V.C. Lord Hatherton, Lord Lieutenant of Staffordshire, had the utmost confidence in Napoleon III as an ally but 'it was their duty as a nation to be prepared for any emergencies'. It was perfectly conceivable that Napoleon III might be replaced by his Army in the same way that he had himself overthrown the Second Republic. In any case, as R.J. Harvey told a meeting at Norwich on 23 May 1859, 'it could not be too widely known that the forces under arms on the Continent were numerically so enormous that ours were as comparatively nothing to them'. In such circumstances as C.J. Selwyn, M.P., stated at Richmond, 'we had not the slightest desire to become embroiled in a Continental war, but at the same time we must not forget the old proverb which told us that if we wished for peace we must be prepared for war'. A resolution passed at the Dartmouth Arms, Forest Hill, on 29 January 1860 to form a Sydenham corps called for such a body since, 'in the present state of Europe and with the view of maintaining an imposing neutrality, it is essential that the defence of the Empire should be such as to defy attack'. Resolutions on this theme are commonplace as, for example, that at a meeting held at the George Inn, Frome, on 7 December 1859 calling for volunteers as a measure to strengthen the system of national defences and thus being 'conducive to the maintenance of peace'.[69]

Another factor in some areas was fear for the safety of property. Sir Thomas Phillipps of Worcester echoed the well worn vision of a licentious soldiery thus: 'if any enemy should land or conquer the country, he will take away your cattle, your sheep, your horses, your pigs, your poulty and your corn, at last, if not first, your wives and daughters'. James Walter recalled that in 1807, or so he claimed, French military hospitals had 62,000 men under treatment 'for diseases induced by their vices'. Indeed all this was not far removed from the more hysterical orations of fifty years previously. Nevertheless, there was the realisation that Britain's wealth and this 'richest and choisest inheritance of God's earth, where all that was valuable, glorious and good was concentrated'[70] might prove a tempting prize to a foreign power. A more sober judgement was that of George Charsley of the proposed Amersham corps who wrote to his brother in February 1860: 'There is a strong feeling that some of the gentry ought to join as the corps is more for the protection of property or of those who have anything to lose than for those who have not.' Lord Chesham of the same corps agreed that the establishment of an efficient corps 'will render every man's property secure from invasion'. Sir John Kennaway also felt that increased defences had added to the value of property.[71]

One inducement to Volunteer recruiting during the Napoleonic Wars had been the suspension of the ballot until 1808 but this was no longer a substantial factor in 1859. Lord Seymour could join the Movement 'rather than see the country disgraced by the ballot being restored to . . .' and because 'the enemy I fear is not France, but the ballot for the Militia'. But the concept of the Volunteers saving the country from conscription was a rather later development. Sir Richard Vyvyan, who would have preferred the Militia to volunteers, felt 'the proposed exemption from the Militia ballot is of little value when people believe that it will never be enforced, as the government of the day neglected to do so, when the Militia was reorganised'.[72]

It is far from uncommon to find clergymen prominent in the promotion of the Volunteer Movement at local level. This might at first appear unusual but there were justifications for a military organisation in the eyes of at least the established church. A number of sermons delivered to Volunteer corps in 1860 make this abundantly clear. Lincoln Volunteers were exhorted in June 1860 to repel an invasion that threatened property, political freedom and the church for 'there is no cause so holy as the defence of our native land'. This was echoed in a sermon to the 13th Somerset (Frome) R.V.C. in November 1860 where the Rev. Daniel reminded his audience that the knee that bowed lowest before God would be the last to bow to an enemy. A sermon to the 9th Dorset (Shaftesbury) R.V.C. in May 1860 had dwelt on similar themes and also noted that as Volunteers were a defensive force they could never be a source of danger to the government. A sermon to the 2nd Wilts (Trowbridge) R.V.C., on the other hand, had found the source of all Europe's current problems in the 'usurped authority, with which, under the blasphemous title of Vicars of Christ, the Popes have tyrannised for more than 1200 years . . .'[73]

It would be wrong to suppose that the formation of Volunteer corps went entirely unopposed in the localities in 1859. Sir Walter Trevelyan of the Temperance Society for one had written to the Mayor of Morpeth that the invasion scare 'is an insane and groundless panic'. Pamphleteers like Barrett, active in 1852, railed against the scare:

From *The Times* to the *Eatonsville Gazette* everyone here has used unbounded freedom of comment on our French neighbours and yet when the French press has taken a leaf out of our own book, and when ultramontaine journals and obscure pamphlets have reciprocated the hatred and anger we have so capriciously poured forth, we immediately raise a scream of astonishment . . . declare these intemperate scum are the proof of a deliberate design on the part of the Government to invade England.[74]

One leading Buckinghamshire pacifist, Dr John Lee, in whose papers many of Barrett's pamphlets survive, was deeply worried by the 'immense power and influence now in the possession of our Army and Navy' but, at least, Volunteers had the merit of proving additional arguments for reducing the standing Army. At Aylesbury a coal merchant named Shaw attempted unsuccessfully to disrupt the public meeting and subsequently communicated his feelings to the local press. In his view the public had soon forgotten the lessons of the Crimea for had not everyone cried for war in 1854 and then discovered the 'miserable' results. A pamphlet circulated in Dorset outlined twelve reasons why 'thoughtful and serious minded' persons should not join the Volunteers. These differed little from the arguments of 1852 — war was opposed to the spirit of the Bible; it would lower the character of the individual to kill; volunteering would arouse evil passions such as drunkenness, bad company and the music and glitter that would act on young minds and counteract the teaching of Sunday schools![75]

In northern areas in particular there was also a feeling that the formation of the Volunteers represented a plot to kill interest in domestic reform. At Huddersfield the Chairman of the public meeting in June 1859, William Moore, accused those most favourable to reform of being afraid to trust the people with arms. Another speaker, however, called the Volunteers a 'Tory dodge' to divert attentions from reform. An attempt to tack an amendment on the resolution to form the corps led to uproar, £5 worth of damage to furniture and the break up of the meeting in utter confusion. There were similar accusations of a 'Tory device' at Rochdale in December 1859 and a resolution at Oldham condemning attempts to lead the public away from reform of representation and taxation.[76] There is little enough evidence of any such motivation on behalf of those advocating Volunteer corps. Nevertheless Tennyson's poem had certainly implied dropping reform issues to concentrate on national defence and in January 1860 W.H. Russell called for the extension of the 'disease' of rifle fever 'because we believe it will ensure our body politic against much more terrible disorders'. Lord Monson also considered the Volunteers as important a safeguard against 'destructive democratic feeling among ourselves' as against invasion.[77]

Despite such moral strictures many men who might have been expected to heed them nevertheless became involved in the Moverment. Charles Dickens, though feeling that there was no greater sin than an unnecessary war, felt that:

> the next greatest sin that can be committed by those who have accepted the responsibility of Government is to leave the people under their direction ill prepared to resist war . . . For assuredly it is but reasonable that any man who has a stake in this country — and what man has not who has a life in it? — should be trained in the use of arms in its defence.[78]

George Cruikshank, the cartoonist and Vice President of the

Temperance League, was angered by 'an affront by the Peace Society and others against the Rifle Volunteers' when he sent a recruiting party to Deptford in November 1861 for his 24th Surrey R.V.C. W.E. Forster, the Quaker M.P., frequently recalled his earlier days in the Movement when he had joined though a man of peace, for it stemmed panics. Another leading Quaker Volunteer was J.W. Pease of the Hull Volunteers.[79] Captain Toynbee reflected the views of many when he spoke at Aylesbury that he had 'heard something of Peace Societies, and when he saw that Frenchmen loved Englishmen, or Englishmen loved Frenchmen as well as they loved themselves, he would join the Peace Society'. One J. James, a solicitor, was loudly cheered at the same meeting when he said: 'If any gentleman was desirous, on peace principles, of having his nose pulled by a Frenchman, he must go to France and have it done, for they could not suffer it in Aylesbury market-place.'[80]

It is now fashionable to be unduly cynical about motives of patriotism and, although there were other elements involved in 1859, it cannot be denied that the predominant motive force behind the Volunteer Movement was patriotism and the sense of duty. It was viewed at the same time by the great majority of the participants as a spontaneous patriotic reaction:

> like a snowball throughout the United Kingdom — it only required a slight move to become a mass of overwhelming power and if called upon to protect the country it will explode like a fulminated still and scatter an enemy in the most precipitate manner.[81]

If this enthusiasm quickly died it is not evidence that it was not genuinely felt at the time. Few in 1861 would have quarrelled with Earl Spencer when he said: 'When he joined the Volunteer Movement it was not because he feared an invasion from France but because he thought such a movement was necessary for the defence of the Country.'[82]

The actual process behind the formation of a typical rifle volunteer corps can be traced by examining in some detail the Amersham and Chelsham R.V.C. which ironically failed to materialise as a permanent unit.[83] Frederick Charsley — an Amersham solicitor, Clerk to the Magistrates, Clerk to the Board of Guardians and Superintendent Registrar — began to canvass support for an Amersham corps in January 1860. Many prominent men approached, such as Lord Howe, had already promised support to other corps such as those at Wycombe and Slough. The Duke of Bedford was also approached but declined, as a resident of Bedfordshire, to support a Buckinghamshire unit. Enthusiasm anyway seemed lacking in the area as George

Charsley, brother of Frederick and a Beconsfield solicitor, noted on 17 January:

> The present generation are very unlike that of yore . . . they are poor here and without any military ardour. From enquiries I have made I much doubt whether you would get a single Volunteer. At any rate, a public meeting would be the only means of stirring them up here.

The situation in Gerrards Cross was described to Charsley on 17 March by Leicester Hibbert, a gentleman of Chalfont St. Peter, 'it is a remarkable fact that all the farmers in the parish are middle aged or elderly, and they have not got a single son among them'.

Charsley issued 269 circulars to local men on 20 January, followed on 26 January by a call for donations:

> I beg to enclose for your perusal the accompanying particulars, relative to the formation of a Volunteer Rifle Corps for the District of Amersham and its vicinity; and at the same time, earnestly to solicit the use of your influence in carrying out the proposed measure; as also the favour of your contribution towards its fund.

The public meeting was held at Amersham on 3 February and was similar to those held elsewhere, resulting in the election of a Committee to administer the corps. The tone can be judged from a speech of J. Holt, a butter factor of Amersham:

> Recent events in France had done more to conduce to the peace of the two nations than any other movement. But still, in the event of a force coming some fine morning to invade us, it was quite essential that we should have riflemen who would be able to plant a few effective shots in the proper quarter.

Included on the seven man committee were Lord Chesham, T.T. Drake (whose family had formerly controlled the old Amersham pocket borough); the Lord Lieutenant, Lord Carrington; Charsley; Hibbert and other assorted gentry and clergy. Three more men were brought on to the committee on 21 February including J.D. Francis, Charsley's counterpart in Chesham, to draw more Chesham men into the corps. A sub-committee chose the Hon. W.G. Cavendish, M.P., a Whig backbencher, as first Commanding Officer.

By 20 March 1860 they had 45 enrolled members, of whom 34 were effectives, plus £190 13s. 6d. in donation and £99 18s. 0d. in subscriptions. A suggestion to drop the subscription to enable more men to join was rejected. The proposed range was to be in Frame

Field, part of Drake's Shardeloes estate, and the armoury in Amersham Market House. At this point the proposed corps ran foul of authority. Firstly, Sergeant-Major Cross of the Royal Bucks. King's Own Militia, sent by Carrington to inspect the armoury, discovered on 12 April that a clergyman was in occupation with a school; 'the clergymen will not give up the possession of the room until a fit and proper place be provided for the said books and cases . . . the walls and ceiling are out of repair, the lock on the door a very weak one'. Worse, the custodian demanded by government circular was revealed as an ex-Militiaman who had deserted to the Royal Navy in 1852. After a period of about a month an officer arrived to inspect the range. George Isaacson, aide to Charsley, informed him that the officer 'cannot certify a safe range anywhere; the fields beyond are all arable fields and his opinion is that many bullets, from whatever place, would traverse these fields, or glance off the trees at the back of the butt in all kinds of directions'. On 4 June 1860 Sidney Herbert informed Carrington that the Corps could not be accepted until a safe range had been found. Lord Chesham lamented that 'Chesham and Amersham people had been so slack in coming forward'. Ideas swung to a mounted corps as Charsley explained in a further circular on 28 August. On 18 September the Committee decided their enquiries 'did not leave them to believe that it was practicable to establish a mounted corps', Leicester Hibbert remarking that he did not even have a horse.

A similar process can be traced in most cases. Once a corps was accepted it was given a county number and its officers were appointed by the Lord Lieutenant.

Seeds of Permanence

The growth of the Volunteer Movement exceeded most estimates in 1859 and 1860 and surprised such observers as Bright who predicted in January 1860 that the enthusiasm would not last long.[84] In fact such figures as are available indicate that the number of recruits increased in the autumn of 1859 and spring of 1860. It was estimated that in November and December 1859 alone there were 700 recruits daily and an average monthly increase over the two years to May 1861 of 7,000 recruits. Certainly, whereas only 133 rifle corps were formed in 1859, a total of 578 were formed in 1860 and a further 36 rifle corps in 1861 and this did not include artillery units or those corps which had failed to materialise.[85] Why then did this enthusiasm for the Volunteer Movement persist long after most observers had expected it to decline swiftly?

The main factor, of course, was the continuing suspicion of Napoleon III long after the Franco-Austrian war had been concluded by the

Peace of Villafranca in July 1859. A survey of 'war scare' articles in the *Saturday Review* reveals that there was a total of 15 such articles in 1858, 47 in 1859, 44 in 1860, 33 in 1861 and still as many as 25 in 1862.[86] Napoleon III still appeared the embodiment of militarism. There was no decrease in French naval expenditure and in November 1859 the French launched the first sea going iron clad, *La Gloire*. There was general suspicion of French offers of aid in China which a conciliatory letter of Napoleon III to Persigny published in *The Times* in August 1860 did little to abate. Such fears extended to the Government. Neither Sidney Herbert nor de Grey and Ripon were scare mongers but Herbert believed war possible. As late as June 1860 de Grey was voicing the opinion that war 'stands close to us'.[87] Palmerston, Lord John Russell and Herbert were all particularly wary of Napoleon III's offer to co-operate in the expedition to China to ratify the Treaty of Tientsin. Palmerston had long continued to believe in Napoleon's fair intentions but by November 1859 his opinion had changed. He now felt it 'unwise not to make all our preparations for the gale which the political barometer thus indicates'.[88] The Cobden Trade Treaty negotiated with France in January 1860 did little to lull supicions notably at Court and the effect on the public mood was far outweighed by the reaction to French annexation of Savoy, the price of French intervention in Italy in 1859.[89]

In fact, Herbert had undertaken a review of defensive requirements before Palmerston's conversion to national defences. Although a Defence Committee was at work in the War Office, Herbert responded to a suggestion of the Prince Consort and set up a Royal Commission on National Defences to show that the Government was prepared to act and to secure public support for the financial outlay that might result from its recommendations. The Royal Commission, authorised on 20 August 1859, reported on 7 February that:

> . . . we are led to the opinion that neither our Fleet, our standing Army, nor our Volunteer Forces, nor even the three combined, can be relied on as sufficient in themselves for the security of the Kingdom against foreign invasion.[90]

The Commission recommended that the ports should be fortified rather than London which was not so vital to the defence. The resulting controversy over the merits of fortifications as opposed to manpower and the conflict over the increased expenditure on defences between Palmerston and Gladstone need not concern us here but they indicate the continuing tensions.[91] In April 1861 Palmerston was still wary of France and there were now indications of approaching conflict with the United States. Relations with the Northern States came near to war in November 1861 with the seizing of the Confederate diplomats, Mason and Slidell, from the British steamer *Trent* and throughout the American Civil War Britain maintained a large number of troops in Canada.[92] This continuing international tension was to prove a major stimulus to Volunteer recruiting.

The two most overt signs of permanency in 1859 were the foundation of Volunteer journals and newspapers and of the National Rifle Association. The *Volunteer Times*, the *Volunteer Journal for Lancashire and Cheshire*, and *The Volunteer* were not destined to survive long but the *Volunteer Service Gazette* soon achieved the status of the official organ of the Volunteer Movement. Originally designed for easier publication of company orders in the metropolis, the *Volunteer Service Gazette* was established as a limited company by prominent metropolitan officers such as Lord Ranelagh (South Middx. R.V.C), Charles Lindsay (St. Georgès R.V.C.), Lt.-Col. Montagu Hicks (London Rifle Brigade), Josiah Wilkinson (14th Middx. R.V.C.), William Roupell (19th Surrey R.V.C.) and Sir John Lubbock (H.A.C.). Hicks was the first editor but in January 1861 the company was taken over. The new editor was John C. Templer of the Harrow Rifles, agent for Rajah James Brooke of Sarawak and younger brother of Henry Templer, who had attempted to form the rifle corps at Bridport in 1852. Templer's coadjutor and deputy editor was none other than Thomas Hughes, author of *Tom Brown's Schooldays* and commanding officer of the 19th Middx. R.V.C.[93]

The National Rifle Association, rather like the Volunteer Movement itself, had no real 'master builder'. A Committee had been set up to organise such an association in October 1859 led by Earl Spencer, Adam Gladstone, Proctor Beauchamp, Archibald Boyle, Henry Templer, Wilbraham Taylor (12th Middx. R.V.C.) and Edmund Warre of Eton College. At the same time other metropolitan units including the London Rifle Brigade had organised their own committee headed by Lord Elcho (London Scottish R.V.C.) and Earl Grosvenor (Queen's Westminsters R.V.C.). The two groups met at Spencer's London home and on 16 November 1859 held a joint meeting at the Thatched House Tavern in St. James's. A Council was established for the new Association which would seek to promote the Movement and encourage the spread of rifle shooting as a pastime. It was proposed to create an annual meeting on the lines of the Swiss *Tir Fédéral* to assist the permanence of the Movement. An appeal for funds was not too successful but at the suggestion of the secretary, Edmund Mildmay, the first meeting was held at Wimbledon on 2 July 1860.[94]

Queen Victoria opened the meeting with a bullet fired to the bullseye from a carefully aimed and wired Armstrong rifle. The Queen noted the way the ancient fondness for sports had been harnessed to the defensive needs of the country for it was the purpose of the Association 'to make the rifle what the bow was in the days of the Plantagenets'.[95] This in many ways had always been the aim of the Volunteer advocates in the years before 1859. Appropriately, the medals of the National Rifle Association showed an archer of the period 1300-1500 and a rifleman of 1860 standing together with the motto 'Sit perpetum'.

In the face of French ambitions and the growing evidence of Britain's military deficiencies, there arose within Victorian society pressure for the revival of the Volunteer Movement despite considerable reservations on the part of both soldiers and politicians. In 1859 the culmination of events led to a reluctant acceptance by the Government of Volunteers largely as a convenient and cheap solution to what seemed temporary enthusiasm. But the Volunteer Movement proved rather more than a temporary phenomenon and was largely a spontaneous and patriotic national response to the seeming threat of invasion. Assisted by a change of Government and the continuing international tensions, the seeds of permanency were already becoming evident by the close of 1859. But who were the Volunteers?

[1] B. Bond, 'The Prelude to the Cardwell Reforms', *JRUSI* CVL (1961), p 229-36.
[2] J.P. Baxter, *The Introduction of the Ironclad Warship* (Harvard 1933), p 1-47.
[3] Baxter, op cit, p 115.
[4] Wellington to Peel, 27.12.44 and 7.8.45 quoted C.S. Parker, *Sir Robert Peel* (London 1899), III, p 199-206; Hon. G. Wrottesley, *The Military Opinions of General Sir John Fox Burgoyne* (London 1859), p 1-23; Wrottesley, *The Life and Correspondence of F.M. Sir John Fox Burgoyne* (London 1873), I, 434-51; Spencer Walpole, *The Life of Lord John Russell* (London 1889), II, p 14-16.
[5] Wrottesley, *Life*, op cit, I, p 486-7; Wrottesley, *Opinions*, op cit, p 24-61; Sir Francis Head, *The Defenceless State of Great Britain* (London 1850); H.A. Bruce, *The Life of General Sir William Napier* (London 1864), II, p 249-51; Montefiore, op cit, p 357-8.
[6] Burgoyne, 'On the Defence of Great Britain', PRO WO 33/5 No 4.
[7] H. Perkin, *The Origins of Modern English Society* (London 1969) passim; Asa Briggs, *Victorian People* (London 1954), p 223-30; O. Anderson, 'The Growth of Christian Militarism in Mid-Victorian Britain' *EHR* 86 (1971) No 338, p 46-72; O. Anderson, *A Liberal State at War* (London 1967).
[8] Richard Barrett, *Reasons Against the Proposed Enrolment of the Militia* (London 1852); 'Cobden's Three Panics Dispelled' *USM* (1862) Pt III, p 159-80, 334-352.
[9] I.F. Clarke, *Voices Prophesying War, 1763-1984* (Oxford 1966) p 22-6.
[10] J.R. Vincent, *The Formation of the British Liberal Party, 1857-1868* (London 1966), p 58-65.

[11] Wrottesley, *Opinions*, op cit, p 112-127; Wrottesley, *Life*, op cit, p 434-451; Parker, op cit, III, p 197-206.

[12] Charles Napier, 'Letter on the Defence of England by Volunteer Corps and Militia' 8.2.1852 quoted Montefiore, p 357-8; Napier to Kennedy, 7.2.52 *PRO* 30/64/16.

[13] Bruce, op cit, II, p 331-5, 516-22.

[14] Burgoyne, 'Militia and Volunteers' *USM* (1853) Pt 1, p 405-14; G. Douglas and G.D. Ramsay, *The Panmure Papers* (London 1908), II, p 435-44; W. Verner, *The Military Life of HRH George, Duke of Cambridge* (London 1905), I, p 162-7.

[15] Parker, op cit, III, p 196-7, 207-16, 400-12; Walpole, op cit, II, p 13-14; G.P. Gooch, *Later Correspondence of Lord John Russell* (London 1925), I, p 236-40; Palmerston, 13.6.1845 *Hansard* LXXXI, 518-28.

[16] C.S. Parker, *Life and Letters of Sir James Graham* (London 1907), II, p 16-17.

[17] Walpole, op cit, II, p 15-23; Gooch, op cit, I, p 236-70; Dalling and Ashley, *The Life of Henry John Temple, Viscount Palmerston* (London 1870-4), III, p 390-402.

[18] F.W. Hirst, *The Six Panics and Other Essays* (London 1913), p 11-19; Sir T. Martin, *The Life of the Prince Consort* (London 1876), II, p 433-7; J. Ridley, *Lord Palmerston* (London 1970), p 529-47.

[19] Hirst, op cit, p 14-15; Elihu Burritt, *Aggressive War* (London 1852).

[20] Gooch, op cit, I, p 256-7.

[21] Ellenborough, 18.3.52 *Hansard* CXIX, 1226-8; Evans, 22.3.52 *Hansard* CXIX, 1413-4.

[22] Derby, 18.3.52 *Hansard* CXIX, 1229; Walpole, 22.3.52 *Hansard* CXIX, 1425-6 and 5.4.52 *Hansard* CXX, 646.

[23] Bruce, op cit, II, p 332-3, 522.

[24] Williams, 9.3.55 *Hansard* CXXXVII, 351-2; Douglas and Ramsay, op cit, p 444.

[25] J.B. Payne, *Roots in Support of Lt.-Col. Richards' Claim of Chief Promoter of the Volunteer Movement of 1859* (London 1876); 'F G' *The True History of the Origins of our Volunteer Army* (London 1867); Capt. James Orr, *History of the 7th Lanark Rifle Volunteers* (Glasgow 1884), p 7-13 supports Busk; Woodburne, op cit, was dedicated to Bousfield.

[26] Col. Sir Duncan MacDougall, *History of the Volunteer Movement — Its Promoters up to 16 April 1859* (London 1861).

[27] C.A.C. Keeson, *The History and Records of Queen Victoria's Rifles*, 1792-1922 (London 1923), p 491-521; M. Cunliffe, *Soldiers and Civilians: The Martial Spirit in America, 1775-1865* (London 1969); C.P. Stacey, *Canada and the British Army, 1846-71* (London 1936); G.F.G. Stanley, *Canada's Soldiers: The Military History of an Unmilitary People* (Toronto 1954).

[28] Orr, op cit, p 7-13; Montefiore, op cit, p 358-9; Woodburne, op cit, p 30-2; *VSG* Supplement 6.10.60; R.B. Rose, 'The Volunteers of 1859' *JSAHR* 37 (1959), p 97-110.

[29] B.L. Crapster, 'A.B. Richards, 1820-76: Journalist in Defence of Britain' *JSAHR* XLI (1963) No 166, p 94-7; *VSG* 13.10.60; 24.6.76, p 534 'Obituary'.

[30] R.B. Rose, 'Liverpool Volunteers of 1859' *Liverpool Bulletin* VI (1956), p 47-66; *VSG* 24.2.72, p 200 'Sketch of the 1st Lancs Rifles'; 19.5.83, p 481 'Obituary'.

[31] Berry, op cit, p 119; *USM* (1862), Pt III, p 422-3; C. Cooper-King, *The Story of the British Army* (London 1897), p 243.

[32] D. Hudson, *Martin Tupper: His Rise and Fall* (London 1949) esp p 189-99.

[33] Joanna Richardson, 'Tennyson: The Most English of Englishmen' *History Today* XXIII (1973), p 776-84; *The Times* 9.5.59, p 10.

[34] PRO HO51/96-9.

[35] Woodburne, op cit, p 31-33; 'The Dorset Volunteers are 100 Years Old' *Dorset Year Book* (1960-1), p 132-5; Dorset Military Museum DMM/DRV/220; A. Fell, *A Furness Military Chronicle* (Ulverston 1937), p 174; W.G. Fisher, *The History of Somerset*

Yeomanry, Volunteer and Territorial Units (Taunton 1924), p 98-9; Montefiore, op cit, p 358-9; *VSG* 25.4.74, p 403.

[36] Devon RO *Seymour of Berry Pomeroy Mss* 1392 M/Box 18/12; Papers of 1st Exeter and S. Devon R.V.C. 825 W/V 1-202.

[37] Woodburne, p 32-3; *Times* 25.9.57, p 6.

[38] *Times* 14.9.57, p 8 letter from 'An Old Volunteer'; 25.9.57, p 6; 25.9.57, p 10 letter from 'JO'; 26.9.57, p 11 letter from 'C'.

[39] Cf Earle to Disraeli, 26.1.58 *Hughenden Mss* B/XX/E/28.

[40] Cf *Times* 29.1.58, p 10; 30.1.58, p 10; 8.2.58, p 10; 11.2.58, p 8; 15.2.58, p 8; Claremont to Cowley 21.8.58 PRO FO 27/1258 No 49.

[41] Earle to Disraeli, 15.2.58 *Hughenden* B/XX/E/29; Disraeli — Autobiographical Observations, *Hughenden* A/X/36, 37; Benson (ed), *Letters of Queen Victoria* (London 1907), III, p 375-8; Martin, op cit, IV, p 278.

[42] PRO WO 33/5.1.

[43] Burgoyne, 'Popular fallacies with regard to our security against invasion' *PRO* WO 33/5.9, p 73-9.

[44] *Royal Commission on the Militia of the United Kingdom BPP* 1859 [2553, Sess 2] ix.1 esp paras 3671-3 and 6572-8; *Report of the Select Committee on Military Organisation BPP* 1860 (441) VII.I.

[45] *Times* 18.4.59, p 6.

[46] Cf *Times* 19.4.59, p 9; 27.4.59, p 8; 28.4.59, p 7.

[47] Peel, 5.7.59 *Hansard* CLIV, 690-2; *VSG* 15.4.61, p 311 'A History of the Volunteers'; Woodburne, op cit, p 35; E.T. Morgan, *A Brief History of the Bristol Volunteers* (Bristol 1908), p 8-12.

[48] *Times* 13.5.59, p 8.

[49] Memories of Earl Wemyss *LSRG* 1 (Feb 1896), p 13-14; Sir R. Vyvyan to Lord Vivian, 16.5.59 Cornwall R.O. 22M/BO/34/28.

[50] Peel, 5.7.59 *Hansard* CLIV, 689-92.

[51] *BPP* 1860 (441) VII.I, para 3829.

[52] Elcho speech to 1st VB Royal Scots quoted *LSRG* III (Oct. 1898), p 157; *VSG* 25.2.60, p 201; R.W.S. Norfolk, *Militia, Yeomanry and Volunteer Forces of the East Riding, 1689-1908* (E. Yorks Local History Society 1965), p 35.

[53] The circular is reproduced in Montefiore, op cit, appendix L. See also Verner, op cit, I, p 272-3; Walter, op cit, p 89-90.

[54] Martin, op cit, IV, p 436-7; the second circular is reproduced in Montefiore, op cit, appendix M.

[55] *Times* 28.5.59, p 8.

[56] Peel, 5.7.59 *Hansard* CLIV, 689-92; Cornwall R.O. 22M/BO/34/28.

[57] Derby, 1.7.59 *Hansard* CLIV, 520-1.

[58] *USM* 1859 Pt II (July) p 431-33.

[59] Herbert 1.7.59 and 5.7.59 *Hansard* CLIV, 534-6, 695-7; de Grey 1.7.59 *Hansard* CLIV, 512-5. A description of the 1859 Hythe course by Captain King of the Cheshire Rifles is in Berry, op cit, p 129-30 and a description of the 1862 course by Captain Wickham of 13th Somerset R.V.C. in Somerset RO *Lewis Papers* DD/LW 26.

[60] Lord Stanmore, *Sidney Herbert: A Memoir* (London 1906), II, p 386-9.

[61] Lovelace to G. Young 26.8.59 Surrey R.O. *Mole, Metters and Forster Deposit* Acc. 1011 Box 24.

[62] Berry, op cit, p 493-4.

[63] Berry, op cit, p 134; Grierson, op cit, p 21.22; G.L.R.O. (M) *Lieutenancy* L/C/46 for examples of rules in Middlesex units.

[64] Cf Lewis Palk 5.7.59 *Hansard* CLIV, 678-81; Howden, 1.7.59 *Hansard* CLIV, 518-9; Lyndhurst, *Hansard* CLIV 616-27; Horsman, *Hansard* CLIV, 677-92; Sir T.

Martin, *A Life of Lord Lyndhurst* (London 1883), p 481-90.

65 Devon R.O. *Kennaway Mss* 961 M/51.
66 Oxon R.O. *Lieutenancy* L/M VII. iv/5.
67 W.E. Duncombe, *Hansard*, CLIV, 688; Fell, op cit, p 176.
68 *Bucks Herald* 24.12.59.
69 G.L.R.O. (M) *Lieutenancy* L/C/46; Oxon R.O. *Lieutenancy* L/M VII/iv/5; Archives and Local History Dept., Lewisham Public Libraries, A 58/611/1; Somerset R.O. *Lewis Papers* DD/LW 25; *Times* 24.5.59, p 5.
70 Rose, op cit, *JSAHR*, p 106; Walter, op cit, p 59; Berry, op cit, p 388.
71 Geo. Charsley to F. Charsley and Chesham to Charsley, Bucks R.O. *T.A. Collection* Box 14 Amersham Correspondence; Devon R.O. *Kennaway Mss* 961 M/51.
72 Seymour to Grove, 22.12.59 Wilts R.O. *Troyte Bullock of Zeals House* W.R.O. 865/491; Vyvyan to Vivian, 28.5.59 Cornwall R.O. 22 M/BO/34/28.
73 Rev. E. Larken 'The Christian Patriot' 24.6.60 Lincs. R.O. *Hill 12th Deposit* 12/2/1; *Frome Times* 3.10.60; Rev. J. Reynolds, *A Sermon* (Shaftesbury 1861); Rev. J.D. Hastings, *The Oath of Allegiance to the Sovereign: God's Oath to Man* (London and Trowbridge 1860) in Wilts. Regimental Museum.
74 R. Barrett, *The Volunteer Movement* (London 1860); R. Barrett, *The Invasion Panic Once More* (London 1860) both in Bucks. R.O. *T.A. Coll* Box 14 Lee Mss.
75 *Bucks. Advertiser and Aylesbury News* 31.12.59; *Twelve Reasons why Thoughtful and Serious Minded Persons should not join the Volunteers*, Dorset Military Museum.
76 Berry, op cit, p 384-9; Cunningham, op cit, p 20.
77 *Army and Navy Gazette*, 7.1.60; Monson Mss quoted F.M.L. Thompson, *English Landed Society in the Nineteenth Century* (London 1963), p 271.
78 *VSG* 7.1.60, p 87.
79 Cruikshank to Lovelace, G.L.R.O. (M) *Cruikshank Mss*, Acc 534/1; Forster to 3rd W. Yorks. R.V.C., 16.12.76 quoted *VSG* 23.12.76, p 117; Walter, op cit, p 118.
80 *Bucks Herald* 24.12.59.
81 Capt. Caseuline to Wallingford Volunteer Committee, 10.11.60, Berks. R.O. D/EH Z/10.
82 Northants R.O. Eunson compilation Vol II, p 75-7.
83 Quotations on the Amersham and Chesham R.V.C. drawn from Bucks. R.O. *T.A. Coll*, Box 14 Amersham correspondence.
84 Bright to Cobden, 12.1.60 *Add Mss* 43384.
85 R.D. Baxter, *The Volunteer Movement: Its Progress and Wants* (London 1860), p 19-20; Jacques Steeple Mss, Ogilby Trust; Berry, op cit, p 136-7.
86 M.J. Salevouris, *Riflemen Form: The War Scare of 1859-60 in England* (Unpub. PhD, University of Minnesota, 1971), p 292-3.
87 Baxter, *Ironclad*, op cit, p 92-180; *Times* 1.8.60, p 9; L. Wolf, *The Life of 1st Marquis of Ripon* (London 1921), I, p 183-5; Stanmore, op cit, II, p 208-9.
88 Palmerston to Russell, 4.11.59 *Add Mss* 48581 No 51, f 34; see also Palmerston to Gladstone, 15.12.59 *Add Mss* 48581 No 114, f 66.
89 Cf *VSG* 21.4.60, 28.4.60.
90 Royal Commission on National Defences, *BPP* 1860 [2682] XXIII. 431. para 8; see also Stanmore, op cit, II, p 272-3.
91 See Salevouris, op cit, chapter IX; PRO WO 33/9 No 358 0101 and 33/9 0108; *BPP* 1860 (473) XLI. 621; *USM* 1860 Pt II, p 375-7; *VSG* 23.6.60, p 1; D.P. O'Brien, *The Correspondence of Lord Overstone* (Cambridge 1971), III, p 993-4.
92 See Palmerston to Somerset, 11.4.61 Bucks. R.O. *Ramsden Mss* AR/41/62(1) Box 1; K.H. Bourne, 'British Preparations for War with the North, 1861-2' *EHR* LXXVI (1961), p 600-32.
93 *VSG* 20.6.74, p 533 Obituary of Templer; 1.11.84, p 7-8 Notes; for *VSG* Company

circulars see *Freame Mss*, Gillingham Local History Society Museum.

[94] Lord Cottesloe, *The Englishman and the Rifle* (London 1946), p 55-66; Wemyss Memories *LSRG* (May 1896), p 53; Montefiore op cit, p 380-2; *VSG* 13.11.75, p 23; for NRA circulars see Surrey R.O. *Mole, Metters and Forster Dep* Acc 1011, Box 24.

[95] 'The British Olympia at Wimbledon' *USM* 1860 Pt II, p 512-21.

CHAPTER II

THE SOCIAL COMPOSITION OF THE VOLUNTEER FORCE 1859-1899

"It is a glorious, gallant band,
  A phalanx grand and rare,
That heart linked thus doth firmly stand,
  Let meet it they who dare.
The chivalry of labour, hand
  In hand with knightly crew,
What living belt boasts other land
  As potent, and as true?"

'Our Volunteers'
Alfred Richards, 1867

A glance at the rules of almost any of the early Volunteer corps will indicate at once the character of these units and thus to a large extent the intended 'class' of the membership. The impression from these early rules must be one of a series of exclusive military clubs, maintaining that exclusiveness by the sheer barrier of expense. This at least was the ideal but from the very beginning there were exceptions and by the eve of the South African War the composition of the Volunteer Force was very different from that conceived by Ranelagh and his Rules Committee in August 1859.

Each corps had both honorary and enrolled members. The honorary members could wear the uniform of the corps but had no military function, for which privilege they paid either a life subscription of around ten guineas or an annual subscription of between one and three guineas. Enrolled members were further divided between effectives and non-effectives; the effectives being those who could comply with the modest drill requirements laid down in the government circulars. All enrolled members paid an annual subscription usually ranging from half a guinea to one guinea. In many corps there was also an entrance fee of perhaps half a guinea and possibly further contributions for officers to various corps' funds such as a Band Fund. Membership was further restricted by the proposing and seconding of members. There was essentially little practical difference between officers and men, both were expected to serve on the elected Finance Committee. These published annual accounts for scrutiny and discussion by all the members at annual general meetings. Discipline was simply expected from gentlemen and was enforced only by a system of petty fines. Pointing a rifle at another man for example, could cost 5s. in the Buckingham corps but £1 in the Slough corps. The tone of the whole is perhaps set by a printed circular of the 2nd Bucks. (Wycombe) R.V.C. of December 1859:

> It is the earnest wish of the Committee that the tone of the Corps should be that of gentlemen — and that no cause of offence, either in conduct or language, should ever impair the harmony of its action.[1]

All the rules were drawn up and arrangements made with 'due regard for the convenience of members'. This was hardly the 'rabble' envisaged by the Duke of Cambridge in 1857, at least in a social sense. The level of intelligence in Volunteer ranks was generally considered to be and to remain well above that of the other ranks of the Militia and Regular Army. The prevalence of Volunteer poetry, however bad, also indicates a degree of literacy unlikely to be found in the ranks of the Regular Army (see Appendix 1).

The British Army in the second half of the nineteenth century was by no means representative of society as a whole. Both officers and men came from basically unrepresentative social groups. The Army remained a 'way of life' which bore little relation to the larger structure of English society. In 1857 the Royal Commission on Purchase had recognised that the middle classes in particular had 'no place in the British Army under the present system'. If one can judge the incidence of the middle class in the rank and file of the Army by the prevalence of nonconformism then this was almost non-existent. In the 1860's nonconformists represented only about 3% of the rank and file and still only 6.7% as late as 1913. Middle class officers represented approximately 47% of the officer corps of the British Army in the 1830's and still only 59% in 1912. The balance of aristocratic and landed officers was considerably over-representative in their proportion to the total population. The officers of the Militia remained largely what Michael Howard has termed the 'squirearchy in arms' since they had to fulfil property qualifications for commissions until 1869. The Militia ranks were filled with the unemployed and casual labourers since no one else in regular employment or trade could afford to devote 28 days to Militia training each summer. The Yeomanry were virtually restricted to the landed and farming communities, they alone being able to afford the upkeep of horses and equipment.[2] Much of the inspiration behind the Volunteers in these first few years was the attempt to involve the middle classes of society who previously had had no recognised place in the military sphere. Both the Prince Consort and Sidney Herbert saw the attraction that an exclusive type of volunteer corps might hold for the middle class and this was certainly the ideal expressed in the rules of early units.

Potentially there was a large reservoir of the middle class who could be drawn into the Movement. Professor Best has depicted the 1850's as the decisive turning point in terms of urban growth in Britain. In 1841 approximately 48.3% of Britain's population were to be found in urban areas; by 1851 this had increased to 54%; by 1861 to 58.7% and by 1871 to 65.2%. It is a proportion which continues to increase down to the present time. In 1851 there were only 11 cities with a population of over 100,000 inhabitants but by 1881 this had grown to a total of 26 major urban centres. Figures for the early years of the Volunteer Movement are notoriously inaccurate. Nevertheless some calculations by the statistician Dudley Baxter in 1860 are convincing in substance if not in precise details. Baxter calculated that most of the cities, which contained approximately one third of the total population, had raised Volunteers. Of the towns containing something less than one third of the population, about half of the larger and one third of the smaller had raised corps. In the rural areas, which contained something over a third of the total population about one twentieth had joined the Movement. Table 1 indicates the figures produced by Baxter of town involvement:

Table 1

Town Population	No. of Towns	No. Raising Volunteers	Proportion
Over 20,000	70	66	94%
10-20,000	124	59	47%
3-10,000	609	169	28%
Under 3,000	8,500	750	2%

For all the guesswork involved in Baxter's figures, the table still indicates the factor obvious to most contemporaries — that the most favourable environment for Volunteer corps was where wealth, youth and the middle classes were found to coincide.[3] But how far is even this rough guide applicable to the Volunteers of 1859-60?

There were from the very beginnings of the Volunteer Movement conscious attempts to involve the more intelligent elements of the labouring classes. The middle class ideal as embodied in the rules of Volunteer corps never bore much relation to reality even before 1862-3 when evidence pointed to an increasing dependence upon artisans.

Within the middle class itself there were considerable differences in the pattern of participation and leadership between urban centres and smaller provincial market towns. It is possible, in fact, to construct three separate theoretical profiles of the Volunteer in the period from 1859 to about 1862. These may be termed the Urban Volunteer, the Rural Volunteer and the Mounted Volunteer. Each of these three was profoundly different from the others although by 1862-3 there is little doubt that all were being diluted in the face of the growth of a predominantly working class Volunteer Force.

One of the more difficult exercises in historical study must surely be the definition of class. It has lately been the practice of historians and other students to discover a 'rising' middle class in most centuries yet it was not until the Nineteenth Century that there appears to have been any real consciousness of a class system in England. For the purpose of examining the social composition of the Volunteers, it is necessary to establish a broad definition of 'classes'. This must necessarily be based upon the concepts of social status utilised by contemporaries and by contemporary directories. The difficulty lies with this concept of status which did not necessarily depend upon economic factors. Thus there is a large gap in contemporary terms between a clerk and an artisan though the economic difference may not be marked. It is also necessary to take the professions given in a directory at face value thus a 'merchant', 'farmer' or 'engineer' may well hide the exact status of the individual. Unfortunately, then, an element of risk must enter the definition of class.

The terms 'landed' and 'gentry' are self evident though directories never differentiate between the actual status of the individual. Middle class is taken here to include 'farmers', 'clergy', 'professionals', 'tradesmen' and 'clerks'. There are, of course, varying grades within the middle class and 'professionals', 'clergy' and 'farmers' are assumed to be 'upper middle class' whilst 'tradesmen' and 'clerks' are assumed to be 'lower middle class'. Within these groups are divisions in, for example, the 'professionals'. In the 1841 census only clergy, lawyers and medical men were classed as professional men. Others of a similar status were classed as 'other educated persons'. By 1861 teachers, actors, journalists, artists, musicians, engineers and draftsmen were included but some groups like architects, surveyors and bankers did not achieve professional status on the census until much later.[4] Here the term 'professional' is deemed to include all those listed as professional above and, indeed, all involved in the legal, financial, engineering, commercial and medical worlds and civil servants. The term 'tradesmen' covers shopkeepers of all types, butchers, bakers, brewers and the obviously lower type of merchants such as coal merchants. The labouring classes are also varied and are assumed to comprise craftsmen or artisans and outright labourers. Craftsmen or artisans are assumed to include all those using their hands in basic skills such as plumbers, coach builders, cabinet makers and silversmiths. Using these contemporary divisions between professions and trades, whilst imposing upon them a class definition would seem to provide the best means of examining the actual social composition of the Volunteer Force.

Participation and Leadership

Whatever the difference between urban and rural Volunteers, both were subject to certain common constraints on their ability to recruit and it is necessary to examine these before discussing our theoretical models.

One of the clearest constraints upon participation in the Volunteer Force was the degree of social leadership available in any given locality. Since the Volunteers were intended to fit into the existing pattern of local county government, much could depend initially on the attitude towards the infant force of the Lord Lieutenant. Where support was lacking, problems could arise. In Somerset, for example, Lord Portman took no action to summon a meeting of Deputy Lieutenants and Magistrates to discuss the formation of Volunteer corps. When such a meeting was finally convened in September 1860 it was chaired by a man who had himself expressed considerable reservations on the Movement. In Hampshire the Lord Lieutenant, the Marquis of Winchester, alienated many by attempting to enforce his own preference for knickerbockers as the uniform for Hampshire Volunteers. In particular, this led to a long standing quarrel with Lord Malmesbury of the 10th Hants. (Christchurch) R.V.C. When Malmesbury finally resigned to go abroad in July 1863 after continuing disputes concerning uniforms, annual returns and matters of command, Winchester was much relieved:

> He has chosen to take his own line independent of all authority, and I am very glad he has resigned, and as to his Corps I suspect if the truth was really known it amounts to a sub-division.

Winchester also contrived to fall into disagreement with the inhabitants of Southampton in 1859. He had accepted the 2nd Hants. (Southampton) R.V.C. raised by a Deputy Lieutenant, Thomas Fleming, but other residents wished to raise a separate battalion incorporating Fleming's corps. Winchester was angered that 'these trading people' should attempt to attach Fleming's corps without authority. His refusal to accept any further offers until Fleming's corps was at full strength eventually resulted in a memorial from the town to Sidney Herbert.[5]

Winchester naturally had no desire to encourage the proliferation of countless small and understrength units but this was an argument apparently ignored by prospective patriots. The Marquis of Salisbury faced the same difficulties in Middlesex and was also anxious to conceal how far enrolled numbers were falling below establishment. Thus he incorporated Lord Elcho's proposed 'Euston Road Rifles' in Lord Enfield's 29th Middx. R.V.C. and men from Messrs J. Broadwood and Sons Ltd of Horseferry Road, Westminster, in Earl Grosvenor's 22nd Middx. (Queen's Westminsters) R.V.C. Other offers such as that of Alfred Richards to raise a 'Workmen's Volunteer Brigade' in August 1860 were rejected as being within the jurisdiction of the City of London. Similarly, when George Cruikshank attempted to recruit men for his 24th Surrey (Havelock's Own) R.V.C. in Kent he received a sharp letter from Viscount Sydney, Lord Lieutenant of Kent:

> His Lordship has reported the proceeding to the Secretary of State officially, considering it to be necessary to prevent the recurrance of

proceedings so irregular as Corps belonging to other Counties marching into a County to which they do not belong for the purpose of recruiting.

Cruikshank's own Lord Lieutenant, Lord Lovelace, did little to assist the Movement in Surrey by his insistence that only ex-Regular officers should be appointed to the rank of Lieutenant-Colonel in the Volunteer Force.[6]

The attitude of the Lord Lieutenant was especially crucial when it came to the possibility of raising artisan corps. Lord Leigh of Warwickshire was one who favoured artisan corps but his counterpart in Cambridgeshire, Lord Hardwicke, viewed artisan corps rather differently:

> I always considered they had other duties to perform, and that there was a great difference between men who had property to lose and those who had none, and that if a weapon was given to a man who had no real property, his natural tendency would be to acquire a property which he had not.

In Northamptonshire, Lord Exeter, had misgivings concerning the formation of the 5th Northampton R.V.C. raised from the employees of Messrs. Isaac, Campbell and Co:

> Pray tell me what trade Messrs. Isaac and Campbell follow and what class of men they employ — I should think they must be below the class of Rifle Volunteers and better suited for the Army and Militia.

A month later, in January 1860, Exeter was again trying to reassure himself that the members of the new corps were not 'common work people' but, unfortunately, the identity of the firm remains a mystery although it is likely that it had connections with the shoe trade.[7]

In Middlesex, the Marquis of Salisbury was opposed to units which would 'place upon its class the stamp of inferiority to another'. In consequence there was one protracted quarrel surrounding the formation of the 46th Middx. (London and Westminster) R.V.C. between August 1860 and March 1861. This corps was to be raised from 'persons in steady employment and in the receipt of fair wages who have a stake in the country'. Salisbury, however, refused to accept it even when the Liberal M.P. for Westminster, Sir John Shelley, proposed to change the concept from a purely artisan corps to one composed of both artisans and clerks from banks, printing houses and lawyers' offices. There were allegations of political prejudice and, finally, Sidney Herbert was forced to instruct Salisbury to accept the 46th Middlesex.[8]

The participation of a recognised social leader was considered vital to the success of the Movement. Sir George Osborn recognised this when he pressed the Lord Lieutenant of Bedfordshire, the Duke of Bedford, to appoint Francis Hastings Russell to the command of the Bedfordshire Volunteers:

> I cannot conceal from your Grace that from my personal observations I am satisfied the organisation of the Force, which although in a promising state is still in a primary state, will be greatly prejudiced if the salutary and encouraging countenance of an authorised head be longer withheld . . . a lukewarmness will take root, which may be fatal to a Movement which hitherto has so auspiciously progressed.

This sentiment was echoed by Owen Wethered, later Lieutenant-Colonel of the Bucks. Volunteers and a member of a well known brewing family at Marlow. Wethered envied the situation in Berkshire where, apart from excellent rail connections, 'the vast number of gentlemen's residences in the Royal County provided an ample supply of officers'. Above all, Berkshire had a leading landowner, Robert Loyd-Lindsay, who threw himself into the Volunteer Movement with considerable energy.[9]

It is clear that the first choice in any location was for some member of the landed classes. Mathew Arnold, who joined the Queen's Westminsters, criticised the 'hideous English toadyism' of placing the nobility in command regardless of military ability. He himself attributed it to the vulgar-mindedness and inferiority of the middle classes. Certainly, there is little doubt that the landed classes provided the nucleus of command in most rural areas. In Northamptonshire, for example, the first Lt.-Colonel of the Northants. battalion was the Earl of Euston. His majors were Earl Pomfret and Earl Spencer whilst the Earl of Southampton served in the 2nd Northants. (Towcester) R.V.C. In Bedfordshire, Francis Hastings Russell was indeed appointed as first commanding officer. He was Liberal M.P. for the County from 1847-72 and later succeeded his cousin as 9th Duke of Bedford. The Bedfordshire Volunteer Committee also included Lord St. John of Bletsoe and Lord Wensleydale. Among leading Volunteers in Devon were numbered Sir John Duckworth, Bt., Sir John Kennaway, Bt., Viscount Valletort, the Earl of Mount Edgcumbe and both Sir Thomas Dyke Acland, Bt., and his son Sir Charles Acland. This pattern was equally true of some urban areas. The 3rd Durham (Sunderland) R.V.C. for example, was commanded by Lord Adolphus Vane, the third son of the Marquis of Londonderry.[10] In the metropolis itself aristocratic officers remained immensely influential in the Volunteer Force long after most of their fellows had departed from provincial forces. In 1860 Lord Ranelagh commanded the 2nd Middx.; Lord Radstock, the 9th Middx.; Lord Elcho, the 15th Middx.; Viscount Bury, the 21st Middx.; Earl Grosvenor, the 22nd Middx.; and Lord Enfield, the 29th Middx. Where such natural leaders were not available other social elites had to take their place. As will be seen in the cases of the theoretical 'models' of Volunteer units, the differences between alternative elites in large urban centres and small rural market towns were marked.

Another constraint upon participation could be the sheer expense of joining the Volunteers, particularly for artisans. The accompanying Table 2 of representative examples of uniform and subscription costs indicates the range of initial expense for the prospective Volunteer. Once other incidental expenses such as additional equipment and weapons were also taken into account, total costs could approach £10 or more. In the 2nd Wilts. (Trowbridge) R.V.C. the total cost was £7 10s. 0d., and in the 1st Kent (Maidstone) R.V.C. a total of £10. In a more exclusive unit such as the London Rifle Brigade the total cost of joining came to £14 7s. 6d. Officers were frequently required to pay even more. Sliding scales of donations operated in units such as the 7th Cumberland (Workington) R.V.C., 35th Kent (Westerham) R.V.C., 1st Lincoln (City) R.V.C., 7th Monmouth (Newport) R.V.C., 5th Northants. R.V.C. and 2nd Wilts. (Trowbridge) R.V.C. In the latter case a captain had to donate as much as £100 above his other expenses to the corps. It need hardly be said that large numbers of Englishmen were in no position to afford such expenses even had they wished. In Liverpool, where the average cost of uniform alone was £4 13s. 6d., dock porters earned only 3s. 6d. per day. In rural areas agricultural labourers were earning between 9s. and 12s. per week by 1860-1 although this average was naturally subject to considerable seasonal variations. There appears to have been general agreement that 18s. per week regular wage was the lowest income level at which Volunteers should be recruited without competing directly with the Militia and Regular Army.[11]

Table 2
Examples of Uniform Costs and Subscriptions in Volunteer Corps, 1859-60.

Cost of Uniform		Annual Subscription	
Morpeth	£1 14s. 0d.	Deddington	5s. 0d.
Marlow	£2 5s. 0d.	Maidstone	7s. 6d.
Portsmouth	£2 17s. 6d.	Morpeth	10s. 0d.
Aylesbury	£3 0s. 0d.	Slough	10s. 6d.

Oxford	£3 7s. 0d.	Trowbridge	£1 0s. 0d.
Frome	£3 9s. 10d.	Newport (Mon.)	£1 1s. 0d.
Banbury	£4 0s. 0d.	Maldon	£1 15s. 0d.
Huddersfield	£4 17s. 6d.	Titchfield	£1 11s. 6d.

If artisans, who might themselves subsist barely above that level, were to be recruited in the Volunteer Force then some means had to be found by which they could be relieved of unnecessary expense. That artisans should be recruited was the prevailing view amongst the leaders of the Volunteer Force since the Movement might well decline if it rested on too narrow a social base. Neither Alfred Richards nor Lord Elcho could see any advantage in excluding artisans and perpetuating class distinctions. The *Volunteer Service Gazette* agreed but clearly expected such 'seasoned laborious frames' to be chiefly useful for throwing up earthworks beyond the capacity of gentlemen Volunteers. Elcho believed that the cost could be kept sufficiently low and was prepared to enrol 150 artisans in his 15th Middx. (London Scottish) R.V.C. paying a weekly uniform and equipment instalment of 1s. 3d. Artisans would pay no entrance fee and only a reduced subscription of 5s. in the first year. Earl Grosvenor came to a similar conclusion:

> I think it will be found desirable by us and others to admit members on their paying an annual subscription . . . and to supply them with uniform and accoutrements on their agreeing to pay a weekly instalment of, say, 1s. 6d.

Instalment plans were introduced into many other units such as the 39th Lancs. (Liverpool Welsh), 1st Bucks. (Marlow) and the Chelmsford corps. Other units including the 23rd Essex (Maldon), 7th Monmouth (Newport) and the 13th Somerset (Frome) R.V.C. had schemes whereby honorary members could nominate individuals to receive assistance from the corps committee. In September 1859, for example, W. Phillips nominated a young man employed in his gardens for free equipment in the 13th Surrey (Reigate) R.V.C.[12]

Elsewhere public appeals were made for funds for artisan corps. Such a case occurred in the 8th Kent (Sydenham) R.V.C. in July 1860 when the Rev. J.M. Clark of Forest Hill approached the Committee with the names of 60 artisans willing to join if sufficient funds could be collected to equip them. An Artisans Committee was formed and an appeal launched on 31 July 1860, but the experiment was not a success. There was continual friction between the Volunteer Committee and the Artisans Committee and it was announced to the annual general meeting in 1861 that subscriptions from a 'populous and wealthy neighbourhood' were not sufficient to forward the Movement in Sydenham. The Artisans Committee had considerable difficulty in raising its annual subscriptions, fell into arrears and resigned in February 1862. The Committee of the corps then insisted on issuing summonses to recover the arrears and in September 1863 one man was actually committed for a month to Maidstone Gaol for defaulting on his subscription. On the other hand there were at least two instances in which there were violent reactions to attempts to restrict membership. When Adam Gladstone organised a meeting to raise the 5th Lancs. R.V.C. at Liverpool Sessions House on 20 May 1859, R.J. Tilney 'led his supporters to smash the ballot-boxes by the use of which the founders had hoped to exclude undesirables from membership'. Similarly at Ulverston in December 1859 a proposed subscription met with dissent and many men left the public meeting: 'The malcontents waited outside and gave expression to their indignation by snow-balling their comrades as they came out of the Assembly Rooms . . .'[13]

One constraint of particular relevance in rural areas was the difficulty of securing recruits from a widespread agricultural community. In Cornwall Sir Richard Vyvyan acknowledged this problem as early as May 1859:

> It is only large towns, where the general interest in foreign politics is connected with newspaper reading, that the public at large have any patriotic inducements to arm themselves; and even then, if we are to infer from the small number of those ready to be affiliated in rifle clubs (as compared with the population) the letter of the Secretary of State does not meet with an adequate response, whatever may be the enthusiastic speeches delivered at public meetings.

Another county which well illustrates this kind of problem is Oxfordshire. Reports reaching the Clerk to Lieutenancy, J.M. Davenport, through the summer and autumn of 1859 were hardly encouraging. In May Alexander Forbes of Whitchurch, on the Berkshire border near Sonning, had lamented the preponderance of agricultural labourers and the fact that 'I cannot call to mind more than two or three persons, myself inclusive, whose means or leisure would enable them to volunteer for such a corps as that proposed.' Watlington Magistrates reported that distance to ranges, likely costs and lack of potential officers accounted for their failure to raise men. On 23 July 1859 the (County) Volunteer Committee named 21 possible officers to encourage recruiting but A.R. Tawney of Banbury found little response. By October he was advising Davenport that the 21 'officers' would do better to reduce themselves to the ranks and enlist a few friends each.

Both Tawney and another correspondent, Samuel Gardner, remarked on the unwillingness of the farming community to 'give up any time . . . to anything but their present calling . . .' In November Herbert Wykeham, son of Baroness Wenham of Thame, reported that the middle classes, too, appeared to object to 'having to find their own uniform'. The problem was best summarised by Davenport himself in a memorandum of 19 November 1859:

> it will be in vain to expect a large supply of Volunteers from districts of a purely agricultural character, and that it is expedient to rely chiefly upon the towns as the centre of the several companies or sub-divisions of which it is proposed to form a County Regiment.

In Devon one solution to the problem appeared to be the formation of a central County organisation to collect and diffuse information, stimulate local exertions and advise the Lord Lieutenant on Volunteer matters. A special committee under the chairmanship of Lord Devon was established in December 1859, and in February 1860 a county meeting endorsed its recommendations to establish a Devon County Volunteer Association. This succeeded admirably in its intentions and was to form the model of the County Rifle Associations later developed throughout the country under the auspices of the National Rifle Association.[14]

By contrast urban units frequently had difficulty in satisfying the government inspectors of the safety of their proposed ranges as was discovered at Newport in Monmouthshire where the Committee reported in December 1859:

> We are, of course, endeavouring to surmount this obstacle which settles always on towns near which land is much cultivated and covered with stock or intersected by roads or footpaths . . .

Elsewhere it was simply a question of lack of local support for reasons which are now difficult to explain. In Buckinghamshire, for example, a proposed corps at Newport Pagnell foundered through lack of support in 1860 and another at Princes Risborough, where only a clergyman was available to command it. Martin Tupper's meeting to raise a unit at Albury in July 1859 was attended by only twenty persons and in Sussex Lord Leconfield could find no support at all for the Movement in the Midhurst and Masham area. As a result he was forced to alter his estimate of 'the area of County I calculated upon to produce 100 men of the right class'.[15]

Purely local issues could play a significant part in the fortunes of particular Volunteer corps. In Cornwall it was feared that the original government decision to withhold arms would greatly hamper the progress of the Movement. The Lord Lieutenant, Lord Vivian, warned General Peel on 16 May 1859 that:

> whilst their means are too good to induce them to become Soldiers, they are not sufficiently good to enable them to supply themselves with arms in compliance with the requirement of your circular.

This indeed proved to be the case when T.P. Tyacke attempted to raise recruits in the Helston area and also in the West Kirrier Division generally where Sir Richard Vyvyan also encountered a disinclination to accept the 'discipline requisite' in military units. Vyvyan himself believed that military effort in the county had been adversely effected by the withdrawal of state support from the local Yeomanry in 1828 which had 'so thrown back the military energy of the yeoman and shopkeepers' that it would require years to bring them back to their former bearing. Answers from gentry solicited for subscriptions proved generally unfavourable in Helston in May 1860. In Dorset Robert Freame of the 11th Dorset (Gillingham) R.V.C. was forced to appeal for funds in January 1861 because of the difficulty of raising either money or interest amid a largely non-resident gentry in the Blackmore Vale. In Bedfordshire John Green of the 8th Beds. (Woburn) R.V.C. was convinced that the unattractive nature of the Bedfordshire battalion uniform was the cause of the failure to recruit more men. This thought continued to obsess him for six years, resulting in a stream of letters on the subject to both his commanding officer and the Lord Lieutenant, Earl Cowper. Uniform disputes led to the loss of large numbers of men from one Birmingham corps and the hiving off of the Customs Section of the 21st Middx. (Civil Service) R.V.C. simply because they disagreed with the belt ornaments chosen by the majority of the corps.[16] Bearing in mind these limitations and conditions, we can now turn to consider the three theoretical 'models'.

The Rural Volunteer

The current controversy surrounding the concept of deference in mid-Victorian electoral behaviour lies outside the scope of this work. Nevertheless the historian of the Volunteer Movement in rural areas can only be struck by the marked resemblance of some units to bands of neo-feudal retainers. The 1st Northants. (Althorp) R.V.C., for example, was raised by Earl Spencer from his 17,000 acre estate. In June 1860 it was described as comprising his tenants and friends. The 6th Wilts. (Maiden Bradley) R.V.C., commanded by the Earl of St.

Maur, was raised from the tenant farmers of the Duke of Somerset in the Blackmoor Vale; in Bedfordshire, the 8th Beds. (Woburn) R.V.C. was drawn entirely from the estate of the Duke of Bedford. Such examples are not confined to southern England. The 2nd Northumberland Artillery, commonly called the Percy Artillery, was raised from the tenants of the Duke of Northumberland and commanded by his son for thirty years. At Lord Zetland's estates in the North Riding, all male members of the households were drilled daily and, similarly, companies were raised from the Scottish estates of Lord Tweeddale and the Earl of Wemyss.[17]

Many other units enjoyed the patronage of local landed gentry. Sir George Osborn, Bt., of Chicksands Priory always provided the 7th Beds. (Shefford and Biggleswade) R.V.C. with its annual dinner. Sir Rainald Knightley was a patron to the 8th Northants. (Daventry) R.V.C. and the Hon. G.W. Fitzwilliam, whose family had controlled the former pocket borough, was patron to the 6th Northants. (Peterborough) R.V.C. The participation of local gentry is also marked in several Hampshire units such as the 3rd Hants. (Lymington), 12th Hants. (Petersfield) and 17th Hants. (Titchfield) R.V.C. Outside the larger towns in Lancashire, too, gentlemen can be identified as providing the majority of officers between 1860 and 1871 in such units as the 8th Lancs. (Bury), 9th Lancs. (Warrington) and 11th Lancs. (Preston) R.V.C. The Marquis of Hartington served in the 37th Lancs. (Lonsdale) R.V.C. and, indeed, caused some comment at the Berlin Victory Parade in 1866 when he appeared in the uniform of the unit. Prussian officers were considerably surprised to learn that this 'unassuming young gentleman' in the unknown uniform had been Secretary of State for War only a few weeks before.[18]

To a large extent the success of units in rural areas also depended upon the attitude of the farming community. In many cases this was at best ambivalent. As noted earlier, there was very little interest in the Movement amongst Oxfordshire farmers. A similar attitude can be traced in the agricultural areas around Usk in Monmouthshire where it was found 'impracticable to obtain Volunteers from among the agricultural population in the neighbourhood of Ragland'. Nevertheless, some units do show a large farming influence. Significantly, Earl Spencer mentioned in his speech to the Northants. Volunteers at Althorp in August 1864 that the 2nd Northants. (Towcester) and 8th Northants. (Daventry) R.V.C. had been unable to attend camp because of the early harvest. Close examination of the surviving lists of the Towcester corps indicates that it drew recruits from over twenty different villages and hamlets. Similarly, the 24th Somerset (Somerton) R.V.C. recruited heavily from the surrounding villages of

Kingweston, Long Sutton and Kingdon. The 13th Somerset (Frome) depended upon recruits from the outlying villages of Nunney and Berkeley and the 7th Hants. (Fareham) R.V.C. had a large contingent from Wymering and Porchester. The 18th Cornwall (Meneage) R.V.C. drew men not only from Helston but also from the villages of Constantine, St. Keverne, St. Anthony, Cury, Mawgan, St. Martin, Ruan Major, Ruan Minor, Grade, Mullion and Landewednach. Of 64 men enrolled in this unit in March 1860 some 36 can be identified, of whom 25 were farmers. Farmers also formed the largest identifiable group in the 8th Wilts. (Mere) R.V.C. and the 10th Wilts. (Warminster) R.V.C. maintained its own kennels.[19]

The 7th Somerset (Keynsham) R.V.C. was described in December 1860 as being entirely recruited from farmers, sons of farmers and their labourers; in 1862 a third of the 13th Sussex (Hurstpierpoint) R.V.C. was also indentified as farmers. A muster-roll of the 15th Kent (West Kent) R.V.C. commanded by Sir Edmund Filmer indicates the prominent role that could be played by the farming community. Some 91 men were enrolled in the West Kent corps between 1860 and 1870 drawn from the villages of East Sutton, Sutton Valence, Headcorn and Lintern. Occupations are given for 88 men comprising 3 gentlemen, 1 professional man, 14 tradesmen, 7 clerks, 23 craftsmen and 27 farmers and 13 agricultural labourers. In this unit, then, approximately 45% were drawn from the agricultural community.[20]

In the majority of cases however, units in rural areas were concentrated in the small market towns. Evidence points to the involvement in the Volunteer Movement in such towns of a broad cross section of the local community. In some instances a unit benefited from the presence of a large residential middle class as in the 5th Berks. (Maidenhead) R.V.C. and 2nd Oxford (City) R.V.C. More usually, such provincial units had a predominance of professional gentlemen and tradesmen and a sprinkling of craftsmen. In Northampton, for example, Alexander Barr's 4th Northants. R.V.C. comprised professional men and tradesmen. Of 45 men enrolled in the proposed Amershal corps in March 1860 approximately 54% of identified Volunteers were middle class and in the Winslow Sub-division of the 3rd Bucks. (Buckingham and Winslow) R.V.C. approximately 80% of identified Volunteers were middle class. A similar preponderance of professional men and tradesmen can be found in many other units including the 3rd Dorset (Dorchester), 5th Dorset (Weymouth), 1st Kent (Maidstone), 10th Somerset (Wells), 5th Surrey (Reigate) and 1st Wilts. (Salisbury) R.V.C.[21] But let us examine some typical units for which detailed muster rolls survive more closely.

The 5th Kent (East Kent Tradesmen) R.V.C. was raised at Canterbury with 39 members in 1860. These comprised 3 professionals, 19 tradesmen, 7 clerks and 10 craftsmen or roughly 48% tradesmen. The 29th Kent (Ashford) R.V.C. totalled 44 members in 1860 comprising 2 farmers, 2 professionals, 15 tradesmen, 9 clerks and 16 craftsmen. The 2nd Cinque Ports (Ramsgate) R.V.C. totalled 22 members in 1859 comprising 1 farmer, 1 professional, 10 tradesmen, 9 craftsmen and 1 labourer and the 7th Cinque Ports (Margate) R.V.C. in December 1859 comprised 4 professionals, 10 tradesmen, 2 clerks and 4 craftsmen. The 1st Monmouth (Chepstow) R.V.C. totalled some 61 members in July 1859 comprising 8 gentry, 9 farmers, 10 professionals, 19 tradesmen, 1 clerk and 14 craftsmen. Another typical example of a small town corps is the 2nd Beds. (Toddington) R.V.C. for which a list survives for June 1860 giving details of its membership of 64 men. The leading Volunteer was W.C. Cooper, lord of the manor and patron of the living in a town which boasted only some minor straw-plaiting as a manufacturing industry. The unit comprised 1 gentleman, 20 farmers, 4 professionals, 19 tradesmen, 4 men of miscellaneous occupation, 12 craftsmen and 2 labourers with only 1 man being unidentified. In terms of rough percentage this gives approximately 37% of what might be termed upper middle class, over 35% lower middle class and over 21% artisan class.[22]

Fortunately, it is possible to reconstruct the membership of the entire Oxfordshire county force in 1859-60 from the lists submitted to the Lord Lieutenant, the Duke of Marlborough, for the 2nd City, 3rd Banbury, 4th Henley, 5th Witney, 6th Deddington, 7th Bicester and 8th Thame corps.[23] That of the 5th Witney corps is drawn from separate lists submitted for its component towns of Witney, Woodstock, Bampton and Burford. The information is best presented in the accompanying Table 3.

Within these various categories a broad cross section of the community as a whole emerges. It can be seen that few landed gentry contributed to the Volunteer Force in Oxfordshire — a few officers but nowhere more than 7% of the whole. Both agricultural labourers, as might be expected, and also clerks were scarce. The farming community was only represented significantly in purely agricultural districts such as Deddington and Bicester. The professional classes contributed the most men only in Witney and the backbone of every corps, with the exception of Bicester, was provided by the tradesmen. These shopkeepers, butchers, brewers, drapers and the like joined in large numbers. In Thame, they provided 50% of the whole, in Henley some 46%, in Banbury 38% and 34% in Oxford. Nowhere was the artisan content over 26%. The situation in Oxfordshire in the period 1859-60 gives therefore approximately 43.7% lower middle class and

33.8% upper middle class across the county — an overwhelming 77.5% middle class.

Although there is a tendency to categorise early Volunteer units as middle class, it could be argued that historians have paid too much attention to the wood at the expense of the trees. In the same way that Professor Davis demonstrated that a different perspective could be obtained from approaching Buckinghamshire pollbooks in terms of individuals rather than occupations, so more becomes apparent from considering individual volunteers rather than their collective social origin. In most cases there is no significant concentration of any particular occupation and some men almost defy the analyst by combining a wide variety of occupations. In the 2nd Bucks. (High Wycombe) R.V.C., for example, one Volunteer was both auctioneer and paperhanger. In Aylesbury the Chairman of the Gas Works also ran a wine and spirit business to which he presumably owed his position as quartermaster to the Bucks. Volunteers. But what is important in terms of our contrasting 'models' of the Rural and Urban Volunteer is the type of professional man commonly found in rural units. In rural units where landed gentry were not available to command, leadership commonly devolved upon professional men. In particular the majority of the professional men thus involved in the Movement were what Professor Vincent has characterised as among the 'epiphenomena' and economic dependents of the landed elite — solicitors and others trained in the legal profession.

Thus the Committee elected at Aylesbury in December 1859 to establish the 4th Bucks. (Aylesbury) R.V.C. included Acton Tindal, Clerk of the Peace; E.R. Baynes, his eventual successor; J. James, Secretary to the Savings Bank; J. Parrott who combined the posts of County Coroner, Clerk to the Board of Guardians and Superintendent Registrar of the Workhouse, and Alfred Selfe, the local bank manager. As noted in the previous chapter the guiding hands behind the proposed Amersham corps were three solicitors who held six public appointments between them. The 2nd Bucks. (High Wycombe) R.V.C. similarly included the Clerk to the County Court, C. Harman, and the Clerk to the Union Workshouse, J. Harman. The 7th Northants. (Wellingborough) R.V.C. was raised by two solicitors, William Murphy and George Burnham. Other small town officials occupying precisely similar posts are also to be found in such units as the 5th Surrey (Reigate), 18th Surrey (Farnham), 3rd Somerset (Taunton) and 13th Somerset (Frome) R.V.C.[24]

It might also be assumed that most artisan units would be found in urban areas but, in fact, rural areas also had examples of artisan corps. Normally these were drawn from industries in smaller towns that were

Table 3 — **The Social Composition of Oxfordshire Rifle Corps 1859-1860**

Oxfordshire	2nd City 18.11.59	3rd Banbury 9.12.59	4th Henley 29.11.59	5th Witney 16.3.60	6th Deddington 6.12.59	7th Bicester 23.12.59	8th Thame 10.8.60
Gentry	7.3%	4.7%	2.5%	1.5%	—	15.6%	—
Farmers	—	1.5%	10.2%	18.1%	30.0%	50.0%	10.0%
Professionals	21.1%	28.5%	10.2%	33.8%	12.5%	9.3%	13.3%
Tradesmen	34.8%	38.0%	46.1%	31.8%	32.5%	18.7%	50.0%
Clerks	16.5%	12.6%	5.1%	4.5%	5.0%	—	3.3%
Craftsmen	20.1%	14.2%	23.0%	6.0%	20.0%	6.25%	20.0%
Labourers	—	—	2.5%	3.0%	—	—	3.3%
Total No. of Men	109	63	39	66	40	32	30

basically products of a rural economy such as straw-plaiting in Bedfordshire, agricultural implements works as at Banbury or the blanket manufacturing of Oxfordshire. Thus the 1st Essex Artillery was raised by E.H. Bentall from his iron foundry in Heybridge and the 3rd Essex (Brentwood) R.V.C. had 60 men from the agricultural implements works of William Burgess and Sir K.G. Key. In Cornwall the artillery battery at Polruan was drawn from the Hayle foundry and the Keyham Steam Factory likewise provided the nucleus of the 13th Devon A.V.C. At Bedford the 9th Beds. R.V.C. was raised from 'workmen in the employment of Messrs Howard . . . it is to be stated that Mr Johnson and Mr Lester (the proposed officers) are clerks in the establishment'. The Britannia agricultural implements works at Bedford were owned by Frederick and James Howard. The latter, who was Liberal M.P. for Bedford from 1868 to 1874, took personal command of his employees' corps in December 1860.

In the same way two offers of artisan corps were made by small industrial concerns in Oxfordshire. In February 1860 William Bliss, who manufactured woollen girths, horse cloths, pressbagging and tweeds at Chipping Norton, offered 35 of his employees. These comprised an overlooker, a superintendent, a foreman, 2 clerks, 2 manufacturers and 28 operatives. In May 1860 Bernhard Samuelson, who manufactured agricultural implements at the Britannia Works in Banbury, offered some 91 men. These comprised 2 engineers, a manager, a lawyer, a draftsman, 2 clerks, 5 merchants, 3 pattern-makers, 12 carpenters, 10 moulders, a warehouseman, 51 mechanics and 2 labourers. Samuelson's offer was accepted and the men were attached as second company for the Banbury corps. The offer of Samuel Isaacs, of Messrs Isaac, Campbell and Co, was also accepted, as noted earlier. For the most part, however, artisan participation in rural areas was confined to individual craftsmen in towns and villages. One example of this is the 8th Monmouth (Usk) R.V.C., which in April 1860 comprised 8 gentlemen, 2 farmers, 9 professionals, 15 tradesmen, 2 clerks, 34 craftsmen and 2 labourers. By April 1862 the corps had 7 gentlemen, 8 farmers, 8 professionals, 19 tradesmen, 6 clerks, 43 craftsmen and 8 labourers. Another is the artillery unit at South Stoneham in Hamshire:

> recruited from the mechanics belonging to the workshops of some of the most eminent tradesmen in the town, the scale of wages which they received making it totally impossible for men to enter either the Regular Army or Militia.[25]

The Urban Volunteer

The majority of both middle and artisan classes were to be found, of course, in the larger urban centre rather than in the countryside. Baxter's estimates of participation in the Volunteer Movement in 1860 suggested that the ratio of Volunteers to population reached no higher than 4⅓ Volunteers per 1,000 inhabitants in any English county with an average of only 2 per 1,000. Excluding Oxford and Cambridge, where the university population raised the ratio to 14 Volunteers per 1000 inhabitants, the highest ratios were obtained only in larger cities. Baxter estimated that there were 11 Volunteers per 1,000 inhabitants in Edinburgh and Liverpool and 9 per 1,000 in Glasgow and Manchester. Over 50 rifle corps were raised in Middlesex, some 43 of them before the close of 1859. The City of London raised an additional five corps and the Tower Hamlets some twelve corps. By the end of 1859 Merseyside alone had furnished over 4,000 Volunteers in 26 separate corps. By June 1861 while Newcastle, Hull and Birmingham had each raised over 1,000 Volunteers, Manchester's contribution amounted to some 3,700 Volunteers.

The key note of the larger cities is variety, since units raised there were usually the result of many individual companies and interests combining to form a composite whole. Thus the 1st Newcastle R.V.C. commanded by Sir John Fife, contained a Temperance company, a Kilted company, a Quayside company, an Oddfellows company, a Guards company and a company drawn from the Hamptern factory. A further two companies were drawn from the locomotive works of Robert Stephenson and Co., and men were also recruited from the Elswick Ordnance Works of Armstrong and Partners. The young Joseph Chamberlain failed to gain approval for his offer of a company in Birmingham from the Edgbaston Debating Society, of which he was secretary, but the 1st Warwick (Birmingham) R.V.C. did contain one company raised from a cricket eleven returning from an unsuccessful game at Stowport. It also contained a Press company, a Gunmaker's company, a Scots company and four assorted artisan companies. The 6th Lancs. (1st Manchester) R.V.C., commanded by Viscount Grey de Wilton, was a similar amalgam of local firms such as Messrs J.P. and E. Westhead and Co., and Messrs J. and N. Philips and Co., bodies such as the Royal Exchange and the Athenaeum Gymnastic Club, and purely local units such as the seventh company drawn from Old Trafford and the twelth company drawn from Eccles.[26]

One of the best examples of a wide range of local interests participating in the Movement was the Queen's Edinburgh Rifle Volunteer Brigade comprising 21 different companies in two battalions raised between August 1859 and November 1860. Nine of these companies were professional (advocates, writers to the Signet, University, solicitors, accountants, civil servants, 2 merchants companies, High Constables); four were drawn from miscellaneous interests (freemasons, total abstainers, Highland Society, Highlanders); two were citizens' companies; 2 were lower middle class companies (tailors, bankers' clerks) and four were artisan companies. In Glasgow the 1st Lanark R.V.C. had six professional companies (2 University, bankers, procurators, stockbrokers and accountants, press) and two companies for craftsmen (fine arts including jewellers, watchmakers, silversmiths and engravers; furnishers and undertakers' employees).[27]

Both London and Liverpool illustrate the considerable variations in social composition from some of the wealthiest and most exclusive units in the country to some of the poorest. In London the Honorable Artillery Company and the Victoria Rifles had long operated such devices as ballots to bar anyone 'polluted with trade'. The 11th Middx. (St. George's), commanded by the Hon. Charles Lindsay, had its headquarters in Burlington House and its companies drawn from Bond Street, Grosvenor Square, Hanover Square and Belgravia. The London Rifle Brigade, nominally the 1st City of London R.V.C., was specifically designed to be a select body of clean, healthy and respectable men, which goes some way to explaining its high initial outlay of £14. 7s. 6d. on entrance fee, subscription and distinctive black uniform. It was commanded by Montagu Hicks, Governor of Whitecross Street Prison. The 20th Middx. (Railway Rifles), though drawing on the lower middle class for its ranks, considered itself by the very nature of the men's occupations, 'a peculiar and exclusive corps'. The far more exclusive 23rd Middx. (Inns of Court) was among the wealthiest of the Metropolitan units, the Hon. Society of Lincoln's Inn alone donating £105 in 1859. The Inns of Court corps left many in the legal profession outside the Movement and the 40th Middx. (Central London Rangers) were 'persons chiefly connected with the legal profession who are not members of the Inns of Court and therefore not eligible for the corps of that name'. The 38th Middx. (Artists Rifles) was formed in 1859 at the instigation of Edward Stirling, an art student at Carey's School of Art. It was designed exclusively for painters, sculptors, musicians, architects and actors. Among the original members were numbered Val Prinsep, G.F. Watts, Burne-Jones, Rossetti, William Morris, Millais, Frederick Leighton, Alfred Nicholson and Arthur Lewis. The first commanding officer was the painter Henry Phillips. Another exclusive metropolitan unit was the 1st Surrey (South London) R.V.C. which had grown out of the former Peckham Rifle Club. Its commanding officer was J.H. Macdonald, J.P. and Governor of Alleyn's College of God's Gift at Dulwich.[28]

At the other extreme were purely artisan corps such as the 48th Middx. (Havelock's Temperance) R.V.C., raised by George Cruikshank when he had failed to find sufficient interest in Surrey. The members, the majority of whom were 'total abstainers from intoxicating drinks', were 'nearly all working men, who after purchasing their uniform and accoutrements, acknowledged themselves unable to contribute money sufficient to defray the legitimate and absolutely necessary expenses of the Corps'. Thomas Hughes raised and commanded the 19th Middx. R.V.C. drawn from the pupils of the Christian Socialists Working Men's College in Bloomsbury where he was a lecturer. It was calculated by Hughes that his was the poorest corps in London, taking as it did three companies from the College and the remainder from artisans, clerks, warehousemen and shipmen. In the City of London Alfred Richards, too, was raising an artisan unit — the 3rd City of London — with a thousand working men. The 1st Tower Hamlets Engineers invited gentlemen to become honorary members since 'Volunteer Engineers are eminently a working class'.[29]

The same range of social composition is discernible in Liverpool. The 66th Lancs. (Liverpool Borough Guard) R.V.C. was raised by Joseph Mayer and designed to cater for tradesmen but it contained a large number of skilled craftsmen in addition to specialist retailers. The 80th Lancs. (Liverpool Press Guard) was drawn from the staffs of the *Albion, Mercury* and *Weekly Chronicle.* At the other end of the social scale were corps drawing upon large industrial concerns such as the Mersey Iron Works (25th Lancs.), the shipyard workers of the Cunard Steam Ship Company and Laird's Birkenhead Works. As in the metropolis and other large cities, Liverpool had a range of ethnic units. There was a Liverpool Scottish corps commanded by Robert Buchanan and an 'Irish Brigade', nominally the 64th Lancs. (Liverpool Irish) drawing on the large potential reservoir of the many thousands of Irishmen who had migrated to Liverpool after the famine. The 39th Lancs. (Liverpool Welsh) was raised under the auspices of the Welsh Literary Society and comprised clerks and book keepers.[30]

Despite such a wide range of units in urban areas it is still possible to note some common trends, particularly in the participation of the middle classes, which clearly differentiate urban from rural corps. It is not perhaps surprising that, outside the metropolis, there is little evidence of leadership in urban areas by the traditional landed rural elite. Recent research into urban elites in Victorian England has suggested that social, economic and political life was dominated by the larger manufacturers and merchants. In Leeds, for example, cloth and woollen manufacturers dominated the council from the 1830's and in Birmingham there was actually an increase in the proportion of larger manufacturers on the council from the 1850's onwards. In the Lancashire towns of Bolton, Blackburn, Rochdale and Salford manufacturers and merchants averaged well over 40% of the membership of the councils from the mid 1840's to the 1890's. Manufacturers remained the largest group on the Bolton and Salford councils until 1885, at Rochdale until 1895 and at Blackburn until 1900. In Wolverhampton the large manufacturers and businessmen did not lose their influence over the council until the 1920's. By comparison such men represented only 24% of the membership of the House of Commons as late as 1874, suggesting that the urban middle class found in the local arena a range of economic, social and psychological satisfactions denied them in national politics. Unlike inherited landed influence in rural areas, urban influence had to be created by the individual. Such influence was not just the result of economic substance but of active participation in the local community and its affairs.[31] In urban Volunteer units it was to these same men — manufacturers, merchants and the professional men who were usually the second largest group on councils — that the Volunteers looked for leadership.

This does not necessarily mean that there was absolutely no landed influence in urban units outside London, since many northern gentlemen were also leading industrialists. The town of Workington, for example, owed much to the Curwen family and they donated funds to both the Workington Artillery and the 7th Cumberland R.V.C. The Workington corps appears to have contained a large cross section of the community but continued to look to the Curwen family for leadership. As late as 1883 Henry Fraser Curwen was still captain of the unit and C.J. Valentine of the Derwent Iron Works, his lieutenant. Similarly Seaham in Durham had been built up by the 3rd Marquis of Londonderry who owned the Seaham Colliery. In 1860 the Marchioness of Londonderry equipped a company raised from the Colliery for the 2nd Durham Artillery. Two further companies were raised by the Mann brothers, local timber merchants, and a third from the bottlemakers of John Candlish's Londonderry Bottle Works. The unit continued to rely both on the Colliery and the Londonderry family; indeed there was a minor controversy in 1867 when Lord Ernest Vane Tempest, who had been cashiered from the Army in 1857, was permitted to serve in the unit under his brother, Earl Vane. The 3rd Durham (Sunderland) R.V.C. as related earlier, was commanded by the third son of the Marquis. The 5th Monmouth (Pontypool-Hanbury) R.V.C. was raised from the Hanbury Tinplate Company owned by the Lord Lieutenant, Capel Hanbury Leigh.

Hanbury Leigh controlled not only all iron, coal and tin interests in Pontypool but owned 10,000 acres as well.[32]

More usually as in Manchester and Liverpool officers were drawn from professional men from the commercial and financial worlds rather than from the legal profession, which was so often the case in rural units. The 4th Lancs. Artillery Brigade, for example, raised by the shipowner James Walter, was composed of 'young clerks in Liverpool merchants' counting-houses, the officers being sons of prominent merchants and others'. George Melly, a cotton broker who also served in the unit, believed that 'all officers should be young merchants and all rank and file clerks and apprentices in their employ'. The unit was commanded by another merchant and colliery owner, James Bourne. Similar merchants and manufacturers can be found in other urban units. The 7th Monmouth (Newport Borough) R.V.C., for example, was overwhelmingly professional in character as shown by two lists of December 1859 and January 1860. It comprised 43 professionals, 20 tradesmen, 9 clerks, and 7 craftsmen or approximately 54% professional. The professional men were all involved in one way or another with the ship-building industry at Newport as shipping agents, brokers, etc. The Coventry corps was commanded by Frederick Browett, a trimming and frilling manufacturer in a town known for its riband trade. The 1st Newcastle Artillery was raised by Henry Allhusen, who managed his father's chemical works in Gateshead, and the 1st Northumberland R.V.C. was raised in North Shields and Tynemouth by a coal owner, Edward Potter of Cramlington. The 1st Kent (Maidstone) R.V.C. included leading local paper manufacturers, John Hollingworth and R.J. Balston; a quarry owner, Wm. Benstead; and the three times mayor, William Haynes, J.P.[33]

A large number of metropolitan units was raised from those in direct government employ. Foremost amongst these bastions of middle class participation was the 21st Middx. (Civil Service) R.V.C., inspired by Tom Taylor of the Government Act Office and better known for his connection with the *Morning Chronicle* and *Punch*. The 26th Middx. (Customs and Excise) drew heavily on the professional classes and its officers between 1860 and 1872 included the Principal of Police at the West India Docks, the Inspector General of Customs and the Assistant Comptroller-General of Customs. The 42nd Middx. (St Catherine's Docks) included amongst its officers in the same period the Collector to the Docks, the Comptroller of Charges and the Secretary, T.W. Collet, who commanded the corps.

The Middlesex Record Office possesses the surviving commission forms for nine rifle corps (4th North London, 15th London Scottish, 16th Hounslow, 20th Railway, 26th Customs, 28th London Irish,

42nd St Catherine's, 46th London and Westminster and 48th Havelock's) and three artillery corps (1st, 2nd and 3rd Middx. Artillery). These give details of age, profession, and previous military experience.[34] Some care, however, must be exercised in utilising these forms, as by no means all officers appointed between 1860 and 1872 are included and in many cases neither the rank nor full details are given. In all units except three (16th, 28th and 42nd Middx.) 30 or more names are given. These units have therefore been excluded from some of the accompanying tables; similarly, the 26th Middx. is excluded from the detailed class analysis as it is extremely difficult to distinguish differences in status between those denoted as customs employees. The total sample for rifle corps numbers 413 officers and of these the professions of 300 are given in Table 4, excluding those units specified above and individuals with no known occupation. The artillery sample totals 178 officers of which the professions of 170 are shown in Table 5. Where known ages have been included in Table 6 and military experience in Table 7. Finally and most significantly, Table 8, analyses the general area of occupation of professional officers only, including those members of the 26th Middx., whose professional officers can be indicated accurately.

The tables indicate clearly that the professional classes were predominant in both rifle and artillery officer corps between 1860 and 1872. Together with tradesmen and clerks, the professionals make up an overwhelming 73% of rifle and 84% of artillery officers. Officers of both types of corps tended to be in their early middle age with approximately 46% of rifle officers and 36% of artillery officers having previously served in the ranks of Volunteer units before commission. Comparatively few had previous military experience in Regular Army or Militia. The occupations of purely professional officers indicate a range much wider than that commonly found in rural units. Members of the legal profession, the largest percentage in most rural units, provided only approximately 13% of professional officers in these Middx. corps. The contributions of the commercial, shipping and engineering professions were much larger and that of the educational, medical and clerical professions even higher.

Most metropolitan units appear to have relied on a strong core of lower middle class other ranks with the professional men as officers. The 18th Middx. (Harrow) R.V.C. of John Templer was a fairly typical suburban unit in 1862, comprising 40 tradesmen and 30 others including 5 farmers, 1 clergyman and only 3 artisans. Professionals included 6 or 7 fellows of Oxbridge Colleges and Templer himself, who was a master of the Exchequer. The 5th Hants. (Portsmouth) R.V.C., although benefitting from substantial support from the

Table 4 — The Professions of Middlesex Rifle Volunteer Officers 1860-1872

	Nos.	%		Class
Gentry	44	14.6	14.6% Landed	14.6% Landed
Professionals	159	53.0	53.0% Upper Middle	73.3% Middle
Tradesmen	21	7.0	20.3% Lower Middle	
Clerks	40	13.3		
Craftsmen	36	12.0	12.0% Artisans	12.0% Artisans

Table 5 — **The Professions of Middlesex Artillery Volunteer Officers 1860-1872**

	Nos.	%	Class	
Gentry	19	11.1	11.1% Landed	11.1% Landed
Professionals	115	67.6	67.6% Upper Middle	84.2% Middle
Tradesmen	5	2.5	16.6% Lower Middle	
Clerks	24	14.1		
Craftsmen	7	4.1	4.1% Artisans	4.1% Artisans

Table 6 — **The Average Age of Middlesex Officers, 1860-72**

	Infantry	Artillery
Average Age	32.3 years	32.3 years
Average Age — Ensigns	29.8 years	29.0 years
Average Age — Lieutenants	31.7 years	33.6 years
Average Age — Captains	34.6 years	34.9 years
Average Age — Majors	37.25 years	—

urban middle class, was also heavily dependent upon the lower middle class for its ranks. A muster-roll of November 1859 shows that the corps had 86 non-effectives and honorary members, comprising 9 gentry, 9 servicemen, 2 clergy, 30 professionals, 29 tradesmen, 1 clerk and 6 craftsmen. The unit itself, however, totalled 120 men, comprising 13 gentry or ex-servicemen, 27 professionals, 53 tradesmen, 14 clerks and 13 craftsmen or approximately 22% professional and 44% tradesmen. More usually in the larger urban areas the predominance of tradesmen, so noticeable in rural units, gave way to a dependence upon clerks. As noted earlier, the 4th Lancs. Artillery Brigade relied upon clerks from Liverpool counting houses and the 40th Lancs. (3rd Manchester) R.V.C. was similarly drawn from warehousemen and clerks. By 1864 city firms such as Broadwood, Price, Marshall and Snelgrove, Shoolbred and Coutts' Bank had all raised contingents for the Volunteer Force principally clerks. The frequent appearance of units recruited from railway companies or docks is misleading, since most of these were drawn from their clerical establishments. Examples of these include the 5th Essex (Plaistow and Victoria Docks) R.V.C commanded by the docks manager, Charles Cooper; the 8th Essex (Eastern Counties Railway) R.V.C.; 27th Kent (Deptford Dockyard) R.V.C.; and 12th Devon Artillery drawn from Devonport dockyard. Nominally 'government' or 'civil service' units also relied heavily on clerical staff such as the 27th Middx. (Inland Revenue) R.V.C., 34th Middx. (Admiralty) R.V.C. and 41st Middx. (Royal Small Arms Factory) R.V.C. Elsewhere, employees of naval and military establishments formed the 26th Kent (Royal Arsenal) R.V.C. and the Royal Gunpowder Mills at Waltham Abbey provided the nucleus of the 22nd Essex R.V.C.[35]

It was the urban centres, of course, which provided the majority of the purely artisan corps of which there were large numbers from the

Table 7 — Previous Military Experience of Middlesex Officers, 1860-1872

	Nos. Rifles	% of 413	Nos. Artillery	% of 178
In Volunteer ranks	194	46.9%	65	36.5%
Militia or Yeomanry	14	9.6%	3	6.7%
Army	26		9	
Navy	2		1	

very beginning of the Movement. Frequently such units were raised from individual industrial concerns, although others such as those of Alfred Richards and the 19th Surrey (Lambeth) R.V.C. of William Roupell, M.P., drew on artisans and mechanics from a wide variety of concerns. The 10th Monmouth (Risca) R.V.C., for example, was formed entirely from the Risca Colliery Company and commanded by the manager, Thomas Phillpotts. Detailed lists of the unit for September and November 1860 show 123 enrolled members. Of these the occupations are given for a total of 120 comprising 3 farmers, 11 professionals, 9 tradesmen, 6 clerks and 91 craftsmen and artisans. It is not possible entirely to distinguish between the relative status of these artisans, of whom 41 were described as colliers. In terms of rough percentage the artisans and craftsmen represent 75% of the total. In December 1861 the Risca Colliery disaster cost the lives of 100 men who were also Volunteers. Similarly, an explosion at the Marquis of Londonderry's Seaham Colliery in 1880 killed 36 NCO's and men of the 2nd Durham Artillery. Other units raised from such concerns included the 11th Durham (Chester-le-Street) R.V.C.,

Table 8 — **The Occupations of Professional Officers in Middlesex Units, 1860-1872**

	9 Rifles (200) Nos.	%	3 Artillery (115) Nos	%
Finance and Insurance	40	20	9	7.8
Government Service & Railways	35	17.5	12	10.4
Legal	30	15	16	13.9
Commerce	20	10	20	17.3
Ships Engineering etc.	26	13	21	18.2
Industrial & Manufacturing	12	6	5	4.3
Educational Medical & Clerical	28	14	28	24.3
Others	9	4.5	4	3.4

drawn from the Pelton Colliery, and the 12th Durham (Middleton) R.V.C. drawn from the London Lead Company. Miners and millmen were included in the 37th Staffs (Moorland) R.V.C. raised at Cheadle and comprising 3 gentlemen, 8 farmers, 5 professionals, 12 tradesmen, 9 clerks and other lower middle class elements, 28 craftsmen and 15 labourers.[36]

In London the brewing firms of Truman, Hanbury and Buxton provided the nucleus for the 3rd Tower Hamlets R.V.C., and the 2nd City of London was raised from the printing works of Eyre and Spottiswoode. In Bradford W.E. Forster raised the 23rd West Riding R.V.C. from his own mill hands, and A.J. Mundells raised a corps from his employees in Nottingham. In 1861 the 3rd Durham R.V.C. lamented the absence of companies 'formed of mechanics and headed by their principals', since such units existed at Seaham, West Hartlepool, Middlesbrough, Gateshead and Newcastle. In Manchester the Old Trafford company of the 1st Manchester R.V.C. included contingents from the Commercial Mills at Hulme and from T.G. Hill and Co. In Huddersfield the third company of the 10th West Riding R.V.C. was almost entirely drawn from artisans employed by Learoyd and Sons, Day and Sons and E.T. Monk and Co, silk spinners. The second company comprised one-third small tradesmen, clerks and higher warehousemen but two-thirds artisans who were not self supporting. The original company had shown a much broader cross-section of the community with 10 gentlemen, 21 professional men, 15 tradesmen, 11 clerks and 6 craftsmen. In Scotland of the 107 rifle corps in Lanarkshire alone, Grierson identified 10 corps drawn from ironworks, 9 from shipping and engineering firms, 4 from other firms such as breweries and a further 20 corps as artisan units of one kind or another. Only 11 could be described as being lower middle class in character. Such was the myth of the middle class ideal.[37]

The Mounted Volunteer

Some Volunteers of vision, such as Sir Thomas Acland in Devon and Lt.-Col. John Bower in Hampshire, conceived a force of Light Horse Volunteers as far more attuned to the needs of Rifle Volunteers than auxiliary cavalry such as the existing Yeomanry. It was reasoned that hunting men, accustomed to rapid movement across country, could act as the eyes of their dismounted colleagues. The Light Horse would undertake reconnaissance, picket and outpost duties, assembling rapidly and fighting on foot with the rifle. There was considerably more military potential in such a role than using them merely as

70

vehicles for infantry which the Duke of Manchester feared might prove the limit of War Office intentions.[38]

The factor which determined both the social composition and the eventual collapse of the Light Horse Volunteers was sheer expense. It was because of this difficulty in finding men able and willing to bear the considerable outlay that an attempt failed to raise a corps in Monmouthshire. Similarly it was reported in Essex that only a minority were prepared to become effectives. It was thought that it would cost at least £50 per annum to maintain a horse solely for the purpose of Light Horse drill, which in practise severely restricted the likely number of recruits. It was calculated that the initial outlay for a troop in the proposed 2nd Middx. L.H.V. might well exceed £300 with an annual outlay thereafter of perhaps £100. Subscriptions were not particularly high, ranging from 5s. in the 1st and 2nd Devon M.R.V. to £1 in the 1st Northants. M.R.V. Middlesex units were slightly costlier with a subscription of 2 guineas in the 1st Middlesex and 5 guineas in the 2nd Middx. L.H.V. There was an entrance fee in the 1st Middlesex of one guinea and in the 1st Northants. M.R.V. of £3 but the 6th Devon M.R.V. had no subscription at all, reasoning that members already gave their time and horses. Most expensive were the often fanciful uniforms costing as much as £15 in the 1st Hunts. and 1st Lincs. In the case of the 1st Middx. L.H.V. the Lord Lieutenant, the Marquis of Salisbury, suggested several alterations in the uniform since 'it will be exceedingly expensive and not last through a shower of rain'. It was just this sort of extravagance that prompted one scurrilous circular in Devon announcing the formation of the 'South Devon Irregular Donkeys' armed with carving knives, pledged to 240 days training per annum and wearing a uniform costing £56. 15s. 6d.![39]

The chief recruiting ground for the Light Horse was almost certainly bound to be the farming and hunting communities but here units might find themselves in competition with existing Yeomanry regiments. In the case of the 1st Oxon. L.H.V. raised at Banbury the corps was recruited from sons of farmers who objected to joining the Yeomanry. In Hampshire, however, Bower found himself in direct competition with the Yeomanry. In some other areas the Light Horse was successful because no Yeomanry existed. In Hertfordshire, for example, the 1st Herts. L.H.V. had its headquarters at Bishop's Stortford outside the normal recruiting ground of the South Herts. Yeomanry Cavalry and the 1st Fife L.H.V. was raised in a county in which the Yeomanry had actually ceased to exist. The attraction the Light Horse might have for a farming community which was not always willing to participate in the Rifle Volunteer Movement, was that the Light Horse were considerably cheaper and less socially exclusive than the Yeomanry but somewhat above the status of the Rifle Volunteers. Those who joined the 1st Lincoln L.H.V., for example, did so from a desire not to mix with the Rifle Volunteers.[40]

The fact that the bulk of recruits were to come from the agricultural community naturally brought other limitations. Thus the 6th Devon M.R.V., raised at South Molton, had a drill season from March to June between seed time and harvest. Similarly, the 1st Northants. L.H.V. exercised from March to July and undertook shooting practice from September to November. The 1st Hunts. L.H.V., which drew men from Cambridgeshire, Bedfordshire, Northamptonshire and Buckinghamshire as well as Huntingdonshire, held its drills in April and May at varying venues such as Sharnbrook, Bedford, Putnoe, Huntingdon, Cambridge, Sawston and Kimbolton to offset the difficulties of assembly.[41]

Existing muster-lists and other evidence indicate the dependence upon the farming community. The 1st Northants. L.H.V. was raised at Overstone by Robert Loyd-Lindsay from farmers and members of the Pytchley Hunt. In September 1861 there were 35 members of whom 29 can be identified comprising 3 gentlemen, 14 farmers, 9 farmers sons, 1 professional, 1 tradesman and 1 craftsman. The 1st Surrey L.H.V. was composed chiefly of hunting men and most of the 6th Devon M.R.V. also rode to hounds. A surviving muster-roll for the 1st Devon M.R.V. raised by Sir Thomas Acland gives the names and occupations of all members between 1859 and 1875. Unfortunately this is now too badly damaged to yield an exact analysis but as far as may be deciphered most members were listed as farmers or yeoman. The 1st Hunts. L.H.V., usually known as the Duke of Manchester's L.H.V., was again mostly drawn from farmers, their sons and some professional men and gentry. Of some 41 members of the 1st Essex M.R.V. in November 1860 some 34 can be identified comprising 3 gentlemen, 8 farmers, 2 professional men, 13 tradesmen, 1 clerk and 7 craftsmen. The craftsmen were drawn from what might be termed the 'horse' trade, being saddlers, blacksmiths, farriers and the like. In the same way the 1st Middx. L.H.V. in October 1860 included 3 professionals, 3 ex-Regular soldiers, 3 tradesmen, 2 craftsmen and 7 men from the horse trade-dealers, saddlers, livery stable owners and one manufacturer of patent stable fittings. Lord Truro's 2nd Middx. L.H.V. was more exclusive, being 'worthy of the population, the wealth and the influence of that great City'. Its ranks included 2 peers and 3 M.P.'s in January 1861.[42]

The Light Horse, however, never attracted large numbers, and by the mid-1870's most of the thirty or so original units had disappeared.

Costs rose, which economy measures, such as that in the 2nd Devon M.R.V. of buying the helmets of the disbanding 1st Glos. L.H.V. in 1866, could not avert. The two Middlesex corps were amalgamated as early as July 1861. The 1st Herts. L.H.V. was disbanded in 1879 after the commanding officer had fled abroad leaving the corps with debts of £2000. The more usual reason was that given for the disbandment of the 1st Oxon. L.H.V. in 1869 — the 'paucity of members who muster at its meetings'.[43]

The Light Horse were in many ways in a rather anomalous position being neither Rifle Volunteers nor Yeomanry. They proved an expensive diversion for the farming community in hunting counties and as such did not long survive. The 1st Fife L.H.V. alone lasted long enough to be incorporated in the Imperial Yeomanry in 1901 by which time the value of a mounted arm for the Volunteers had been belatedly recognised. By the mid-1860's, however, the Mounted Volunteer was already a curiosity in much the same way that the theoretical models of Rural and Urban Volunteer were also disappearing into the amorphous shape of a predominantly working class Volunteer Force.

Patterns of Change

It was becoming obvious to many leading Volunteers as early as 1862 that the social composition of the Volunteer Force was decisively changing from the original middle class ideal to a working class reality. One who noticed the change was Owen Wethered of the 1st Bucks, (Marlow) R.V.C.:

> At first we had many gentlemen in our ranks — men of social position equal, and in many cases superior, to that of their officers. These men gradually dropped out and it became the fashion about 1863-4 to deplore the deterioration of the class of recruit . . . It seemed to me unreasonable to suppose that men who might be willing under the stress or supposed stress of a national emergency to give up their dinners, go out to night drills, frequently many miles away, in all weathers, in order to shoulder a rifle and stand in the ranks between say their own gardeners and their grocers' assistants, would continue to do this indefinitely in cold blood after the emergency had passed away. Personally I rather welcome the change because I always considered the artisan chap to be the backbone of the Volunteer Force, and our natural recruiting ground as the agricultural and other day labourers are for the Regular Army and the Militia . . .[44]

Substantial evidence of the changing composition of the Force was recorded by the Royal Commission on the condition of the Volunteer Force in 1862. In Liverpool and Manchester, for example, the professional element of the Force had declined considerably. Bousfield's 1st Lancs. R.V.C. had originally contained sons of gentlemen and professional men such as brokers and merchants from the cotton trade. By 1862 it was dependent upon tradesmen, their sons and assistants and also contained three purely artisan companies. The 4th Lancs. Artillery Brigade still principally depended upon clerks in merchant houses but it had been compelled to enroll 50-60 mechanics though it was stressed these were of the highest class. Cunard contributed a corps commanded by Col. McIver, and in Birkenhead the artillery corps was now utterly dependent upon large firms such as Jackson and Brassey's Canada Works and Laird's Iron Works with some Volunteers earning as low as 20s. a week. In Manchester 2-3,000 Volunteers were now artisans. The 3rd Manchester R.V.C., for example, comprised 77 gentlemen and professionals, 129 tradesmen, 62 clerks, 347 artisans from foundries and 21 labourers or approximately 58% artisan or labourer in content.

Elsewhere the picture was much the same, be it rural or urban unit. In Glasgow the Volunteer Force was dependent upon 6-7,000 artisans and in Edinburgh, too, the professional men were leaving the corps. Working men formed the nucleus of both the 31st Lancs. (Oldham) R.V.C. and the Durham Administrative Battalion, where the members were local workmen supported by their Tyneside employers. The 3rd Sussex Artillery still contained some professional men from the Newhaven Customs House but was mainly composed of master blacksmiths, carpenters, tradesmen, skilled artisans and superior labourers. The 1st Haddington A.B. comprised 7 farmers, 9 professional men, 94 tradesmen, 38 clerks and other lower middle class elements, 205 artisans, 8 fishermen and 89 labourers or approximately 67% artisan or labourers. In London Thomas Hughes' 19th Middx. R.V.C., as already related, was chiefly dependent upon artisans, warehousemen and shopmen. Although the 2nd Cinque Ports Artillery at Sandwich still boasted a mixture of classes the 7th Sussex (Horsham) R.V.C. was finding the best attendance was from mechanics and artisans. The 1st Worcs. A.B. still had two middle class companies but also two to three companies of artisans.[45]

Most other evidence available for the same period indicates a similar pattern. In 1860, for example, the 35th Kent (Westerham) R.V.C. had included most of the town's leading tradesmen. By 1862 it comprised 9 gentlemen, 2 farmers, 24 tradesmen, 7 servants, 14 artisans and 6 labourers with 20 men subsidised by the corps committee, 8 men paying half the cost of equipment and 7 clothed by employers. This had changed yet again by the following year when Lord Hardinge noted:

Many of the gentlemen had retired, the leading tradesmen not being able to give up their time to drill, sent their apprentices and the tenant farmers disappeared from the ranks.

In other rural areas corps were even beginning to recruit agricultural labourers which alone enabled the 1st Devon A.B. to go into camp in July 1864 after the hay harvest and Assizes but before the corn harvest.[46]

Evidence from 1862 onwards illustrates the continuing process of change within the Volunteer Force. In 1868 the 10th Kent Artillery were artisans from the shot and shell factory at the Royal Arsenal, and in 1870 the 14th Kent Artillery had to disband when Woolwich Dockyard closed, since it depended upon artisans employed there. By 1872 there were no professional companies remaining in the 1st Lancs. R.V.C. and it comprised clerks, tradesmen and artisans. The evidence given to the Bury Departmental Committee in 1878 confirmed this trend. Sir Walter Barttelot revealed that the 1st Sussex A.B. formerly composed of at least half farmers was now composed mainly of agricultural labourers, tradesmen and mechanics. The landed gentlemen had completely dropped out and few of Barttelot's men had any military experience at all. The 6th Lancs. (1st Manchester) R.V.C. had become dependent upon clerks, warehousemen and pupils from engineering works. The 2nd Worcs. A.B. contained artisans and agriculturalists but no longer any shopkeepers whereas the 1st Worcs. A.B. contained miners, carpet weavers and agriculturalists. In Edinburgh the men were nearly all artisans and J.H.A. Macdonald was recruiting officers from among young clerks in the civil service. In Derbyshire the majority of Volunteers were again artisans.[47]

Even the elite 'class' corps of the metropolis did not escape this process of change. In 1878 Lt.-Col. Hayter of the London Rifle Brigade was describing his once exclusive corps as consisting of bankers' clerks and men from city houses. The 38th Middx. (Artists Rifles) found it increasingly difficult to maintain the artistic nature of the corps. The two original companies had been composed of painters and musicians. Further companies for painters were added in 1877 and 1880 but, in the meantime, the corps had also had to establish two companies for architects in 1864 and 1875 and two companies of students from London University and the London Hospital in 1865 and 1880 respectively. A survey of 1893 indicates the extent to which the artistic content had declined. Artists, painters and sculptors now comprised only 4.54% of the battalion; architects 11.79%; the legal profession 12.39%; the medical profession 10.33% and civil engineers

5.99%. The remaining 54.96% includes civil servants, bankers, stock brokers, accountants, men in commerce and various miscellaneous occupations. The 15th Middx. (London Scottish) R.V.C. admittedly included 150 artisans in 1859 as well as a company from employees of the Oriental Bank. Lord Elcho recalled that 'men like the Duke of Abercorn and the Marquis of Lorne might be seen in the ranks with the Scottish artisans of London . . .' and by 1896 the corps could claim two Governor-Generals of Canada, one Lord Lieutenant of Ireland, one Governor of New South Wales, the Chairman of the Chartered Company of South Africa and the British Consul in Angola. However, by the 1890's it was becoming increasingly difficult to maintain its national identity and in 1898 Scottish ancestry had to be waived to allow men of Scottish descent through the female line to join although it was made clear to them that they might not easily gain authority in the corps if promoted.[48]

But let us examine the actual process of change more closely. A gradual change is apparent from the example of the 11th Berks. (Wallingford) R.V.C. for which a muster-roll survives listing all members between 1861 and 1877.[49] Wallingford was a typical small market town with trade in corn, timber, cattle and agricultural produce; its only important building was the Corn Exchange built in 1856. The entrance fee to the corps was 10s. 6d. with an annual subscription of 10s. 6d. for other ranks and a sliding scale from one guinea for an Ensign to three guineas for the Captain. The uniform cost four guineas and the corps was commanded by F.L. Austen of Brightwell Park, Tetsworth, just across the Oxfordshire border, since no one else 'with more military knowledge and experience' resided nearer the town. The changing composition is best summarised in the accompanying Table 9.

Average ages are calculated for 27 men in 1861; for 21 men from 1862-9; 48 men for 1870-3 and 16 for the period 1874-7. Some 78 men joined in 1861 and the period of service is known for 72 men and the occupations of 63. Between 1862 and 1869 another 35 men joined and 66 left — the average service is for 43 men and the occupations for 21 men. Between 1870 and 1873 some 51 men joined and 53 left — the service of 46 men is known and the occupations of 50 men. Between 1874 and 1877 only 22 men joined and 33 left — the service of 7 of these is known and the occupations of 18.

The table reveals that in 1861 the corps was a typically broad cross-section of the local community much as elsewhere with local farmers and tradesmen prominent. After 1861 the farming community largely stopped providing recruits and the backbone remained the tradesmen. From 1870 onwards the unit was taking increasingly from

76

Table 9 — **The Social Composition of 11th Berks. (Wallingford) R.V.C. 1861-1877**

WALLINGFORD	1861	1862-69	1870-73	1874-77
Average age on joining	30.29 yrs.	21 yrs.	22.04 yrs.	19.87 yrs.
Average no. of years service	5.6	3.7	3.3	4.1
Gentry	11.12%	9.54%	2.0%	—
Farmers	26.98%	4.76%	12.0%	—
Professionals	6.19%	14.28%	6.0%	11.12%
Tradesman	34.92%	38.09%	28.0%	44.45%
Clerks	12.69%	19.04%	10.0%	11.12%
Craftsmen	7.93%	14.28%	42.0%	33.34%
Joined	78	35	51	22
Left	—	66	53	33
Remaining in 1877	4	1	11	21

artisans. Overall from 1861-77 the lower middle class contributed nearly double the proportion provided by the upper middle class and the artisan class. However the artisan class virtually replaced the upper middle class element in the same period.

In Buckinghamshire the Volunteers became increasingly dependent upon the artisans as the professional classes dropped out. In October 1877 a 6th Company was formed consisting of Wolverton and Stony Stratford men largely drawn from the Carriage Works of the London and North Western Railway Company which had come to Wolverton in 1866. The Committee, elected on 2 October 1877, appealed for funds: 'As the Corps will be principally formed by men who from their circumstances will be unable to defray the whole cost, the Committee hope by the aid of subscriptions to relieve them of a portion of this burden.' Alfred Gilbey, later Lt.-Col. 1900-05, joined the Wycombe company in 1879 noting 'the men of my company were nearly all engaged in chair-making, the staple industry of High

Wycombe. There was a certain independence about them which made them hard to drive but easy to load'.[50]

Wethered was particularly concerned about the lack of officers. He wrote to AR. Baynes, the Clerk of Lieutenancy, on 21 August 1883:

> Cadets of County families of position appear to one to distinguish themselves now-a-days by evincing a supercilious indifference to the duties and responsibilities of their position — and the time will come when they will find that they have forfeited their claim to be regarded by those beneath them in position as their natural leaders.

The 3rd Duke of Buckingham who had succeeded Lord Carrington as Lord Lieutenant in 1868, suggested promoting a few N.C.O.'s to fill the gaps. Wethered recognised that gentlemen no longer served in the ranks and that the N.C.O.'s were tradesmen and artisans. He replied to the Lord Lieutenant:

> I do not think it would answer to promote anyone who is not a gentlemen by education and manners to our commissioned ranks — it might stop a difficult gap for a time, but, at the cost of increased future difficulties — nor do I think the men would like being commanded by any but gentlemen, and I should personally be very unwilling to make so public a recognition of the fact that the natural leaders of the people are willing to ignore their proper responsibilities and duties*.

It would seem that Wethered considered himself and his fellow professionals as deserving of that deference once reserved for the landed gentry. On 6 August 1885 he issued explicit instructions to his recruiting parties:

> Inasmuch as the class of agricultural and day labourers is the natural recruiting ground for the Regular Forces and the Militia, members of that class will not be admitted into the 1st Bucks. R.V.C. In a purely agricultural county like Bucks an agricultural or day labourer may be defined as one who, not being a clerk, tradesman's assistant, artisan or apprentice, does not earn at least 18s. a week regular wages.

Wethered retired from command in 1891, being succeeded by Lord Addington. Wethered sent Addington a copy of his 1885 recruiting

---

* *Arthur Brookfield, Tory M.P. for Rye and Commanding Officer of 1st Cinque Ports Battalion at Hastings, had a similar problem in 1884 when he was trying to persuade busy professional men to take commissions as the local gentry had a rustic distrust of military service.*

orders in October 1893 commenting on a proposed Newport Pagnell company:

> I hope you will be very particular as to the class of men you enrol . . .
> Don't go lower than Artisans and Apprentices. The labouring class
> has not the intelligence enough to become good soldiers with the
> limited instruction we can give them and they are much better in the
> Regular Army or Militia!

The turnover in the Bucks. Volunteers by 1896 was substantial and, for example, on 1 November 1896 some 185 men had joined and 148 left during the year. In terms of service from 23 officers and 788 other ranks roughly 64 per cent had served less than five years and 57 per cent were under 25 years of age. On 20 May 1897 F.O. Wethered applied on behalf of Addington to redistribute the Battalion, as some companies were having difficulty in finding suitable mechanics and artisans, 'no one of a less educated class being enrolled'. The Wycombe chair-makers now provided over a company whereas some companies were near to recruiting agricultural labourers. As a result the War Office sanctioned a redistribution — two companies at Wycombe, one-and-a-half at Wolverton, a half at Buckingham and one each at Marlow, Aylesbury, Slough and Stony Stratford. Alfred Gilbey (magistrate, governor of Wycombe Grammar School and Master of the Old Berkeley Hounds) took over command in 1900 and discovered half the Battalion deficient in physical standard. He still refused to take agricultural labourers and when offered a place in Brodrick's Field Army in 1901 was careful to gain the co-operation of Lord Stalbridge, Chairman of the L.N.W.R., who employed the Wolverton Company in his Carriage Works, 'skilled workmen, who took the same pride in being efficient in their military duties as they did in their work'.[51]

In 1879 the Beds. Battalion was taking over 50 per cent of its recruits from Luton and Bedford and it seems likely that it had become dependent upon the artisans of the straw plait and brick industries of those localities. As early as 1867 Wethered had recorded the trend in Northants. during a joint camp: 'There was not much fraternisation between the two battalions. The Northants. were principally shoemakers and straw plaiters and consequently of a very different class from our men.' The concern, too, with declining standard is evident in the Daventry company of the Northants. Battalion. By 1890 the old 8th Northants. was L Company of the Northants. Battalion and commanded by Frederick Willoughby, the Town Clerk and a solicitor. On 23 December 1890 Willoughby submitted the names of five new recruits — two finishers, two rivetters and a blacksmith — to the Battalion Adjutant, Major E.D. Sandys. On 26 December Sandys replied:

> I think these recruits are too small, their height is miserable but, of course, if you wish I will sign the papers. The Colonel doesn't like them so small. And unless you have reasons I should not send them in simply for the reason of increasing your strength. We want quality not quantity.

A list of May 1899 gives the names of the employers of 86 men in L Company. Only five men were self-employed, four worked for the Railway and six for other public concerns. Some thirteen had assorted employers and of these, one was an outright labourer — a plasterer's mate. The overwhelming majority, fifty-seven, were in the shoe trade. This gives an average of 67.4 per cent in the shoe industry, 11.68 per cent in public employ and only 5 per cent self-employed.[52]

Another example of the increasing dependence upon artisans, this time in an urban context, is the case of the 1st Lincs. (City) R.V.C. for which a muster roll survives recording the names and occupations of those enrolled between 1859 and 1891.[53] Lincoln had a large range of industrial enterprises in 1859 including breweries, malt kilns, corn mills, seed mills and corn warehouses. The three largest manufacturers in the town were Clayton, Shuttleworth and Co., agricultural and general engineers at Stamp End Iron Works; Ruston, Proctor and Co., engineers, millwrights and agricultural machinemakers at the Sheaf Iron Works; and Robey and Co., agricultural steam engine manufacturers, machinists, iron and brass founders at the Perseverance Iron Works. In 1882 these firms were still the town's largest employers with Claytons employing 1,300 men and Ruston and Robey 700 each. The Volunteer Committee included the usual complement of town officials and both Joseph Shuttleworth and Nathaniel Clayton as officers. Clayton and Shuttleworth encouraged their employees to join from the start and offered to provide uniforms which could be repaid in weekly instalments of 1s. 6d. As late as 1890 such patronage remained when Joseph Ruston presented the City with a Drill Hall.

The accompanying Table 10 indicates the changing composition of the 1st Lincoln R.V.C. between 1859 and 1891 broken down into five yearly periods. The figures in each case are the number of men joining the unit for those years and the average ages and length of service are again for those men who joined during that period. The artisans and craftsmen include those designated as 'fitters', 'joiners' and 'turners' or just as 'artisans' or 'labourers'. Employers are also given in many cases and although some artisans and clerks through the years were

80

Table 10 — **The Social Composition of the 1st Lincoln (City) R.V.C. 1859-1891**

LINCOLN	1859-63	1864-68	1869-73	1874-78	1879-83	1884-88	1889-91
Gentry	1	—	—	—	—	—	—
Farmers	17	2	2	—	—	—	—
Clergy	6	1	—	—	—	—	—
Professionals	53	30	21	31	32	16	16
Tradesmen	49	33	19	32	21	14	9
Clerks	41	49	27	36	35	25	28
Artisans and Labourers	81	209	225	225	322	276	199
Average age on joining	25.6 yrs.	21.4 yrs.	21 yrs.	20.7 yrs.	19.6 yrs.	20 yrs.	19.5 yrs.
Average length of service	4.6 yrs.	4.0 yrs.	3.1 yrs.	3.5 yrs.	3.9 yrs.	3.4 yrs.	3.9 yrs.
Nos. joining Army or Militia	—	—	3	10	10	18	11

employees of the *Lincoln Times* or Popletons (confectioners), the overwhelming majority were employees of Claytons, Rustons or Robeys.

The table indicates that for the first few years the 1st Lincoln contained a broad cross section of the community in much the same way as many other provincial town corps throughout the country. Both the upper middle class and lower middle class elements thereafter declined markedly whilst the artisan element rapidly increased from 1863 and maintained its predominance throughout.

It is noticeable that the average age of recruit declined after the early years in Lincoln; indeed the average age in 1859 was 29.2 years and the length of service 6.05 years, both well above that in any subsequent year. This pattern is reflected in other cases where it is possible to discover the age of recruit. In Wallingford, for example, the average age fell from 30.2 years in 1861 to 19.8 years in 1874-7 and the length of service from 5.6 years in 1861 to 4.1 years in 1874-7. Similarly, in the Coventry corps the average age fell from 27.2 years in 1859 to 24.3 years in 1863. This is, of course, a reflection of the decline in upper middle class Volunteers. In the 8th Monmouth (Usk) R.V.C. in 1860, for example, the average age of gentlemen joining the Volunteers was 44.5 years; for professional men it was 28.1 years; for clerks 26.8 years; for tradesmen 25.6 years; for craftsmen 25.1 years; for labourers 24 years; and for farmers 23.1 years. The range of ages in the early years could be very wide indeed. In the 18th Surrey (Farnham) R.V.C. there were 14 men under 21 years, 30 men aged 21-30 years, 21 men aged 30-40 years and 5 aged over 40 years. Similarly ages in the 37th Staffs. (Moorland) R.V.C. ranged from 17 to 49 with an average of 24.8 years. The average age of the 5th Surrey (Reigate) R.V.C. in 1859 was 21.6 years; in the 15th Kent (West Kent) between 1860 and 1870 it was 28.5 years. Annual figures available for Force from 1895 onwards confirm both declining age and length of service.[54] Figures are not often available for the number of Volunteers who joined the Regular Army or Militia from individual units. The figures for the 1st Lincs. R.V.C. do, however, appear to follow a general pattern with a small but increasing percentage of men enlisting each year. In the 2nd Durham Artillery only 2% transferred to the Regular Army between 1860 and 1908. Although several witnesses to the Norfolk Commission in 1904 mentioned their belief that the Volunteers were resembling Militia and Regular Army more and more, the balance of opinion was that Volunteers were still essentially above the class of Militia and Regular recruits. The Norfolk Commission itself produced figures for the social composition of the Volunteer Force based on the replies of 218 commanding officers. The results set out in the accompanying

Table 11 indicates just how far the composition of the Force had changed since 1859.[55]

Table 11 — **Social Composition of the Volunteer Force, 1904**

Officers		Rank and File	
Gentlemen	6.5%	Professional men	1.8%
Professionals	29.2%	Clerks	9.6%
Men in business		Shopmen	5.3%
on their own account	33.5%	Artisans	35.5%
Employees	22.6%	Men in business on their	
Students	3.5%	own account	3.2%
Others	4.8%	Agricultural Labourers	4.2%
		Town Labourers	8.6%
		Miners	6.0%
		Factory Hands	12.9%
		Men in private employ	
		(gardeners etc)	2.0%
		Men in government employ	2.9%
		Others	8.0%

What general conclusions can be drawn then respecting the social composition of the Volunteer Force between 1859 and 1908?

At first the Movement embraced, as indeed its founders had intended, the upper middle class elements of society who had previously shown no particular interest in military affairs. These groups, rather than the landed gentry, were, in many instances, the leaders of local town communities whose individual consciousness of identity had developed only during the first half of the Nineteenth Century. These professional men were frequently drawn from the legal world in the provinces though tending to be manufacturers or other businessmen in the larger cities. It is clear that the majority of the upper middle class dropped out of the Movement about 1862-63 though some remained throughout, almost as a quasi-Volunteer officer class.

Local gentry played an important initial role in many provincial areas and their presence and financial support often gave added impetus to the progress of the Movement. In the Metropolis, too, the lead came from the nobility and these acknowledged leaders of society were among the most influential officers of the entire Volunteer Force. The gentry, however, tended very largely to drop out of the Movement by the mid-1860's and this, coupled with the loss of the professional men, significantly reduced the monetary income of the Force as a whole. The farming community did not, on the whole, show great attachment to the Movement except in the South-East and

South-West, where the centres of population and industry were less widespread.

The great majority of the Volunteers in 1859 and 1860 were drawn from the lower middle class who had also not previously been the target for Regular or Militia recruiting. The lower middle class members were usually clerks of one kind or another in the cities, but in the rural areas the tradesmen and shopkeepers formed the backbone of the Volunteer Force. Though steadily decreasing in numbers as the years passed, the lower middle class was always an element in the Movement and came to be regarded almost as the natural source of non-commissioned officers.

The last component of the Force in the early years was provided by the craftsmen and artisans. In the larger cities there were artisan companies drawing men from no particular industrial concern but more often artisans were led into the Movement by their employers. The lowest level of income, below which men were seldom accepted in the Volunteers, was generally regarded as about 18s. to 20s. regular weekly wage.

Altogether this represented in the early years a broad cross-section of both the local and national community though the middle class element was the largest group. It was frequently argued in later years that the essential middle class 'character' of the Volunteer Force had been changed by the Government issue of arms which enabled artisans to join, but this 'character' was really a fiction from the very start. It was clear by 1862 that the upper middle class was dropping out of the Movement and that there was a growing dependence upon the artisan class throughout the country. Indeed it became more difficult to find middle class officers than artisan other ranks. In some rural areas even agricultural labourers were eventually recruited which would have been unthinkable in 1859. By 1899 the Volunteer Movement, though it might still cling to middle class concepts and ideals, could no longer be regarded as middle class.

At the beginning there is no doubt that the Movement was a national one in terms of social and political composition. It embraced, as has been seen, many differing creeds and aspirations. The social consequences and aspects of this will be discussed in the next chapter but it is important, having discussed the social composition, to put the Movement into perspective in terms of its size and popularity in proportion to the total population of the country.

Over the whole country Dudley Baxter estimated in 1860 that the average proportion of Volunteers to population was 3.5 Volunteers per 1,000 inhabitants. For England the average was 3 per 1,000; for Wales the average was 2.5 Volunteers per 1,000 and in Scotland it

84

reached 5 per 1,000 inhabitants. Indeed, for reasons that remain obscure, Scotland always did better than England in terms of numbers in proportion to population.

The Volunteer Force proved unable to maintain this ratio as the population increased and it was only due to the enthusiasm for the Movement in Scotland that the ratio was as high as it was. The situation is given in the following Table 12.[56]

Volunteers per 100 of total population	England	Wales	Scotland
1861	0.629	0.655	1.119
1871	0.655	0.620	1.316
1881	0.613	0.627	1.310

The thinly populated areas largely maintained their ratio over these years and that of the rural counties in fact increased. Most Scottish counties showed at least one Volunteer per 100 and in some cases over two Volunteers per 100.

By 1884 the percentage of the population in the Volunteers was 0.72 per cent (0.72 per 100 inhabitants) which compared most unfavourably with the 3.52 per cent of 1806 though, of course, the danger had been more apparent in 1806. In terms of the whole of the Auxiliary Forces in proportion to the population, in 1877 the total number of Auxiliaries (Yeomanry, Militia and Volunteers) represented 6.36 per cent of the male population of military age (15-35 years). The *Volunteer Service Gazette* commented that this was barely sufficient to indicate that the material was there somewhere! In all, some 632,911 Volunteers had passed through the ranks by 1877, exclusive of the enrolled strength in 1877 of 185,501 Volunteers.[57]

By 1901 the situation was no better, as indicated in the following Table 13.[58]

Auxiliaries per 10,000 of the male population — 1901	Yeomanry	Militia	Volunteers
England and Wales	13.4	43.4	129.6
Scotland	16.5	51.2	249.4
United Kingdom	12.4	48.5	127.8

Total Regulars/Auxiliaries — 319.4 per 10,000. Total for the Regular Army 130.7 per 10,000.

It is clear that the Volunteer Movement, despite its broadly based social and political composition, was never really a popular Movement when considered in proportion to the population as a whole, but then this applied equally to the Regular Army and Auxiliary Forces. The Volunteer Movement was, however, more representative of the country as a whole than the other branches of the Armed Services. Precisely what the attitude of the public and society as a whole towards the Volunteer Movement was must now be considered.

[1] Bucks. RO *TA Coll* Box 14.
[2] B.J. Bond 'Recruiting the Victorian Army, 1870-1892' *VS* V (1962), p 331-8; A.V. Tucker, 'Army and Society in England, 1870-1900: A Reassessment of the Cardwell Reforms' *JBS* II (1963), p 110-41; P.E. Razzell, 'Social Origins of Officers in the Indian and British Home Armies' *British Journal of Sociology* XIV (1963), p 248-60; H.J. Hanham, 'Religion and Nationality in the Mid-Victorian Army' in M.R.D. Foot (ed), *War and Society* (London 1973), p 159-181; G. Harries-Jenkins, *The Army in Victorian Society* (London 1977), p 12-58; G. Ramsay Skelley, *The Victorian Army at Home* (London 1977); M. Howard, *Studies in War and Peace* (London 1970), p 86-7.
[3] Best, op cit, p 23-40; R.D. Baxter, *The Volunteer Movement: Its Progress and Wants* (London 1860), p 15-17; *VSG* 4.10.60.
[4] Reader, op cit, p 147-53.
[5] W.G. Fisher, *The History of Somerset Yeomanry, Volunteer and Territorial Units* (Taunton 1924), p 100-1; T. Sturmy Cave, *History of the 1st VB Hampshire Regt, 1859-89* (London 1905), p 75; Hants R.O. L.L.61 Winchester to Earle, 27.7.63; L.L.52 Winchester to Earle, 23.12.59 and 19.1.60.
[6] G.L.R.O. (M) L/C/40 Salisbury to Elcho 8.10.60; Salisbury to Grosvenor, 23.10.60; Salisbury to Richards 4.9.60; *Cruikshank Papers* Acc 534/1; J.M.A. Tamplin, *The Lambeth and Southwark Volunteers* (Regimental Historical Fund 1965) p 3.
[7] C.J. Hart, *The History of the 1st V.B. Royal Warwickshire Regiment* (Birmingham 1906), p 101; *VSG* 14.7.60, p 1; Northants R.O. Box 320 Markham correspondence, Exeter to Markham, 18.12.59 and 6.1.60.
[8] G.L.R.O. (M) L/C/74 Salisbury to Shelley 6.11.60; Walmisley to Salisbury, 9.8.60.
[9] Beds. R.O. *Lieutenancy* L.C.V.4 Osborn to Bedford 9.6.60; Bucks R.O. *TA Coll* Box 15 Wethered Mss, p 5; Lady Wantage, *Lord Wantage: A Memoir by his Wife* (London 1908), p 151-2.
[10] Notes, *JSAHR* No 37 (1959), p 43; Northants R.O. Eunson, II 'The Volunteers'; Beds R.O. *Papers of Beds Rifle Assoc.* X 67/540; Devon R.O. *Seymour of Berry Pomeroy* 1392M/Box 18/10.
[11] Bucks. R.O. *TA Coll* Box 14; Cumbria R.O. *Curwen Mss* loose file, unlisted; Essex R.O. D/DOp, F4; Gwent R.O. LLCM+V 8/189; Haynes Mss, Hollingbourne, Kent; Hants. R.O. L.L.68; Lincs. R.O. *Hill 12th Deposit*, 12/2/1; Northants. R.O. Box X320; Northumberland R.O. BMO/B16; Oxon. R.O. L/M XI/i/5; *QOG* X no 12 (1892), p 913-4 and XI No 3 (1893), p 937-8; Somerset R.O. *Lewis Papers* DD/LW 25; Wilts. Regt. Museum file A16; Rose, *L Bulletin*, op cit, p 58; *VSG* 31.5.73, p 488 'Sketch of LRB'; Berry, op cit, p 409; for wage levels see Lord Ernle, *English Farming Past and Present* (London 6th edition 1961), App IX, p 524-5; Pamela Horn, *Labouring Life in the Victorian Countryside* (Dublin 1976), App G.
[12] *VSG* 14.7.60, p 5; G.L.R.O. (M) L/C/40 Elcho to Salisbury, 6.10.60; L/C/74 Elcho to *Times* 13.8.60; Grosvenor to Salisbury 18.8.60; Surrey R.O. *Mole, Metters and Forster Dep* Acc 1011, Box 24.
[13] Archives and Local Hist. Dept, Lewisham Public Libraries A58/6/1,2,4; Rose *Bulletin*, op cit, quoting Liverpool R.O. Topographical Collection; Fell, op cit, p 190.

[14] Cornwall R.O. 22M/BO/34/28 Vyvyan to Vivian, 16.5.59; Oxon. R.O. *Lieutenancy* L/M I/ix/1 and VII/iv/5; Devon R.O. *Seymour of Berry Pomeroy* 1392 M/Box 18/12.
[15] Gwent R.O. *Lieutenancy* LLCM+V 9/32 Gerthing to Prothero 31.12.59; Bucks R.O. *T.A. Coll* Box 15 Wethered Mss; Hudson, op cit, p 198-9; West Sussex R.O. *Lavington Archives* Mss 81 Leconfield to Lavington, 18.12.59.
[16] Cornwall R.O. 22M/BO/34/28 Vivian to Peel, 16,5,59; Tyacke to Vyvyan 26.5.59; Vyvyan to Vivian 16.5.59 and 28.5.59; Gillingham Local History Society Museum, *Freame Mss*; Beds. R.O. Papers of 7th Earl Cowper X 95/216 Nos 27, 53-5, 60, 70-4; Hart, op cit, p 109-10; E. Merrick, *A History of the Civil Service Rifle Volunteers* (London 1891), p 12.
[17] Northants. R.O. Eunson, p 61, 181; N.C.E. Kenrick, *The Wiltshire Regiment* (Aldershot 1963), p 285; Beds R.O. *Lieutenancy* L.C.V.4; J.G. Hicks, *The Percy Artillery* (London 1899), p 13-51, 56; Grierson, op cit, p 193; *VSG* 24.12.59.
[18] Hants. R.O. *Lieutenancy* L.L. 54, 63, 68; Lancs. R.O. *Lieutenancy* LA 10; Fell, op cit, p 187.
[19] Gwent R.O. D.766, 54 Minute Book of 8th Monmouth R.V.C. Bosanquet to Prothero 10.4.60; Northants. R.O. Eunson, p 111, 211; Somerset R.O. *Dickinson Family Papers* DD/DN 386 and *Lewis Papers* DD/LW 25; Hants. R.O. *Lieutenancy* L.L.59; Cornwall R.O. 22M/BO/34/28; Wilts. R.O. *Troyte Bullock of Zeals House* W.R.O. 865/491 muster roll; Kenrick, op cit, p 285.
[20] *VSG* 8.12.60, p 166 letter of F. Haviland; *BPP* 1862 (3053) XXVII 89, 2455-7; Woodburne, op cit, p 110; Kent R.O. K.A.O. U 120 07.
[21] Northants. R.O. Eunson, p 61; Bucks. R.O. *T.A. Coll* Box 14; Dorset R.O. J.C.1 muster roll of 5th Dorset R.V.C. and D 264/1 muster roll of 3rd Dorset R.V.C.; Haynes Papers, Hollingbourne, Kent; Somerset R.O. *Lewis Papers* DD/LW 26; Surrey R.O. *Mole, Metters and Forster* Acc 1011, Box 24; Wilts. Regimental Museum 64/33. Order Book of 1st Wilts.
[22] C. Igglesden, *History of the East Kent Volunteers* (Ashford and London 1899), p 75-6, 87-8, 125, 136-7; Gwent R.O. LLCM+V 5/4; Beds. R.O. L.C.V.4.
[23] Oxon. R.O. L/M. I/ix/3,4,5,6,7,8,9.
[24] J.R. Vincent, *Pollbooks: How Victorians Voted* (Cambridge 1967) p 15; Bucks. R.O. *T.A. Coll* Box 14; Northants. R.O. YZ 1228; Surrey R.O. Acc 1011, Box 24; Somerset R.O. Papers of Somerset Archaeological Society DD/SAS/SY 2 Minute Book 3rd Somerset R.V.C. and *Lewis Papers* DD/LW/25.
[25] William White, *Directory of Essex* (1863), p 221, 574; *VSG* 10.2.72, p 166-7 'Sketch of Duke of Cornwall's Artillery'; Devon R.O. *Seymour of Berry Pomeroy* 1392M/Box 18/10; Beds. R.O. L.C.V. 4 and 5; Oxon. R.O. L/M I/ix/1; Gwent R.O. LLCM+V 17/1 and D.766.54 Minute Book of 8th Monmouth R.V.C.; Hants. R.O. L.L.52.
[26] Rose, *Liverpool Bulletin*, op cit, p 55; *Sunderland Daily News and Shipping List* 25.6.61; Baxter, op cit, p 3.13; Army Museums Ogilby Trust, *Steeple Mss*; J.G.H. Warren, *A Century of Locomotive Building by Robert Stephenson and Co, 1823-1923* (London 1923); J.D. Scott, *Vickers: A History* (London 1962); J.L. Garvin, *The Life of Joseph Chamberlain* (London 1932), I, p 61-3; T.H. Gamm, *The History of the 1st Warwicks Batt of Rifle Volunteers* (Birmingham 1876), p 5; Manchester Central Library M25/5/5/6.
[27] Grierson, op cit, p 178-9, 221-3.
[28] W.H. Blanch, *The Volunteer's Book of Facts: An Annual Record* (London and Liverpool 1862), p 4; G.L.R.O.(M) L/C/46,58,72(i); H.A.R. May, *Memories of the Artists Rifles* (London 1929), p 8, 74; *VSG* 31.5.73, p 488 Sketch of LRB; 25.5.72, p 406 Macdonald Obituary.
[29] G.L.R.O.(M) *Cruikshank Mss* Acc 534/2; *BPP* 1862 (3053) XXVII 89, evidence of Hughes, 1171-5; *VSG* 13.10.60; Crapster, *JSAHR*, op cit, p 96-7.

[30] Rose, *Bulletin*, op cit, p 58-60; *Lancashire and Cheshire Volunteer*, I (1895), No 8; Woodburne, op cit, p 108; F. Forde, 'The Liverpool Irish Volunteers' *The Irish Sword* X (Winter 1971) No 39, p 106-23; Liverpool Public Libraries, *Twemlow Papers* J.T.3.

[31] E.P. Hennock, *Fit and Proper Persons: Ideal and Reality in Nineteenth Century Urban Government* (London 1973); G.W. Jones, *Borough Politics* (London 1969); J. Garrard, *Leaders and Politics in Nineteenth Century Salford: A Historical Analysis of Urban Political Power* (University of Salford 1977); J. Garrard 'The Middle Class and Nineteenth Century National and Local Politics' in J. Garrard, M. Goldsmith and D. Jary (eds) *The Middle Class in Politics* (London 1978) p 35-67. An indication of the independence of urban elites can also be gauged from the view in Birmingham that a city Volunteer corps would be free of 'county and club influence' — see R. Quinault and J. Stevenson (eds) *Popular Politics and Public Order* (London 1974), p 210.

[32] Cumbria R.O. *Curwen Papers* D/Cu/1/44 Minute Bk of 7th Cumb. R.V.C. and Loose File, unlisted misc papers; Durham R.O. *Londonderry Mss* D/Lo/F 541 Memoirs of 2nd Durham A.V. by G.H. Aird, 10.9.1909 and D/Lo/D 235 Correspondence of 3rd Durham R.V.C.; *VSG* 26.10.67, p 753; Gwent R.O. LLCM+V 12; *Usk Gleaner and Monmouthshire Record*, VII (July 1878) XI (Nov. 1878) biography of Leigh.

[33] Lancs. R.O. LA 10; Walter, op cit, p 32-3; G. Melly, *Recollections of Sixty Years* (Coventry 1893), p 103; *VSG* 18.3.82, p 310; Gwent R.O. LLCM+V 8/4; Warwicks. R.O. AC/CR 33; *VSG* 2.9.71, p 665; *The Monthly Chronicle of North Country Lore and Legend* (Newcastle 1888), p 54-5; Haynes Papers, Hollingbourne, Kent; *QOG* X No 11 (1892), p 909-10.

[34] Wolf, op cit, I, p 185-6; G.L.R.O.(M) L/C/56 (b), 60, 61, 63 (ii), 66, 73, 74, 75, 76(iv), 77, 78 (iii), 85.

[35] Woodburne, op cit, p 100; Hants. R.O. L.L.56; *VSG* 27.8.64, p 613; Ogilby Trust, *Steeple Mss*.

[36] J.M.A. Tamplin, The Surrey Rifle Volunteers, 1859-1959 (typescript), p 3 and *Lambeth and Southwark*, op cit, p 3; Gwent R.O. LLCM+V 14/2 and 14/10; *VSG* 19.1.61; Durham R.O. D/Lo/F 541; Staffs. R.O. D797/9.

[37] G.L.R.O.(M) L/C/40; Wolf, op cit, I, p 185-6; Durham R.O. D/Lo/D 235; Manchester Central Library D/1/A/26 Roll of 1st Manchester (Old Trafford Coy); Berry, op cit, p 397-8, 435-7; Grierson, op cit, passim.

[38] *VSG* 18.2.60, p 192 'The Surrey Light Horse'; Essex R.O. D/DOp F4 Manchester to Parker, 25.10.60.

[39] Beds. R.O. X25/38; Devon R.O. *Acland* 1148 M/18/4/2; Essex R.O. DOp F4; G.L.R.O. (M) L/C/79 Salisbury to Nicholson 10.12.60; Lincs. R.O. 12/2/1, p 30; Northants. R.O. Box X319; *VSG* 22.2.73, p 259; G. Brennan, 'The Light Horse and Mounted Rifle Volunteer Corps', *JSAHR* XXI (1942), No 81, p 3-16.

[40] *VSG* 23.3.72, p 257; *BPP* 1878-9 [c2235] XV 181 evidence of Lt.-Col. Thomson, 1154, 1182, 1201; J.D. Sainsbury, *Hertfordshire Soldiers* (Hitchin 1969), p 30; Essex R.O. D/DOp F4; Oxon. R.O. L/M I/v/3 Clerks Letter Book, 4.11.63.

[41] Beds. R.O. *Wade-Gery Papers* CRT. 190/141 bundle 270; Northants. R.O. Box X319; *VSG* 23.3.72, p 257 'Sketch of Duke of Manchester's L.H.V.'; 22.2.73, p 259 'Sketch of South Molton M.R.V.'

[42] Wantage, op cit, p 155-6; Northants. R.O. Box X319; Devon R.O. *Acland* 1148 M/18/4/1; Beds. R.O. X 25/38; Essex R.O. D/DOp F4; G.L.R.O.(M) L/C/79 Richardson to Salisbury, 24.10.60.

[43] Devon R.O. *Seymour of Berry Pomeroy* 1392 M/Box 18/3 Conran to Fortescue, 11.8.66; Oxon. R.O. L/M. I/v/3 and VII/iii/2; J.D. Sainsbury, 'The History of the 1st Herts. L.H.V.' *Herts. Countryside* XVIII No 69 (1963), p 12-13.

[44] Bucks. R.O. *T.A. Coll*, Box 15 Wethered Mss, p 4.

[45] *BPP* 1862 (3053) XXVII 89, 2184-93, 2277, 2455-7, 2540-2, 2597-9, 2829, 3019-21,

3173-4, 3383, 3344, 3431, 3444, 3550, 3573; *BPP* 1862 (118. xxxii 833) Return of Address to the House of Commons including a Report of the Committee of the Commissioners of Supply for Haddington; Woodburne, op cit, p 107-10.

[46] *QOG* XI 3(214) (1893), p 937-8; Dorset Military Museum, Batt. Order, 11.4.64.

[47] *VSG* 15.2.68, p 164; 23.4.70, p 325; 24.2.72, p 200; *BPP* 1878-9 [c2235] XV 181, 694-4, 866, 1358-60, 1366-8, 2684-5, 2830, 3582-4.

[48] Ibid, *BPP* 1878-9, 1479; May, op cit, p 13-15, 53, 260-3; *LSRG* I (Jan 1899), p 7-9, I (Feb 1896), p 13; II (July 1897), p 77-8; IV (Feb 1899), p 40.

[49] Berks. R.O. Papers of Wallingford M Division D/EH. Z 1, 3, 10.

[50] Bucks. R.O. *Fremantle Mss* D/FR 135/13; *T.A. Coll*, Box 15 Gilbey Mss, Chap 1, p 4.

[51] Ibid, *T.A. Coll* Box 15 Wethered Letter Book; Battalion Order Book 1889-98 Loose File, 1894-8; Gilbey Mss, Chap 11, p 2; A.M. Brookfield, *Annals of a Chequered Life* (London 1930), p 207.

[52] Beds. R.O. L.C.V.4; Bucks. R.O. *T.A. Coll* Box 15 Wethered, p 13; Northants. R.O. Daventry Volunteer Papers, Box X4230, bundles 188-93, 1898-1900.

[53] Lincs. R.O. *Hill 12th Dep* 12/3.

[54] Ibid; Berks. R.O. D/EH.Z 3; Gwent R.O. LLCM+V 17/1 and D.766.54; Surrey R.O. Acc 1011, Box 24; Staffs. R.O. D 797/9; Kent R.O. K.A.O. U120 07.

[55] Durham R.O. D/Lo/F 541; *BPP* 1904. [c 2064] xxxi, 587 Pt IV, p 250, 253.

[56] *VSG* 29.4.82, p 408, 413; 8.11.84, p 16-17; Grierson, op cit p 56-7.

[57] *VSG* 3.3.77, p 277; 9.6.77, p 503; 22.9.77, p 754; 3.10.85, p 823.

[58] *BPP* 1904 [c 2064] xxxi, 587. Appendix XXXIII.

CHAPTER III

THE VOLUNTEERS AND SOCIETY 1859-1899

"Up, tradesman, up! and rally round,
  Defend your homes, as sacred ground,
Your children's smiles a sweet reward,
  When you join the Patriot Borough Guard."

'The Liverpool Borough Guard'
A Private in the Band, 1859.

The relationship between the Volunteers and society in general can be seen largely in terms of a correlation between recruitment figures and international crises. Thus a pattern of apathy and even antipathy interspersed with short periods of interest characterised the public attitude towards the Volunteer Movement. Given the general apathy shown in Victorian England towards the Regular Army it could hardly be expected that the Volunteers would be treated any differently once the initial enthusiasm of 1859-61 had subsided. Indeed the foundation of the National Rifle Association had been specifically designed to prepare for such a contingency. But the public's attitude was also conditioned by a number of factors peculiar to the Volunteer Movement. Yet despite such sources of opposition from the public the Volunteer Movement continued more or less to flourish even during periods of international calm. This leads to the problems of motivations behind participation in the Movement especially among the artisans who contributed the bulk of recruits after 1863. In the light of such consideration conclusions can perhaps be drawn upon the role of the Volunteer Movement in Victorian society.

The early enthusiasm and support for the Movement was considerable with almost no donation too lavish. Land-owners such as Sir B.W. Bridges, Bt., were usually more than willing to grant permission to units such as the 1st Essex R.V.C. to drill or shoot on their land — in this case Danbury Common: 'It will be a satisfaction to me to promote by any means in my power the convenience of the Volunteer corps.' Prizes were willingly given for rifle matches and entertainments were commonplace. The 8th Monmouth (Usk) R.V.C., for example, marched on Good Friday 1861 to Llangibby Castle where the owner, W.A. Williams, threw open his cellars to the Volunteers, receiving in return three cheers for his liberality. In Berkshire, too, 'Lords and gentlemen . . . were apt to be kind to us and find us a good dinner or some refreshments'. As Volunteer corps could not carry colours, a widespread practice was the presentation of suitably inscribed silver bugles by Ladies' committees. In August 1860 Aylesbury Ladies presented one to the 4th Bucks. R.V.C. 'in acknowledgement of the zeal with which they have devoted themselves in their duties'. In July 1860 Frome ladies had been approached to relieve the 13th Somerset R.V.C. of band expenses and in April 1862 a four day bazaar organised by the Ladies Committee raised an astonishing £1784 16s. 9d. for the Stockport Volunteers.[1]

However, enthusiasm declined amongst many Volunteers and much of the public. As early as May 1859 the Duke of Bedford had predicted success in towns 'but in a flat country, a dispersed popula-

93

tion, some miles to walk to parade, much time lost in giving instruction . . . and none of the fair sex to look on and to encourage, I fear it will soon become dull . . .'. This indeed seemed the case as Captain Brunnell noted with bad drill attendance in the 3rd Northumberland (Morpeth) R.V.C. in May 1860: 'and the excuse for their non-attendance cannot be want of time, as on each evening members were dressed in plain clothes walking about the streets and even on the drill ground itself . . .'. Time was, in fact, a crucial factor for both upper middle class and artisan members, and this posed considerable difficulties for commanding officers in arranging drill times for 'the officer has to consider not only the convenience of the Man but Fair days, market days and other local circumstances and snatch at will as he best can'. In January 1862 Viscount Bury was appealing to men, who could not afford the time, to stay on as non-effectives rather than resign completely. Later the same year Lt.-Col. Colvill, Governor of Coldbathfields Prison, was forced to relinquish the command of the 39th Middx. (Clerkenwell) R.V.C. by Middlesex magistrates, who regarded it as incompatible with his prison duties.[2]

The other crucial factor was increasing expense. In many cases there had been unnecessary extravagance at the start and the level of public subscription simply could not be maintained beyond the first few years. The problem was common throughout the country. In January 1862 H. Jefferson wrote to Lord Leconfield concerning debts of £90 incurred by the 10th Cumberland R.V.C.:

> Under these circumstances we are compelled to look for aid from your Lordship and one or two other owners of property in the parish and neighbourhood, the annual subscription in Egremont being very limited.

In the same year the 3rd Oxon. (Banbury) R.V.C. was finding its funds 'scarcely sufficient to pay the necessary annual expenses'. Volunteer self sufficiency had never been a reality and by 1862 some corps already required reclothing. The officers of the 1st Hants. A.B. offset the cost of reclothing in 1862 by raising subscriptions among the officers on a sliding scale from £2 each for Ensigns to £50 from the Colonel. Though it could be argued that donations to the Volunteer Movement saved the country from considerably more expense on a large standing Army, the general feeling among Volunteers was that the early subscriptions had set almost a precedent and were in danger of becoming virtually an annual indirect tax upon the public. In short, donations were a horse ridden too hard by the Volunteers.[3]

The provision of a Government capitation grant in 1863 was, in fact, a further stimulus to the decline in public support. Expenses continued to mount despite state aid and in 1869, for example, the 13th Essex (Stow Valley) R.V.C. was disbanded due to expense. Its late commanding officer faced with a War Office claim for damage to weapons returned to the Government did not intend to be put to any more expense 'having already been very much more than I anticipated when I took the Movement up'. Even greater difficulties faced purely artisan units. In Cruikshank's 48th Middx. the financial situation was not measurably improved until 1868, when Cruikshank resigned in favour of a wealthy ship owner, Cuthbert Vickers. Similarly, Alfred Richards declined the honorary colonelcy of his own 3rd City of London R.V.C. in 1867 in favour of a wealthier man. As it happened Richards' corps had come in for some ridicule in January 1862 for proposing a costly changeover from képis and shakos to bearskins at a time when other corps were appealing for state aid. Government aid could do little to provide the £25,000 required by the London Scottish for a new headquarters to resolve its considerable difficulties in finding adequate premises in the heart of the capital in 1886. The Artists Rifles raised much of the sum required for their new headquarters in 1887-9 by such measures as raffling paintings donated by leading artists and sponsoring concerts supported by celebrated musicians.[4]

It was in the context of this declining public financial support in 1861 and 1862 that Volunteer agitation began both within and outside Parliament for Government pecuniary aid. This agitation, which will be discussed in a later chapter, marked the decline of popular support for the Movement. Henceforth this would be temporarily reawakened only by the recurrence of such international crises and invasion panics as had aroused the public in the 1840's and 1850's. However, before examining this pattern it is necessary to illustrate the general public attitude towards the Volunteer Movement which prevailed during periods of calm and which affected recruiting. This general public attitude derived from a number of contributory factors which can be conveniently divided as follows: the image projected by the Volunteer Movement in its early years; the issue of common rights and drill space; the question of the status of a Volunteer commission; the relationship of Volunteer and employer and the growth of recreational opportunities in Victorian England.

The Public and the Volunteers

To a certain extent the early Volunteers invited public ridicule by their military pretensions and often fanciful uniforms. Lord Seymour of the 6th Wilts. R.V.C. regretted the common mistake of spending money upon fanciful imitations of the more colourful costumes to be seen in Continental Armies, and indeed there were some oddly assorted combinations of uniforms. George Melly of the 4th Lancs. Artillery Brigade complained that his 'fancy dress affair' was not only uncomfortable and similar to a chimney pot in appearance but exposed him 'to the ridicule of small boys'. William Lamont, later Lt.-Col. of the 1st Renfrew V.B., similarly recalled that it required moral courage to appear alone on the streets in uniform because of the taunts of 'hooligans', and J.G. Macdonald and his colleagues of the 1st Northumberland R.V.C. 'were looked upon by many as a lot of enthusiasts, and were sneered at and shouted at through the streets as "noodles" '.[5] Such gibes, coupled with the widespread notion that the Volunteers were 'playing at soldiers', were fostered not only by the popular press and *Punch* but by politicians. Col. Dunne, M.P., spoke of Volunteers as 'amusing playthings for the people' and Sir Robert Peel 'could find no duty more dignified for our great national force than shooting their neighbours' cats . . .'. Such ridicule died hard; in 1874 Henry Spenser Wilkinson 'was prepared to be laughed at' when he joined the Oxford University R.V.C. and in June 1878 the *Volunteer Service Gazette* noted with satisfaction that Trowbridge Magistrates had given 14 days to a sweep for attempting to disrupt and assault Volunteers.[6]

A source of continual antipathy between Volunteers and public concerned age-old common rights which in many cases the Volunteers appeared to threaten by their urgent need for drill space and ranges. A proposal to erect a parapet wall and range on South Common, Lincoln, provoked considerable opposition in October 1859 from those who claimed common land rights. It was argued that the land was unfit for the recreation of the townspeople, 'who not infrequently step into a bog', but in June 1860 a mob of 200 freemen demolished the parapet. Similarly, during the first encampment of the 1st Bucks. A.B. at Marlow in 1865 a mob, claiming access to parish ground, attempted to disrupt the 'camp fire' but

> fortunately the fences round the ground were in good order, and when the leaders realised that, if they broke down the field-gate, they would have to impale themselves on our fence of cold steel before they could attain their object . . . the mob gradually melted away . . .

There was also plain vandalism to contend with. Thus the Committee of the 13th Surrey R.V.C. reported in the same year: 'It is to be regretted that the stack of Faggots which were placed above the Butts should have been destroyed on the 5th of November last . . .'.[7]

The need for drill space was particularly critical in the Metropolitan area but here the public could hardly be expected to respond to Volunteer requirements when successive governments proved unco-operative. There was a serious clash between Volunteers and crowds in Regent's Park on Whit Monday 1861, where mobs threw stones, broke up the ranks and injured horses. Subsequent requests by both Josiah Wilkinson and Thomas Hughes for mounted police at future parades and reviews were refused by the Metropolitan Commissioner of Police, Sir Richard Mayne, on the grounds of lack of men. Mayne, Commissioner of Metropolitan Police from 1829 to 1869, and his successors continued to refuse to spare police even though Volunteers pointed out that plenty seemed available to patrol Rotten Row and cricket pitches in Regent's Park and Battersea. The *Volunteer Service Gazette* warned in 1870 that with ranges beset by enemies and drill grounds swarming with crowds and idlers there was actual danger to the public, and in June 1875 there was a clash between Volunteers and cricketers in Regent's Park although not serious enough to impress the Government of the need to act. Again in June 1881 crowds disrupted an inspection in Regent's Park of the 2nd Tower Hamlets and 10th Middlesex R.V.C.[8] In 1880 and 1881 the Police combined with the Home Office, Commissioner of Works and the Duke of Cambridge as Park Ranger, to ban Volunteer reviews from Hyde Park both for fear of damage to flower beds and also crowd and traffic problems. Yet in July 1884 large crowds were allowed to attend a franchise demonstration in the Park which seemed a clear case of double standards being applied to the Volunteer Movement.[9]

In view of such treatment at the hands of central authority it is not surprising that local authorities followed the example. In 1878 the Marylebone Vestry applied to demolish a drill shed previously erected under the authority of the Metropolitan Board of Works. There was a determined effort in December 1881 by Putney and Wandsworth Vestries to prevent the annual meeting of the National Rifle Association on Wimbledon Common. The Vestries threatened to take complaints of damage to trees, disorderly crowds and noise at night to the Conservators of the Common and Surrey J.P.'s. In the following year in deference to the local inhabitants it was agreed to restrict the selling of liquor and to clear the enclosures earlier than usual, but in 1890 the N.R.A. was finally evicted from Wimbledon because bullets were reaching the Duke of Cambridge's land at Coombe, and the meetings were moved to Bisley. The Putney Vestry had hinted in 1882 that, in any case, they doubted the value of prize shooting, and similar arguments were used by the Local Board of Hampton Wick in banning Volunteers from Bushey Park in 1883 because of an annual bicycle meeting. The reaction of the *Volunteer Service Gazette* to such complaints was that there were more important considerations than the interests of mere leisure seekers and Wimbledon inhabitants on a few nights of the year. Opposition to Volunteer activities was also encountered outside the Metropolis. In 1883, for example, Tynemouth Town Council complained that the noise from the Volunteer Artillery range disturbed holiday-makers and local salmon fishermen.[10]

There could be, however, certain circumstances in which some localities welcomed the Volunteers. The great Easter Monday reviews, organised between 1861 and 1877 by the Metropolitan Commanding Officers at such venues as Brighton or Portsmouth attracted considerable trade to the chosen town — in 1863 at Brighton, Volunteers and their families alone spent £50,000 cash over the Easter weekend. To a certain extent this gave the Volunteers a lever with which to extract more favourable terms and in 1866 Brighton was warned that rail conditions must be improved or the review would go elsewhere. Representatives of the rail companies and towns usually attended meetings of the Metropolitan C.O.'s to press their respective claims; for example, in February 1868 representatives attended from Brighton, Dover and Portsmouth. A circular from Dover rail companies, shopkeepers and hoteliers in 1867 stressed: 'Volunteers would be able not only to inspect a celebrated and most extensive modern fortification, but also avail themselves of steamboat trips at cheap rates to the coast of France.' Such reviews were attractive to many other elements of society as at Guildford in 1864:

> The heath was infested by an abundance of sharpers of every grade, from the black-eyed and bullet-headed rogues, who laid snares for the unwary in exceedingly transparent games of chance, to the well-got-up scoundrels whom you might have got beside with the most easy confidence in the world.[11]

However, with the passing of the Bank Holiday Act, the rail companies had sufficient civilian traffic to refuse to convey the Volunteers and the review was abandoned in 1874 and 1875, forced out to Tring in 1876 and Dunstable in 1877 and finally abandoned in 1878.[12]

The factors of time and expense continued to be of particular importance in the recruitment of Volunteer officers, especially as the artisan classes, upon whom the Force increasingly relied to fill the ranks, could give little more than their leisure time. The problem was given added dimensions by the virtual ostracism of Volunteer officers in society. As the upper middle class elements dropped out so it became more difficult to find candidates for commission. The 5th

Oxon. (Witney) R.V.C. was disbanded in June 1864 through a lack of candidates and the 7th Oxon. (Bicester) R.V.C. went the same way in June 1870 having failed to revitalise itself during a year's grace. The 4th Beds. (Dunstable) R.V.C. provides a good example of the problems beginning to be encountered in finding suitable officer candidates. By June 1868 William Medland, a solicitor, was the only remaining officer. An innkeeper named Merefield of the Saracens, Dunstable, was accepted as Ensign only after the Lord Lieutenant, Earl Cowper, had been assured of his suitability and that there was no objection from the unit itself. A candidate for the vacant Lieutenancy was refused after he had been convicted at Woburn Petty Sessions for 'driving wildly about the streets of Hockcliffe to the danger of other persons so that the Police Constable was obliged to interfere'. In March 1869 Medland himself was struck off the Roll of Attornies by the Incorporated Law Society for misconduct and fled to Belgium, from whence he submitted his resignation on the grounds that he had moved abroad! Merefield resigned in July 1872 and the Mayor of Dunstable refused to take over because of the expense.[13]

Despite similar objections to men of 'trade' becoming officers as at Lyncombe in Somerset and at Evesham in 1870 it became necessary in many instances to accept men who previously would have seen non-commissioned rank as the limit of their ambitions and, indeed, any man who could afford time and money, which was not always conducive to military efficiency and also laid the Force open to social 'climbers'. But, in fact, Volunteer commissions proved no passport to social influence and position. As early as 1862 it was reported in the 3rd Durham R.V.C. that 'young men of respectability have been deterred from joining from the fact of the officers being men of no position or influence in the town or county'.[14] Officers increasingly became the target for social stigma in satirical magazines such as *Tomahawk, Britannia* and *Whitehall Review* for their allegedly low breeding and poor professional standing; the attitude being summed up as 'a greengrocer presented with a major's commission is a greengrocer pleased'. Society journals such as *Vanity Fair* and *Metropolitan* and indeed the press generally refused to accord military rank to the Volunteers. Thus many Volunteer M.P.'s preferred not to use titles which were, in any case, usually ignored in both press reports and military journals such as the *Army and Navy Gazette* and Foreign Office clerks habitually left Volunteer ranks off passports.[15] Volunteers regarded this treatment as an attack upon their dignity although public attitudes were perhaps understandable in this respect in view of the misuse of military titles in the experience of the United States. On 7 March 1860 some 2,000 officers of the infant Volunteer Force had been presented to Queen Victoria at a special levee but this was never repeated and thereafter presentation of officers at Court by virtue of their Volunteer commissions was consistently refused by the Lord Chamberlain. It was particularly galling to Volunteer officers, especially after 1871 when all Auxiliary commissions emanated from the Crown, that Militia officers who did ony one month's duty per annum and Yeomanry officers who did even less enjoyed such privileges. It was in short no advantage to a young man to be known as a Volunteer subaltern in provincial middle class society.[16] Volunteers were theoretically exempt from tolls when in uniform but this, too, was often contested and caused problems, for example, in August 1873 when men of the 80th Lancs. R.V.C. were involved in a fight with officials at Woodside Ferry. Paradoxically, it can be noted that, despite occasional complaints of rowdyism, any Volunteer in uniform could attend theatres such as the Alhambra or the Crystal Palace and obtain first-class tickets without qualms, which contrasted strongly with the discrimination against Regular soldiers at public entertainments.[17]

The issue of honours and privileges became, as will be discussed in a later chapter, another platform for Volunteer agitation in Parliament, as it was generally believed that some mark of official favour would give an impetus to recruiting by inducing press and public to recognise Volunteer officers. In 1862 Lt. Reed of the 3rd Durham R.V.C. expressed his belief that 'a privilege of some sort, such as being free from Juries or a reduced scale of taxation for all really effective Volunteers, in lieu of exemption from the Duty on Hair Powder, would probably give an impetus to the Movement'. Jury exemption was the most common demand and hopes were raised in 1879 when Lord Justice Thesiger granted exemption to a Volunteer officer on duty, but this remained a matter for individual judges, and in 1882 Mr Justice Grove incensed Volunteers by comparing their titles to those of the Salvation Army.[18] Some concessions were gained — in 1881 Hugh Childers granted 5 K.C.B.'s, 25 C.B.'s and 4 A.D.C.'s to the Volunteer Force; in July 1884 the Board of Inland Revenue finally exempted Volunteers from the Gun Tax; in 1890 Volunteers were finally placed on the same footing as Militia and Yeomanry officers for Court presentation; a Volunteer Decoration was granted to officers in 1892 and a Long Service Medal to other ranks in 1893.[19] Jury exemption was recommended by the Harris Departmental Committee in 1887 and again by the Select Committee on Volunteer Acts in 1894 but, despite its favourable consideration by successive governments, never materialised. However, expenses did not fall, and the burden of meeting the gap between Government grant and actual expenditure continued to fall on the officers; finance was thus both cause and effect of the deficiency of officers. The problem was never solved: in 1873 there were 2,233 officer vacancies; in 1886 1,096 vacancies; in 1891 1,401 vacancies; in 1893 1,677 vacancies; in 1894 1,841 vacancies; in 1895 1,907 vacancies; in 1896 1,800 vacancies and in 1904 the Volunteer Force was still short of 2,360 officers or 24.9 per cent of establishment.[20]

In the early years of the Volunteer Force it was thought that the moral assumptions underlying the Movement would prove especially attractive in inducing employers to favour their men joining. This did not prove the case in the long term. Although many employers originally supported the Movement there were some opposed from the very beginning, notably Northern spinning manufacturers and mill owners in towns such as Rochdale, Huddersfield and Manchester. Indications of this opposition continued to appear — in August 1861 Cook, Son and Co., of St. Paul's Churchyard, Manchester, ordered their warehousemen to leave the Force and in January 1862 the Director of the Lincoln and Lindsay Bank similarly refused to release his clerks. The need to co-operate with local employers did not make it easier to arrange drills and parades as Captain Warburton wrote to Earl Vane Tempest in January 1862: 'I fear we shall not be able to get even a tolerable muster of the Corps, as there is no holiday before Easter and the members cannot leave their work.'[21]

Relations between Metropolitan employers and Commanding Officers were somewhat better and officers such as Lord Elcho, Lord Grosvenor, Lord Radstock and Thomas Hughes also enjoyed close co-operation with the Early Closing Movement. Metropolitan C.O.'s made the first step towards shorter hours with an agreement with London employers in September 1860 on earlier Saturday closing, which it was hoped would enable more working men to join the Volunteer Force. This was followed in 1866 by the first half holiday experiments with 30-40 leading Metropolitan employers. However, Government requirements in terms of time made little provision for the condition of a man's employment and as Government requirements on the Volunteers increased so did opposition from employers as, for example, in 1874 when Messrs. Geekie and Black of Coupar Angus refused to release men for an inspection of the 2nd Perth A.B. In 1881 Lord Ranelagh, Charles Lindsay and the Lord Mayor of London all appealed to employers to allow men to attend the Royal Review at Windsor in July and on this particular occasion the Stock Exchange closed for the review and the Government, not always very co-operative, released its own civil servants.[22] The argument on the part of the Volunteers that their existence safeguarded employers' business interests looked less persuasive after the first few years, and by 1881 the *Volunteer Service Gazette* considered that most employers were now opposed to the Movement, severely discouraging men if not actually prohibiting them from joining. Volunteer M.P.'s continually called attention to the opposition of employers to increased requirements, but this had little effect. The position was best summed up by John Swan in his annual statement to the 1st Lincoln R.V.C. in November 1870:

> It cannot reasonably be expected that the employers of labour should suffer a heavy pecuniary loss by the absence of their employees on the one hand, or that the employees should, on the other hand, be asked to run the risk of losing their employment for absenting themselves without leave.[23]

The advent of the Volunteer Movement in 1859 opened up new recreational opportunities in Victorian England but rather in the same way that the half holiday back-fired against the Volunteers with respect to the Easter reviews, so too did the growth of sports which they had encouraged. Contemporaries attached more importance to this factor than it perhaps warranted, for example, in 1895 the *Lancashire and Cheshire Volunteer* considered that 'the love for golf, football and other recreations has for the moment placed volunteering in the background'. Robert Potter Berry, writing in 1902 on the decline of the Force in the years after 1869, blamed the growth of sports: 'It might be added that the increase of professional football, with its inevitably attendant gambling, is steadily lowering the morale of the classes from which Volunteers are mainly recruited.' It was recalled that even Napoleon III had assured James Walter that 'your young men will never substitute rifle practice and drill for cricket'.[24] The recreational factor does, however, seem to have played an important role in the decline of the Oxford University R.V.C. In 1879 recruiting material stressed 'while the Corps does not in any way interfere with boating or cricketing interest, it opens a career to many men useful to themselves and in some measure honourable to the University'. Matters did not improve and in October 1888 new Merton undergraduates were informed: 'We do not pretend that, considered as an amusement, Volunteering comes up to boating, cricket or football' but that the Corps would not interfere 'the least seriously with the ordinary amusements of this place'. The Oxford University R.V.C. came near to disbandment in 1888 but survived with further appeals in 1893 and 1897. A similar instance is the case of the 1st Essex A.B. at Colchester where it was reported in 1871 that men 'preferred the regatta and their wives and families to their inspection' showing 'how lightly they think of duty and Volunteering and hardly deserve the name of Volunteers'.[25] Certainly the growth of sports outside the Movement contributed to the difficulties of recruitment but it was not as important as the opposition of employers.

The Pattern of Recruitment

Of course, to a large extent, public attitudes depended upon the climate of international affairs at any one time and the resulting assessment by the public of the likelihood of the Volunteer Force being required for national defence. It is possible to detect a correlation between Volunteer recruitment figures and such major international crises as came nearest to threatening Britain. This is especially true in the case of the resignations and new appointments of Volunteer officers who had a far greater burden of expense to consider prior to joining than other ranks. The fluctuations of Volunteer recruitment are indicated in the following Tables — 14 and 15.

There was a steady growth in the numbers of Volunteers in the early years which were not short of international tensions. In 1863 it was possible to find conflicts in New Zealand, China, Japan, West Africa, Poland, Canada, the Cape and, of course, the American Civil War. This was followed by the crisis over Denmark in 1864 and domestic problems in Russia, Poland and Italy. In 1866 came the Austro-

Table 14 — The Recruitment Pattern of Volunteer Officers, 1872-1885

	Resignations*	New Appointments	Net effect
1872-3	1112	839	−273
1873-4	886	764	−122
1874-5	826	746	− 80
1875-6	690	740	+ 50
1876-7	716	799	+ 83
1877-8	592	883	+291
1878-9	772	728	− 44
1879-80	727	708	− 19
1880-1	631	690	+ 59
1881-2	676	763	+ 87
1882-3	662	673	+ 11
1883-4	667	649	− 18
1884-5	583	815	+232

Average loss: 17-18 per cent.
* *excluding deaths.*
Figures derived from the *Volunteer Service Gazette.*

Table 15 — **The Enrolled Strength of the Volunteer Force,**
1861-1908

Year	Enrolled	Year	Enrolled
1861	161,239	1885	224,012
1862	157,818	1886	226,752
1863	162,935	1887	228,038
1864	170,544	1888	226,469
1865	178,484	1889	224,021
1866	181,565	1890	221,048
1867	187,864	1891	222,046
1868	199,194	1892	225,423
1869	195,287	1893	227,741
1870	193,893	1894	231,328
1871	192,608	1895	231,704
1872	178,279	1896	236,059
1873	171,937	1897	231,798
1874	175,387	1898	230,678
1875	181,086	1899	229,854
1876	185,501	1900	277,628
1877	193,026	1901	288,476
1878	203,213	1902	268,550
1879	206,265	1903	253,281
1880	206,537	1904	253,909
1881	208,308	1905	249,611
1882	207,336	1906	255,854
1883	209,365	1907	252,791
1884	215,015	1908 1st Apr.	224,217

Average turnover 25 per cent
Figures from the annual returns of the Volunteer Force 1863-1907

Prussian War and in 1867 there were Fenian threats both in Canada and Britain. The significance of these crises to the Volunteers, judging from editorials in the *Volunteer Service Gazette*, was not that they posed an actual threat of invasion but that Britain might be unavoidably embroiled in a general European conflagration. In fact, none of them proved a really major stimulus to recruiting in terms of the perceptions of Volunteers themselves. Indeed the 'sober' reactions to 1864 and 1866 were largely attributed by Volunteers to the existence of the Force as a guarantee of security and an influence against panic. Viewing a situation of the 'most profound peace' in September 1869, the *Volunteer Service Gazette* could find problems only in Cuba, Paraguay and New Zealand.[26]

The years 1868-1872 proved less successful for the Volunteer Force despite the Franco-Prussian War and the brief recurrence of invasion alarms induced by the literary efforts of such as Alfred Richards in his *Invasion of England* and George Chesney's famous *Battle of Dorking* in January 1871, which was narrated through the eyes of a Volunteer.[27] Between 1868 and 1873 some 27,267 men were lost, with 1872 showing a decrease of 14,329 men which was the third worst year for recruitment in the entire existence of the Volunteer Force. These were the years when military and press criticism of the Volunteers was at its zenith in journals such as the *Pall Mall Gazette, United Service Magazine, Broad Arrow* and the *Times*. This criticism of Volunteer military efficiency, which will be examined in a later chapter, culminated with a most unfavourable report on the 1871 Brighton review by Sir James Hope Grant. These were also the years of Cardwell and increased Government requirements, to be examined in the next chapter, which were held responsible for the resignation of nearly 2,000 officers between 1872 and 1874 which represented a net loss, after new appointments, of nearly 400 officers. The Franco-Prussian War did not prove the stimulus that Lord Derby for one had predicted and, indeed, in 1869 the *London Gazette* had begun to print less details of Volunteer resignations 'in consequence . . . of observations made by foreigners on the frequent changes in the Volunteer Force'.[28]

The major crisis which the *Volunteer Service Gazette* hoped would revive public interest in the Movement came with the Balkan Crisis of 1876-78, when the Army Reserve was called out, Indian troops brought to the Mediterranean, the Fleet dispatched to Besika Bay and Sir Robert Napier and Sir Garnet Wolseley nominated respectively Commander-in-Chief and Chief of Staff of any British expeditionary force.[29] Under the impact of the crisis the Volunteer Force increased by 17,712 men between 1877 and 1878 and there was a net increase of 291 officers; indeed, 163 new officers were appointed in April 1878 alone. This seemed to prove what Volunteers had always maintained that, in the event of a war or invasion, men would flock back to the Force, but with the passing of the crisis there came the expected reaction. Colonial campaigns in Afghanistan and South Africa posed little threat to the British public and the disaster at Maiwand did not revive as much interest as the *Volunteer Service Gazette* hoped. By January 1881 there had been a heavy retirement rate for the previous two months. Added to the decline in tension was a continuing trade depression which certainly had some effect on businessmen contemplating the expense of a commission, though not as serious as had been expected, and J.H.A. Macdonald always maintained that the true barometer of Volunteer recruitment was officers and not the state of trade.[30] It can be noted that any depression in trade had a completely different effect upon the Regular Army, the 'compulsion of destitution', as Sir William Nicholson later called it, being a major influence on Regular recruiting figures.[31]

There were renewed domestic tensions in 1882 with the agitation against the Channel Tunnel project and the naval scare of 1884, but these were largely press affairs and had little effect upon the Volunteer Movement, the *Volunteer Service Gazette* noting that the public would soon forget any lessons to be learned. However, in 1885 there occurred once more a major international crisis with the perilous situation of British troops in the Sudan following the failure to relieve Gordon and the continuing Russian threat to India as emphasised in the Penjdeh crisis. This brought an increase of 14,647 men in two years and the appointment of 800 new officers of whom 298 were recruited in only nine weeks.[32] The trouble, of course, with such a sudden influx of new officers was that in the event of war they would in any case be untrained. There followed the customary reaction in officer recruitment and only minor fluctuations in the Force as a whole occurred in the remaining years of the century. There was, in fact, an actual fall in numbers during the height of the Boulanger affair in France and the War Office/Admiralty disputes on invasion. The revival of invasion literature appears to have had no appreciable effect in the 1890's and indeed the public itself did not seem unduly concerned even though it was a period when the French and German General Staffs were seriously tackling the problems of invading Britain. Rather like the *Volunteer Service Gazette* in 1882, the *Lancashire and Cheshire Volunteer* hoped in 1895 for a 'slight hitch' in European affairs to bring home to the public their sense of responsibility for the unsatisfactory treatment of the Volunteers and in 1896 Col. W.J. Alt of the 22nd Middlesex spoke at the Royal United Service Institution of the hour of danger likely to fall on Britain 'like a thief in the night'.[33]

The 'slight hitch' occurred, of course, in 1899 but not in Europe. The Volunteer Force reacted to the South African War in the way in which it had always been predicted that it would in a major crisis. Between 1900 and 1901 the Force increased by some 58,622 men and over 19,000 Volunteers served in South Afica, but this was followed by the predictable loss of some 35,195 men in the two years following the cessation of hostilities — 1902, with a decrease of 19,926 men, was the worst year in the history of the Force. Thereafter, the uncertainties of Arnold-Forster's plans and the Territorial scheme of Haldane further affected recruiting.

A condition of peace was thus regarded as something of a threat to support for the Movement. On the other hand, despite the frequently voiced fears of the Volunteers themselves, there was an overall steady rate of growth. The fact that, despite the apparent setbacks, the Force continued to enjoy the support of nearly a quarter of a million men for much of the period after 1885, when public perceptions of danger were slight, was also remarkable in a society traditionally hostile to participation in military affairs. That there was such support tended to be lost on those individuals or organs like the *Volunteer Service Gazette* which modelled Volunteer 'opinion' and who naturally enough believed that, given the encouragement they demanded from the state, so much more would have been achieved. In part this line of thinking can be seen in the later conversion of Lord Elcho to the idea of reviving conscription as a means of inducing the whole manhood of the nation to serve in its defence in a way that the Volunteers could not. These same contemporaries, however, rightly viewed the main achievement of the Volunteers, as will be discussed in a later chapter, in terms of encouraging the growth of a 'military spirit' in Britain. A case, perhaps, of having a cake and eating it too!

Having examined those factors which tended to work to the disadvantage of the Volunteers, it is necessary to explain the motives which induced men to join in the face of the 'unexampled discouragement'[34] which Volunteers believed characterised public attitudes in times of peace and which enabled the Force to survive so well.

Recruitment and Motivation

Motives, as expressed in the accounts of Volunteers who joined in later years, varied greatly. For many officers like Howard Vincent, who was to become a leading Volunteer M.P., patriotism was still the primary motive:

> I have always held and still hold that it is the duty of a man to his sovereign and his country, if under forty years of age and not serving in the Regular Army, the Militia or the Yeomanry, to join the Volunteer Force.

Indeed, it required a considerable sense of duty to undertake the responsibilities and sacrifices required of a Volunteer officer who risked, as Haldane later remarked, not only his life but his fortune. Spenser Wilkinson became interested in military affairs by what he saw on a European tour in 1874 of the contrast between Britain's Army and the large Continental conscript armies, but Alfred Gilbey, who joined the Bucks. Volunteers in 1879, admitted that he was fired by neither military ardour nor patriotism: 'It was all arranged without my being consulted by Col. Wethered and my father when I was 17 years of age.' H.A.R. May joined the Artist Rifles in 1882 through the 'contagious' enthusiasm of a friend after an Easter camp.[35]

What, then, were the motives for other ranks in sacrificing their leisure hours for no apparent reward? Contemporaries and especially critics attributed to the Volunteers motives of social climbing, the attraction and prestige of a uniform and the evil influence of military ardour. These cannot be entirely discounted but it is unlikely that they were an important stimulus in later years when it appeared that Volunteering conferred no social distinction. As has been shown, Volunteer rank was no real social advantage and a Volunteer uniform was more likely to attract ridicule than respect as, for example, in Bedfordshire where the Battalion uniform was customarily hissed at: 'the dislike to the uniform worn by the Battalion manifested by the public in such a manner is very trying to Volunteers who work hard at the sacrifice of much time to do their duty.' In Sunderland it was felt that any uniform change to scarlet would prove of only temporary benefit.[36] Pressure from employers to join can certainly be discounted as a motive and indeed the reverse was increasingly the case. Organs of Nonconformism such as *Morning Star* and the *Methodist Recorder* argued that military ardour as represented by the Volunteers was an evil influence tending to draw youths away from mechanics' institutes, reading rooms and teetotal pledges, and Joseph Pearce of the Peace Society similarly believed: 'Take away the tinsel of women's smiles and attractions of brandy and water and cigars and the military ardour would soon evaporate.' To a certain extent Pearce was right, for what the Volunteers did offer was unrivalled recreational opportunities. Recreation was not only a major stimulus to the Movement among the artisan and lower middle class but also gave the Volunteer Force a moral purpose in an intensely serious age — that of combining recreation with patriotism in an atmosphere of social intercourse between differing classes. As T.F. Fremantle wrote: 'There must have been many to whom an interesting and outdoor recreation, with a strong flavour of drilling and patriotism accompanying it, was very welcome.'[37]

Volunteer activities were seen as a great advantage to both the Volunteers themselves and to their employers. It is no accident that Thomas Hughes, whose *Tom Brown's Schooldays* appeared in 1858, and Samuel Smiles, whose *Self Help* appeared in 1859, were such strong supporters of the Movement. George Melly and James Walter in Liverpool both believed that drill and discipline would inspire men with habits of order, silence, obedience, cleanliness, punctuality and courtesy. Such habits could not be practised continually 'without exercising a strong attraction over men of naturally healthy, orderly and decent character, and exhorting some respect even from ruder natures . . .'. The combination of drill, exercise and fresh air was naturally healthy as Mathew Arnold recorded: 'It braces one's muscles and does one a world of good.' This would obviously have a beneficial effect upon, for example, young Londoners whose physical recreation amounted at best to perhaps an occasional walk or cricket game. As a result, 'the toils of the countinghouse, the warehouse and the shop would be undertaken in a new spirit of dutiful delight . . .'[38] These early hopes appear to have been realised as far as most middle class Volunteers were concerned. Many witnesses before the Royal Commission in 1862 testified to the success of the Movement in claiming the 'idle' and stemming 'dissipation'. Indeed it was claimed that a Volunteeer was worth 3s. a week more to a jobbing master and that Volunteers were generally more respectful towards authority and more attached to the government, even in former Chartists areas such as John Street and Fitzroy Square where Lord Elcho recruited his artisan companies for the London Scottish. Social and moral benefit was also claimed in many other areas of the country. In Egremont in Cumberland the social benefit conferred on a small community was 'very great' and in Sunderland the Force 'was putting its elevating stamp on the people in their holiday hours'. The *Volunteer Service Gazette* went so far as to claim that there had been a general improvement in the appearance and carriage of town populations between 1859 and 1862.[39]

Much the same arguments were used for the creation of the many public school cadet corps which were attached to Volunteer Units, such as the Eton corps, which was designated the 8th Bucks. R.V.C. and then the 2nd Bucks. (Eton) V.B. In the 1880's this spread to the larger cities with independent cadet corps and battalions for working boys in Birmingham, Liverpool, Manchester, Glasgow and London. By 1899 there were 37 separate cadet corps and 6 cadet battalions. The working boys' corps were designed to exercise moral influence over school leavers and instil boys with 'habits of self respect, subordination, punctuality, smartness, loyalty to their Queen and love for their Country'. Volunteers officers were closely associated with these units, for example, Lt. Fordyce of the 2nd V.B. South Staffs with the Birmingham Home for Destitute Boys, Major Bower of the 7th Surrey in South London, Freeman Willis of the Finsbury Polytechnic and Sir Francis Vane with the London Cadet corps at Toynbee Hall. Both William A. Smith of Glasgow, who founded the Boys' Brigades in 1883, and Walter Gee, who founded the Church Lads' Brigade in

1891, were also Volunteers.[40]

It was not just, of course, that as Col. Gordon stated in 1859, 'a dissipated man rarely makes a good shot'. Moral and social benefits of volunteering also implied a measure of social control and conditioning of the lower orders of society by the middle classes. There were instances in which discipline in Volunteer corps was maintained under pain of dismissal from civilian employment as in the Wolverton company of the Bucks Volunteer Battalion drawn from the L.N.W.R., McIver's corps in Liverpool drawn from the Cunard company and in the 24th Middx. (Post Office) R.V.C.[41] More commonly, the process of social control was more subtle. The Boys Brigades and the Volunteer cadet battalions have been characterised by Dr. Springhall as conscious attempts to penetrate the leisure of the working-class adolescent as an antidote to restlessness. The largest of the cadet battalions was that of Southwark, catering mainly for apprentices to skilled trades such as printing and book binding. Here, the battalion was much influenced by Octavia Hill and formed only one of the means by which the Charity Organisation Society pursued the reinforcement of social conformity in the area. But participation in these units also conferred upon the working-class boys a *rite de passage* between classes for the upwardly aspiring which is precisely similar to the function of the Volunteer corps in relation to the clerical workers in Liverpool and Manchester examined by Dr. Anderson. As far as employers of clerks were concerned, participation in the Volunteers not only promoted 'punctuality and submission to authority in business' but by allowing clerks to 'rub shoulders' with employers also compensated them for declining opportunities of upward social mobility. In turn, search for security by clerks in face of increasing competition, not only from female and foreign clerks but from the erosion of social and economic differentials between them and the 'labour aristocracy', led them to re-express their commitment to the social system through membership of voluntary organisations such as the Volunteers and the Y.M.C.A.[42]

The search for respectability through participation was also marked among the 'labour aristocracy'. Recent research on skilled workers in Edinburgh and the London boroughs of Deptford, Greenwich and Woolwich has suggested that such participation fell far short of acceptance of direct forms of social control by the middle classes and represented a situation of 'implicitly negotiated compromise' between middle class leadership and working class resistance. The concept of upward mobility to the labour aristocracy implied a claim to status recognition and citizenship on behalf of skilled workers as a whole sharing the aspirations of the middle class but seeking autonomy and

110

independence of outright middle class control. The Volunteers in Edinburgh have been identified by Dr. Gray as one of the best examples of ways in which skilled men sought to distinguish themselves from their fellows and to stake their claim to be 'brought within the pale of civic respectability'. The individual's ability to achieve upward mobility within the working class was linked to 'respectable behaviour patterns'. In this the work discipline inculcated by Volunteer training was thought to be most advantageous, as the contemporary historian of the Queen's Edinburgh Rifle Brigade noted in 1881.[43]

Whatever the differing concepts involved, the Volunteers were thought to be acting as a means by which certain social values were transmitted to the working class. There is little doubt that social intercourse between classes did result from Volunteer activities. At first it had been feared by some, such as Mathew Arnold and Ernest Jones, the former Chartist leader, that the Volunteer Force would become a 'class' movement beyond the participation of the artisan classes. This, of course, proved mistaken and it was generally recognised that class feeling would have been potentially very dangerous within the Movement. The spirit of the early conception of the Force in which officers and men had frequently been social equals persisted. In the 1st Bucks. (Marlow) R.V.C. in 1859 officers had been 'mortally afraid of offending their men — many of whom were of equal social standing with themselves'. In the 1st Berks. (Reading) R.V.C. men 'all worked together very harmoniously', and in Wiltshire Lord Seymour had gone as far as to suggest that 'where gentlemen serve in the ranks, unnecessary commissions are only invidious distinctions'. In later years this spirit posed some problems in terms of military discipline, but it did mean that most Volunteer officers continued to feel it essential to achieve social harmony within their units. The apparent class conflict between the professional man of the 'Fighting Fifth' Kent (East Kent Tradesmen) R.V.C. and artisans of the 'Drunken Sixth' Kent (East Kent Artisans) R.V.C., which 'led to a great deal of unpleasantness at the time' was rare. In 1862, for example, Captain Chapman of the 3rd Durham R.V.C. engaged the services of a man to teach marching songs in the evenings as he found it 'necessary to get the men together at night' and believed this would prove popular. Similarly, the Adjutant of the 48th Middx. R.V.C. advised officers in April 1863 to take an active interest in their men:

> I would propose inviting all members to a march out into the country, having a little drink, and their giving them some refreshment. I think it would bring the members together.[44]

Lord Elcho for one believed that the degree of social harmony

111

achieved was highly beneficial and demonstrated the willingness of the artisan class as a whole to accept social recognition in preference to political reform. This explained the charge of his political opponents that he would not extend the franchise to men he was prepared to arm. It was further illustrated by his close contact with the 'respectable' Scottish mining leader Alexander MacDonald, and his sponsorship of the Master and Servant Amendment Bill in 1866. More usually, as in the 49th Middx. (Post Office) R.V.C., considerable social benefit was thought to derive from social intercourse in the Volunteers:

> It has brought all the branches and departments of the Post Office into close relationship and lifetime friendships have been formed at the camps, drill fields and ranges, which would have been impossible when there existed no common ground on which Post Office employees met[45].

Some junior officers, who came to be known as the 'Advanced School' and whose contribution to the military aspect of the Force will be examined in a later chapter, advocated a greater demarcation line between officers and men as part of a general tightening up of Volunteer regulations. However, it was generally recognised that authority on the parade ground could not be translated into civilian life and that any attempt to lower the status of the ordinary Volunteer through mistaken notions of dignity would impair the harmony of the Force. Owen Wethered had, as was recorded in the last chapter, very definite views on the status required of a Volunteer officer. However, when he admitted Eton boys as honorary members of the Officers' Mess in 1872, he was careful to allow any man to mess with the officers if introduced by his company Captain, as he was 'unwilling to make any distinction between them (Eton boys) and the other Volunteers',[46] but few men took advantage of this.

A further expression of the mixing of social groups within the Force was the incidence of masonic lodges attached to Volunteer corps, as in the City, West Kent and Wolverhampton, though it can be noted that in practice these tended to be confined to nominally 'class' corps such as the London Scottish, London Rifle Brigade, Victoria's, 1st Surrey and South Middlesex R.V.C.[47]

Once a man had joined, what types of activity would he find?

Leisure and other Activities

The actual variety of Volunteer activities can now be illustrated. The pattern of Volunteer life did not basically change through the existence of the Force and, indeed, most activities continued in the

'The Noble and the Brave . . .'

*Top left: Lord Elcho, M.P.; Lt.-Col. 15th Middlesex (London Scottish) R.V.C.,
1859-1878.*
Top right: Captain Edmund Bellairs; Adjutant of 1st Norfolk A.B., 1861-1864.
*Bottom left: Charles Ichabod Wright, M.P.; Lt.-Col. 1st Notts. (Robin Hood Rifles)
R.V.C., 1861-1875.*
*Bottom right: Nathaniel Creswick; Officer Commanding 4th West Riding (Sheffield)
A.V., 1861-1897 (pictured as a Major,* circa *1862).*

'Skilled at the Butts . . .'

Top: Queen Victoria performing the opening ceremony at the National Rifle
Association's first meeting on Wimbledon Common, 2 July 1860 (as photographed by
Roger Fenton).
Bottom: Fenton's photograph of the competitions on the opening day at Wimbledon.

'Who Shot the Dog? . . .'

Top: Officers of the 4th Durham (Teesdale) R.V.C. circa 1861.
Middle: Lord Bury, Lt.-Col. 21st Middx. (Civil Service) R.V.C. (seated second left) and Lt.-Col. Robert Loyd-Lindsay of 1st Berks. R.V.C. (third from right) with Belgian and French officers in Brussels during the Tir National, October 1866.
Bottom: 1st Middlesex (Queen Victoria's Rifles) R.V.C. on the road to Wimbledon, July 1864.

'The Future of War: Reality'

Top: A group of 3rd London R.V.C. (11th V.B., King's Royal Rifle Corps) with Gatling Gun, 1896.
Bottom: 22nd Middlesex (Central London Rangers) R.V.C. (8th V.B., King's Royal Rifle Corps) with the Nordenfelt machine guns purchased in 1882.

'The Future of War: Speculation'

Top: Cyclists of the 4th V.B., East Surrey Regiment, photographed at Winchester.
Bottom: Cyclists of the 2nd V.B., Hampshire Regiment, and friends on manoeuvres,
in 1898; probably at Easter.

'2 Chevaux, 40 Hommes . . .'

Top: Members of the 1st Hants (Droxford Light Horse) M.R.V.
Bottom: A detachment of the 2nd Cambridge (University) V.B. in training at Colchester, March 1886.

'The War God's Call . . .'

*Top: Captain A. L. Careless and other volunteers for South Africa from E Company
(Builth Wells), 1st V.B., South Wales Borderers, 1900.*
*Bottom: The Return of the Second Volunteer Service Company of the King's
Shropshire Light Infantry to Shrewsbury, 1902.*

'Despatches from the Seat of War . . .'

Three members of the City Imperial Volunteers.

Territorial Force after 1908. These activities can be loosely divided into those of military necessity such as drills, musketry, reviews and camps; those of financial necessity such as balls, concerts, bands and theatrical performances, and those of an internal social nature such as clubs.

For the period 1859-1899 the basic requirement was to attend 6 company drills, 3 battalion drills and the Annual Inspection, though in practice many men completed far more than the minimum. Recruit drills were initially 30 in the first 18 months but this was increased to 60 drills in 2 years in 1881 and musketry requirements were raised in 1872 and 1887. The Volunteer year began in October from 1859-62, in December from 1863 to 1871 and thereafter in November. Drills were normally completed by the Inspection in May or June and a certain number had to be completed before a man could attend an Easter review or camp in March or April. It would be impossible to illustrate every regimental variation but a few examples can be given of typical weekly programmes.

In the first few years drills were held both in the early morning and the evening. Thus the 1st Kent (Maidstone) R.V.C. held its drills at 6.45 a.m. on two mornings per week and at 7 p.m. on a further two evenings per week. The programme of the 36th Middlesex (Paddington) R.V.C. for the week 8-13 July 1861 was as follows: Monday 6.45 a.m. snapping practice and blank firing, 6.45 p.m. Coy. drill; Tuesdays 6.15 p.m. class firing, 7 p.m. snapping practice and blank firing, 7 to 9 p.m. position drill and arms cleaning drill; Wednesday 6.45 a.m. preliminary ball practice, 6.45 p.m. battalion drill in full dress; Thursday 5.45 p.m. preliminary ball practice, 7 to 8 p.m. position drill and arms cleaning drill, 8 p.m. general meeting; Friday 6.45 a.m. class firing, 6.45 p.m. Coy. drill; Saturday Wimbledon review. In March 1867 the 48th Middlesex (Havelock's) R.V.C. held squad and company drill at various venues at 8 p.m. on Tuesdays and Thursdays with musketry at 8 p.m. on Mondays, target practice at Willesden range on Wednesdays and Battalion parades at Somerset House on Saturday evenings at 6.30 or 7. In 1899 the Wolverton detachment of the 1st Bucks. V.B. held company drill on Tuesdays at 7.30 p.m.; Adjutant's drill on Thursdays at 7.30 p.m.; recruit drill on Tuesdays and Thursdays at 7.30 p.m. and band practice on Mondays at 7.45 p.m.[48]

The most important activity after drill was musketry, and upon this the Volunteers largely depended to maintain interest among the members as 'that interesting, healthful and manly exercise which the Rifle Movement is supposed to supply, and which is calculated, perhaps more than anything else, to keep alive the enthusiasm of the

Volunteers . . .' In the mid-1860's County Rifle Associations were formed to organise annual rifle competitions and to finance camps. In most cases, this necessitated further appeals to public liberality: 'Between us (Owen Wethered and T.F. Fremantle) we sent out over 3,000 circulars to all and sundry, taking the County Directory parish by parish, and by the Spring of 1864 we had nearly £300 promised in donations and more than £300 in subscriptions.' Large numbers of prizes were offered at such regimental and company matches, for example, in 1865 the 7th Beds. R.V.C. shot for silverware, editions of Shakespeare, writing cases, field glasses and a Ladies' Challenge Cup. The Bucks. Volunteers had the (Florence) Nightingale Vase presented by Sir Harry Verney which emphasised his continuing support for the Movement. In 1871 prizes for the 3rd Northumberland R.V.C. included ale, mutton, potatoes, ox tongue, umbrella stands and medals. Such matches were in themselves a social event with accompanying dinners and entertainments, though weather could dampen enthusiasm, as with the case of the Bucks. County meeting in 1864:

> The Volunteers were cheered in no small way by the presence of a good sprinkling of the Ladies, who with a bravery not common to their sex, boldly faced the wind and appeared to take great interest in the proceedings . . .'[49]

The National Rifle Association also arranged the visit of Robert Loyd-Lindsay, Lord Bury and 11,000 Volunteers to Brussels for the *Tir National* in October 1866, where the Volunteers were welcomed with balls, open air concerts, balloon ascents and operas and paraded before the King and Queen of the Belgians. The attraction of such a trip abroad to men whose travel opportunities were limited was immense. The Belgians visited Wimbledon in 1867; an Anglo-Belgian Prize Fund was established in 1868; a further British contingent visited Liége and Spa in 1869; a presentation was made to the King of the Belgians when he visited London in November 1869 and there was another visit to Ghent in 1872. However, such visits were suspended to avoid political complications,[50] though Volunteer teams continued to compete in America and Canada under leading marksmen such as Sir Henry Halford, Bt.

At the same time relations between public and Volunteers were marred on occasions by accidents on ranges. In 1868, for example, a boy was killed on the range of the 36th Middlesex, but T.F. Fremantle, who joined the 1st Bucks. V.B. in 1885, could recall only 'a vague tradition of damage to a cow' in Bucks. There were criticisms that rifle shooting was becoming too much of a pastime and merely encouraged

114

'pot hunters' whilst doing little to improve the shooting of indifferent marksmen.[51]

Camps, which began to be held from about 1864-5 in most parts of the country, were primarily of a military nature but also took on the appearance of major social events. The camp at Althorp in August 1864 had specially furnished tents for officers with flower borders, an officers' mess under the direction of Earl Spencer's own cook, athletics, shooting, pony races, cricket matches and a music hall:

> The Volunteers filled the tent, seated upon forms or stretched upon the ground at their ease, smoking their pipes, and quaffing hot punch with which they were regaled by Earl Spencer. The band, stationed outside the tent, played at intervals and good songs were sung . . .

Of course, camp life could also introduce the Volunteer to some of the privations of military life as in the case of the camp of the Monmouth and Worcester Artillery Volunteers at Port Skerret in June 1875: 'Rain, rain, rain had come on day after day, until one's very spirits were damped. To go was to incur the risk of rheumatic fever and ills most dire — to stay at home, when duty called, was to play the part of a shirker.' Similarly, the camps of the Bucks. Volunteers were severely hit by bad weather in both 1867 and 1879. Camps were turned increasingly to practical military experiments but never entirely lost the early spirit as in 1872 when the church parade of the 1st Bucks. Volunteers was held in blazing sunshine: 'A stiff dose of brandy and water was administered to the first man who fell out and this had the instantaneous effect of intensifying the sun's powers, and man after man succumbed.'[52]

The Easter reviews, field days and marching columns were similarly of a dual military and social nature — so much so that many doubed their military value:

> The march . . . up to the Downs was delightful, and on the whole so was the time up there, for often it resolved itself into lying on the grass in the sunshine, eating our sandwiches and enjoying the fine exhilarating atmosphere. I question if on any one of these Brighton reviews we did more than an hour's real military movements apart from the march to the ground, the march past, and the march back to the level.[53]

Owen Wethered, feeling that the Brighton review had little to offer a country unit, discouraged Bucks. corps attending and equally expressed doubts on the value to Metropolitan units:

for a vast number of their members made it an excuse for spending three or four days at the seaside — in a semi-military capacity — but under no effective military control, and when their Corps reached Brighton on the Monday morning, these men fell in or didn't fall in, preferring to be spectators than actors in the day's proceedings . . .

It was generally felt, however, that such reviews popularised the Movement and induced recruiting, especially Royal reviews as in 1860, 1863, 1866 and 1881.[54]

Bands were generally considered a necessary ingredient of Volunteer life, for example, that of the 2nd Oxon. (City) R.V.C.: 'It is a great gratification that to the primary duty of the Band (march outs) can be added Musical Entertainments for the enjoyment of the Public in the College Gardens and Public Buildings.' The Government never considered bands to come within the provisions of the necessary expenses covered by the capitation grant, and individual corps frequently had to enter into costly contracts with civilian bands — in 1874 the Penrith Volunteer Band was costing £52 per annum and the Whitehaven Band some £74 per annum. Very little control could be exercised over a civilian band and in August 1862 the entire band of the 1st Lincoln R.V.C. was dismissed for failure to appear at a parade. Money could, however, be raised from public concerts such as those held by the 1st Lincoln Band when it was reformed in 1867, but Wethered considered that to organise marches just to utilise a band was 'a deliberate waste of good opportunities for drill'.[55] The Volunteers do seem to have simulated the revival of amateur bands throughout the country.

Volunteer bands could be utilised to raise additional funds and a wide variety of Volunteer activities served the same purpose. These took the form of balls, such as the Grand Ball of the Surrey Light Horse in February 1867 or the concert given by the 48th Middlesex in May 1862 at the Queen's Rooms in Hanover Square. In 1896 L Company of the 1st V.B. Dorset were still holding weekly dances and entertainments such as the 'Snowflake Minstrels' to raise ready cash. Other features of fund raising were bazaars and fetes, such as that of the 49th Middlesex at the Crystal Palace in August 1871, which included cricket and athletics, or the annual fetes of the 13th Surrey R.V.C. which included steam roundabouts, Punch and Judy, fortune-tellers, shooting galleries, magical illusions, athletics, dancing and special exhibitions such as sketches of the Franco-Prussian War at the 1871 fete.[56] The Grand Military Bazaar held in aid of funds for the 1st Manchester R.V.C. in St. James's Hall, Oxford Street, in November 1884 included a waxworks, shooting gallery, exhibition of Lady Butler's paintings, the Minehaha Amateur Minstrels and examples of such novelties as galvanic batteries and seamless umbrellas. Another popular pastime was theatrical performances, as in the 8th Kent, 1st Lincs., 18th Hants. and the 3rd Somerset R.V.C., where in 1876 costumes were borrowed from the County Lunatic Assylum. The 13th Surrey R.V.C. gave annual performances of burlesque and farces which, originally designed to aid only regimental funds, were also devoted to charities such as the 'Fund for the Relief of Widows and Orphans of the 24th Foot at Isandula (*sic*)' in 1879.[57]

Finally, there were the social functions of primary interest to the Volunteers themselves. Officers' messes existed in some units but these were regarded as tending to work against social harmony. Most battalions, and indeed companies, had annual balls and dinners, for example, the regimental ball of the 49th Middlesex at Cannon Street Hotel in January 1870, or the annual dinner of G Company, London Rifle Brigade, at the Broad Street Restaurant in 1892. There were annual prize givings and also impromptu feasts such as that of the 1st Kent (Maidstone) R.V.C. in 1878:

> In the orchard adjoining the Captain's residence were set out in tempting array large piles of 'Volunteer fare' with supplementary dishes of fruit, which rapidly disappeared under the vigorous assault of the men, whose appetites had doubtless been sharpened by an instructive drill.[58]

There was, of course, the opportunity to serve on various Shooting, Band and Finance committees and many clubs, especially where a drill hall was available as a social centre — the 18th Middlesex had an athletic club; the 1st Surrey had a lawn tennis club; the 49th Middlesex had a cricket club and the London Scottish had a shooting club, a school of arms, a swimming club, a golf club, a cycling club, a revolver club, a football club and so on.[59] It was in this way that Volunteers were seen as primarily responsible for the popularisation of sports, particularly athletics, in both ordered clubs and in the streets, whereas previously many sports had been confined to the wealthier classes.[60] The Volunteer Force, in other words, opened up tremendous opportunities of recreation and companionship to the lower middle and artisan elements who filled its ranks and, as a result, it was considerably easier to find recruits for the ranks than to find candidates for commission.

What, then, can be deduced of the importance of the Volunteer Movement in terms of Victorian society? To a certain extent the early years showed the willingness of the upper middle, and particularly professional, elements of society to assume responsibilities for national defence traditionally held by the landed class, but these men had largely dropped out by 1863. Their involvement was no more than one step among many in the process by which the 'moneyed' classes became assimilated to the 'landed': in this sense the Volunteers were a product of the times rather than an influence shaping the times. The popularity of the Volunteers with the public depended upon international events and, during periods of international calm, society as a whole was indifferent to the Movement as indeed it was to the Regular Army. As a result the Volunteer Movement was no passport to social distinction and indeed membership could be a disadvantage in society. Notwithstanding these difficulties, however, the Force did show a remarkable ability to maintain a reasonably steady growth rate throughout its existence probably due largely to the range of opportunities it offered its members.

So far from being a divisive force in society, it can be argued that the Volunteer Movement was a cohesive factor in that it tended to draw the differing classes which composed its strength together, although middle class and artisan class Volunteers might have radically differing views as to why this was beneficial. Its greatest contribution to the social field was the recreational aspect which not only left a Volunteer 'better in every respect than when he joined'[61] but also seems to have encouraged the growth of sports on a national basis amongst the lower middle and artisan classes of Victorian England.

[1] *VSG* 19.11.70, p 805-6 'Patronising'; Essex R.O. D/DOp F4 Bridges to Parker, 14.11.60; Gwent R.O. *Usk Gleaner* X (Oct 1878); 'Reminiscences of an Old Volunteer' in *Lancashire and Cheshire Volunteer* I (July 1895) No 7; Bucks R.O. *T.A. Coll*, Box 14 *Lee Mss*; Somerset R.O. *Lewis* DD/LW 25 Minute Book, 9.7.60; J. Christie-Miller, *A Record of the Stockport Volunteers and their Armoury* (Stockport 1969), p 4.
[2] Beds R.O. *Lieutenancy* L.C.V.4; Northumberland R.O. BMO/B 15 Order, 28.5.60; Oxon R.O. L/M XI/i/10 North to Marlborough, 10.2.61; *VSG* 18.1.62, p 202; 10.5.62, p 457.
[3] West Sussex R.O. *Petworth House Archives* Ms 773 Jefferson to Leconfield, 28.1.60; Oxon. R.O. L/M I/ix/5; Cave, op cit, p 114; *VSG* 28.3.68, p 255; 1.3.79, p 277-8 'The Volunteer and the Tax Payer'; 8.12.83, p 83 speech by W.E. Forster.
[4] Essex R.O. Papers of 1st Essex A.B. D/DTu. Acc 4723-1869 and 1870 bundles; G.L.R.O. (M) Acc. 534/7 and L/C/75; *VSG* 25.1.62, p 216; Crapster, op cit, p 96-7; *LRSG* IV(Jan 1899), p 7-9; May, op cit, p 260-1.
[5] Wilts. R.O. *Troyte Bullock* W.R.O. 865/491 Seymour to Grove 22.12.59 and 2.1.60; Melly quoted Rose, *Bulletin*, op cit, p 60-1; William Lamont, *Volunteer Memories* (Greenock 1911), p 37; 'Reminiscences of J.G. Macdonald', *Monthly Chronicle of North Country Lore and Legend* (Feb. 1888), p 54-5.
[6] Col. Dunne, 5.7.59 *Hansard* CLIV, 693-4 *VSG* 21.7.60, p 5; H. Spenser Wilkinson, *Thirty Five Years* (London 1933), p 5-6; *VSG* 8.6.78, p 517.
[7] Lincs. R.O. *Hill 12th Dep* 12/2/1 Scrap Book for 1859-65, p 5, 8, 12; Wethered, op cit, p 10; Guildford Muniment Room, 122/4/4 Annual Report of 13th Surrey, 31.3.65.
[8] F. Engels, 'The War Office and the Volunteers' in *Volunteer Journal for Lancashire*

and Cheshire II, No 40, p 125; *PRO* HO 45/OS 7217 Wilkinson to Lewis, 3.7.61 and Hughes to Mayne, 5.6.61; *VSG* 28.5.70, p 405; 5.6.75, p 501; 13.5.76, p 438; 19.2.77, p 247 Metrop. CO's meeting; 25.6.81, p 550.

[9] The opposition based on alleged damage to the Park during the 1876 review to welcome the Prince of Wales on his return from India can be traced in *VSG* 29.5.80, p 493; 12.4.80, p 527-8; 19.6.80, p 547-8; 14.5.81, p 439; 26.7.84, p 649-50.

[10] *VSG* 24.1.78, p 204; 3.12.81, p 69-70; 27.5.82, p 477; 23.6.83 Edit; 18.8.63, p 705.

[11] *VSG* 27.2.64, p 196; 19.5.66, p 39; 20.2.68, p 198; 7.3.68, p 214; G.L.R.O. (M) Acc 534/12 Misc for Dover circulars; Surrey Archaeological Society PF/GFD/87 copy of *Surrey Gazette* of 29.3.64.

[12] *VSG* 21.2.74, p 262; 27.2.75, p 263; 25.3.76, p 325-7; 19.2.77, p 247; 30.3.78, p 352-3; 6.4.78, p 369.

[13] Oxon. R.O. L/M I/ix/8; Beds. R.O. L/C.V.4 and X 95/216 Nos 78-81.

[14] Fisher, op cit, p 104-4; *VSG* 2.7.70, p 485; 30.7.70, p 544; 18.1.73, p 181-2, 'The Want of Officers'; 9.8.73, p 646 'The Status of Volunteer Officers'; 16.10.80, p 846-7; Durham R.O. *Londonderry* D/Lo/C 235/37 Warburton to Vane Tempest, 28.3.62.

[15] *VSG* 4.12.69, p 6; 22.1.70, p 117; 10.4.75, p 357; 29.7.73, p 757; 6.3.75, p 278 'The Position of Volunteer Officers'; 21.2.77, p 198-9; 2.2.78, p 220-1; 16.10.80, p 846-7; Brookfield, op cit, p 165; Captain R.W. Phipps, *Our Sham Army* (Exeter 1868), p 27; T.D. Acland, *Volunteer Organisation* (London 1868), p xvii.

[16] Cunliffe, op cit, p 74-5; 'Account of the Presentation of Volunteers to the Queen' and 'The Volunteer Levee, Dinner and Ball' *USM* (1860) Pt 1, p 498-504 and 635-54; *VSG* 5.10.72, p 708; 5.4.73, p 357; 9.8.73, p 646; 7.11.74, p 7; 18.5.78, p 46; 13.5.82, p 446 'The Supply of Officers'; 21.4.83, p 7-8; 7.7.84, p 510-1 'The Prospect of the Future'.

[17] *VSG* 31.10.68, p 752; 31.8.78, p 723; B.J. Bond, 'The Effect of the Cardwell Reforms, 1874-1904' *JRUSI* CV (1960), p 515-24; Tucker, op cit, *JBS* II (1963), p 110-41.

[18] *VSG* 18.1.73, p 181-2; 9.8.73, p 646; 7.11.74, p 7; 2.2.78, p 221 'Officers'; 1.2.79, p 212; 29.4.82, p 413; Durham R.O. *Londonderry* D/Lo/C 235/30 Reed to Vane Tempest, 12.3.62.

[19] *VSG* 5.3.81, p 277; 3.3.81, p 281; 19.7.84, p 627; Egerton and Stanhope, 4.8.90 *Army Debates* (1890), 715-6; Stanhope 10.6.92 *AD* (1892). 494-5; Campbell-Bannerman, 12.9.93 *AD* (1893), 1042-3.

[20] Volunteer Capitation Committee *BPP* [c4951] XVI. 271; Select Committee on Volunteer Acts *BPP* 1894 (224) XV. 631; Jury Exemption Bills *BPP* 1892 (131) x.555 and 1893-4 (141) VIII.531; *VSG* 26.7.73, p 608-10; Vincent, 19.3.86 *AD* (1886), 184; Vincent, 19.2.91 *AD* (1891), 101; Brown, 2.3.93 *AD* (1893), 41; Col. Alt, 'The Dearth of Officers in the Volunteer Force' *JRUSI* XL (1896), p 1309ff; Royal Commission on the Militia and Volunteers, *BPP* 1904 [Cd 2064] xxxi, 587 Appendix XXXVII.

[21] *BPP* 1862 [3053] XXVII 89, 2374, 3534; Berry, op cit, p 393; *VSG* 31.8.61, p 716; Lincs. R.O. *Hill 12th Dep* 12/2/1 scrap book 21.1.62; Durham R.O. *Londonderry* D/Lo/F 494 Warburton to Vane Tempest, 8.1.62.

[22] *VSG* 13.12.62, p 127 'The Early Closing Movement'; 6.12.62, p 100; 5.5.66, p 357 'Saturday Half Holiday'; 22.9.66 'Volunteers Half Holiday'; 12.9.74, p 725; 10.12.75, p 24; 25.6.81, p 549; 25.8.81, p 477; D.J. Rowe, 'Movements to Reduce Hours of Labour before 1871' in E. Allen, J.F. Clarke, N. McCord and D.J. Rowe (eds) *The North-East Engineers' Strikes of 1871* (Newcastle 1971), p 29-57.

[23] *VSG* 18.9.69, p 661; 29.11.73, p 69 'Loyd-Lindsay's Scheme of Volunteer Reform'; 28.12.78, p 133 'Christmas 1878'; 25.8.81, p 477; 15.10.81, p 847; Lincs. R.O. *Hill 12th Dep* 12/2/2. `

[24] *VSG* 15.11.62, p 57; *Lancs. and Cheshire Volunteer* I (1895), No 2; Berry, op cit, p

119

181; Walter, op cit, p 135-42; Macdonald, op cit, p 45.

[25] Bodleian Library Papers of 1st Oxon. R.V.C. G A Oxon. c 92 Vol 1; G A Oxon. c 281 (f 56) Merton College scrapbook; *VSG* 4.11.85, p 24 and 21.11.85, p 39 'From a Correspondent' Parts 1 and 2; *INMM* II (1889), p 1253; Essex R.O. D/DTu. Acc 4723 inspection report, 5.8.71 in 1871 bundle.

[26] Cf *VSG* 10.10.63, p 809-10; 19.12.63, p 43 'Origins and Intent'; 2.1.64, p 71; 25.6.64, p 469; 9.6.66, p 436-7 'The War Crisis'; 25.8.66, p 613 'The Sober Panic of 1866'; 25.9.69, p 675.

[27] *VSG* 1.7.71, Edit; Crapster, op cit, p 96-7; Clarke, op cit, p 30-63.

[28] *VSG* 7.11.74, p 7; 13.8.70, p 583; Kent R.O. *Cinque Ports Mss* CPW/RP/1 Phillips to Knocker, 15.9.69.

[29] *VSG* 3.9.70, p 629; 21.11.74, p 37-8 'The Volunteers and the Country'; 29.5.76, p 470-1; 24.2.77, p 262-3 'The Defence of England'; 2.3.78, p 286 'The Volunteers and the Crisis'; 15.6.78, p 537 'The Political Situation and the Auxiliary Forces'; A.W. Preston, *British Military Policy and the Defence of India: A Study of British Military Policy, Plans and Preparations during the Russian Crisis, 1875-80* (Unpub Ph.D London, 1966); A.W. Preston (ed) *Sir Garnet Wolseley's South African Diaries, 1875* (Cape Town 1971) and *Sir Garnet Wolseley's South African Journal, 1879-80* (Cape Town 1971) esp introductions.

[30] *VSG* 10.11.77, p 21; 19.1.78, p 181-2; 1.9.78, p 741; 26.10.78, p 853; 30.11.78, p 69; 28.12.78, p 133; 16.8.79, p 689; 25.10.79, p 849-53 'The Past Year'; 1.1.81, p 133; 8.1.81, p 149; Macdonald, op cit, p 266.

[31] *PRO* WO 105/41 Nicholson to Roberts, 10.11.1906; *VSG* 14.2.85, p 246-7; Tucker, op cit, p 110-41.

[32] *VSG* 4.3.82, p 277; 15.7.82, p 817; 27.9.84, p 798 'The Navy Alarm'; 14.2.85, p 246-7 'The Crisis and the Auxiliaries'; 7.3.85, p 294; 11.4.85, p 373; 16.5.85, p 466 'The Present Position'; 31.10.85, p 890-4 'The Past Year'.

[33] *VSG* 27.5.82, p 478-9 'Compulsion versus Voluntary Service'; *Lancashire* and *Cheshire Volunteer* I (1895), No 3; W.J. Alt, 'The Dearth of Officers in the Volunteer Force' *JRUSI* XL (1896), p 1309; for the invasion debate generally see H B Moon, *The Invasion of the United Kingdom: Public Controversy and Official Planning* (Unpub Ph.D London 1968) 2 volumes, esp I, chaps 1-2.

[34] *VSG* 21.11.74, p 37-8 'The Volunteers and the Country'.

[35] S.H. Jeyes and F.D. How, *The Life of Sir Howard Vincent* (London 1912), p 264; R.B. Haldane, 25.2.1907 *AD* (1907), 65-95; Wilkinson, op cit, p 5-6; Bucks. R.O. *T.A. Coll* Box 15 Gilbey Mss, chap 1, p 1; May, op cit, p 17-20.

[36] Beds. R.O. *Cowper Mss* X 95/216 No 54 Green to Cowper, 18.5.64; Durham R.O. *Londonderry* D/Lo/C 235/35 Chapman to Vane Tempest 21.4.62.

[37] *VSG* 24.9.70 p 677; 21.5.64, p 389; Cottesloe, op cit, p 65.

[38] Briggs, op cit, p 136 and 205-39; Thomas Hughes, 'The Volunteer Force' in *British Army Review* I (1864) p 81-7, Melly, op cit, p 104; Walter, op cit, p 32-5, 195-214; *VSG* 16.11.59 Edit, 30.3.61, p 361 'Workers and Volunteers'; *JSAHR* 37 (1959) p 43.

[39] *VSG* 15.9.60, p 10; Woodburne, op cit, p 113-6; *BPP* 1862 (3053) XXVII 89, 851, 1554-6, 1573-5, 2573-5, 2605-8, 3537-9, 4274-6; West Sussex R.O. *Petworth House Archives* Ms 773 Jefferson to Leconfield, 28.1.62; Durham R.O. *Londonderry* D/Lo/f 49 Misc joint report 1st Durham A.C. and 3rd Durham R.V.C., *VSG* 19.4.62, p 409 'Physical Education'.

[40] *Naval and Military Magazine* IV (1899), p 282-90; *VSG* 19.1.67, p 116, 26.9.85, p 809; Sir Francis Vane, *Agin the Governments* (London 1928), p 61-7; Hanham, op cit, p 159-181; F.P. Gibson, *William A Smith of the Boys' Brigades* (London and Glasgow 1934); J.O. Springhall, *Youth, Empire and Society* (London 1977), p 71-80.

120

[41] Rose, *JSAHR*, op cit, p 108; Bucks. R.O. *T.A. Coll*, Box 15 Wethered, p 26; Cunningham, op cit, p 29.

[42] Springhall, op cit, p 71-80; G. Anderson, *Victorian Clerks* (Manchester 1976), p 30-51, 74-86.

[43] G. Crossick, 'The Labour Aristocracy and Its Values: A Study of Mid-Victorian Kentish London' *VS* XX (1976) p 301-28; R.Q. Gray, *The Labour Aristocracy in Victorian Edinburgh* (Oxford 1976) p 91-143 esp p 102-3, 130, 139-42.

[44] *VSG* 25.2.60, p 203; 14.1.65, p 101 'Social Intercourse Amongst Volunteers'; 23.12.76, p 117; *PRO* WO 33/22 0453 Aikman to Cardwell, 24.12.70; *Lancs. and Cheshire Volunteer* I (1895) No 7; Wilts. R.O. *Troyte Bullock* W.R.O. 865/491 Seymour to Grove, 22.12.59; Igglesden, op cit, p 88-9; Durham R.O. *Londonderry* D/Lo/C 235/31 Chapman to Vane Tempest 12.12.60; G.L.R.O. (M) *Cruikshank Mss* Acc. 534/10 Walton to Cruikshank, 20.4.63.

[45] *VSG* 30.6.66, p 485 'Party Politics in the Force'; C.J. Kauffman, 'Lord Elcho, Trade Unionism and Democracy' in K.D. Brown (ed) *Essays in Anti-Labour History* (London 1974), p 183-207; Post Office R.O. R7/2(c).

[46] *VSG* 14.7.77, p 590; 18.6.81, p 529-30 'Volunteers and Officers'; 17.10.85, p 858 'Officers and Men'; 28.2.80, p 278 'Members'; Bucks. R.O. *T.A. Coll*, Box 15 Wethered, p 18-19.

[47] *VSG* 17.4.75, p 370; 3.11.77, p 10; 22.4.82, p 395; 2.12.83, p 65; 7.7.84, p 504; 30.1.69, p 128.

[48] *QOG* X (1892) No 11, p 909-10; *PRO* WO 70/7, p 62 Order Book of 36th Middx.; G.L.R.O. (M) Acc. 534/8; Bucks. R.O. *T.A. Coll*, Box 14.

[49] Guildford Muniment Room 122/4/1 Annual Report 13th Surrey R.V.C., 31.3.62; Wethered, op cit, p 7; Beds. R.O. X67/534; (Claydon House) *Verney Papers*, Fremantle to Verney, 29.8.67; Northumberland R.O. BMO/B 20 Record of Shooting in 3rd Northumb. R.V.C.; *Bucks. Herald*, 2.4.64.

[50] Cottesloe, op cit, p 151; Berry, op cit, p 182-3; Woodburne, op cit, p 131-8; 'Volunteer Fetes in Belgium' *USM* 1866 Pt III, p 42-3; Lady Wantage, op cit, p 157-60; *VSG* 20.11.69, p 805; 17.8.72, p 597; 5.6.75, p 487; 11.8.83, p 607.

[51] G.L.R.O. (M) L/C/70; Cottesloe, op cit, p 236; Woodburne, op cit, p 161-2; *VSG* 27.8.64, p 613; 'Wimbledon' *USM* 1865 Pt II, p 595-7.

[52] Northants. R.O. Eunson, III, p 89-115; *Usk Gleaner* 111 (1878) 'The Camp at Port Skerret'; Wethered, op cit, p 9, 13, 20, 27-8.

[53] 'Notes on the old Easter Monday Review by a Participant' *LSRG* IV (1899), p 15-16 (January).

[54] Wethered, op cit, p 8; *VSG* 21.5.81, p 458; 5.11.81, p 7-8.

[55] Oxon. R.O. L/M I/ix/3; Cumbria R.O. *Curwen Papers* D/Cu/1/44 Minute Book 1868-74; Lincs. R.O. *Hill 12th Dep* 12/1/1 Minute Book, 14.8.62 and 12/2/2 Annual Report, 30.11.67; Wethered, op cit, p 13.

[56] G.L.R.O. (M) *Cruikshank Mss* Acc. 534/12 and 534/8; Gillingham Local History Society Museum, L Coy Diaries, 1895-1906; Guildhall Mss 9408 No 188 Orders of 49th Middx.; Guildford Museum G 7911, LG648/7 and 650/2; Manchester Central Library M25/5/5/6.

[57] Lincs. R.O. *Hill 12th Dep* 12/2/1; Cave, op cit, p 95; Lewisham Public Libraries Archives and Local History Dept A 58/6/7; Somerset R.O. *Foster Mss* DD/FS Box 77 Medlicott to Foster, 14.4.76; Guildford Museum LG 648/1-6, 8-16; G 709-10, 712-5, 717-20, 722-4; E.C. Ellis, 'The Dramatic Club of the Old 13th Surrey Volunteers', *The Keep* (Oct 1915), p 6-7.

[58] *VSG* 5.11.64, p 772-3; Lincs. R.O. *Hill 12th Dep* 12/2/1; Guildhall Mss 9408 No 99; Guildhall Mss 9387, p 76 *Records of London Rifle Brigade*, Minute Book of G. Coy (Ward of Bassishaw), 1887-1913; Haynes Papers, Hollingbourne, Kent.

[59] *VSG* 2.4.70, p 277; 6.12.84, p 96; Guildhall Mss 9408 No 106; *VSG* 20.1.66, p 117; *LSRG* I (Marc 1896), p 29 and IV (Jan. 1899) p 7-8.
[60] Berry, op cit, p 181; *VSG* 15.11.62, p 57; 'The Advance and Influence of the Volunteer Movement', *Lancs. and Cheshire Volunteer* I (Aug. 1895), No 8.
[61] Ibid.

CHAPTER IV

THE VOLUNTEERS AND THE
STATE-ADMINISTRATION AND FINANCE
1859-1899

"Q — Quartermaster; his good beef and mutton,
His greens and potatoes would make you a glutton."

"X — for the X-aminations we suffer;
but you pass for promotion unless you're a duffer."

'Camp Alphabet'
T.F. Fremantle, 1904.

In order to examine the role of the Volunteer in both politics and national defence, it is important to outline the general administrative background and changing constitution of the Volunteer Force. This is a task of some complexity since, to give one example, by 1906 there were some twenty-two different means by which the Force was financed.[1] There is, in fact, little point in attempting to record every minor variation in grants and regulations which are, in any case, to be found elsewhere.[2] Therefore, this outline which of necessity is largely chronological is confined to the developments of major significance.

Early rationalisation

The first phase of administrative development resulted from the rapid growth of the Volunteer Movement in 1859 and 1860. The weekly volume of Volunteer correspondence reaching the War Office increased so much that the staff dealing with it had to be increased from five to fifteen clerks by the end of 1860. The ailing Sidney Herbert, who died in August 1861, gave the responsibility for the expanding Force to his Under Secretary of State, Earl de Grey and Ripon. Herbert and de Grey were concerned to develop further the organisation and military efficiency of the Volunteer Force over which they had secured a measure of control by the issue of Government arms in July 1859. It was not their intention, however, that the Force should become a charge upon public funds. Thus their measures, codified in the first Volunteer Regulations of January 1861, were designed to increase Government control whilst maintaining the convenient fiction of the 'character' of the Volunteers.[3] By 'character' was meant financial self-sufficiency.

The key-note of the measures was uniformity and thus a series of circulars attempted to curb the worst excesses of Volunteer costume by banning Regular Army distinguishing marks such as sashes and gold lace; prohibiting other ranks from wearing swords and laying down some general uniform recommendations. In the same way uniformity of arms calibre was secured by the further issue of 25 per cent of rifle requirements on 14 October 1859 and of the remaining 50 per cent on 20 December 1859. This was coupled with the promise of the more modern Short Enfield rifle to replace the Long Enfield and an offer in January 1861 to buy back non-regulation private weapons. It should not be assumed, however, that the Volunteers' rifles were always promptly replaced. Thus, in September 1863, the 3rd Durham (Sunderland) R.V.C. had still got 356 Long Enfields and only 18 Short Enfields.[4]

There was also a series of measures to increase military efficiency,

125

again by introducing some kind of uniformity, in this case in drill. On 8 February 1860 Corps were authorised to obtain the services of Regular drill instructors for three month periods at 2/6d. per day with lodgings provided by the Corps. On 29 February 1860 Corps were further authorised to appoint adjutants from ex-officers of four years' military experience who could provide testimonials and a certificate of fitness. Adjutants would be paid 8s. per day with a 2s. forage and travelling allowance, to which was added in September 1860 a further travelling and stationery allowance. In most cases adjutants had considerably more than four years military service, which was just as well, since many represented the only members of their respective corps with military experience. Thus Robert Beatty, Adjutant of the 46th Middlesex (London and Westminster) R.V.C., had served for 19 years in the 21st Foot and Ceylon Rifles; H.J. de Cateret, of the 48th Middlesex (Havelock's Own) R.V.C. had served 13 years in the Royal Marine Light Infantry; Major W.B. Stevens of the 1st Middlesex A.V. had served 21 years in the Madras Army, and R. Crowe of the 2nd Middlesex A.B. had served 9 years in the 93rd and 60th Foot. Many, as will be noted later, continued to serve for long periods after the introduction of serving Regular Adjutants in May 1872. Thus Captain H. Landon, for example, having retired from the 55th Foot, served as Adjutant of the 1st Northants. A.B. from 1860 until 1886. In the interests of greater efficiency the Horse Guards authorised Volunteer field days on 6 June 1860 and reviews on the 20 July provided permission was sought to obtain Regular reviewing officers. On 16 August 1860 Regular guards were ordered to salute Volunteer officers and Volunteers under arms. The further concession of permission to brigade with Regular troops in camps at Aldershot and Shorncliffe was given in November 1861.[5]

The most important step towards both efficiency and uniformity was the authorisation of a battalion organisation for the Volunteers on 24 March 1860. By this circular 'consolidated' and 'administrative' battalions could be formed from between four and twelve companies. A 'consolidated' battalion was confined in practice to the larger towns where a number of companies in close proximity could combine easily to form a composite battalion, as in the case of the 1st Newcastle R.V.C. In country areas individual corps were frequently scattered widely and the expense of drill instructors and adjutants could be considerably reduced by the formation of an 'administrative' battalion. Such battalions were combined for 'administrative' purposes only, as in the case of the 2nd Oxon. A.B. 'to effect a unity of system in correspondence, drill, inspection and returns'.[6] Each corps retained control of its own finances and internal affairs and continued to be governed by its own committees; indeed corps could not be brought together for battalion parades without the consent of the individual corps. The Commanding Officer of an administrative battalion had only general charge of drill and discipline. He was responsible for enforcing the directions of the Secretary of State and acted as the means of communication between the Corps and the Secretary of State through the Lord Lieutenant. The Battalion Adjutant was responsible for maintaining contact with the individual Corps and conducted general battalion correspondence such as official returns. The Commanding Officer of the Corps, usually a Captain, retained control of the arms, stores and payments of the Corps and conducted correspondence through the Adjutant. The advantage of the administrative system was that it naturally tended to lead to a more united system of drill and dress than would have existed otherwise. To give an example, when Josiah Wilkinson took command of the 2nd Middlesex A.B. in January 1862 there was such a wide variety of uniforms amongst the six component corps that he ordered that 'In battalion parades the light grey will compose the Right Wing, dark colours the Left Wing'![7]

There were, however, drawbacks, for the Lt.-Col. was in the anomalous position of having no theoretical authority over individual Corps except when on parade with two or more of them. He could only recommend and advise but could not compel attendance. Thus the whole system depended upon the goodwill of the participants, as Earl Fortescue reminded Devon Lieutenant-Colonels in September 1860: 'I am sure I need not impress on you the necessity of fully considering their (corps) wishes and their convenience before taking any steps towards it (battalion parades) and then of proposing to bring together only such as are really desirous of it.' In practice the situation could be overcome with tact as Owen Wethered recalled:

> As a rule this did not lead to serious difficulty partly because Colonels were careful not to ignore the strict rights of officers commanding Corps — partly because the latter's good sense taught them that the Colonel's recommendations or wishes were for the good of their Corps.[8]

In terms of higher organisation a Volunteer branch was created at the War Office with the appointment of Colonel W.M.S. McMurdo, C.B., as Inspector General of Volunteers on 22 January 1860. McMurdo and the Deputy Inspector General, Colonel G. Erskine, headed the ten Assistant Inspectors appointed in March 1860 to regulate the transmission of returns, enforce Government regulations and to inspect the Volunteer Force in accordance with the provisions of the circular of the 13 July 1859. The Select Committee on Military

Organisation, which reported in July 1860, endorsed the appointment of an Inspector of Volunteers reporting direct to the Under Secretary of State, and by the end of 1860 the Militia and Volunteer branches at the War Office had grown to four staff-officers and twenty-nine clerks.

The second major stage in development was initiated on 16 May 1862 by the appointment, in response to Volunteer agitation, of a Royal Commission to enquire into the condition of the Force and the means of improving efficiency. The recommendations of the Royal Commission, chaired by Lord Eversley, were incorporated into the Volunteer Act of 1863.[9] The Commission accepted that financial burdens were increasing and that a Government grant would be necessary, although it was hoped that the provision of such a grant would not weaken public support for the movement. The advantage of the capitation grant, recommended by the Commission, was that it could be made conditional upon a certain standard of military efficiency. Thus, to earn the basic 20s. grant a Rifle Volunteer must complete nine drills (three battalion, six company) and attend the Annual Inspection. An additional 10s. could be earned for extra efficiency which consisted of no more than firing off 60 rounds at a target. Secondly, a measure of internal economy could be guaranteed by defining the 'necessary expenses' upon which the capitation grant could be expended. These comprised, for Rifle Volunteer Corps, headquarters, drill grounds, care and repair of arms, ranges, clothing and accoutrements, conveyance, postage, stationery and forage. The advantage of the administrative battalion was also stressed by the Commission and the Volunteer Act made adjutants paymasters for the capitation grant, thus encouraging smaller units to combine to receive their grant through one adjutant. An additional 4s. was granted to Administrative battalions for men of all corps beyond five miles from the Battalion H.Q. and, as an indication of their new responsibilities, adjutants' pay was increased to 10s. per day with allowances for lodgings, forage and servants. The new efficiency conditions for Rifle, Artillery, Engineer and Mounted corps, which varied slightly from each other, were brought into operation by the Order-in-Council of 23 July 1863.

It was clear that the Constitution of the Volunteer Force had changed radically from the autonomous and self-sufficient corps of 1859, but successive Governments persisted in the belief that any additional aid would violate the 'voluntary character' of the Force. Thus Governments did not accept the view of the Volunteers that a bargain had been struck in 1863 between the State and themselves and that if they found the grant insufficient they would be entitled to a review of expenditure. Sir John Pakington, as Secretary of State from 1867-68, refused to bow to Volunteer pressure for an increased capitation grant. However, Pakington did relieve adjutants of the responsibility for the grant, which was now entrusted to the commanding officer advised by his Finance Committee. Pakington further rationalised the command structure at the War Office by combining the Militia, Volunteer and Reserve branches in a new Reserve Forces Division headed by an Inspector General of Reserve Forces under the immediate order of the Secretary of State.[10] Major-General the Hon. James Lindsay was appointed Inspector-General in January 1868 with Col. E.W.C. Wright as Deputy-Inspector. It was felt at the time that Col. Erskine, who had succeeded McMurdo as Inspector of Volunteers in 1865, had been treated badly by his sudden transfer to the Military Train. Pakington pointed out that the new Division required an officer of higher rank and, in any case, Erskine was replacing an officer who had died unexpectedly.[11]

The changes in the constitution of the Volunteer Force effected by Cardwell reforms, which mark the next stage of administrative development, proved highly unpopular with the majority of the Volunteers and provoked considerable opposition in Parliament from Volunteer M.P.'s.

The Cardwell Reforms and After

Cardwell aroused the animosity of the Volunteers from the beginning by a refusal to consider that any increase in the capitation grant was necessary, coupled with the opinion that if more money was to be granted in the future it would require considerably more efficiency from a force grown too large.[12]

His popularity was not enhanced by his adoption of the recommendations of a Departmental Committee, headed by Major-General Lindsay, which remained the basis of the Cardwellian approach to the Volunteer Force. By means of some rather doubtful mathematical calculations, Lindsay's Committee had concluded that the average annual expenditure of a Corps on what they considered necessary expenses (Headquarters, care and repair of arms, ranges, conveyance, clothing and bugles) totalled £53 10s. 0d. This was more than covered by the existing 30s. grant for extra efficients, assuming an average strength of 80 men per Corps or company. They therefore recommended the abolition of the basic 20s. grant compelling all Volunteers to attain the musketry requirements which had previously earned the extra 10s. and to this musketry standard was added 10 rounds volley firing. The Committee further recommended a new certificate of proficiency for officers and N.C.O.'s, the amalgamation of smaller units, the consolidation of administrative battalions, and a maximum limit to the Force of 260,000 men. These measures, plus a return to the adjutant's responsibility for the grant, a suggestion that uniforms should be made to last five years and a scale of minimum numbers required to attend before a drill counted towards efficiency, were all adopted by Cardwell.

The opposition was such, particularly to adjutant finance and minimum numbers, that in February 1870 Cardwell agreed that volley firing, adjutant finance and consolidation would not be pressed.[13] Cardwell was prepared in July 1870 to raise the capitation grant from 30s. to 35s. per man but only in the form of a new certificate of proficiency: like the calculations of the Lindsay Committee this was based on 8 officers and N.C.O.s per corps or company earning the equivalent of 5s. to each of 80 men. The certificate would be granted for knowledge of drill, command, musketry supervision and general military duties such as guard and picquet duty. In order to gain the certificate an officer could attend a month's course at a school of instruction (set up at Aldershot, London, Manchester and Glasgow for Rifle Corps) which would be rewarded by the letters 'PS' in the Army List, or a month's attachment to a Regular or Militia regiment which would gain the letter 'P' in the Army List; N.C.O.'s would be examined by the adjutant. The accompanying liberal allowances and the issue of the Snider breech-loading rifle to the Volunteers in September 1870 went some way towards restoring a measure of confidence in Cardwell's aims. However, opposition was renewed by the further tightening of efficiency regulations by the Auxiliary and Reserve Forces circular of 28 May 1872.[14] The certificate of proficiency was now made compulsory for an officer within one year of his appointment, and retirement at 60 years of age was instituted although extensions of 5 years might be granted. One compulsory brigade drill per annum was ordered, and a scale of minimum attendances laid down including the necessity for two-thirds of a unit to be present at its inspection before the capitation grant could be paid. The only concessions were some small allowances to encourage camps. It was generally felt that such increased requirements would not be tolerated by employers and that the introduction of a virtual examination for officers would lead to a further decline in the number of candidates for commission.

The implementation of Cardwell's major reforms was equally unwelcome to many Volunteers in that it made the future of the Force largely dependent upon the goodwill of Regular officers. By the Regulation of the Forces Act of 1871, Volunteer commissions were to be issued by the Crown, and the Lords Lieutenant were reduced to recommendations on first appointments. Under the same Act Volunteers were also made liable, when brigaded with Regulars or Militia, to the provisions of the Mutiny Act, which provoked bitter opposition from some leading Volunteer M.P.s. The May 1872 circular changed the title from 'Reserve' to 'Auxiliary Forces' and Lindsay was now designated Inspector-General of Auxiliary Forces and his division transferred from the Secretary of State's Department to the Commander-in-Chief's Department. The responsibility for inspection, permanent staff (adjutants and instructors) and training now rested with the Commander-in-Chief, whose orders were to be passed to G.O.C.'s of Districts through the Inspector-General of Auxiliary Forces, whereas disciplinary questions were to be passed to the Adjutant-General for transmission to the Secretary of State. To assist the I.G.A.F. two A.A.G.'s were appointed in June 1873 (Brevet Colonel E.K. Bulwer, C.B., and Brevet Colonel R. Biddulph, R.A.), and the staff of the division was increased to one confidential clerk and eighteen other clerks.

Under the Localisation Scheme, which was applied to the Force by the Auxiliary and Reserve Forces circular of 21 April 1873, Volunteer units were put into the new Sub-District with two Regular 'linked battalions' and two militia battalions. The responsibility for inspection and training the Volunteers was now vested in the hands of the Lt.-Col. commanding the Sub-District brigade depot. Volunteer adjutants, by the provisions of the May 1872 circular, were to be gradually replaced by Regular officers on five years' attachment. However, under the Localisation Scheme, the 'old' adjutants were gazetted back as Regular captains, placed under the O.C. Brigade Depot, given additional duties in recruiting and made liable for depot duties such as courts martial. This was greatly resented by the adjutants, who became something of a pressure group. They sought adequate pensions and retirement concessions, such as honorary rank, to compensate for their increased work load and loss of allowances. One additional source of income had been the occasional sale of adjutancies, but this was curbed by Lords Lieutenant refusing to accept any recommendations from retiring adjutants as to their successors. The 'Old Adjutants' of whom only 47 were still serving in 1885, failed to enlist the support of the Metropolitan Commanding Officers in March 1870 because the latter considered their grievances to be outside their jurisdiction. However, they did secure the support of Sir Walter Barttelot, who unsuccessfully attempted to move for a Commons Select Committee to investigate their case in 1878.[15] Thus the future of the Volunteer Force largely depended upon the interest and co-operation of the Regular adjutants, who could hardly be expected to adjust to Volunteer conditions quickly, and the O.C.'s of the brigade depots. It is in these terms that the success of the Cardwell reforms, as far as the Volunteers are concerned, will be judged in a later chapter.

Gathorne-Hardy, as Secretary of State, made a few minor concessions to the Volunteers but there was no further major development until the appointment of a Departmental Committee headed by Lord Bury on 22 February 1878.[16] It can be noted that both the Under-Secretary of State, Bury, and the Financial Secretary to the War Office, Loyd-Lindsay, were Volunteers. Further, the committee was partly established in response to the renewed Volunteer agitation initiated by the Volunteer Conference at the Royal United Service Institution in January 1878. The stated object, however, was fully to assimilate the Volunteer Force into the Cardwell system, which had been taken to its rational conclusion of territorialisation by the Stanley Committee of 1876 despite disturbing signs that Cardwell's ideals were falling far short of the realities of Army requirements.[17]

The exhaustive enquiry into Volunteer finance and organisation, undertaken by the Bury Committee revealed that 240 Volunteer units spent more than the annual capitation grant and only 38 spent less. It was concluded, however, that there had been excessive and unnecessary expenditure in many cases, particularly on bands, and the existing capitation grant was sufficient to cover necessary expenses (defined as Headquarters, drill grounds, drill sheds, armouries, care and repair of arms, ranges, conveyance, clothing and equipment). The best means of both increasing efficiency and reducing costs whilst complying with Cardwellian organisational principles seemed to lie in the consolidation of all administrative battalions. Uniformity of dress was also considered desirable, especially assimilation to the scarlet of the Regulars, and it was proposed that the Government should issue all cloth, which would further reduce costs and the likelihood of units incurring debts by having to raise loans for uniforms. Additional camping and travelling allowances were recommended but no changes in either constitution or disciplinary system of the Force. It was proposed to increase recruit drills to 60 in two years and to enforce a limit of 250,000 men which Cardwell had failed to do.

The Bury Committee recommendations were accepted by the Government[18] and gradually introduced. Two circulars of 3 February and 17 April 1880 laid down guide-lines for consolidation. Many administrative battalions had already consolidated in the years before the Bury report, the individual Corps becoming companies of the new Volunteer battalion — Berkshire had done so in 1869 and Buckinghamshire in 1875.[19] The only clue to what had existed before was the number of chaplains and surgeons attached to the Volunteer battalions, thus the 2nd Derby V.B. had some 6 chaplains and 10 surgeons carried over from the former independent corps. The Committee had not found it necessary to recommend the abolition of the right to resign on 14 days' notice, though they favoured the increasing introduction of four year agreements between Commanding Officers and men, whereby a man agreed to remain efficient for four years or pay a fine by way of compensation for the lost capitation grant. The retention of the 14 days' principle contrasted strongly with Stanley's introduction of the Army Discipline and Regulation Bill in February 1879. This seemed to go beyond the Mutiny Act in applying Army punishments to Volunteers and was strongly opposed by Volunteer M.P.s.[20] Whilst the Bury Committee had not materially changed the constitution of the Volunteer Force, a distinct change had taken place in the status of the movement with the War Office. In 1878 the Auxiliary Forces Division was transferred from the C-in-C's department to that of the Adjutant-General and its work divided between A.G. 1, 2, 3, 4 and 5. The I.G.A.F. was reduced to a D.A.F. acting as I.G.A.F., his two A.A.G.'s abolished and his staff reduced to one confidential clerk. The I.G.A.F. had not only lost direct access to the Secretary of State but was responsible only for those matters not decided elsewhere in the A.G.'s department. In February 1879, A.G. 1, 2, 3, 4 and 5. The I.G.A.F. was reduced to a D.A.G. acting as I.G.A.F. under the general supervision of the Military Secretary, though this new responsibility was briefly given to the C-in-C from February to July 1880. The independence of the Auxiliary Forces branch had been destroyed; indeed, when Lt.-Gen. Armstrong died in April 1880 it seemed at first as if a new D.A.G. would not be appointed, but Major-General J.H.F. Elkington was appointed on 28 April 1880.[21]

Hugh Childers completed the introduction of the Bury Committee recommendations with new efficiency regulations in August 1880, including the necessity of completing battalion drills in camp which many Volunteers feared would prove difficult to achieve. On 1 July 1881 full territorialisation came into effect with the 215 Volunteer battalions becoming Volunteer battalions of Regular regiments. Childers could hardly reverse the policy upon which the Liberal Government stood, despite renewed criticism of Cardwell's system by the Airey Committee. Territorialisation not only utilised the depots, upon which a large amount of money had been spent, but also held out the hope that local recruiting would be stimulated.[22] Consolidation had posed many problems of assimilation for Volunteer corps and territorialisation introduced the prospect of considerable expense upon changing titles and uniform. The renumbering recommended by the Committee under the A.G., Sir Charles Ellice, was not always popular; for example, the 1st Bucks. Volunteer Battalion not only consistently refused to refer to themselves as the 3rd Volunteer Battalion, Oxfordshire Light Infantry, but fought a long rearguard action to retain their grey uniforms. The metropolitan units were renumbered and divided between the depots of the King's Royal Rifle Corps and the Rifle Brigade at Winchester and the depots of the Middlesex Regiment and Royal Fusiliers in London, which was hardly conducive to rational military organisation and training. A measure of the gradual progress can be seen in the change in uniforms to the recommended scarlet, which was now the only change permitted — in 1879 some 91 Volunteer battalions wore scarlet, 66 green and 57 grey but by 1881 some 107 battalions wore scarlet and in 1885 some 116 wore scarlet. Mindful of the need to save costs, Childers announced in June 1882 that units need only change to scarlet when they could afford it.[23]

Childers, as was noted in the previous chapter, granted new honours to the Volunteers in 1881 and in January 1882 instituted a voluntary examination in tactics for officers above the rank of Captain, which earned 10s. grant and the letter 't' in the Army list.[24] The examinations, conducted by the Department of Military Education in January and July, were extended to subalterns in September 1883 by Hartington. Hartington, as Secretary of State, also completed the issue of the Martini-Henry breech loading rifle to the Volunteers by 31 March, 1885, the gradual adoption of which had been begun by Stanley in 1879. He also authorised the establishment of a Volunteer Medical Staff Corps in 1885, the same year in which a Volunteer transport experiment was conducted by the 1st V.B. Hampshire Regiment, commanded by Sir William Humphery.[25]

Renewed Volunteer agitation led to the appointment by W.H. Smith of a further Departmental Committee which reported in January 1887.[26] Rather like the Lindsay Committee in 1869, the Volunteer Capitation Committee chaired by Lord Harris indulged in some complicated calculations to conclude that the deficiency between the existing capitation grant and necessary expenditure averaged 4s. 7d. per head. They therefore recommended an increase in the capitation grant of 5s., but to earn the new 35s. grant a Volunteer must achieve 2nd class in musketry. A man could still earn 30s. by hitting the target at least twelve times in sixty rounds, but if he failed to achieve 2nd class standard in three consecutive years then the capitation grant would be forfeited. The Committee further recommended an additional 4s. for travelling to ranges and an increase to 30s. for the tactics examination and 30s. for a signalling certificate. It was left to a new Secretary of State, Edward Stanhope, to implement these recommendations.

Stanhope is, perhaps, the most elusive of all British Secretaries of State, yet he did more to define a place for the Volunteers in national defence, and to develop Volunteer organisation accordingly, than any previous occupant of the War Office. His aim was to fill Volunteer deficiencies and integrate the Force fully into the new Mobilisation Scheme, which would adequately correct the old Volunteer grievance that too little attention had been shown to them in the past and too little value was placed on their potential. Stanhope adopted the Harris Committee recommendations with the exception that there would be one 35s. grant dependent upon a Volunteer achieving 2nd class musketry, but in the face of Volunteer opposition Stanhope conceded a grant of 10s. to men failing the standard for two consecutive years after which the grant would be forfeited. Similarly, in face of opposition, he dropped the clause in the National Defence Bill by which Volunteers could be called out when the Militia was embodied in imminent national danger or emergency, instead of upon actual or apprehended invasion. However, Stanhope was able to give encouragement to Volunteer supporting services such as the Medical Staff Corps, Submarine Miners and cyclists, and he gave a grant of £45 to each of ten Volunteer battalions conducting further transport experiments.[27]

There was a large number of departmental committees on various aspects of the Volunteer Force designed primarily to save expense; also increased camping grants in 1889 and the provision of position batteries for the long neglected Volunteer artillery.[28] The major development was, of course, the creation in 1888 of Volunteer brigades from those battalions not allocated to garrison duties in the Mobilisation Scheme. The role of the Volunteers in the Mobilisation Scheme will be examined in a later chapter. It need only be noted here that the main drawback was that the new brigadiers, many of whom were prominent Volunteers, were in much the same position as the commanding officers of the old administrative battalions in that they had only nominal control over their brigades and could be overruled by the OC's of Regimental Districts who retained responsibility for inspection and training.[29]

In March 1889 Stanhope in his speech on the Estimates could claim: 'I have been and am doing my best, within the limits created by the peculiar circumstances of the Force, to organise and utilise it to the utmost extent of which it can be made capable.'[30] It was singularly unfortunate, in such circumstances, that Stanhope became the first Secretary of State to be defeated in a Parliamentery vote by Volunteer pressure group activity. In March 1889 the War Office Council drew up schedules of the equipment required by Volunteers on mobilisation determining what articles would be provided gratis by the Government, what articles would be covered by a special mobilisation grant of two guineas per man and what articles the Volunteers should provide through their capitation grant. The resulting schedules, issued under the authority of Wolseley as Adjutant-General in May 1889, compelled Volunteers to provide such necessities as water-bottles, haversacks and greatcoats by a certain date upon pain of losing the capitation grant entirely. The resulting appeals for public support failed, and the Volunteers were forced on 13 March 1890 to introduce a motion demanding that the Government make good deficiencies and cancel all Volunteer debts. The significance of the Government defeat on this vote will be examined in the next chapter but as a result Stanhope, though refusing to cancel debts, which might prove a dangerous precedent, was prepared to issue a grant of 12s. per man to make up the deficiencies. Metropolitan units were excluded from the grant as the 'Lord Mayor's Patriotic Volunteer Fund' had been exclusively restricted to their requirements at the expense of provincial units. Greatcoats would be issued gratis unless units already had them, in which case a further 12s. would be given, and Stanhope promised a maintenance grant of 1s. in the following year for equipment.[31] In 1891 Stanhope increased the equipment grant to 13s. for black and brown equipment and 15s. for buff equipment to offset rising prices. In 1892 Stanhope turned his attention to the dearth of officers and introduced a Volunteer Decoration for twenty year's commissioned service; a Military Lands Act was passed to enable Volunteers to acquire land for ranges with the aid of loans from the Public Works Loan Commissioners and when the Government fell jury exemption was being actively considered.[32]

In his earlier short tenure of the War Office in 1886, Henry Campbell-Bannerman had not been noted for his sympathy towards Volunteer aspirations. Between 1892 and 1895 his attitude did not materially change; indeed, Sir Frances Grenfell recalled that Campbell-Bannerman 'only asked me to let him know, from time to time, how the Force was getting on, to enable him on all occasions to answer questions connected with it in the House of Commons'. Since February 1888 the Auxiliary Forces division had been designated A.G.3 and since 1891 the D.A.G. acting as I.G.A.F. had been designated D.A.G. for Militia, Yeomanry and Volunteers. In 1894 Grenfell, as D.A.G., agreed to take over the duties of the

Inspector-General of Recruiting, since he could visit recruiting officers during his inspections and Volunteer Adjutants were frequently recruiting agents. As a result he was designated Inspector-General of Auxiliary Forces and Recruiting, and was given an A.A.G. and a D.A.A.G. to assist in his increased work load.[33]

Campbell-Bannerman did, however, institute a Long Services Medal for N.C.O's and men in response to Volunteer pressure and authorised the issue of the Lee-Metford magazine rifle to the Volunteers in 1895. The major development of his period at the War Office derived from the recommendations of a Select Committee on Volunteer Acts which had, in fact, been suggested by Stanhope. The Select Committee[34] recommended that loans should be made available for the construction of buildings on land purchased under the Military Lands Act; that Volunteers should be liable to actual military service in a condition of imminent national danger and that some provision should be made for accepting Volunteer offers of service in situations short of grave emergencies. In response Campbell-Bannerman introduced the Volunteers (Military Service) Bill which received the Royal Assent in July 1895.[35] Under this Act Volunteer offers could be accepted after the Militia had been embodied, which was a considerable departure from the original conditions for service in the event of invasion, but it did not go quite as far as the conditions Stanhope had attempted to introduce in the National Defence Bill.

Grenfell later remarked that 'there were few of us that were not glad to see a Conservative Government in again', and indeed the new ministry made immediate concessions to the Volunteers. It is possible that these were, in some measure, a reward for the Volunteers' role in the defeat of Campbell-Bannerman on the cordite vote in June 1895 which had been masterminded by the new Under-Secretary, St. John Brodrick. In March 1896 Brodrick announced the payment in advance of half the year's capitation grant, which would help clear debts; a new outfit allowance of £10, and an allowance of £10 for a school of instruction course for new officers, which it was hoped would attract more candidates for commissions. In return, a recruit was now required to attend twelve drills in this third and fourth years instead of nine and a medical standard was introduced for the first time. In 1897 an amended Military Lands Act and a new Military Works Act were passed to enable Volunteers to bear the cost of new ranges for the greatly increased range of the Lee-Metford, which had caused some concern to the public over the safety of existing ranges. A Volunteers' Bill was passed also to enable Volunteers to recover fines through summary jurisdiction.[36] On the eve of the South African War musketry requirements were once more increased. There were still financial problems and officer deficiences but the Volunteer Force of 1899 had progressed considerably from that of 1859.

In 1860 the Volunteer Force had cost the taxpayer barely £3,000 but in 1897 the Volunteer Vote stood at £627,200.[37] This steadily increasing Government expenditure is the key to Volunteer administrative development. Volunteer self-sufficiency was never a reality and the price of Government aid was Government control of the once highly individual and independent corps. Successive governments refused to increase aid without a corresponding increase in efficiency or regulations, thus the Force gradually progressed towards, first, a battalion, and then a brigade organisation. The political activities which accompanied this process and the resulting effects on the military efficiency of the Volunteer Force between 1859 and 1899 can now be examined.

[1] R.B. Haldane, 25.2.1907 *AD* (1907), 65-6; Sir George Clarke, 3.4.1906. *PRO* Cab 38/11/16.
[2] Cf Volunteer Regulations for 1861, 1863, 1878, 1881, 1884, 1887, 1890, 1891, 1892, 1893, 1894, 1895, 1896, 1897, 1898, 1899; Auxiliary Forces Circulars 1870-8, *BPP* 1904 [cd 2065] 58 Appendix XC11 'History of Volunteer Grants'.
[3] de Grey and Ripon, 6.2.60. *Hansard* CLVI, 553-6; Stanhope, op cit, II, p 389-92; Wolf, op cit, I, p 186-90; *BPP* 1904 [Cd 2064] 587 Appendix XXXI 'History of the Auxiliary Forces Branch at the War Office' by Major General Sir Alfred Turner, I.G.A.F.
[4] Circulars of 14.10.59, 20.12.59, 23.1.60, 15.2.60, 24.4.60, 30.4.60, 31.10.60 and 7.1.61; Durham RO D/Lo/F 494 Misc.
[5] Circulars of 8.2.60, 29.2.60, 6.6.60, 12.6.60, 7.7.60, 20.7.60, 1.8.60, 16.8.60, 8.9.60, 8.10.60, 8.10.61; *VSG* 19.10.61, p 828-9; G.L.R.O. (M), L/C/74,75,76,80; Northants. R.O., Eunson, p 19.
[6] Oxon. R.O. L/M I/V/3 Memo of 23.4.60.
[7] Circulars of 24.3.60 and 4.9.60; G.L.R.O. (M) L/C/80 Memos of Josiah Wilkinson, 31.1.62; Woodburne, op cit, p 87-91.
[8] Devon R.O. *Seymour of Berry Pomeroy* 1392 M/Box 18/1 Memo of Fortescue 19.9.60; Bucks. R.O. *T.A.Coll* Box 15, Wethered Mss, p 11.
[9] *BPP* 1862 (3053) XXVII 89; 26,27 Vict c 65 Volunteer Act of 1863.
[10] *VSG* 1.2.68, p 132; 4.1.68. Edit; 28.3.68, p 255-6.
[11] *VSG* 28.3.68, p 257-8.
[12] Cf *VSG* 16.1.69, p 1-101, 109; 13.3.69, p 224; 12.6.69, p 432-5; 'The War Office and the Volunteer Force' in West Sussex R.O. *Barttelot Papers* Add Mss 324/2; Sir R. Biddulph, *Lord Cardwell at the War Office* (London 1904), p 26
[13] *PRO* WO 33/21 B Report on the Financial State and Internal Organisation of the Volunteer Force; *VSG* 25.12.69, p 52; 1.1.70, p 100-1; 28.5.70, p 406.
[14] *VSG* 27.8.70, p 613; 3.9.70, p 628-9, 630-3; 8.6.72, p 437 'The New Volunteer Regulations'.
[15] VSG 23.10.69, p 740 'Sale of Adjutancies'; 26.3.70, p 262, 276-7; 22.2.73, p 263 'Adjutants'; 11.1.73, p 165 'Adjutant Grievances'; 9.3.78, p 295-6; 3.10.85, p 841 'The Old Adjutants'; West Sussex R.O. *Barttelot Papers* Add Mss 324/23-5.

[16] *BPP* 1878-9 [c 2235] XV 181, *PRO* WO 32/5975 Report on the Financial State and Internal Organisation of the Volunteer Force; *VSG* 15.2.79, p 238-43 'The Bury Report'.

[17] *VSG* 24.1.78, p 191-210 'The Conference on the Requirements of the Volunteer Force'; Tucker op cit p 110-41.

[18] *PRO* WO 163/2 Minutes of War Office Council meetings of 4.2.79 and 24.6.79; WO 33/33 0740 Report of the Sub-Committee on certain paragraphs of the report of the Volunteer Committee.

[19] Wethered, op cit, p 21; *VSG* 24.4.80, p 409 'The Two War Office Letters on Consolidation'.

[20] *VSG* 8.3.79, p 288; 22.3.79, p 325-6 'The Army Discipline Bill and the Volunteers'.

[21] *VSG* 24.4.80, p 410, 'The Inspector Generalship'; 1.5.80, p 425.

[22] *VSG* 14.8.80 p 691-2 'The New Scheme of Efficiency'; 1.10.81, p 800 'Territorial Organisation'; Lt.-Col. Spencer Childers, *The Life and Correspondence of the Rt. Hon. Hugh Culling Eardley Childers* (London 1901), II, p 61-3.

[23] Wethered, op cit, p 24; *PRO* WO 163/2 meeting of WO Council of 4.2.79; WO 33/33 0740 Appendix IV; *BPP* 1878-9 [c 2235] XV 181 Appendix XXV; Howard Vincent, 14.3.95. *AD* (1895), 41; *VSG* 8.1.81 p 149-50; 10.6.82, p 510; 14.11.85 p 21-2.

[24] Wilkinson, op cit, p 23/25; *VSG* 31.12.81, p 133-4 'Education of Officers'; 7.1.82, p 149-50 'Examination in Tactics'; 18.3.82 p 309 Notes.

[25] *VSG* 8.9.83, p 753; 10.11.85 p 165; 27.6.85, p 580 'The Change of Government'; N. Cantlie and G. Seaver, *Sir James Cantlie* (London 1939) p 30-58.

[26] *BPP* 1887 (c 4951) XVI 271 Report of the Volunteer Capitation Committee; *VSG* 9.5.85, p 449 for report of WO Conference on musketry requirements.

[27] Stanhope, 14.3.87. *AD* (1887) 312-5 27.2.88, *AD* (1888) 65-100, 3.5.88, *AD* (1888), 383-6; 9.8.88 *AD* (1888), 1145; *PRO* 33/49 A160 Report of Volunteer Cycling Committee. See also I.F.W. Beckett, 'Edward Stanhope at the War Office, 1887-1892, *Journal of Strategic Studies* V, 2 (1982), p 279-307.

[28] *PRO* WO 33/49 A180 Report of Committee on Volunteer Forms; WO 33/48 A147 Report of Committee on Volunteer Medical Services; WO 33/49 A181 Report of Committee on Volunteer Camps and Allowances; WO 33/45 A31 Report of Commmittee on Volunteer Signalling.

[29] The fullest source for the brigade system is *Ardagh Papers PRO* 30/40/13, 14; see also WO 33/48 A116, A124, A138; WO 163/4; WO 33/86 A484 Committee on the Command of Volunteer Brigades.

[30] Stanhope, 11.3.89 *AD* (1889), 69-70.

[31] *PRO* WO 163/4 meeting of WO Council of 28.3.89 and 17.4.90; Cab 37/26 No 22 Stanhope to Cabinet of 25.3.90; Stanhope, 12.5.90. *AD* (1890), 251-2.

[32] Stanhope 16.3.91, *AD* (1891), 386-7; Volunteer Vote, 10.6.92, *AD* (1892), 494-5; *BPP* 1890-1 (223) XVI 701 Report of Select Committee on Rifle Ranges; Brodrick 17.6.92 *AD* (1892), 572.

[33] Field Marshal Lord Grenfell, *Memoirs* (London 1925), p 115-8; Campbell-Bannerman, 12.9.93, *AD* (1893), 1042-3 and Stanhope 1049-50.

[34] *BPP* 1894 (224) XV. 631; see also Eustace Balfour, 'Volunteer Law' *LSRG* III (Feb 1898), p 30.

[35] *BPP* 1895 (281 sess. 1) VI 473.

[36] Grenfell, op cit, p 120; Brodrick, 12.3.96 *AD* (1896), 74-9; Lansdowne 18.2.97. *AD* (1897), 301-5.

[37] Howard Vincent, *Naval and Military Magazine* I (June 1897), p 56-7; *PRO* Cab 38/11/16 Memo by Sir George Clarke.

CHAPTER V

THE VOLUNTEERS AND POLITICS
1859-1899

"Let your reforms for a moment go!
　　Look to your butts and take good aims!
Better a rotten borough or so,
　　Than a rotten flesh and a city in flames!
Storm, storm, riflemen, form!
　　Ready, be ready, against the storm!
Riflemen, riflemen, riflemen, form!"

'The War'
Lord Tennyson, 1859.

In March 1907, when Haldane was about to introduce the Territorial and Reserve Forces Bill into the House of Commons, the consensus of opinion was that the Secretary of State was altogether too confident in the face of the coming confrontation with Parliamentary representatives of the Auxiliary Forces which would be swept away by the Bill. The only part of the military reforms of the previous incumbent of the War Office to reach the floor of the House had been utterly destroyed there by the small but vociferous group of Volunteer M.P.'s between February and July 1905. Both the Secretary of the Committee of Imperial Defence, Sir George Clarke, and that eminence grise of Edwardian politics, Lord Esher, were led to the view that the influence of the Volunteers, who now monopolised virtually all military debates in the House of Commons, was becoming a grave public and political danger. Indeed Esher hoped that the new Territorial County Associations proposed by Haldane would break the 'trade unionism' of the Volunteers by creating regional groups of conflicting interests and competing aims.[1]

The most remarkable feature of this supposed political influence was that it came from representatives of a Movement which had gone to elaborate lengths to avoid partisan gestures although, in common with other contemporary interest groups, the Volunteers became increasingly identifiable with one political party. This chapter seeks, firstly, to examine the way in which the Volunteers attempted to remain aloof from party politics, but were none the less drawn into becoming a potentially influential interest group in defence of the Force as a whole. Secondly, it identifies the aims, members and changing methods of the Volunteer interest in face of the growth of ministerial control and party discipline in the House of Commons.

In recent years the outcome of the major issues in mid- and late Victorian politics, such as Irish Home Rule and the extension of the franchise, has been interpreted in terms of the interaction by small groups of key politicians. The corresponding role of the ordinary backbencher and even the junior minister has been dismissed as the 'unimportance of the unimportant'.[2] Yet as Alderman argued in his study of the railway interest and Berrington in his revisionist study of party discipline in the House of Commons, examination of major issues can do little to explain either the day-to-day workings of the political system or the day-to-day relationship between the private Member and the party leadership. Most Parliamentary business was devoted to less emotional issues.[3] For all the attention focussed on Irish problems in Gladstone's short and eventful third ministry of 1886 it was also a session in which fifty-nine public general acts received the Royal assent. Indeed the great issues appear hardly more relevant to the explanation of election results when compared to long term electoral trends.[4] However, despite these correctives to the treatment of minor issues in Victorian politics, there has been relatively little research on interest groups within the House of Commons. With the exception of the colonial and railway interests far more attention has been paid to what amount to major political sub-groups such as the Peelites, Liberal Imperialists and Unionist Free Traders.[5] The study of an interest group lacking a distinctive economic or political stance, and differentiated from most others by its peculiar para-military status under the constitution, may therefore be of some wider interest. It would, for example, be particularly interesting if the development of the Volunteer interest was found to conform to the pattern observed of other Parliamentary interest groups in mid and late Victorian politics.

Parties, Factions and aid to the civil power

It was shown in the second chapter that the Volunteer Movement embraced a wide variety of unlikely political bed-fellows representing a broad cross-section of the political community. Thus members ranged from Tories such as Lord Ranelagh and Charles Lindsay to Whigs such as Earl Grosvenor, to Liberals such as Earl Spencer and to Radicals such as William Roupell. The Movement was certainly not the monopoly of any particular political persuasion:

> We have Whig Lords in command, Conservative captains of companies and Radical privates, or vice versa, getting on together most pleasantly and good humouredly, without even a sign of that discord which is so likely to follow the discussion of politics.

Indeed, it was widely recognised that party disputes could prove disruptive of that social harmony which the Volunteer Force was thought to promote. In any case 'no Englishman would ask another whether he was for Reform or Church Rates on his way to the coast to resist an armed landing'. In such circumstances, as the *Volunteer Service Gazette* stressed in only its second issue, Volunteers could have 'but one political motive — it is the defence of the country; they can therefore, have but one political inspiration — it is patriotism'.[6]

There is little evidence of party disputes within the Force itself but, Sir Thomas Acland, for instance, refused to accept the Lt.-Colonelcy of the Devon A.B. in 1865 because he could not consent on political grounds to be appointed over Sir John Duckworth. In December 1863 there was some trouble at a Volunteer dinner in Lincoln when a Tory

M.P. accused the Liberal Town Clerk of 'elasticity' with Corporation funds but this was not primarily of concern to the Volunteers.[7] In 1864, however, a major political dispute involving the Volunteers was brought about in Bucks. through the actions of the Liberal Lord Lieutenant, Lord Carrington. In August 1861 Robert Bateson Harvey had succeeded Lord Seymour in command of the 5th Bucks (Slough) R.V.C., despite Carrington's objections to a Corps memorial in Harvey's favour, which seemed to run against the Lord Lieutenant's authority to appoint whom he pleased. The popular Harvey was the obvious choice for the Lt.-Colonelcy of the newly formed Administrative Battalion in 1864 but was passed over by Carrington, who appointed the Hon. Percy Barrington. As Harvey was the newly elected Tory M.P. for Bucks. and the brother-in-law of the Duke of Buckingham, 'between whom and the Lord Lieutenant no love was lost', it appeared that Carrington had been motivated by political considerations. Harvey, having consulted with Disraeli, resigned and protested his case in the County press. No one could be found to accept command of the Slough corps until Owen Wethered stepped in to prevent disbandment in November 1864.[8] In February 1868 the Chairman of the Watch Committee at Ashton-under-Lyne refused to allow the local Volunteers to use the Town Hall as an armoury, not because of security reasons, but because they had disrupted a meeting he had chaired in favour of the dis-establishment of the Irish Church.[9] Such political disputes within the Force were, however, largely isolated cases.

After the uncontested Tiverton by-election of April 1861, where Volunteers in uniform had escorted Lord Palmerston to the poll, Sidney Herbert imposed a ban on Volunteers in uniform attending any meetings not for drill or other military purposes or assembling for any purpose at all between the issue of election writs and the poll. The spirit of Herbert's circular was largely maintained, for example, in 1880 when the projected Easter Review was abandoned due to the general election. However, there were occasional breaches of the ruling. In particular, the appearance of Volunteer bands, which were often under only nominal military control, in political processions was a recurring problem. In August 1868 the band of the 2nd Cambs. R.V.C. was accused of escorting the Liberal candidate in Wisbech; in July 1873 the band of the 5th Fife A.V. illegally took part in a Trade Union demonstration; in January 1883 the band of the 1st Worcs. A.V. gave a concert in aid of the Conservative Working Men's Association at Newport and in August 1883 a Renfrew Volunteer band was accused of taking part in a procession of the Orange Grand Black Chapter in Glasgow.[10]

145

By far the worst offenders were the press. For example, the connection of a captain of the 10th Gloucestershire R.V.C. with an organisation known as the Young Conservative Volunteers in Cheltenham in February 1866 was magnified although there was no link between this organisation and the Volunteers. Similarly, the *Standard* canvassed support for Lord Ranelagh as Tory candidate for Middlesex in 1865 on his merits as a Volunteer, and the *Daily Telegraph* urged Volunteers to vote only for Reform candidates in 1866.[11] The political issues surrounding Disraelian foreign policy seems to have put a severe strain on the neutrality of some Volunteers. Volunteer gatherings were increasingly made a platform for political speeches of one kind and another, the Regular Adjutant of the Gloucestershire A.B. going as far as to make a political speech on the parade ground. In response to this activity and in particular to a speech by Lord Lytton to the 23rd Middlesex in December 1880, in which he defended his Indian policies, the Duke of Cambridge reiterated Herbert's circular and imposed a ban upon political speeches at Voluteer meetings.[12] The Commanding Officer or senior officer present was now empowered to disperse any meeting at which such a political speech was attempted.

In view of the widely differing political dictates of individual Volunteers, it is not surprising that the Movement rarely took a definite stand on any particular issue of domestic or foreign politics. Political gestures were on the whole carefully avoided. Thus in November 1862 a plea for Volunteers to aid the 'distressed North' was turned down except as individual civilians, and in November 1866 the 1st Middlesex A.V. were accused of supporting the 'Eyre Defence Fund' for Governor Eyre of Jamaica. Objections of political motivation could not be levelled against such charities as the 'Volunteer Prince Imperial Memorial Fund' in 1879 or the funds raised by West Kent Volunteers for widows of the Egyptian campaign in 1882, and these received official support. However, even the 'Isandhlwana Fund' of 1879 was open to objection by Volunteers on the grounds that it provided only for the families of Regular soldiers and not for those of Colonial Volunteers who had died with them.[13]

In terms of domestic politics there was some talk, encouraged by Lord John Russell, of extending the franchise to Volunteers in 1860 but nothing came of it. With the renewal of franchise agitation in 1865 and in 1866 there was again some attempt to involve the Volunteers by attacks upon Lord Elcho's alleged double standards in arming men to whom he denied the franchise. Elcho was mobbed by pro-franchise demonstrators after a Hyde Park parade in June 1866 and even accused in 1867 in the House of Commons of threatening to disperse meetings of the Reform League with Volunteers.[14] The Volunteers were, of course, involved in the Early Closing Movement and Saturday Half-holiday movements but, as was seen in the third chapter, the success of this agitation worked against Volunteer interests in the long term.

Foreign policy issues were also largely avoided by the Movement as a whole. As was noted in the third chapter, the link with Belgium was severed in 1875 to avoid political embarrassment to the Government. Similarly, in 1864 moves by the 3rd City of London R.V.C. to entertain Garibaldi, the epitome of Volunteer military prowess, were discouraged. In January 1871 the I.G.R.F., Major-General Lindsay, firmly banned Radical Volunteers in uniform from welcoming the French Republican, Jules Favre, and, as a result, some Volunteers were dismissed. A measure of the embarrassment which could have resulted was illustrated in the case of the 10th Kent A.V. who solicited a prize from the exiled Napoleon III in October 1872.[15] There seems to have been considerable sympathy for the Confederate States of America among many Volunteers, as well as among many Regular officers. The Confederate Army seemed not unlike the Volunteers in composition, and the Marquis of Hartington echoed many when he spoke of the Confederates as being animated by the same feelings and drawn from the same classes as the Volunteers. The historical validity of the Southern military tradition has since been challenged by Professor Cunliffe, but it was of course widely believed at the time.[16]

It was the almost universal opinion of the Force that, relying as it did upon a mixture of classes, any clash between Volunteers and the general public would prove fatal to the Volunteer Movement. As was seen in the third chapter, relations between Volunteers and the public were frequently strained over such issues as drill space, but the most potentially dangerous issue of all was the role of the Volunteers in aid of the civil power. The Volunteers were emphatically not meant to be an internal police force, in the way in which the Yeomanry were, unless insurrection followed an enemy invasion.

A suggestion by the *Daily Telegraph* in November 1862 that armed Volunteers should patrol the streets of London at night was strongly opposed by the *Volunteer Service Gazette*. The exact role of the Volunteers in the event of civil disorder was not clearly defined and Volunteers were called out for the first time in April 1861 at Weston-super-Mare when a riot broke out between supporters of the two sides in a divorce case. In this instance the Volunteers arrived too late to invervene but on 1 July 1862 at Chesterfield the 1st Derby L.H.V., on the initiative of their Captain, cleared the streets though there was in fact no sign of any disturbance! It transpired that the officer in question, Captain Brown, had determined that a lecturer should deliver a lecture which was anathema to the local Catholic population. The Government wisely turned down a request from Birkenhead Magistrates to use the Volunteers during the Garibaldi riots of October 1862. The local authorities considered Volunteers likely to prove more reliable than special constables, who were 'in cases where a question arises between Orange and Green, even dangerous to call into action'.[17] At the same time, considerable fears were expressed, particularly in Liverpool, for the safety of Volunteer armouries which might fall into the hands of the mob. In October 1864 a Volunteer guard set over the arms of the 1st Warwick R.V.C. in Bingley Hall was misrepresented as an attempt to disrupt the South Staffs. Colliers' strike.[18] The Volunteer Act of 1863 had not mentioned aid to the civil power and it was increasingly clear that some definition must be attempted. The Fenian attempt on Chester in February 1867, in the prevention of which Volunteers played a major part, provided the stimulus for Government action.

Rumours of Fenian activities had already caused the Secretary of State, General Peel, to issue arms chests to Volunteer units in Lancashire, Cheshire, the West Riding, Cardiff, Glasgow and Liverpool in December 1866. In Liverpool rifles stolen from Metropolitan Volunteers were discovered and guards were once more placed over Volunteer armouries. On 11 February 1867, to forestall a Fenian plot to seize the arms and ammunition in Chester Castle, the 6th Cheshire R.V.C., under Major Humberston, was called out and sworn in as special constables with arms but no cartridges. They deferred attack until the arrival of a company of the 54th Foot and later the Scots Fusilier Guards, sent by train from London. The incident, which undoubtedly disrupted the Fenian plot, provoked much debate in Parliament where W.E. Forster led the demand for clarity from the Government. Many feared that Volunteers, if forced to fire upon demonstrators, might suffer the fate of Governor Eyre, 'marked out for the murderous hostility of pseudo-philanthropists and "advanced thinkers" '.[19] The Metropolitan Commanding Officers meeting on 27 February, 1867 opposed the use of Volunteers in aid of the civil power and defeated a motion by J.C. Templer and Earl Grosvenor, who argued that the use of Volunteers in such an emergency as Chester 'fermented by foreign influence' was justified. There was considerable confusion over the exact legal implications, which the first Government circular on the problem in June 1867 did little to dispel. A revised circular issued in October 1867 seemed to define the position satisfactorily. Volunteers could not be used as an armed body but only as individual citizens acting as special constables and armed with staves. They could, however, use their military knowledge to combine and in cases where a riot was aimed at insurrection, felony or subversion of authority, magistrates could use them as a body with arms if necessary. Under common law Volunteers could defend their armouries with arms.[20]

Peel also instituted a major review of security arrangements with a circular to Lords Lieutenent on 21 February 1867 instructing them to report upon the safety of Volunteer and Militia armouries in the event of sudden attack. Arrangements varied but it was generally considered best for Volunteers to keep their own arms at home, subject to periodic inspection, with the spares and locks for stored arms distributed amongst them. Some inland counties felt the possibility of sudden attack to be remote but the enquiries did reveal poor security in many cases, for example, the headquarters of the Bucks. Militia at Wycombe Abbey was condemned. The 11th Berks. R.V.C. was refused permission to deposit ammunition in local police stations, a frequent practice, on the grounds that the Police could not adequately guard it and in the event of accidents the fire insurance policy would not come into effect.[21] There were other instances in 1867 of Volunteers being called out at Birmingham, Sheffield, Salford and Sidmouth and, after the Fenian attempt to blow up Clerkenwell Prison in February 1868, it was suggested that the Fenians were technically 'invaders', therefore Volunteers could be utilised against them. However, the second circular largely prevented the use of Volunteers in aid of the civil power and there were only occasional breaches thereafter — in 1875 Volunteers were on call in Glasgow; in May 1878 the 17th Lancs. R.V.C. enrolled as special constables in Burnley and there were renewed Fenian alarms in 1881.[22] The Force thus successfully avoided open conflict with their fellow citizens. However, their largely negative attitude towards partisan involvement was not to be repeated in the House of Commons, where Volunteer M.P.'s proved diligent in bringing their grievances to the attention of successive Secretaries of State for War.

The Volunteer Interest — The First Phase

The grievances of the Force have already been indicated in previous chapters and may be conveniently divided into financial, social and military. The basic demand, of course, was for increasing amounts of state pecuniary aid, Volunteers arguing that time given freely to the state should be rewarded with the means to serve the state efficiently. In view of the widely differing requirements of rural and urban corps this would best be distributed as a block monetary grant rather than as aid in kind. At the same time, they sought to relieve officers of the burden of meeting income deficiencies and to encourage officer recruitment by gaining concessions such as jury exemption or presentation at Court by virtue of Volunteer rank. Volunteers also sought recognition of their military value as an integral part of national defence but this remained largely in the background compared with financial demands. Volunteers were careful to stress, moreover, that they could not undertake increased commitments conflicting with their civil employment. This naturally contrasted with the views of successive Secretaries of State that any increase in state assistance must be met with a corresponding guaranteed increase in efficiency and therefore commitment. In their favour Volunteers could emphasise their relative cheapness as a military force and their supposed position as the last resort before the re-adoption of the ballot.

Volunteer agitation in pursuit of these aims may be conveniently divided into two main phases. The first phase, from 1861 to around 1873, was marked by primarily extra-Parliamentary activity. This largely failed to achieve its objectives through the inability and unwillingness of the Volunteers to capitalise upon their voting potential in the House of Commons. The second phase, from 1878 onwards, saw the revival of organised Volunteer activity, so that by 1895 the Volunteers could be reckoned as a potentially influential interest within the House, their effectiveness increasing in proportion to their assimilation within one political party.

The first initiative in Volunteer agitation was taken on 23 February 1861 when twenty-four Metropolitan Commanding Officers headed by Lord Elcho unanimously passed resolutions calling for proper state provision for drill and musketry instruction, care of ranges and arms. Support for these resolutions emerged from a specially convened meeting of provincial representatives at the Thatched House Tavern in St. James's at which demands were made for a capitation grant of 20s. per effective. Elcho was to raise the matter in the House of Commons, Volunteers were urged to lobby M.P.'s and a number of memorials were addressed to the Secretary of State. In February 1862 there was a further meeting of the Metropolitan Commanding Officers followed in March by a meeting of 62 peers and M.P.'s both supporters and members, in the Commons Committee Rooms and a deputation to the Secretary of State. The result of the agitation was a Royal Commission established in May 1862 to ascertain the varying requirements of rural and urban units.[23] Its recommendations for a capitation grant of 20s. in return for completion of nine drills and attendance at the annual inspection, with an additional 10s. for extra efficiency, were subsequently incorporated into the Volunteer Act of 1863.

This comparative success established the pattern of agitation in the first phase. When in 1866 Volunteers began to seek a review of the level of state aid, the initiative was again taken outside Parliament; in this case by Captain Thomas Kinnear of the Leeds Rifles and a partner in Benjamin Gott and Son, who had himself lent over £1,100 of his own money to the unit to offset debts. Kinnear issued the first of two circulars distributed throughout the country in December 1866 which revealed general agreement on the insufficiency of the grant. This resulted in renewed agitation accompanied by further deputations to the Secretary of State. The Metropolitan Commanding Officers undertook three major surveys of Volunteer opinion in the course of the agitation; in February 1867 to confirm the findings of the Kinnear circulars; in February 1869 to investigate detailed requirements of the Volunteer Force; and in January 1870 to report on the reaction of the Force to the recommendations of a Departmental Committee established by Edward Cardwell. In both 1867 and 1870 Elcho and Josiah Wilkinson of the 14th Middlesex (Highgate) R.V.C. utilised the facilities of the National Rifle Association to ensure wide distribution of the circulars.[24] The 1869 inquiry, stemming from a meeting held in the Commons Tea Rooms, was designed to produce evidence on which Parliament could judge what was needed. By the time Elcho submitted the resulting memorial in April 1869 it had been signed by some 76 peers and M.P.'s.[25]

However, the agitation failed to convince either Sir John Pakington or Edward Cardwell of the merits of the Volunteer case. Pakington clung to the somewhat dubious argument that further pecuniary aid would violate the 'voluntary character' of the Force, by which he meant self-sufficiency. He also pointed to the varying requirements on which Volunteers in urban and rural units could not apparently agree. Early deputations to discover Cardwell's attitude towards the Force indicated that he was even less sympathetic to a Force he considered had grown too large. Further cause for concern came with the recommendation of the Departmental Committee in December 1869 that the basic 20s. capitation grant should be abolished, compelling all Volunteers to attain the extra efficiency standards which had previously earned the additional 10s.[26] In response to the 1870 agitation, however, Cardwell made only minor concessions, which marked the end of Volunteer success. Thereafter the Force fought a losing battle against the implementation of the Cardwell reforms, notably the application of the Mutiny Act to the Volunteer Force. There were no more deputations and in Parliament both Lord

Elcho and the Hon. Charles Lindsay consistently failed to raise sufficient support to achieve success. The motion against the application of the Mutiny Act, which Lindsay claimed was inapplicable to a body of men who were not only unpaid but capable of resigning on fourteen days notice, was lost by 212 votes to 30 votes in June 1870. Lindsay again raised the issue on the Volunteer vote in June 1872 but was forced to withdraw his motion through lack of support. Similarly, a motion by Elcho and Lindsay in July 1873 for an inquiry into the 2,233 officer vacancies in the Volunteer Force failed.[27] Why had the Volunteers, who in 1869 numbered well over a hundred M.P.'s, failed to act?

In April 1867 the *Volunteer Service Gazette* had stressed that 'none but a very strong Government would venture to take issue against them (Volunteer M.P.'s) on any matter not absolutely inadmissable upon which they settled to go as one man'. But the editor was falling into the common trap of equating the nominal total of an interest group with the number of M.P.'s who might actually constitute the effective membership. There is a considerable difference. The railway interest is a case in point, for whereas earlier histories before him produced nominal totals of M.P.'s connected in some way with the railways, Dr Alderman substantially modified the figures in terms of the actual effective railway interest. In 1868, for example, only 39 out of a total of 125 railway directors in the House of Commons could be considered effective members of the railway interest.[28] The Volunteer interest presents similar problems.

It is difficult in some ways to judge the precise voting strength of Volunteer M.P.'s at any one time due to the rapid turnover in both Volunteer ranks and Parliamentary elections and by-elections. The biographical details given to such publications as *Dod's Parliamentary Companion* often differ from year to year and it should be added that many Volunteer M.P.'s preferred not to use military titles commonly ignored in press reports and debates. *The Volunteer Service Gazette* is similarly subject to omission and errors in its lists of both M.P.'s and Parliamentary candidates. The accompanying Table 16 represents as accurate an analysis of Volunteer voting potential as is possible. The 'nominal' column includes all former Volunteers, many of whom might not continue to represent the interest of the Force. Of the seventy-two Volunteer M.P.'s in 1886 under thirty were actually serving in the Force at the time, with the remainder either former Volunteers or holders of honorary rank. The total number of Volunteer M.P.'s always contained a small number of Honorary Colonels and these, too, are included in the nominal column. The proportion of former Volunteers to those serving increased progres-

Table 16
THE VOLUNTEER INTEREST IN THE HOUSE OF COMMONS

YEAR	CONSERVATIVES*		LIBERALS		TOTALS		
	Nominal Interest	Effective Interest	Nominal Interest	Effective Interest	Nominal Interest	Effective Interest	% effective to nominal (to nearest whole number)
1861	21	4	27	11	48	15	31%
1865	32	9	41	16	73	25	34%
1869	52	13	78	21	130	34	26%
1875	74	12	56	10	130	22	17%
1880	66	13	50	10	116	23	20%
1886	54	21	18	4	72	25	35%
1890-1	53	22	17	4	70	26	37%
1895	37	17	9	1	46	18	39%

*Includes those designated Liberal Conservatives and Liberal Unionists

Drawn from *Dod's Parliamentary Companion, McCalmont's Parliamentary Poll Book* and the *Volunteer Service Gazette*

153

sively towards the end of the century.

The greatest potential strength of the Volunteer interest was thus the 130 M.P.'s between 1868 and 1880. It is a curious fact that their greatest potential in the House of Commons occurred at the very time at which the Force itself was suffering most social and military criticism in the press. Yet the absolute maximum effective support may be taken as the forty-nine Volunteer M.P.'s (together with fifteen peers and twelve other M.P.'s) who signed the memorial on the Volunteer Capitation Grant in April 1869. This itself is by no means a clear indication of the actual effective strength, and a truer estimate may perhaps be attempted by utilising the evidence of those who were either members of deputations, signatories of memorials or frequent speakers on Volunteer matters in the House. This can best be judged between March 1867 and February 1870, when two important documents were signed by M.P.'s and three major deputations undertaken to successive Secretaries of State. When this information is co-ordinated with the numbers present at the meeting in 1862 and those who spoke most frequently in the House, a total of thirty-seven M.P.'s is arrived at as representing the effective Volunteer interest between 1862 and 1874. Naturally, not all of these M.P.'s whose details are given in Appendix III sat in the House at the same time. The effective column in Table 16 therefore represents the *minimun* effective support that the Volunteers could mobilise. As in 1869 the effective interest could probably count on a degree of support from other Volunteers and also from some others interested in the Force who were not members such as C.D. Griffith, the Hon. H.G. Liddell and Sir Harry Verney.

Thus at most the Volunteer effective interest numbered only thirty-four M.P.'s in 1869 or roughly 26% of the nominal total of Volunteer M.P.'s at the same time. This figure can be compared with that of the railway interest which had an effective interest of forty-one M.P.'s or roughly 26% out of its greatest nominal total of 157 M.P.'s in 1865. Just as the effective railway interest comprised the main line railway directors, and the colonial interest was dependent upon a closely knit group linked by membership of missionary and evangelical societies,[29] so also did the Volunteer effective interest depend upon a fairly small sub-group for its impetus. In the case of the Volunteers this was supplied by the members of the Metropolitan Commanding Officers including leading Volunteer spokesmen such as Charles Buxton, Sir Thomas Fowell Buxton, Viscount Bury, Lord Elcho, Lord Enfield, Earl Grosvenor, the Hon. Charles Lindsay and Robert Loyd-Lindsay, who held a commission in the Honourable Artillery Company as well as in the Berkshire Volunteers.

The reliance upon the Metropolitan Commanding Officers indicates one further problem of the Volunteer interest, which was the lack of a central co-ordinating body which could exert pressure on behalf of the Movement as a whole. The National Rifle Association had no real representative authority and, before the mid 1860's, had only a few constituent County Rifle Associations which might have provided a channel of communications between London and the provinces. The only other organisation was that provided by the regular meetings of the Metropolitan Commanding Officers which had begun in May 1860, at the instigation of Lord Ranelagh, to co-ordinate Metropolitan reviews and field days. In such circumstances agitation could only be loosely co-ordinated by the Metropolitan Commanding Officers with the resulting petitions, memorials and deputations informally supported by Volunteer peers and M.P.'s. There were some complaints that matters had been settled so as to favour Metropolitan rather than provincial units but there was an extreme reluctance to find alternative means for the more effective co-ordination of the Volunteer interest. The reason for this reluctance may be glimpsed in an editorial by the *Volunteer Service Gazette* in December 1868. The editorial pressed for unity of action among Volunteer M.P.'s, stating that 'if they do not obtain whatever may be needful in the shape of Government grants and national rifle ranges it will certainly not be from want of power'! However, the editor also warned against forcing measures upon the Government 'bearing the faintest imputation of jobbery' or combining for purposes adverse to the national interest in the way in which the railway directors had done.[30] His concern was very much in keeping with the overall attitude of Volunteers towards political involvement.

Another manifestation of the suspicion of appearing to be a Parliamentary caucus was the hostility to Lord Ranelagh's proposed 'Association of Volunteer Colonels' in February 1870. The volatile Ranelagh was already something of a controversial figure, noted for his view that the Volunteers should form a distinct and separate force from the Army, and from his hostility to any interference by War Office officials in Volunteer affairs. His concept of a permanent monitoring body sitting in London during Parliamentary sessions to lobby M.P.'s horrified many Volunteers, especially when the premises offered by Ranelagh in Norfolk Street were found to house the Conservative Land Society of which he was President. Elcho argued that there was already adequate representation through the Metropolitan Commanding Officers. Finally, it was the Volunteers para-military status which firmly quashed the idea when the Duke of Cambridge implied that he would consider any such body as that proposed by Ranelagh as an unconstitutional armed body within the United Kingdom.[31]

Another obstacle to joint Parliamentary action was that the Volunteers, as Pakington had noted, could seldom agree on a uniform demand due to the varied wants of the localities. At the March 1862 meeting of peers and M.P.'s the majority of speakers had even been concerned that the Volunteers should not appear as 'beggars' before Parliament. On many issues, too, Volunteer M.P's took entirely different stand-points. The Mutiny Act is a case in point, for leading Conservatives such as Barttelot, Loyd-Lindsay and Egerton did not agree with their own colleague, Charles Lindsay, that the measure was an insult to the Volunteer Force. On the contrary, they believed that the Force had little to fear from the Act's provisions.[32] On issues not primarily concerned with the Volunteer Movement M.P.'s naturally tended to follow party lines. Barttelot, Lindsay and Loyd-Lindsay were all in favour of the retention of purchase, whereas Liberal Volunteers such as H.R. Brand, E.T. Gourley and W.S. Roden spoke in favour of abolition. Similarly, Liberals such as R.S. Aytoun, Bury, S.S. Dickinson, G. Loch, W.E. Price, J.S.C. Stepney and John Whitwell had all voted for the disestablishment of the Irish Church in 1869. Conservatives such as Elcho, Charles Lindsay, T.W. Mellor, T.O. Wethered and C.I. Wright had voted against disestablishment. There were some curious juxtapositions amongst Volunteer M.P.'s with Liberals such as Sir Thomas Buxton, prominent in the Aboriginy Protection Society, the Anti-Slavery Society and the Jamaica Committee, on the one hand and fellow Liberals such as Aytoun and R.A. Macfie, both prominent in the Colonial Society, on the other.[33]

The conflicting opinions of the Volunteer M.P.'s not only on the actual needs of the Force but also in party allegiance emphasises the problem facing all Parliamentary interest groups in mid-Victorian politics. This was the growth of party discipline within the House of Commons itself. Thirty-one Liberal Volunteers might be willing to sign Elcho's motion as they had done in April 1869, but voting against their own Government was a very different matter. In 1901 Lowell produced figures indicating a steady increase from the 1860's onwards in the number of divisions in which the majorities of the two main parties voted on different sides. Berrington's more detailed analysis of the pattern of dissidence in the House has shown that the steady growth in party voting was not as smooth a process as Lowell imagined. However, Berrington's figures do show that backbench revolts tended on the whole to strengthen the Government of the day, since most revolts were increasingly of an 'extremist' nature in which the dominant centre could be relied upon to redress the balance.[34]

156

The Volunteers, on the other hand, were not a popular cause. They did not have the support of the national press and their activities in such circumstances could not match the propaganda exercises of the evangelical and missionary societies or the National Education League, which had a network of local branches, a monthly journal and a series of pamphlets financed by industrial concerns.[35] It is unlikely that the *Volunteer Service Gazette* was ever read outside Volunteer circles. In terms of overall organisation the Volunteers also suffered, as already described, from lack of unswerving dedication to a single objective such as united widely disparate elements in the later Transvaal and South Africa Conciliation Committee.[36] They also suffered from the lack of permanent premises from which to co-ordinate a campaign, such as the Canada Building in King Street used by most of the colonial interest groups and also by the Parliamentary Committee on the Eastern Question. Due to the reluctance to approve Ranelagh's scheme in 1870 they also lacked a body capable of monitoring Parliamentary legislation such as the Railway Companies Association, which met monthly during Parliamentary sessions and which was able to negotiate directly with the Government in advance of contentious legislation. The ability of the private Member to obstruct Parliamentary business had in any case been gradually curtailed since the 1830's. Although it was still possible to delay legislation after the procedural reforms of 1872 and 1881-2, notably in the Committee of Supply, the sheer volume of legislation coming before the House and the executive's need to control the Parliamentary timetable both pointed to the assimilation of peripheral interest groups and individual causes within one of the main parties.[37] Thus, interest groups such as the railway directors and the Volunteers themselves became closely identified with the Conservatives. However, during the first phase of their interest group activity between 1861 and 1874 it can be seen that the Volunteers were less able to operate effectively than many other interest groups.

More might have been achieved but for the increasing want of leadership of the Volunteer interest in the House of Commons. For this Elcho was partly to blame. Several Volunteer M.P.'s had experience in other interest groups, such as Sir Thomas Buxton and Macfie in the evangelical groups and James Bourne, Lewis Dillwyn and C.R.M. Talbot in the railway interest, but it was Elcho more than any other who personified the Volunteer interest. Elcho himself almost defies neat party classification since he had served as Lord of Treasury under Aberdeen and had become a leading Adullamite, leaving himself open to accusations of double standards in denying the franchise to men he was prepared to arm as Volunteers. Elcho was by no means against labour generally and he had been one of the first Metropolitan Commanding Officers to admit artisans to his regiment, but he favoured social rather than political advancement. His belief in the former was indicated by his close association with the Scottish mining leader, Alexander MacDonald, and his successful reform of the Master and Servant Act in 1866. Elcho was also suspicious of increasing state control in any form, this being reflected in his enthusiastic support for the Liberty and Property Defence League. In short, as one recent writer has rightly commented, Elcho was never happier than when leading a minority.[38]

However, from around 1867 onwards, Elcho became diverted, if not obsessed, by the need to reintroduce the Militia ballot. He believed that a form of conscription for a home defence army would provide Britain with adequate numbers of reserves so releasing the Regular Army for its duties abroad. The Volunteer Force could then be exempted from the ballot but only at the price of much higher efficiency and a return to self-sufficiency without the capitation grant. Conscription in any form was not guaranteed to prove popular with the Commons, as demonstrated by two motions for the ballot introduced by the Liberal M.P., Myles O'Reilly, in May and July 1871 which were both counted out; junior Government ministers had stood in the lobby to prevent M.P.'s attending in the July vote. As a result Elcho's periodic motions for the reintroduction of the ballot gained little support. Worse, he tended to drift on to the ballot issue in his speeches on the Volunteers which, for example, enabled Cardwell in July 1873 to concentrate his reply upon the ballot issue rather than upon Charles Lindsay's detailed exposition of Volunteer grievances.[39] Elcho retired from command of the London Scottish in 1878, succeeding to the peerage as 10th Earl of Wemyss in 1883.

At the same time other leading Volunteer M.P.'s were leaving the Commons. In 1874 many Volunteers including Charles Lindsay lost their seats and in 1869 Earl Grosvenor had gone to the Lords as Marquis of Westminster. In 1875 Viscount Bury also went to the Lords and in 1885 his cousin, Robert Loyd-Lindsay, followed him as Lord Wantage. The younger generation of Volunteer Officers was far more willing to accept increasing commitments as part of the process by which they became more assimilated to the Regular Army, but the older officers considered that the 'Advanced School' as these younger officers had become known, was running dangerously close to the point where a civilian could no longer meet the requirements without risking his employment. In May 1874 the *Liverpool Daily Courier* had commented on how few Volunteer M.P.'s now took 'any part in debates affecting their interests.' In July 1877 the *Volunteer Service*

Gazette went as far as to complain of the indolence of Volunteer M.P.'s[40] but already a subtle change was occurring in the political composition of the Volunteer interest which was to transform its nature in the second phase of its agitation between 1878 and 1895.

The general trend towards the alliance of land and business in late Victorian politics as seen in the context of the drift of both landowners and business men from the Liberals to the Conservatives in the House is well-known. Whereas in the 1840's, for example, M.P.'s following certain occupations were as likely to be in one party as the other, by the 1880's there was a clear concentration of most landed and business interests in the Conservative party. The decline in the number of Liberal Volunteer M.P.'s, both nominal and effective members of the interest, as illustrated in Table 16, clearly reflects that of other groups within the Commons. The figures bear close comparison with the tables produced by Professor Perkin for the years 1868-1910, notably the decline in Liberal military and naval M.P.'s. Similarly they bear comparison with the railway interest.[41]

The decline in Liberal Volunteer representation also appears to follow the general trend towards the Conservatives when seen in the context of Volunteer M.P.'s occupations. The evidence here is persuasive rather than conclusive. Table 17 show the distribution between the two main parties of 172 Volunteer M.P.'s whose occupations are known between 1861 and 1886. The overall proportion of known occupations differs from year to year. In the same way the proportion of known occupations of the majority of M.P.'s in one particular party vary. It can be seen, however, that the Liberals' proportion of most occupational categories declined after 1869. This was especially true of landowners, brewers and those in the legal profession. The Liberals never had a high proportion of former Regular Officers, but their share of businessmen was always likely to be higher than that of the Conservatives. Yet by 1886 many of the Liberal Volunteer businessmen had also left the House without being replaced. The reasons for the drift of land and business interests to the Conservatives had been variously attributed to the major realignment of the parties after the Irish Home Rule crisis of 1885-6 and to the unmistakable and indiscriminate Radical challenge to all wealth perceived by landowners and businessmen alike in such controversial issues as land reform. Certainly the decline of the Liberal railway directors has been linked with the movement of the Liberal party towards collectivism as epitomised by Mundella's Railway and Canal Traffic Bill.[42] The motives of Liberal Volunteers are by no means clear since they appear quite unrelated to the grievances of the Volunteer Movement. There was certainly a number of Liberal

Table 17
The occupations of Volunteer M.P.'s 1861-1886

	LAND OWNERS (33)		FARMERS (4)		EX-REGULAR OFFICERS (42)		EX-NAVAL OFFICERS (4)		LEGAL PROFESSION (30)		OTHER PROFESSIONS (6)		BREWERS (8)		IRON MASTERS (7)		TEXTILE MANUFACTURERS (11)		OTHER MANUFACTURERS AND INDUSTRIALISTS (6)		MERCHANTS AND SHIPOWNERS (13)		RAILWAY AND MINING INTERESTS (8)	
	C	L	C	L	C	L	C	L	C	L	C	L	C	L	C	L	C	L	C	L	C	L	C	L
(41) 1861	5	7	—	—	11	3	—	2	2	4	—	—	1	1	1	—	—	1	—	1	1	1	—	—
(62) 1865	7	8	—	—	15	4	—	1	3	6	1	1	1	2	1	—	—	3	—	1	3	2	1	2
(85) 1869	9	9	1	1	14	5	1	—	5	9	3	2	2	3	—	5	—	2	1	3	2	4	1	3
(87) 1875	10	8	—	2	16	4	—	—	10	5	1	—	5	1	—	1	3	6	2	3	—	4	3	3
(79) 1880	10	5	—	1	15	5	—	—	7	4	1	—	4	1	—	3	2	5	2	3	—	4	4	3
(35) 1886	6	2	1	—	6	—	—	—	4	1	—	—	1	1	—	1	—	2	—	2	2	2	2	2

Unionists in the Volunteer interest such as H.F. Beaumont and A.H. Brown, who had previously sat as Liberals. However, exception can be found to every rule. Viscount Bury, for example, left the Liberals and stood as Conservative candidate for Stroud in an 1875 by-election not because of land reform but because he disagreed with the abolition of purchase by Royal Warrant. Whatever the reasons the general effect was clear. Henceforth the Volunteer interest was to be closely associated with the Conservative party.

The Volunteer interest — The Second Phase

The period between 1878 and 1885 marks almost a transitional stage in which the Volunteers slowly forsook older methods of extra-Parliamentary pressures as it became increasingly apparent that only Parliament could serve as a real platform for successful agitation.

In January 1878, for example, a conference was held at the Royal United Service Institution at the instigation of Howard Vincent, then Lt.-Col. of the 40th Middlesex (Central London Rangers) and shortly to become Director of Criminal Investigation at Scotland Yard. The object was to invite discussion upon the necessity and practicability of improvement and reform within the Force. General agreement was reached on a demand for a basic increase of 10s in the capitation grant and for a Royal Commission. Hopes were raised when a Departmental Committee was established under the chairmanship of Bury, now Under Secretary at the War Office. However, after an exhaustive investigation of Volunteer finance, the Committee concluded that there had been excessive and unnecessary expenditure in many cases and that the existing grant was sufficient for necessary expenses.[43] A second conference held at the Institution in April 1885 to discuss the views of Sir Edward Hamley on the military role of the Force was similarly turned into a debate on the need for an additional 10s. on the capitation grant.[44] The difference was that it was followed by an attempt to raise the matter in the House of Commons on the Volunteer Vote, which in recent years had either provoked no discussion at all as in 1882 and 1883, or had been disrupted by Irish M.P.'s seeking to extend the Force to Ireland as in 1878 and 1881.* In the following month a motion on equipment deficiencies was lost by only 23 votes to 20 in the House of Lords and might have succeeded had not Wemyss once more strayed on to the ballot issue and alienated his fellow peers.

What made concentration on Parliament more pressing was the fact that the meetings of the Metropolitan Commanding Officers had been abolished. In January 1884 the Metropolitan Commanding Officers,

*See Appendix V

161

led by Col. Alt of the Central London Rangers and Major Stanley Bird, had strayed from their strict terms of reference and discussed the requirements of the Force as a whole behind closed doors. Further meetings were prohibited by the Adjutant-General and it was clear that they could only be convened in future under the supervision of the G.O.C., Home District.[45] This left only Parliament as a focus for Volunteer grievances and in both 1886 and 1890 the Volunteers made major attempts to defeat the Government on the floor of the House itself. Both occasions resulted in more tangible success than the traditional reliance on extra-Parliamentary pressure.

The first indication of the new determination to use Parliament effectively came on 22 March 1886 when Vincent, now Lt.-Col. of the 22nd Middlesex (Queen's Westminsters) and M.P. for Sheffield Central, called in the Committee of Supply for an immediate increase of 10s. in the capitation grant as absolutely and urgently necessary. Gladstone surprised all present by a violent attack upon the motion, insisting that any change in the estimates effected by the Commons would by a usurpation of the role of the executive. Campbell-Bannerman, the Secretary of State for War, tried to ward off the Volunteers by promising a call for returns of expenditure to investigate whether any increase was justified. The Government only narrowly avoided defeat by 187 votes to 166 votes.[46] It was, of course, a peculiarly chaotic time in politics, especially for the Liberals, and in such circumstances it is not surprising that twelve Liberals voted for the motion including two Volunteers and Sir Charles Dilke. Including the tellers, twenty-three Volunteers supported the motion. Only nine Liberal Volunteers or former Volunteers voted with the Government including E.T. Gourley. The Volunteers had thus demonstrated for the first time their greater cohesion and their ability to achieve some degree of success at least when allied with the majority of one particular party. Campbell-Bannerman's Conservative successor, W.H. Smith, called for returns of expenditure and established a new departmental Committee as a result of continuing agitation. This did in fact recommend an increase of 5s. in the capitation grant in 1887 although accompanied by increased musketry requirements.

The second instance in which the new methods won concessions came in March 1890. As related in the previous chapter, in March 1889 the War Office Council drew up schedules of mobilisation equipment required by Volunteers, compelling the Volunteers themselves to provide certain items by a certain date on pain of forfeiting the capitation grant entirely. Various public appeals were made but by 1890 it was clear that the attempts to raise the necessary funds from the public, which Stanhope had hoped to encourage, had failed.[47] On 13 March 1890 Sir Edward Hamley, seconded by Vincent, introduced a motion calling upon the Government to make up deficiencies and to cancel all Volunteer debts. Many speakers including Joseph Chamberlain testified to the almost universal failure of the public appeals. The motion came to the vote, encouraged by the Liberals, and Stanhope was defeated by 133 votes to 102 votes. Thirty-three Conservative and Liberal Unionists including twelve Volunteers voted with the Opposition. A further nine of the dissidents were service members including Hamley, General Crauford Fraser and the eccentric Sir Henry Havelock-Allan. However, some leading Conservative Volunteers including Sir Walter Barttelot, Sir Henry Fletcher, Henry Eyre and twelve others did not vote against the Government, feeling that the Volunteers had assisted a party manoeuvre by a 'faction which can scarcely congratulate itself on its own treatment of the Volunteers.'[48] As related in the previous chapter, the defeat brought immediate concessions from the Cabinet although Stanhope refused to cancel debts for fear of creating a precedent.

Other Parliamentary activity also brought its rewards. The campaign for jury exemption, for example, involved the introduction of two bills by the Volunteers. In 1892 Stanhope agreed to draft a Government bill despite the obvious opposition of the Lord Chancellor, Halsbury, to anything but individual exemption at the discretion of the magistrates. In the event there was no time to bring in the Bill and in February 1893 a second Bill was brought forward by Vincent. The new Secretary of State, Campbell-Bannerman, indicated that the War Office had no particular objection but it encountered heavy opposition from the Treasury and Home Office in committee. When in September 1893 the Secretary of State refused either to help or hinder the Bill it was lost.[49] He did accept the suggestion of both Stanhope and the Volunteers to establish a Select Committee on Volunteer Acts in 1894, and accepted its recommendations, largely formulated by Volunteers, of making provision to accept Volunteers' offers of service in situations short of grave national emergency. Ironically, the resulting Volunteers (Military Service) Bill had its third reading immediately after the Cordite Vote in June 1895, in which the Volunteers combined with the other service members to defeat Rosebery's ministry.

Throughout the second phase of agitation, the Volunteers were far more willing to use Parliamentary tactics such as continued questions or the procedure for going into Supply as they had done in 1886 and to vote against their own party if necessary. This can be attributed to two main factors. Firstly, although overall Volunteer representation had fallen to around seventy M.P.'s, the actual effective interest had increased. Between 1874 and 1884 what little agitation there was had been carried by some of the survivors of the earlier period such as Anderson, Barttelot, Loyd-Lindsay and Whitwell. To these were added a few newcomers such as E.H. Kennard, Sir Arthur Hayter and David McIver. From 1886 onwards, however, more new members could be said to be joining the effective interest. The evidence for the members of the effective interest in this second phase is again based on speeches and questions in the House but also involvement in the abortive jury bills of 1892 and 1893, involvement in the Select Committees on Rifle Ranges in 1890 and on Volunteer Acts in 1894 and, lastly, attendance at the crucial Parliamentary divisions of 1886, 1890 and 1895. The details of twenty-one members of the effective interest between 1886 and 1895 are given in Appendix IV. It should be noted that by no means all of those active in the first phase continued to support the Volunteers to the same extent in the second phase. Similarly, some who had been in the House before 1886 only really became members of the effective interest after that date such as T.W. Boord and Sir Richard Paget. They are therefore only included as members of the effective interest after 1886.

The fact that approximately 70% of the nominal interest and 84% of the effective interest was Conservative by 1890 gave the Volunteers far more cohesion than at any previous time. The second important factor was more effective leadership. Three key M.P.'s all entered the House in 1885 — Howard Vincent, Edward Hamley and Arthur Brookfield. Vincent, who also advocated selected issues such as Imperial federation, Colonial preference and Immigration controls as well as Volunteer grievances, was not altogether popular with fellow M.P.'s, who regarded him as something of a bore. Salisbury and other Conservative ministers were highly contemptuous of his protectionist agitation in 1885-6 and Arnold-Forster was later to describe him as:

> a tiresome ass, absolutely incapable of comprehending any view of the British Army which is not from the standpoint of the Queen's Westminsters and the glorification of Sir Howard Vincent.[50]

It was Vincent, of course, who virtually revived the flagging Volunteer interest with his conference in 1878 and few could equal the prodigiousness with which he raised matters in the House. Yet for all his scene-stealing, it was Arthur Brookfield who provided the real administrative ability behind the Volunteers. Brookfield noted the general lack of planning between interested M.P.'s before the estimates and consequently helped to resurrect the moribund Service

Members Committee with himself as secretary and a Militia officer, Sir James Fergusson, as Chairman. A further indication of growing organisation was the speech by Sir Henry Fletcher in the debate on the Volunteers (Military Service) Bill on behalf of a 'large and influential' body — the Institute of Commanding Officers of Volunteers. The Institute became sufficiently involved in Volunteer political activity after the South African War to prompt an official inquiry into its somewhat obscure origins. The War Office could only discover that no records apparently existed and that it had appeared about 'twenty-five years' previously (i.e. 1880) as a means of discussing internal economy and training with a view to achieving greater uniformity and efficiency. Significantly its first secretary was Stanley Bird, whose activities had led to the demise of the Metropolitan Commanding Officers in 1884, and the Institute was certainly a far more effective focus of Volunteer opinion than the former had ever been.[51]

The Cordite Vote

By 1895 the Volunteer interest was virtually indistinguishable from the Conservative party. As in the case of the railway interest, whose acknowledged leader, W.L. Jackson, was also a Volunteer, the Volunteers were associated with the right wing of the party. Howard Vincent was one of the party's earliest protectionists and only Sir Albert Rollit of the Volunteers elected before the South African War was later a Free Trader. Edwin Hughes, another prominent Volunteer, had employed his regiment to break up rival demonstrations during his own deep involvement in jingoism in 1877.[52] This did not necessarily mean that the Volunteers had completely lost their independence of a Conservative Government, and after the South African War Volunteers succumbed to the instinct of self-preservation in the face of the plans of both Brodrick and Arnold-Forster. But since it was to be expected that a Conservative ministry would normally adopt policies more acceptable to its Volunteer backbenchers than a Liberal ministry, it is not surprising to find the Volunteers combining with other service members in the Cordite Vote of 21 June 1895.

St. John Brodrick, later Unionist Secretary of State for War, conceived the idea of using the shortage of small-arms ammunition, due to the changeover to cordite, as a means of defeating Rosebery's Government. Brodrick later claimed that his actions had revived the Service Members' Committee but this was, of course, erroneous. It is clear that both Arthur Brookfield and the Conservative Whips,

Akers-Douglas and Harry Anstruther, who had himself served in the Volunteers, were closely involved in the planning of the debate. Campbell-Bannerman had just announced the resignation of the Duke of Cambridge as Commander-in-Chief and most M.P.'s had left the Chamber. The Secretary of State did not expect the censure motion, moved by Brodrick and Joseph Chamberlain, to reduce his salary by £100. Brookfield had persuaded 'so many of them (service M.P.'s) to come down to the House that they in fact mustered twelve more than I had expected', and when the vote was called these 'forty or fifty M.P.'s' and their other supporters returned in large numbers from the terrace where they had been waiting. This, as Brodrick recalled, took the Liberal Whips completely by surprise and the 'usual flurry to recall 250 absent members set in with severity . . .'.[53] After an initial mix-up over the actual voting figures the result was announced as a defeat for the Government by 132 votes to 125 votes. Of the 132 Conservatives and Liberal Unionists, fifty-three were service M.P.'s including fifteen Volunteers. Three Liberals voted with the Conservatives, including the Volunteer T.H. Bolton, and five Liberal Volunteers or former Volunteers voted with their Government — C.E. Shaw, Sir George Trevelyan, A.J. Mundella, Gourley, who had also followed his party line in 1886, and, not surprisingly, Campbell-Bannerman.

Earlier in the week the Government had been defeated in the Standing Committee on the Factory Bill and had narrowly survived a vote on the Welsh Church Bill with a majority of only seven. Campbell-Bannerman himself called the defeat at the hands of the service Members 'a snap vote in a thin house on a side issue', but Rosebery had tired of office, the Cabinet was disintegrating and, in any case, the Government was widely expected to fall on the Welsh Church Bill in the following week. Thus the Liberals seized on the unexpected reverse and resigned.[54] The weakness of the Government detracted in some ways from the success of the Volunteers and their fellow service members, but the Cordite vote remained an object lesson in what might be achieved by military M.P.'s acting in concert.

The Volunteer Movement was not designed to operate as a political faction nor as the instrument of any particular party. On the whole a neutral stance was successfully maintained upon party political issues and in the same way the Volunteers were able to avoid a role in aid of the civil power which might have exposed the Force to political pressures. This attitude towards politics was reflected in the reluctance of Volunteer M.P.'s to capitalise upon their voting strength in the period from 1861 to 1873 and the resulting memorials and deputations, which served as the main focus of Volunteer pressure group activity, largely failed to achieve their objectives unless a Government was prepared to grant concessions. It might be noted that Volunteers showed a faith in Royal Commissions and official enquiries which was never fully justified by the results achieved from such bodies. By 1885, after a revival of Volunteer agitation, the attitude of a new generation of Volunteer M.P.'s towards politics had changed and they showed themselves prepared to vote against both Liberal and Conservative ministries in pursuit of their interests. The Cordite vote of 1895 was not only a clear indication of the growing organisational strength of service members generally but also served as a warning of what was to come after the South African War.

The experience of the Volunteer Interest in the House of Commons during the nineteenth century correlates closely with what has been observed of other Parliamentary pressure groups, despite what on the surface appear to be major differences between the para-military status of the Volunteers and the socio-economic or overtly political motivation of other groups. Thus in common with most other interest groups in the same period, the Volunteers became increasingly associated with one of the main political parties through the recognition that success in the face of the growth of party and ministerial control in the House necessitated assimilation. That the Volunteers became largely assimilated within the Conservatives rather than the Liberals is a reflection of the social, economic and political affinities drawing men of similar class and outlook together in the late nineteenth century. The railway interest for one discovered that assimilation, although conferring certain advantanges, did not confer protection against other groups within the same party representing rail users.[55] This was a lesson which the Volunteers failed to learn. By 1899 they considered that they had won much of the recognition for which their M.P.'s had striven since 1859. This was especially apparant when sheer necessity forced the Government to acknowledge the Force as the only means of defence against raids on the United Kingdom during the South African War.[56] The bitterness of the Volunteers' reaction to Conservative policies after the War suggests that the Volunteer interest had confused assimilation with immunity. It was the success of the Volunteers in their rearguard action against, firstly, Brodrick and, secondly, Arnold-Forster, which brought Lord Esher and Sir George Clarke to fear for the constitution.

[1] *BM* Add Mss 49702 Clarke to Balfour, 9.8.1905 and Add Mss 49723 Arnold-Forster to Balfour, 19.3.1907; M.V. Brett (ed) *The Journals and Letters of Reginald, Viscount Esher* (London 1934), II, p 167-9, 205, 227-9.
[2] Cf J. Vincent and A.B. Cooke, *The Governing Passion: Cabinet Government and Party*

Politics in Britain, 1885-6 (London 1974); Andrew Jones, *The Politics of Reform, 1884* (London 1972); Maurice Cowling, *Disraeli, Gladstone and Revolution: The Passing of the Second Reform Bill* (London 1967).

[3] G. Alderman, *The Railway Interest* (Leicester 1973), p 9-10; H Berrington, 'Partisanship and Dissidence in the Nineteenth Century House of Commons' *PA* XXI (1967-8), p 338-74.

[4] J. Cornford 'The Transformation of Conservatism in the Late Nineteenth Century' *VS* VII (1963-4), p 36-8.

[5] Cf. H.C.G. Mather, *The Liberal Imperialists* (Oxford 1973); J.B. Conacher, *The Peelites and the Party System* (Newton Abbot 1972); R.A. Rempel, *Unionists Divided* (Newton Abbot 1972).

[6] *VSG* 26.3.64, p 255; 29.7.65, p 549-50 'The New Parliament'; 9.11.59, p 17.

[7] Devon R.O. *Seymour of Berry Pomeroy* 1392 M-Box 18/2 Acland to Somerset, 13.4.65; Lincs R.O. *Hill 12th Dep* 12/2/1, p 87, 97.

[8] Devon R.O. *Seymour of Berry Pomeroy* 1392 M/Box 18/14 Brown to Seymour, 26.7.61 and 1.8.61; Bucks. R.O. *TA. Coll* Box 15 Wethered Mss, p 6-8; *Hughenden Papers* B/XXI/H 275-8.

[9] *VSG* 20.2.68, p 196; 14.3.68, p 229.

[10] *VSG* 27.4.61, p 430; 19.9.68, p 660-1 'The Election and the Volunteers'; 14.6.73, p 521; 13.3.80, p 309-11; 27.1.83, p 198; 25.8.83, p 724.

[11] *VSG* 24.2.66, p 197 'Election Volunteers'; 8.7.65, p 501 'Perilous Electioneering'; 3.3.66 Edit.

[12] *VSG* 9.2.78, p 237-8 'Volunteers and Politics'; 26.10.78, p 853-7 'The Past Year'; 25.9.80, p 796 'Volunteers and Politics'; 26.10.78, p 853-7; 25.12.80, p 117-8; 1.1.81, p 133.

[13] *VSG* 29.11.62, p 89; 24.11.66, p 824; 19.7.79, p 621-2; 5.4.79, p 357; 12.4.79, p 373; *QOG* V (Jan 1883) No 1.

[14] *VSG* 30.1.60, p 117; 31.12.59, p 77; 13.5.65, p 372-3 'Party Politics in the Force'; 30.6.66, p 485 'Lord Elcho and the Mob'; 17.8.67, p 592-3 'Mr P.A. Taylor and Lord Elcho'.

[15] *VSG* 26.3.64, p 255; 14.1.71, p 101; 21.1.71, p 117 'Political Demonstrations'; 28.1.71, p 133; 26.10.72, p 754.

[16] F.M. Viscount Wolseley, *The Story of a Soldier's Life* (London 1903) II, p 130-41; Sir Alfred Turner, *Sixty Years of a Soldier's Life* (London 1912), p 36; Vane, op cit, p 3-5; W.J. Tansig, *Confederate Military Land Units* (London and New York 1967); B. Holland, *The Life of the Duke of Devonshire* (London 1911), I, p 59; Hartington, *Hansard* CLXX, 1698-9 and CLXXI, 964; Cunliffe, op cit, p 337-84.

[17] *VSG* 29.11.62, p 90 'Volunteer Police'; 13.4.61, p 392; 25.10.62, p 9 'Volunteers and Rioters'; *PRO* HO 45/OS 7322, 1-3; 7326, 6-18; S. Gilley, 'The Garibaldi Riots of 1862 *HJ* (1973), p 697-732.

[18] *PRO* HO 45/OS 7341, 1-5; *VSG* 15.10.64, p 724-5 'The Colliers' Strike and the Birmingham Volunteers'; 22.10.64, p 740-1.

[19] *PRO* HO 45/OS 7799, 120, 150-1, 163, 167-9, 173; *VSG* 8.12.66, p 27; 22.12.66, p 58, 16.2.67, p 175; 23.2.67, p 190-1; 2.3.67, p 208-9; 16.3.67, p 240-3; 30.3.67, p 271; *USM* 1867 Pt II (July), p 427-9; F. Simpson, *The Chester Volunteers* (Chester 1920), p 9-12; G. Huxley, *Victorian Duke* (Oxford 1967) p 86-7.

[20] *VSG* 2.3.67, p 216; 15.6.67, p 449 'The War Office Memo'; 22.6.67, p 463; 6.7.67, p 498; 5.10.67, p 705 'The New Memo'; 12.10.67, p 720-1 'Custody of Arms and Defence of Armouries'; *PRO* HO 45/OS 8060, 1-10; *BPP* 1867 (364) XLI 821.

[21] Oxon, R.O. Lieutenancy L-M I/v/2; Beds. R.O. L/C/V 4 Green to Cowper, 15.3.67; Bucks. R.O. *Carrington Papers* Box 28/3 bundle 33; Berks. R.O. D/EH Z/l Blaudy to Wallingford Committee, 4.1.68.

[22] *VSG* 19.10.67, p 736 'Fenian Alarms'; 23.11.67, p 816; 23.3.67, p 257; 22.6.67, p 463; 8.2.68, p 148-9 'Rioters or Invaders?'; 14.8.75, p 645; 18.5.78, p 465; 25.5.78, p 486 'Volunteers and Civil Tumults'; 8.1.81, p 149-50.

[23] *BPP* 1862 (118. xxxii 833); *VSG* 9.3.61, p 312-5; 18.10.62, p 833 'Government Aid'; Berry, p 163ff.

[24] *VSG* 9.2.67, p 165-8; 23.2.67, p 199; 2.3.67, p 216; 30.3.67, p 277; 13.4.67, p 302-3; *BPP* 1867 (184) XLI 813 Report of Volunteer Committee on the Capitation Grant. I owe additional information on Kinnear to Mrs P.M. Morris, University of Leeds.

[25] *VSG* 16.1.69, p 100-1, 116-7, 'The Sequel to Mr Cardwell's Declaration'; 13.2.69, p 166; 20.2.69, p 183; 17.4.69, p 310; *BPP* 1868-9 (142) XXXVI 593 Memorial of Peers and M.P.'s.

[26] *VSG* 15.6.67, p 449 'Volunteers and their Maintenance'; 22.6.67, p 466 'The Extra Grant'; 21.3.68, p 245 'The Government and the Capitation Grant'; 28.3.68, p 257-8 'The Press and the Capitation Grant'; 17.10.68, p 724-5 'The Capitation Grant'; 18.12.69, p 36-7 'The Secretary for War and the Volunteers'; *PRO* WO 33/21 B Report of the Committee on the Financial State and Internal Organisation of the Volunteer Force.

[27] *VSG* 8.7.71, p 501-2 'The Mutiny Act'; 29.6.72, p 480-2; 19.7.73, p 597; 26.7.73, p 608-10.

[28] *VSG* 20.4.67, p 321-2 'The Increase of the Capitation Grant'; J.A. Thomas *The House of Commons 1832-1901: A Study of its Economic and Functional Character* (Cardiff 1939), p 4-6; P.S. Bagwell, 'The Railway Interest: Its Organisation and Influence, 1839-1914' *J Trans Hist* VII (1965-6), p 65-86; Alderman, op cit, p 24-31.

[29] Alderman, op cit, p 24-31; for colonial interests, see C.C. Eldridge, *England's Mission: The Imperial Idea in the Age of Gladstone and Disraeli, 1868-1888* (London 1973), p 163-8.

[30] *VSG* 5.12.68, p 6-7 'Volunteers in the New House'; 25.2.71, p 197 'Mr Cardwell's Bill and the Volunteers'; 21.3.68 p 245 'The Government and the Capitation Grant'; 19.12.68 p 36-7 'Volunteers in Parliament'.

[31] *VSG* 19.2.70, p 182; 26.2.70, p 196-9; 5.3.70, p 213 'Norfolk Street Versus Pall Mall'; 12.3.70, p 228 'The Representation of the Force'.

[32] *VSG* 11.10.62, p 816; 18.10.62, p 833 'Government Aid'; 22.4.71, p 318-22; 8.7.71, p 503-4.

[33] *VSG* 11.3.71, p 222-7; 18.3.71, p 239-43, 247-8; 25.3.71, p 254-7; Eldridge op cit, p 163-8.

[34] Berrington, op cit; A.L. Lowell 'The Influence of Party Upon Legislation in England and America' in *Annual Report of the American Historical Association* (Washington 1902), I, p 319-542; Eldridge, op cit, p 159-68.

[35] G. Wootton, *Pressure Groups in Britain, 1720-1970* (London 1975), p 88-9.

[36] S. Koss, *The Pro-Boers* (Chicago 1973), p xxiv-xxxii.

[37] For changes in Commons procedures see P. Fraser, 'The Growth of Ministerial Control in the Nineteenth Centry House of Commons' *EHR* LXXV (1960), p 444-663; D.E.D. Beales 'Parliamentary Parties and the Independent Member, 1810-60' in R. Robson (ed) *Ideas and Institutions of Victorian Britain* (London 1967), p 1-19; V. Cromwell, 'The Losing of the Initiative by the House of Commons', 1780-1914' *TRHS* (1968), p 1-24.

[38] *VSG* 13.5.63, p 372-3 'Party Politics in the Force'; 30.6.66, p 592-3 'Mr Taylor and Lord Elcho'; N. Seldon, 'Laissez Faire as Dogma: The Liberty and Property Defence League, 1882-1914' and C.J. Kauffman, 'Lord Elcho: Trade Unionism and Democracy' both in K.D. Brown (ed) *Essays in Anti-Labour History* (London 1974), p 183-207, 208-233.

[39] *VSG* 15.7.71, p 517 'The last Word on National Armament'; 29.1.76, p 197-8 'Lord

169

Elcho's Proposals'; 12.2.76, p 229-30 'Lord Elcho and the Capitation Grant'; Lord Elcho, *Letters on Military Organisation* (London 1871).

[40] *VSG* 30.5.74, p 485; 7.7.77, p 574-5 'Mondays Debate'.

[41] For the significance or otherwise of M.P.'s occupations in the 1840's' see W.O. Aydelotte, 'The House of Commons in the 1840's *History* XXXIX (1954), p 249-62 and 'The Conservative and Radical Interpretations of Early Victorian Social Legislation' *VS* XI (1967), p 225-36; Thomas, op cit, p 14-16; Alderman, op cit, p 229-50; H.J. Perkin, 'Land Reform and Class Conflict in Victorian Britain' in J. Butt and I.F. Clarke (eds) *The Victorians and Social Protest* (Newton Abbot 1973); 177-217.

[42] W.H.G. Armytage, 'The Railway Rates Question and the Fall of the Third Gladstone Ministry' *EHR* LXV (1950), p 18-51; P.M. Williams, 'Public Opinion and the Railway Rates Question of 1886' *EHR* LXVII (1952), p 37-73; Alderman op cit, p 110-5.

[43] *VSG* 24.1.78, p 191-210; *BPP* 1878-9 [c 2235] XV 181 Report on the Financial State and Internal Organisation of the Volunteer Force; I.F.W. Beckett 'The Volunteers and the R.U.S.I.' *JRUSI* 122 (1977) No. 1, p 58-63.

[44] Sir Edward Hamley 'The Volunteers in Time of Need' *Nineteenth Century* XVII (March 1885), p 405-23; *JRUSI* XXIX (1885) No 130, p 629ff; *VSG* 2.5.85, p 433-4 'The Discussion of Sir Edward Hamley's Paper'.

[45] *VSG* 12.1.84, p 165-6 'The Requirements of the Volunteers'; 5.12.84, p 150 'Next Monday's Meeting'; 25.10.84, p 862-5 'The Past Year'.

[46] *Army Debates* (1886), 192-223; A.I. Shand, *The Life of Sir Edward Hamley* (London and Edinburgh 1895), II, p 272-3; S.H. Jeyes and F.D. How, *The Life of Sir Howard Vincent* (London 1912), p 189-191; J.A. Spender, *The Life of Sir Henry Campbell-Bannerman* (London 1923), I, p 102-3.

[47] The fullest source for the Mobilisation Scheme and Brigades is in *PRO* 30/40/13, 14. Papers of Sir John Ardagh; see also *PRO* WO 163/4 for War Office Council meeting of 28.3.89; for public appeals see *Illustrated Naval and Military Magazine* II (1889), p 927-1100; for Stanhope's encouragement of the appeals see Fleetwood-Wilson to MacDonnell, 11.3.89 in Salisbury Papers at Christ Church, Oxford.

[48] *INMM* IV (1890) Notes for April; *AD* (1890) 61-86 for debate and *AD* (1890) 97-143; Shand, op cit, II, p 292-3.

[49] Halsbury, 20.5.92 *AD* (1892), 366-73; Vincent, 25.7.93, *AD* (1893), 847; Campbell-Bannerman, 12.9.93 *AD* (1893), 1054-5; *BPP* 1892 (131) x.555 and 1893-4 (141) VIII.531 for the abortive jury bills.

[50] Jeyes and How, op cit, passim; Arnold Forster's Diary, 3.3.1905 Add Mss 50345. Vincent was knighted in 1896.

[51] A.M. Brookfield, *Annals of a Chequered Life* (London 1930), p 202-4; Add Mss 50312 Section 49.

[52] H. Cunningham, 'Jingoism in 1887-8' *VS* XV (1971), p 429-53.

[53] The account of the debate is drawn from Brookfield, op cit, p 235-9; Earl of Middleton, *Records and Reactions, 1856-1939*, (London 1939), p 87-91; Austen Chamberlain *Down the Years* (London 1935), p 89-91; A.S.T. Griffith-Boscawen, *Fourteen Years in Parliament* (London 1907), p 71-3; J. Wilson, *The Life of Sir H. Campbell-Bannerman* (London 1973), p 202-5; Spender, op cit, p 155-61; *AD* (1895), 169-188.

[54] R. Rhodes-James, *Rosebery* (London 1963), p 364-84.

[55] Alderman, op cit, p 190.

[56] George Wyndham, 12.2.1900 *AD* (1900), I, p 1178-96.

CHAPTER VI

THE VOLUNTEERS AND NATIONAL DEFENCE
1859-99

'Tis not for Greed of Conquest,
　Tis not for Pomp of War,
That we in willing thousands,
　Together banded are:
No Call to Arms, for Menace,
　Has summoned our array,
No scheme of Fierce Agression
　We muster to assay!'

'The Volunteer National Song'
by Lt.-Col. Buck, 26th Kent R.V.C., 1876.

Arthur Brookfield recalled in his memoirs his belief that the official view of the Volunteer Force was that 'while it represented a popular national Movement which it might be a pity to discourage, it was still essential that it should never be regarded as an asset that would be turned to any useful purpose in actual warfare . . .'.[1] Brookfield's theory throws considerable light on the crucial question of the relationship between the Volunteer Force and the Regular Army, upon which ultimately depended the contribution or otherwise of the Volunteers to the military capacity of the Empire. It is a relationship which can only be explained against a background of the problems facing any civilian volunteer force in terms of military discipline, problems which indeed coloured the respective views of both Volunteers and Regulars on the exact role to be played by the Volunteer Force in national defence.

Professionals and Amateurs: Mutual Failings

The early reaction of Regular officers to the Volunteer Force was frequently unfavourable, as Owen Wethered recalled: 'I think that Regular officers, as a rule, regarded us at the very best as harmless lunatics, and at the worst, as utterly valueless as a military force, and, in any case, as a great nuisance.'[2] As was noted in the first chapter, both the Duke of Cambridge and Sir John Fox Burgoyne expressed reservations upon the value of Volunteers and they repeated their criticisms to the Select Committee on Military Organisation in the summer of 1859. The Duke of Cambridge was inclined to believe that Volunteers would 'get in the way', whereas Burgoyne, though favouring the training of the general populace in the use of arms, likened the Volunteers to a 'mob'. Such criticisms were echoed by General Sir Robert Gardiner and the C.-in-C., Scotland, Lord Melville, whose opinion that no general officer would command Volunteers provoked an angry reaction in the Commons. Not all soldiers shared Burgoyne's pessimistic forecast that nothing could make Auxiliaries efficient and that only highly trained troops could act as Light Infantry. Two Peninsular veterans, Sir John Scott Lillie and Sir Harry Smith, testified to the value of large numbers of auxiliary riflemen in support of Regulars. Sir William Napier believed that the higher intelligence of Volunteers and the longer range of the modern rifle would overcome the problems of partisan warfare, the only role in which it was felt that Volunteers could act.[3] The Royal Commission on National Defence, reporting in February 1860, saw some value in the Volunteers as a partial remedy for the 'glaring inferiority' of numbers available for home defence[4] but no Regular seriously believed that

Volunteers could meet trained Continental troops on equal terms in the field.

The general view of the Volunteer Force among Regular officers outlined above prevailed in some quarters until well after the Cardwell reforms. Its roots lay largely in the failure of Regular Army officers to comprehend the special problems facing a Volunteer Force held together by mutual consent rather than a strict code of conduct. The Regular Army had, in fact, little contact with the Volunteers before the Cardwell reforms. It is therefore not surprising that so many Regular officers, often woefully ignorant of their own profession, failed to recognise the problems when they viewed the drill, discipline and public appearance of the Volunteer Force at home and the performances of Auxiliary troops abroad.

It was generally considered by Volunteers that 'what the Army lost in discipline it would gain in intelligence',[5] but it must be said that in many cases the notion of drill and discipline was extremely rudimentary in the early years of the Volunteer Movement. It must be remembered of course that very few Volunteers, beyond perhaps the Commanding Officer and the Adjutant, had any previous military experience. In Bucks., for example, only two officers had any previous military experience. Similarly, only 35 out of the 591 Middlesex officers analysed in the second chapter had served in the Regular Army. As a result there was considerable ignorance. To give one example, J.H.A. Macdonald observed of one lieutenant in Edinburgh: 'it was quite a common thing to see him, when he was drilling the company facing towards it, turn tail three-quarters about to make sure by experiment on himself whether he ought to say 'right turn' or 'left turn'!' Similarly, Richard Clynton, an Adjutant with a Metropolitan unit, had difficulty in getting men to pay the proper compliments to general officers as he recalled when one sentry was confronted by a divisional general:

> He had presented arms to the Brigadier, but a greater man stood before him and deserved therefor a higher compliment, so holding his rifle with his left hand he let go the small of the butt with his right, and seizing his forage cap took it off and held it at arms length in a slanting position . . .[6]

There are many other examples of such occurrences as talking in the ranks, or of men leaving the ranks, as in the case of the members of the 3rd Northumberland (Morpeth) R.V.C., who simply fell out of a march in April 1861 and left their arms piled by the roadside.[7] Such cases were mainly the result of general ignorance of military affairs and would be corrected with time, but much depended upon the quality of Volunteer officers.

Unfortunately, in the early years officers were frequently elected by their fellows rather than appointed for their military skills. Actual examples of ballot papers survive for the 3rd Somerset (Taunton) R.V.C. and the 3rd Monmouth (Newport) R.V.C., but the practice was widespread. In Liverpool the 1st Lancs. R.V.C. circularised its members on the appointment of officers; Joseph Mayer was elected by 'round robin' to the command of the 66th Lancs. (Borough Guard) R.V.C. and the 39th Lancs. (Liverpool Welsh) had frequent elections. This did not of course guarantee that the best men, from a military point of view, were chosen, and in the 3rd Durham (Sunderland) R.V.C. it was felt by 1862 that the corps had suffered from electing the wrong men at the start. Elections were officially discouraged but the old custom died hard — the 1st Lincs. R.V.C. for example, was still electing officers in 1864. There were also cases of corps refusing to accept officers appointed by commanding officers of whom they disapproved, as in the 17th Somerset (Lyncombe) R.V.C. and 2nd Somerset (Weston-super-Mare) A.V. in 1860; in the 18th Somerset R.V.C. in March 1873 and in Truro in November 1873. As late as September 1883 men were still being selected for promotion by ballot in Liverpool and the 1st Cheshire R.V.C.[8] Such concepts as elections and the ability of Volunteers to criticise their officers at general meetings upon financial matters were completely alien to the Regular officer.

It was, in fact, extremely difficult for Volunteer officers to enforce discipline among freely assembled men who were frequently of the same social rank as the officers themselves. It was important that men both recognised and respected the authority of their officers and, indeed, in December 1860 Earl de Grey and Ripon urged Volunteer officers to acquire a greater knowledge of their duties in order to maintain their authority.[9] Discipline and subordination were, however, often lacking amongst officers themselves and there were many cases of internal disputes involving officers. In 1861 the Commanding Officer of the 36th Middlesex (Paddington) R.V.C., Major-General Downing, was openly criticised in the *Paddington Newsman* by his officers. His successor, Lt.-Col. Wood, received the same treatment in the *Paddington Times* in April 1868. In April 1864 two officers came to blows in the 48th Middlesex R.V.C., and in the same year Captain Chapman was dismissed from the 3rd Durham R.V.C. for gross insubordination when he was passed over for promotion.

Such cases continued to occur as, for example, in the 1st Bucks. A.B. in 1874 when there were bitter exchanges in the County press between Owen Wethered and Captain W.H. Cutler, who resented his passing over for promotion to the vacant majority. With only fines and, at most, the power of dismissal (to which was attached a certain amount of public stigma) the Volunteer officer had to rely upon what Alfred Gilbey called an appeal 'to all that is best in human nature'.[10] Thus in December 1860, Major-General Downing of the 36th Middlesex appealed to his men to avoid insubordination as 'one of the worst qualities appertaining to any man who attempts to gain the honourable position of a good soldier; in quarters it will cause confusion and disgrace, in the field it may cause the lives of many to be in jeopardy if not lost'.[11] Discipline had to be gradually instilled, largely by example, and Owen Wethered's account of how one such problem was overcome in the 1st Bucks. (Marlow) R.V.C. is worth recording at length:

> I well remember that soon after we commenced our nightly drills my brother came to my home one evening on his way to drill and said, "look here, Owen: I notice that, when I give the word 'fall in' many of the men fall in with their pipes in their mouths. Now I am sure that can't be right, so I want you to fall in tonight with your pipe in your mouth. I shall then pitch into you, and after that I can blow up anyone else who does it" . . . I was roundly pitched into — and after that evening pipes were duly pocketed at the fall in.[12]

The most frequent contact between the Regulars and the Volunteers was when the former acted in official capacities at Volunteers' inspections, sham fights and reviews. Such contacts do not appear to have improved the Regulars' opinion of the Volunteers in the early years of the Movement. Volunteers generally considered that the inspection system was 'egregiously wrong' in that Inspectors neither tested real efficiency nor appeared to know the contents of the 'Green Book'. Many Regular Inspectors were either excessively polite or completely lacked tact as in the case of the Inspector of the Bucks. Volunteers in 1863, who 'left us in no doubt as to his sentiments towards us and conspicuously failed to gain our affection'.[13] In either case it was unlikely that such a 'one-day man', as J.H.A. Macdonald termed Inspectors, could stimulate Volunteer energy in the right direction. Sham fights and reviews, as noted in the third chapter, often resolved themselves into social occasions or public spectacles. As such, few outside the Volunteer Force regarded them in a favourable light, Sidney Herbert writing to the Duke of Cambridge in February 1861 that he felt their value 'very doubtful beyond amusing the Volunteers'.[14] It was also unfortunate that some of the worst instances of Volunteer indiscipline occurred at such public performances. In August 1861, for example, Earl de Grey was forced to issue a circular condemning the firing of rifles out of railway carriage windows after reviews. At the Easter review at Guildford in March 1864, the 18th Hants. (Basingstoke) R.V.C. refused to be broken up to reinforce other units and the corps was ordered to be disbanded despite efforts by the people of Basingstoke to save the unit and thereby their own prestige.[15]

Considerable confusion and indiscipline was caused at the Windsor review in June 1868 when trains were delayed at Datchet railway station, Thomas Hughes restoring some semblance of order to the affair. This resulted in questions in the Commons and the disbanding of the 9th Essex R.V.C. and the 2nd Herts. (Watford) R.V.C., though this was later rescinded.[16] In a lighter vein the worst incident in Bucks. occurred at the Stowe field day in October 1875 when, by mistake, the Volunteers were plied with neat port as refreshment:

> I shall never forget the march down the long Stowe Avenue, and I trust that I shall never see such a sight again. Man after man staggered to the roadside, where they lay like logs and for these we impressed farm waggons in which they were conveyed to the station like corpses. Many others could just keep their feet, and for these we detailed men to help them along. At least half the Battalion were out of the ranks, either incapable or helping along incapables, so that our march through the streets of Buckingham was the reverse of triumphal.[17]

On the other hand, at the Easter review at Dover in March 1869 the Volunteers, who had been allowed to disperse to local taverns by Sir James Hope Grant in view of bad weather, reassembled remarkably quickly when the Duke of Cambridge ordered their recall. It must be said that the reviews were often unrealistic as, for example, at Portsmouth in 1868, when a train passed between opposing troops. At Brighton on one occasion one unit executed a flanking attack under cover of the crowds of spectators. General Erskine remarked that 'the troops are so penned in by their friends that they cannot possibly see their enemies'.[18] However, it must also be remembered that the drill, upon which the manoeuvres were based and judged, was itself anachronistic.

Opinions upon the value of the Volunteer Force were also conditioned by the performance of Auxiliary troops abroad. Volunteers had done well in Italy, New Zealand and Canada but it was the setbacks which were seen as the more significant. Thus Volunteers could argue that the Confederate Army, which it was claimed was less well disciplined than the Volunteer Force, had had considerable success. However, as the Prince Consort wrote to the Earl of

Ellenborough in November 1861, America showed both the advantages and disadvantages of irregular troops. In particular, the rout of the Union Army, also largely composed of untrained volunteers, at Bull Run in July 1861 was seen as more indicative of the likely fate of Volunteers in the field than the success of the Confederates in the same battle. British observers of the American Civil War, such as Colonel Henry Fletcher or Charles Chesney, took little note of tactical developments but they did stress the need for trained officers and sound discipline in Volunteer forces. The defeat of Garibaldi's Army at Mentana on 3 November 1867 was taken as further proof of the weakness of untrained auxiliaries pitted against trained troops, although both Lord Elcho and Earl Spencer argued that Mentana was not applicable to the British Volunteer Force. Similarly, the collapse of the French Garde Mobile and other irregular units in the Franco-Prussian War provided the basis for further attacks in the press on the efficiency of the Volunteer Force.[19]

To a certain extent the criticism by Regular officers and by the military journals was also conceived in a spirit of narrow professionalism if not quite professional jealousy. There were some fears expressed by both Yeomanry and Militia, as well as by Regular officers, that the existence of the Volunteer Force would either interfere with their own recruiting or be used by a government as an excuse for economy. These fears proved unfounded and Volunteers continued to stress that the Volunteer Force was recruited from elements who would enter neither the Militia nor the Regular Army — indeed that they would resign rather than allow their existence to be used against the interests of the Regular Army. There was one long standing dispute between the City of London Volunteer Committee and the Honourable Artillery Company over the use by Volunteers of the Finsbury drill ground, leased by the H.A.C. The Volunteers claimed they were entitled to its use as the true successors of the Trained Bands. The matter was raised in Parliament by Sir John Lubbock in 1873, 1874, 1875 and 1889 but, on each occasion, the Government of the day declined to intervene.[20]

The clearest example of 'professionalism' on the part of the Regular Army was the refusal to accept that Volunteer field artillery was a feasible possibility. Captain Darby of the 3rd Sussex A.V., a former M.P. for Sussex, conceived the idea of Volunteer position batteries armed with smooth-bore guns and pulled by agricultural horses. The theory was put into practice at the Easter review in 1862 by the 1st Middlesex A.V., who contracted with Messrs. Pickford to supply the horses. The concept was welcomed by the Royal Commission in 1862 and field-guns became a feature of the Easter reviews, earning the praise of Sir Robert Walpole at Brighton in 1865. However, most Regulars still considered that Volunteers had neither the time nor the ability to learn the use of field-guns. There was growing criticism beginning in the *Army and Navy Gazette* in 1866 and continuing with attacks by the 'Military Critic' of *The Times*, Captain (later Major-General) C.B. Brackenbury, who considered that field artillery was beyond the capacity of Volunteers. This was followed by criticism by the 'Military Correspondent' of *The Times* in 1869 and by Sir James Hope Grant at the Easter review in 1871. Despite the argument put forward in defence of Volunteer field artillery by such as Lord Elcho, Henry Allhusen of the 1st Newcastle A.V. and Lt.-Col. Shakespear of the 1st Middlesex A.V., Cardwell refused to allow the upkeep of horses, harness and field-guns to be paid from the capitation grant. Increasing expense spelt the end of the field artillery arm. The 1st Newcastle A.V. were forced to sell their 9 pdr. Armstrongs in April 1871 and in the same year the 1st Middlesex A.V. merged into the 1st London A.V. Subsequently the first Mobilisation Scheme of 1875 revealed crippling deficiencies in the number of Royal Artillery field batteries available for home defence.[21]

In the light of the many instances of Volunteer inefficiency both at home and abroad, and the certain amount of prejudice entertained against such amateur forces, it was not surprising that the Volunteer Force was subjected to much criticism in the military journals and the press generally. Most of the criticism, notably that in the *Pall Mall Gazette* and the *United Services Gazette* was levelled at Volunteer officers who were commonly described as the 'weak point' of the Force, a view shared by Engels in his articles for the *Volunteer Journal for Lancashire and Cheshire*.[22] The climax of the press campaign against the Volunteer Force was reached in the period between 1868 and 1871 and was marked by the attacks of the 'Military Critic' in *The Times* in 1868, by the 'Military Correspondent' of *The Times* and by *The Times* correspondent, 'Hippophylax', in 1869. The campaign was given added impetus in 1871 by the critical report on the Brighton review by Sir James Hope Grant. On the whole the reports upon the Easter Reviews had been satisfactory in former years, although Sir John Pennefather had recommended steadier drill in 1864 and Sir George Buller had criticised 'slovenly' movements in 1868. Hope Grant, however, was extremely critical of Volunteer drill and discipline and the 'ignorance' of the officers and he recommended that the reviews be discontinued.[23]

It is clear that many Regular officers remained unconvinced of the capabilities of the Volunteer Force and this can be detected in their consideration of the proper role to be played by the Force in national defence.

The Role of the Amateur: The Professional View

In 1869 only the two former Inspector-Generals of Volunteers, McMurdo and Erskine, seriously considered that the Volunteers could be utilised in the field against an invading Army and even then only after a period of continuous training. The more general view was that held by Captain H. Schaw, Professor of Artillery and Fortification at the Staff College, who maintained in June 1870 that the Volunteers were only fit for garrison duties.[24] Some of what may be termed the more 'intellectual' Regulars did forsee that the Volunteers might be utilised. In a series of lectures to Volunteer officers held at the Royal United Service Institution in February and March 1873, three lecturers spoke of a larger role for the Volunteers — Lt. Frederick Maurice, winner of the Wellington prize essay in 1872; Major Knollys, Garrison Instructor of the Home District, and Captain Robert Home, attached to the Topographical and Statistical Branch at the War Office. Maurice, though stressing the need for Volunteers to acquire 'habits' of discipline, considered that the Volunteers could release the Regular Army for service abroad, whereas Knollys believed that the Volunteers could retard the progress of an invasion in a partisan role. Home, speaking on 'The Recent War (Franco-Prussian) with reference to Militia and Volunteers', dismissed the charges then current that the Volunteers would prove as inefficient as the French Garde Mobile, and insisted that the Volunteer Force must assist the Regular Army in the event of an invasion.[25] However, in the first Mobilisation Scheme drawn up by Home in 1875, only 40,000 Volunteers, or roughly one quarter of the Force, were utilised and all in garrisons. Some Volunteers such as Owen Wethered and Lt.-Col. Birt of the 5th Essex R.V.C. considered that garrison duty would enable the Volunteers to acquire a greater efficiency but there was bitter disappointment at the small role allocated to the Volunteer Force. As Lord Elcho discovered, there was a likelihood that the Volunteers would be used in the field around local defensive positions. It was further revealed to the Bury Departmental Committee in 1878 that coastal brigades of Volunteers were now contemplated with one quarter of the inland Volunteers in garrison. The Metropolitan Volunteers, for example, were allocated to the entrenched camp at Tilbury, the remainder of the Volunteer Force acting as reliefs for the garrisons.[26]

Even this comparatively limited role was criticised and doubts about the value of the Volunteer Force remained in many quarters. In 1877, for example, General Stephenson turned in a critical report on the Dunstable review, but much of the criticism came from younger Regular officers. Ian Hamilton, them a subaltern in India, had written to his brother after spending a night out on the snow at over 16,000 feet with no shelter in May 1876; 'I wonder what some of our Volunteers who make such a fuss about camping out at Wimbledon would say to it'? Similarly, at a lecture to the R.U.S.I. by Col. Harrison, R.E., A.A.G. at Aldershot, in July 1885, several younger Regulars voiced the opinion that the Volunteers were not only unfit for war but might not turn up at all in the event of an invasion. In March 1890 Captain Walter Adye of the Royal Irish Rifles, who was to gain a certain notoriety in Volunteer circles after the South African War, criticised the training and the officers of the Volunteer Force in his lecture to the Royal United Service Institution.[27] C.E. Callwell, R.A., was another younger officer with a misplaced contempt for the amateur officer:

> You got the impression, indeed, that all Artillery Volunteer Officers were solicitors or barristers, if they weren't worse; for they were as clever as monkeys in putting posers about points of no interest or consequence, and they gloried in finding the poor Regular officer unable to answer them off hand.[28]

However, the official view of the Volunteer Force and its role in national defence was increasingly tempered by the growing contact between Volunteers and Regulars and by considerations of official necessity.

The Cardwell reforms were partly designed, of course, to effect greater co-operation between the Regular Army and the Auxiliary Forces, but this largely depended upon the inclinations of the G.O.C.s of Districts and, especially, the O.C.s of the new Sub-Districts. The O.C.s were theoretically charged with correcting and advising Volunteer Commanding Officers upon defects in drill, discipline, inspection and internal economy but it is clear that many did not take sufficient interest in the Volunteers under their supervision. The 1st Bucks. V.B., for example, saw little of the O.C. Sub-District based at Oxford, and when the Battalion arrived at Port Meadow in pouring rain for the first brigade drill in May 1877 it was over an hour before an orderly sergeant appeared to inform Wethered that the drill had been cancelled: 'The authorities at Cowley Barracks had forgotten all about us.'[29] A lecture on March 1879 by Lt. Col. Sprot, O.C. 47th Sub-District, on how the Volunteers could make the best use of their limited time, was the exception rather than the rule.[30] In this sense localisation can be said to have largely failed and its logical successor, territorialisation, proved equally unsuccessful in promoting closer co-operation.[31]

Nevertheless, there were some Regular officers in positions of responsibility who proved particularly sympathetic to the Volunteers — Col. Henry Fletcher; Lord Abinger, Lt.-Col. of the Scots Fusilier Guards, 1874-78; Lt.-Gen. Prince Edward of Saxe-Weimar, G.O.C. Southern District, 1878-84; Maj.-Gen. W.G. Cameron, G.O.C. Northern District, 1881-84 and Maj.-Gen. Sir George Higginson, G.O.C. Home District, 1878-85.[32] Higginson, whose close co-operation with the Metropolitan Commanding Officers was noted in the previous chapter, allowed Volunteer officers to attend war games at the Horse Guards in November 1883. He also supervised the Easter marching columns revived in 1881. It had been the custom at the old Easter review before 1872 for the troops to march part of the way to the venue. The idea of marching columns on a more systematic basis was conceived by Col. Drew of the 1st London E.V. and executed with the aid of Higginson and his A.A.G., Col. Methuen, who arranged for the billeting and supply of the men. The Easter marching column became a popular event in such regiments as the Artist Rifles and the London Scottish, who organised a march through Scotland in August 1898 covering 123½ miles in a week. Higginson had also persuaded the Duke of Cambridge to allow Metropolitan Volunteers to line the route on the occasion of Queen Victoria reviewing Wolseley's troops on their return from Egypt in November 1882.[33]

Much continued to depend upon those Regular officers prepared to assiste the Volunteers, such as Higginson's successor, Maj.-Gen. R. Gipps (later D.A.G. for the Militia, Yeomanry and Volunteers, 1891-92) who allowed the Volunteers to take part in winter field-sketching and reconnaisance exercises in October 1884. Another was Lt.-Gen. Sir George Willis, Prince Edward's successor at Southern District, who supervised Sir William Humphery's transport experiments with the 1st V.B. Hants. in August 1885.[34] Captain G.F.R. Henderson's *Campaign of Fredericksburg* (1886) was specifically intended as a text book for Volunteer officers to improve their practical and theoretical training. Henderson considered that military history was the best substitute for combat experience and that, if the Volunteers studied with intelligence, they would take the correct action instinctively.[35] Evelyn Wood gave preference to the Volunteers on the Aldershot ranges in 1890 because of the limited time at their disposal.

Such consideration as shown by these Regular officers, and I.G.A.F.'s such as Elkington, who made a point of attending as many Volunteer prize givings as possible, and Maj.-Gen. A.J. Lyon Fremantle (D.A.G. as I.G.A.F. 1886-91) was greatly appreciated by the

Volunteers.[36] At lower levels, too, there was growing contact between Regulars and Volunteers as, for example, at the short-lived autumn manoeuvres which were partly arranged with the co-operation of Robert Loyd-Lindsay. There was a cordial relationship between Regulars and Volunteers at the manoeuvres, even though J.H.A. Macdonald considered that there was a fatal tendency to take for granted that the Regulars could brush aside Volunteers without regard for the tactical situation. Only comparatively small numbers of Volunteers attended these manoeuvres (4,000 in 1872) and Volunteers were not admitted to the summer drills which took place from 1874 onwards, but there were contacts at brigade camps and the courses of instruction undertaken by Volunteer officers at such venues as Aldershot, Shoeburyness and Chatham. The lectures to Volunteer officers at the Royal United Service Institution, given by leading Regular theorists such as Capt. H. MacGregor, former Professor of Military History at the R.M.C., Sandhurst, and Captain Henry Brackenbury, Professor of Military History at the R.M.A., Woolwich, and first organised by Captain Flood-Page (Adjutant of the London Scottish, 1861-73) in February 1872, were a further sign that Regular officers were prepared to assist the Volunteers.[37]

Generally, the Volunteers considered that their steady improvement and the growing contact between Regulars and Volunteers was winning the goodwill of the Regular Army; indeed, the Hon. J.C. Dormer told Henry Spenser Wilkinson that he had only accepted the appointment of D.A.G. as I.G.A.F. in 1885 because of the improvement in the Force during his absence in Egypt. [38] It was, however, growing official necessity which brought a greater role for the Volunteer Force in national defence.

The first indication of this necessity was the Eastern Crisis of 1876-78. It was envisaged that the degree of British military support required to maintain the Turks against the advancing Russians would certainly entail the embodiment of the Militia for garrison duties in Britain, Ireland and the Mediterranean and possibly the calling out of the Volunteer Force. In his memorandum, 'Preparing for War with Russia', in March 1878 Wolseley went as far as to advocate the employment of Volunteers commanded by retired Regulars in his imaginative, if hardly practicable, scheme to launch British forces into the Baltic, the Balkans and the Khanates. In the event the considerable deficiencies in the Army Reserve, the legal difficulties of employing Volunteers abroad and the sheer lack of sufficient resources to wage a major war against Russia made such planning largely academic. Indeed, in July 1878 Wolseley, in what the Duke of Cambridge termed 'an able but hastily written' submission to the

Bury Departmental Committee,* modified his earlier opinions considerably. He now rejected the idea of Volunteers entering into a commitment to serve abroad for fear that any such commitment would adversely affect Volunteer recruitment. Col. Henry Fletcher had expressed the view at the R.U.S.I. in 1877 that foreign service would prove a great stimulus to the Volunteer Force but most Regulars including the Duke of Cambridge and McMurdo agreed with Wolseley.[39] Yet in August 1882 two officers and one hundred men from the 24th (formerly 49th) Middlesex (Post Office) R.V.C. sailed for Egypt to perform the duties of an Army Post Office Corps. The Corps was authorised by Hugh Childers on 22 July 1882 following the recommendation of a Committee on the lack of a proper postal organisation and the likely cost of employing civilian personnel. Some of the men actually came under fire at Kassassin on 9 September 1882 and Wolseley praised their efforts in the campaign: 'Their services have been so valuable that I hope a similar Corps may be employed on any future occasion on which it may be necessary to despatch an expeditionary force from this country.' The War Office had also contemplated sending detachments of Volunteer Engineers, but the campaign ended before arrangements could be made.[40] Following the 'triumphal return' of the Volunteers from Egypt, which earned the 24th Middlesex the rare Volunteer battle honour of 'Egypt 1882', Lt.-Col. du Plat Taylor formed two Field Telegraph companies in January 1883. The War Office authorised a Field Telegraph Corps in 1884 drawn from these companies and in March 1885 one officer and twenty men from the Post Office Corps and twelve men from the Field Telegraph Corps were sent to Suakin. On the initiative of Sir Andrew Clarke, Inspector-General of Fortifications from 1882-86, some forty men drawn from the 1st Newcastle and Durham E.V. and the 1st Lancashire E.V. also went to Suakin with the 10th Coy., Royal Engineers, to undertake railway work.[41]

Thus Volunteers had proved useful auxiliaries to the Regular Army on active service, and Clarke further utilised Volunteer Engineers to make up some of the deficiences in the numbers of Royal Engineers available to man submarine mining defences in mercantile ports. The first experiments were conducted on the Tyne with the 1st Newcastle and Durham E.V., commanded by Lt.-Col. C.M. Palmer, M.P., in February 1884 and the system was successfully extended to the Tay,

* The bulk of Wolseley's submission was devoted, however, to an attack upon the dress of the Regular Army, 'more suitable for the stage than for active service', and the practice of carrying colours in action. As a result of pressure from the Duke of Cambridge the offending passages were omitted from the report printed in the Blue Book of evidence to the Committee.

Forth, Humber, Tees, Clyde, Mersey, Severn and Falmouth port defences.[42] Similarly, both the Duke of Cambridge and Wolseley, now Adjutant-General, realised the value of encouraging the Volunteers to set up their own regimental transport. They therefore urged the Government not to suspend the transport experiments begun by Sir William Humphery of the 1st V.B. Hants, in view of the crippling deficiences in transport available for the Regular Army:

> Here is an opportunity of providing at least one Battalion in our Home Army with Transport and we are disposed to put the papers on the subject in a pigeon-hole because it would add a few more men to the strength of the Battalion for whom, when they had become efficient drivers, the normal capitation grant would be drawn. There seems also to be some supposition that possibly by and by this system, if authorised, might lead to further demands being made upon the annual Army Estimates.[43]

Above all, in the 1880s what may be termed the 'Home Army' school, led by Wolseley and his mentors, such as Maurice and Henry Brackenbury, was increasingly embattled, firstly by those advocating the shifting of the centre of gravity in Imperial strategy to India, and secondly by those domestic politicians and bureaucrats seeking retrenchment in military expenditure. The reaction of Wolseley and his colleagues to the growing influence of the 'Indians' was to raise the spectre of the possibility of invasion which, in turn, brought them into conflict with the Admiralty and 'Blue Water' school who denounced the invasion theory as essentially bogus. The result of the financial strictures of the sort advocated by Lord Randolph Churchill from 1886-87 was that the plans for home defence had to be drawn up on the basis of what was available rather that what was thought necessary.[44] Conscription of any kind for a Home Army was politically and financially impossible and, in such a situation, there remained only the Volunteers as a viable and cheap 'second line'.

Sir Edward Hamley had been one of the first to acknowledge the need to press the Volunteers into use as a second line in view of what he conceived to be the increasingly hostile posture of Europe towards Britain. In his article for *Nineteenth Century* in March 1885 and the subsequent debate at the R.U.S.I. Hamley foresaw the Volunteer Force providing two-thirds of the Home defensive Army. He was careful to stress however, that the Force required more money, equipment and encouragement to render it effective. Hamley only saw the Volunteers as a defensive force in garrisons and indeed suggested that they should only be trained to fire at a maximum range of 300 yards. In particular, Hamley was concerned for the safety of

London and advocated a garrison of 60,000 Volunteers holding a line of entrenched positions and forts around the capital where they could be trained 'in situ' during peace. The Mobilisation Scheme evolved between September and December 1886 by Henry Brackenbury (D.A.Q.M.G., Intelligence Division 1886, A.A.G. Mobilisation 1887 and D.M.I. from 1888-1891) with the aid of Ralph Thompson, Captain Percy Lake and Major F.W. Stopford, utilised only 97 Volunteer battalions out of the 209 available. The large scale use of Volunteers in garrisons was restriced by the need to avoid disrupting trade and business before an actual invasion. Brackenbury further considered that the Volunteer Force was in excess of requirements but that any financial saving would be too slight to justify reduction and would create discontent in the Force as a whole. Some 21,000 Volunteers were allocated to the defence of London, but there was no decision on exactly how they should be utilised. Brackenbury had recognised that Volunteers could supply the deficiencies in fortress and submarine mining companies. In February 1887 Stanhope gave notice that the Volunteers must fill the gaps in the Mobilisation Scheme, to which end the raising of 21 Volunteer batteries of position and 10 new Submarine Mining companies was authorised in February 1888.[45]

Colonel (later Major-General) John Ardagh, charged with the arrangements for the defence of the United Kingdom in 1887, took a more favourable view of the capabilities of the Volunteer Force than Brackenbury. Indeed, in January 1888 Ardagh proposed exercises 'in situ' for the Metropolitan Volunteers but these were ruled out by Stanhope on the grounds of expense. Ardagh's memorandum 'On the Defence of England', dated 17 April 1888 and accepted by the War Office Council on 30 April, became the basis of a revised Mobilisation Scheme. Ardagh considered that the Volunteer coastal brigades proposed by Home in 1875 were no longer practicable and would simply 'fritter away' men on the beaches. He now proposed that eighteen Volunteer brigades of six battalions each should be placed in six large entrenched camps at Aldershot, Caterham, Chatham, Tilbury, Warley and Epping, connected into a continuous defensive line. The brigades, determined simply by the number of battalions available after garrisons had been told off, would thus occupy a line between the two Regular Army Corps, operating to the south of the chalk escarpment of the Weald and Kent and the defences of London. There were objections from Hamley that the proposed camps were not only too far apart but too far from London. By contrast Ardagh considered that the scheme had not only defined the formerly vague notion of the role of the Volunteers in an invasion but had placed them under the most favourable conditions and in the strongest positions which could be found for them. Only one-third of the Volunteer Force would be utilised before actual invasion for fear of disrupting business. Ardagh expressed a desire for the changes in the Volunteer Act proposed by Stanhope's National Defence Bill, but he was also well aware of the problem facing the Volunteers and laid down instructions for the command, training and equipment of the new brigade system, which he hoped would be allowed to develop unhurried. Unfortunately, the equipment required for the brigades became the subject of Wolseley's controversial equipment order in May 1889 which caused, as was seen in previous chapter, so much disarray in the Volunteer Force. Like Stanhope, Ardagh considered that the greatest danger to England was lack of preparation: 'It may be said shortly that, although the ultimate object of calling out the Volunteer Force is the repulse and defeat of an invader, the immediate aim is by antecedent organisation to render the success of an invasion so improbable that it may never be attempted.'[46]

In a further memorandum entitled 'The Defence of London' and dated 16 July 1888, Ardagh suggested that the most economical method of defending the capital would be by Volunteers manning fortified positions. A War Office Committee headed by Wolseley proposed thirty-four such positions in November 1888 and, under the Imperial Defence Loan, some thirteen sites were purchased in addition to three sites already under development. By January 1889 all Volunteer battalions were told off into garrisons or mobile brigades except a few University, school and isolated units and, similarly, the Volunteer batteries of position had been allocated to brigades or local defence. In August 1889 Fleetwood Wilson wrote to Ardagh, now private secretary to the Viceroy: 'Nothing could work better than the Brigade system and I warmly congratulate you on a plan which meets with universal approval.'[47] The same could not be said for the fortifications around London. Although the War Office threw its energies into the scheme for the defence of London, Gerald Ellison of the War Office Mobilisation Section noting that the scheme filled the picture 'to the exclusion of all other considerations' when he joined A.G.7 in 1890, the strategic debate had been won on the one hand by the 'Blue Water School' and on the other by the 'Indians'.[48] As a result, Stanhope's 'Storehouses' were destined to remain uncompleted. Yet, whatever the faults in the War Office arguments and whatever motives underlaid the employment of the Volunteers, the Volunteer Force had, nonetheless, attained an important place in the national defences. If there was now more willingness to assist the Volunteer Force on the part of the Regular Army, this did not, of course, mean that more financial resources would be forthcoming. In such a situation much still depended upon the efforts of the Volunteers to fit themselves for a role in national defence, but views as to what that role should be were conflicting.

The Role of the Amateur: The Amateur View

It is possible to detect two distinct schools of thought within the Volunteer Force upon the direction which the Volunteers should take. The first 'school', largely comprising the first generation of Volunteer officers, was well aware of the limitations of a civilian and voluntary Force. The second group, which became known as the 'Advanced School', welcomed greater commitments as the price of greater integration with the Regular Army without regard for the crucial factors such as time and employers. The 'Advanced School' did not come to the forefront until the later 1870's but there were progressive elements in the Volunteer Force from the very beginning.

The forerunner of the 'Advanced School' was Lord Ranelagh, who headed, as Elcho later recalled:

> the — as some of us thought — too go-ahead party in our Force, in the sense of wishing to act independently of military official author-ity. While others, of whom I was one, endeavoured to retain our autonomy but to act, in hearty union with, and in dependence upon, the authority whose approval we sought to gain for all our projects, as, indeed without their help we were powerless; and success depended on their hearty sympathy, encouragement and support.[49]

Ranelagh, with an uncertain temperament coupled with his experi-ence of irregular warfare, was deeply distrustful of the ability of Regular officers to realise the capabilities of the Volunteer Force. As a result he was convinced that the Volunteer Force should remain independent of military control in any form and he became suspicious and resentful of any attempt on the part of those at the Horse Guards to intervene in Volunteer affairs. In November 1860 Ranelagh sug-gested to Elcho, following a successful sham fight at Chislehurst during the summer, that the Metropolitan Volunteers should hold a review at Brighton on Easter Monday 1861. This would test transport facilities for large bodies of men in a short time and the conduct of the Volunteers in transit. However, Elcho and Lord Bury took the view that it was too early to undertake any projects on such an extensive scale and it would be better to hold a review nearer to London. As a result on 30 March 1861, while Bury lead a contingent of Metropolitan Volunteers to Wimbledon, Ranelagh took between 4 and 5,000 Volunteers to Brighton. The first Easter review was a success even though some men arrived at Brighton with no weapons owing to the fact that their units had chosen to go to Wimbledon.[50]

The dispute between what Engels contemptuously termed 'London generals' prompted the Duke of Cambridge to reflect that the Volunteers were attempting to run before they could walk. It led to a stormy meeting of the Metropolitan Commanding Officers on 20 April 1861 at which it was decided that Regular officers should be invited to command at future reviews. Ranelagh accepted the judgement of the Metropolitan C.O.'s and attended the Easter review at Brighton in 1862, presided over by Lord Clyde, but, on 9 June 1862 at Panshanger, he quarrelled with an officer sent by the Horse Guards to supervise the sham fight using what Sir George Lewis termed 'disrespectful expressions' towards the War Office and the Horse Guards. In February 1863 Ranelagh was again accused of dictating to the Metropolitan C.O.'s on the choice of venue for Easter and in January 1868 he caused further controversy by calling the Volunteer Force a 'sham'. There was some confusion over his actual meaning, for which Ranelagh blamed the *Volunteer Service Gazette* with whose editor, J.C. Templer, he had not spoken since the dispute of 1861. But at a speech on 8 February 1868 he indicated that the Volunteer Force was a 'sham' as an Army and he called for one to be created: 'I hold that the Volunteers should form a distinct and separate force from the Army.'[51] This was clearly impracticable and those of a progressive nature who followed Ranelagh were not so much concerned with creating a separate Army as with assimilating the Volunteer Force to the Regular Army. Ranelagh's idea was largely discarded, although Lt.-Col. Eyre of 1st Notts. A.B., a conscriptionist, revived it in 1874. As late as 1882 Lord Truro, who had supported Ranelagh in 1861-62, still clung to the idea of a separate Volunteer Army.[52]

The majority of the older Volunteer officers were well aware of the practical difficulties of Volunteer discipline, as Sir Thomas Acland wrote in 1868:

> Volunteers, for want of time, cannot form military habits; but they may be inspired by a military spirit, and they may end where the soldier begins, by absolute obedience, that obedience being willingly rendered from a matured conviction of its necessity.[53]

As a result, the Mutiny Act was strongly resisted in 1871, especially by Charles Lindsay, as inapplicable to a body of men who were not only unpaid but capable of resigning on fourteen days' notice, which negated the penal clauses essentially designed to combat desertion from the Regular Army. However, officers entering the Force after

1871 saw the solution to Volunteer inefficiency in more organisation, more discipline and inevitably more commitment on the part of the Volunteer. Such men, who formed the new 'Advanced School', were usually either young subalterns, such as Lt. George Hoste of the 21st (later 12th) Middlesex (Civil Service) R.V.C. and Captain H.W. Hummell of the 11th (later 6th) Middlesex (St George's) R.V.C. or ex-Regular officers such as Howard Vincent or Lt.-Col. Gore-Browne, former Adjutant of the 49th Foot and Lt.-Col. of the 20th (later 11th) Middlesex (Railway) R.V.C. from 1876 to 1883.[54]

On 13 April 1877 a lecture by Hoste at the Royal United Service Institution was the occasion for the first detailed expression of the views of the 'Advanced School'. Hoste himself concentrated upon the need for a higher brigade organisation but speakers from the floor such as Howard Vincent (then Lt.-Col. of the Central London Rangers), Lt.-Col. Malet and Major Rolleston of the 4th Middlesex R.V.C., called for the Volunteer Force to be officered entirely by ex-Regular officers. On 9 July 1877, in a lecture to the Royal United Service Institution well received by the many Volunteer subalterns in the audience, Hummell called for more discipline and the introduction of minor punishments such as extra drills. There was, in fact, no reason to suppose that ex-Regular officers were especially well qualified to command the Volunteer Force. Many Volunteers argued that there was no guarantee that an ex-Regular could adapt himself to the peculiar conditions of the Volunteer Force and that, in any event, it would be wise to ascertain the reason why such an officer had retired from the Regular Army. On the whole, most Volunteers wished to avoid service in the Volunteer Force being made a condition of retirement from the Regular Army, and it was generally considered that excluding civilian members of the Force from command would be harmful.[55]

The argument used against the call for more discipline derived from long standing experience of Volunteer conditions. At the Volunteer Conference held at the Royal United Service Institution in January 1878 most speakers were either in favour of the continued application of the Mutiny Act to the Volunteer Force, which was rarely utilised, or at least they expressed no objections. The Bury Departmental Committee found no desire to introduce tougher discipline: in reply to the circulars 210 corps considered that disciplinary powers were sufficient, while only 75 corps considered more powers necessary; 257 corps felt dismissal effective while only 14 corps felt it served no purpose. The Committee concluded: 'It would appear that any lack of discipline has usually arisen from a want of acquaintance with military usages, which will be remedied by a more frequent association with the Regular Forces.' The Bury Departmental report and the Army Discipline Act of 1879 did not meet the wishes of the 'Advanced School'. Their theories on discipline and officers remained in the background, being occasionally revived as in 1885 when Gore-Browne published a pamphlet advocating the command of Volunteer battalions by serving Regular officers.[56] However, the thoughts of most Volunteers were rapidly turning towards more practical considerations, such as the military education of Volunteer officers and the means to make up the deficiencies in the Volunteer Force. In this the more progressive Volunteers were to play an important role.

The military education of Volunteer officers was one major area in which the Volunteers were left largely to their own devices. Before Cardwell instituted the certificate of proficiency for N.C.O.'s and officers in 1870, the instruction of officers in their duties had rested with the Adjutant and his staff. Junior officers rarely had the chance to drill their own companies as, naturally, the Commanding Officer took precedence on the comparatively few occasions when the Battalion was assembled. The attachments of officers to Line or Militia regiments at least guaranteed sufficient number of disciplined men with which an officer could work. Cardwell's certificates, which became compulsory in 1872, were regarded as an additional burden which might deter men from joining the Volunteers. Indeed, in July 1873, Charles Lindsay called the certificates a harassing and unnecessary ordeal. The schools of instruction, which granted the certificates, were themselves far from satisfactory as they taught only the contents of the drill book which an officer could just as well learn on his own drill ground. There was no instruction in tactics or even interior economy and acquaintance with the ordinary duties of an officer had to be picked up at camps and manoeuvres. Yet most Volunteer C.O.'s expressed themselves satisfied with the schools and the Bury Departmental Committee considered there was sufficient provision for the military education of Volunteer officers.[57]

In February 1881 Henry Spenser Wilkinson and six fellow officers of the 2nd Manchester R.V.C. (successively the 28th, 33rd and 20th Lancs.) formed the Manchester Tactical Society to apply their drill and other training to the actual problems of war by way of discussions, tactical exercises, tactical excursions and wargames. In July 1881 Wilkinson wrote a memorandum suggesting a voluntary examination on tactical theory based on Major Wilkinson Shaw's *Elements of Modern Tactics*, which had been specially produced for Auxiliary officers as part of a series supervised by Lt.-Col. C.B. Brackenbury, then a Superintendent of Garrison Instruction. The merit of the examination, which would be rewarded with an appropriate letter in the Army List, was that it would stimulate military study at practically no cost, whereas a central school for Volunteer officers on the model of the Kingston School of Gunnery in Canada, as suggested by the *Volunteer Service Gazette*, would prove expensive. The memorandum, supported by Wilkinson and his colleagues in the press, was submitted to Hugh Childers in December 1881 by Henry Summers, Liberal M.P. for Stalybridge, and authorised in January 1882 for officers of the rank of captain and above.[58] The initial reaction to the examination, which was opened to subalterns in 1884, was enthusiastic as indicated in the following table — 18:

Table 18
Results of the Tactical Examination, 1882-1885

		Entrants	**Pass**	**Fail**
June	1882	398	360	38
January	1883	172	141	31
January	1884 — Senior	91	62	29
	— Junior	145	106	39
July	1884 — Senior	37	28	9
	— Junior	70	47	23
July	1885 — Senior	35	28	7
	— Junior	68	48	20

The examination in 1882 and 1883 was open only to officers of the rank of captain and above. From January 1884 captains and field officers took the senior examination and subalterns the junior examination. In each case the figures include a relatively small proportion of Militia and Yeomanry officers who also took the examinations. In 1882, for example, 20 Militia and 7 Yeomanry officers took the examination. The Director-General of Military Education, Sir Beauchamp Walker, who was responsible for the administration of the examination, was sufficiently impressed by the results to become a supporter of the Volunteer Force.[59]

Wargames became popular as a result of the tactical examinations and other areas followed Manchester's lead in forming Tactical Societies. In 1887 the West of Scotland Tactical Society was formed in Glasgow and West Riding Tactical Society at Bradford in 1885, the same year in which Lieutenants Horsley and Todd of the Artists Rifles designed special wargames equipment for sale by the *Volunteer Service Gazette*. By 1894 over 1,400 Volunteer officers had passed the tactics examination, but interest seemed to be declining and only 60 officers had passed the examinations in military topography, military law and field fortifications opened to the Volunteers in 1889, only 12 passing in all three subjects. By the 1890's, although the value of Tactical

Societies was fully recognised, Volunteers such as Lt.-Col. T. Sturmy Cave (Lt.-Col. of 1st V.B. Hants.), and Lt.-Col. Eustace Balfour (Lt.-Col. of London Scottish, 1894-1903) favoured more practical outdoor exercises as the best means of training officers in tactics. Their view was shared by Sir Francis Grenfell, who had been impressed by the work of the Arundel Open Air Tactical Association.[60] In the meantime, the Manchester Tactical Society had branched out into the field of publications and the translation of foreign military works such as the German Order of Field Service in 1893. Wilkinson himself was far from happy with the condition of the Volunteer Force. In his *Citizen Soldiers*, articles reprinted from the *Manchester Guardian* in 1883, he declared the Force utterly unfit for war in training, organisation and equipment, and called for a higher standard of musketry, simpler drill and a brigade organisation. Wilkinson considered that the improvements in the Force after 1883 were only caricatures of the reforms he considered necessary and the 1894 edition of *Citizen Soldiers* showed little modification in his views. But, as one recent writer has suggested, what Wilkinson required of the Volunteers would have been hard enough to find in the Regular Army.[61]

The older generation of Volunteers maintained that in their 'contract' with the State they had never undertaken to provide transport or supply facilities for the Volunteer Force, and that it was the duty of the Government to provide such facilities in the event of invasion.[62] The Bury Departmental Committee similarly assumed that the Regular Army would provide all necessary services, but by the mid-1880's many Volunteers began to suspect that the supporting departments of the Regular Army were not sufficiently expansive to serve the needs of the Volunteer Force in war.[63] Although Volunteers still believed that to provide for such contingencies was the duty of the Government, it was felt that it would be better if the Volunteer Force developed its own auxiliary departments to supplement those of the Regular Army and to prevent disaster in a crisis. Some reflected, indeed, that Ranelagh's idea of an independent Volunteer Army had had some merit after all.[64] The Volunteers were used to helping themselves. In 1861, for example, a Volunteer Training Ground and Rifle Range Company was established to buy a site at Sutton with quarters for 1,500 men. Similarly in 1874 a Volunteer Co-operative and General Equipment Company was devised to provide equipment at 20% under current prices. Volunteer departments, too, were not entirely a new concept. In 1865, for example, McMurdo had established the Engineeer and Railway Volunteer Staff Corps, an idea originally suggested by Charles Manby, Secretary to the Institution of Civil Engineers. The corps consisted entirely of officers drawn from civil engineers, labour contractors and railway company managers. It was designed not only to draw up elaborate mobilisation timetables for the transit of the Volunteers and other troops in war, but also to advise the Army on engineering problems and to supply up to 20,000 navvies for work on defensive positions in the event of invasion. The Army itself did not form a railway section until the conversion of the 8th Company, Royal Engineers, in 1882. The corps remained the only organised body able to advise the Army on the technical working and facilities of railways for military purposes until the establishment of the War Railway Council in 1896 under the supervision of the Deputy-Quartermaster-General.[65] The main areas in which supporting services were required were medical services and transport and commissariat facilities.

Sergeant (later Lt.) Andrew Maclure of the London Scottish had begun stretcher companies in the Volunteer Force and had developed a Volunteer Ambulance Department by 1880 but Maclure's organisation, although successful, was merely a motley collection of companies from various regiments. It was James Cantlie, former Assistant Surgeon of the London Scottish, who conceived the idea in 1883 of a Volunteer Medical Staff Corps. Cantlie was able to persuade Wolseley, then Adjutant-General, of the merit of the scheme by parading his embryonic Volunteer Medical Association, drawn from his students at Charing Cross Hospital, at a prize-giving which Wolseley attended at the Hospital on 8 July 1883. The idea spread to other hospitals and Cantlie secured the support of General Hunter of the Army Medical Staff Corps and the D.A.G. acting as I.G.A.F., Elikington, and deputations met the Secretary of State, Hartington. As a result the Volunteer Medical Staff Corps of four companies was authorised on 1 April 1885 with Cantlie as Surgeon-Commandant.[66] The other pressing need was for some form of Volunteer Transport and Commissariat Department, and in February 1885 Lt.-Col. Farrell's 3rd V.B. Royal West Kent attempted to form an ordnance corps. In the same year Captain A.B. Williams of the 2nd V.B. Royal West Kent suggested a transport department and Captain London of the 1st V.B. Essex Regiment suggested a transport conference at the Volunteer Service Club. In August 1885 Humphery began his transport experiment with the 1st V.B. Hants., collecting 21 waggons and horses from local farmers to carry regimental baggage. Stanhope extended these experiments, but little progress was made and, as a result of two Volunteer Transport Committees in 1891 and 1896, the responsibility for the mobility of the Volunteer Force was left to the Commanding Officers of the individual battalions.[67]

The precise role of the Volunteer Force in national defence was also a matter of some controversy between the opposing schools of thought. Leading Volunteers such as Lord Elcho, Charles Lindsay, Walter Barttelot and Sir Arthur Hayter opposed any suggestion that the Volunteers should be used in any other capacity than as a home defence force against invasion. The *Volunteer Service Gazette* agreed that 'We have no more to do with war out of the United Kingdom than the Police Force.'[68] They considered that no Volunteer could undertake in peacetime any commitment of foreign service for the future without prejudicing his civil employment. In any case the employment of Volunteers in any contingency short of actual or apprehended invasion was impossible without special legislation. Nevertheless, as early as December 1861, two Volunteer units, one of which was the 1st Renfrew A.B., offered to serve in Canada following the 'Trent Affair'. This prompted the *Volunteer Service Gazette* to counsel 'in the name of commonsense, and for the sake of our own characters, let us hold our tongues'. Schemes for the use of the Volunteers abroad were put forward by Major (later Lt.-Col.) James Baker of the Queen's Westminsters in 1870, by the correspondent 'H.M.' in 1874 and, as noted earlier, by Colonel Henry Fletcher in 1877. All these schemes involved 'creaming off' an élite picked body from the Volunteers, thus dividing the Force into 'two classes' and running the risk of the home element suffering from comparison with the foreign service men.[69]

The Eastern Crisis brought new interest in the question of foreign service, and by March 1878 the 3rd Lanark, 8th West Yorks, and 20th Middlesex R.V.C. had all offered to serve in home garrisons while the 55th Lancs. R.V.C. offered to go to Gibralter or Malta. 'Advanced School' advocates such as Lt.-Col. Bushby of the Queen's Westminsters and Lt. George Hoste expressed themselves in favour of such offers and a demonstration in Hyde Park in support was only averted by warnings from the G.O.C. Home District and the Under Secretary of State, Lord Bury. Disraeli deprecated any call on the Volunteers but the Government had, as indicated earlier, been forced to at least consider employing Volunteers. It was thus prepared to respond to the pressures by referring the proposal for a 'British Legion of Active Service' drawn from the Volunteers to the Bury Departmental Committee, which was about to begin its work. This particular proposal originated with a meeting at Exeter Hall on 25 April 1878 and a subsequent deputation to the Secretary of State, in which the leading figures were Captain Bedford Pim, R.N., M.P., G.W. Hambledon, Lt.-Gen. Raines, W.W. Forsyth, M.P., Mr Wheelhouse, M.P. and T. Brassey, M.P., later one of the first officers in the Royal Naval Artillery Volunteers. Few witnesses favoured such a new body and the Committee declared itself firmly against the proposal in a preliminary

195

report of July 1878.[70] In the event, of course, no Volunteers were required though individuals continued to appear in various colonial campaigns. In 1874, for example, the Adjutant of the 1st Hants. A.B. was killed in Ashanti. Lt. Villiers of the 24th Middlesex was artist to the *Graphic* in Egypt in 1882 and a sergeant of the same regiment served with Valentine Baker in 1883. Officers from the Leeds Rifles and 5th Surrey R.V.C. served in the Natal Light Horse in Zululand. C.E. Fripp of the Artists Rifles was present during the Zulu War and also represented the *Graphic* at Suakin in 1885, and in 1884 Volunteers were recruited for Col. Methuen's mounted corps in Bechuanaland. Back in 1859 many artisan members of Scottish Corps had joined Garibaldi's 'British Legion' in defiance of the provisions of the Foreign Enlistment Act. In 1863 Volunteers were also warned against joining the Polish Legion contrary to the Act.[71]

By the 1880's the debate had moved to the question of Volunteers serving in the Army Reserve, an idea strongly supported by such as Howard Vincent and Robert Loyd-Lindsay. Loyd-Lindsay, who can be numbered among the more progressive elements of the Volunteer Force, was strongly in favour of closer assimilation to the Regular Army and saw no difficulties in establishing two classes in the Volunteer Force. He had also been a pioneer in the organisation of Volunteer camps. However, once more the scheme was open to objection on the grounds of opposition by employers. There were no such objections to a specific Volunteer Reserve as advocated, for example, by Major Stanley Bird in 1884. The same objection was also not applicable to the 24th Middlesex R.V.C. contingent sent to Egypt in 1882 because they were all Government employees and, as such, guaranteed their jobs on their return. The Volunteer Engineers, who were not in fact sent to Egypt, were enrolled on special engagements carrying automatic discharge from the Army at the end of the campaign. The existing legislation prevented anything but this type of engagement, and even the limited and qualified offers of home garrison service given by Lt.-Col. Lumsden of the London Scottish (Lt.-Col. 1878-1891) and Lord Bury in 1885 could not be accepted.[72] The climate of opinion was still against any major change in Volunteer law when Stanhope introduced his National Defence Bill in 1888 but, by 1895, the Volunteers were in favour of a wider interpretation of their duties. As a result, as was seen in an earlier chapter, the Volunteers (Military Service) Bill enabled Volunteer offers to be accepted after the embodiment of the Militia. This legislation did not, however, enable the Volunteers to serve abroad and hasty provisions would have to be made in 1899. Although considerable progress had been made by 1899, the Volunteer Force was still deficient in officers, equipment, training, field artillery, cavalry and supporting services. What, then, did the Volunteers contribute to the military potential of the British Empire?

The Contribution of the Amateur

The military capacity of a Force which was never called upon to fulfil its *raison d'etre* in resisting an invasion is difficult to gauge. Indeed speculation on such matters is hardly fruitful. However, the value of the Volunteer Force may be measured in other ways. Firstly, contemporaries credited the Volunteers with a number of intangible achievements such as adding strength to the influence of British foreign policy, imbuing the British public with a military spirit and bringing a fresh approach to military problems. Secondly, the Volunteers can be seen to have influenced the Regular Army in a number of important ways.

The influence of the Volunteer Force on foreign diplomats and attachés was alleged, from time to time, by such British politicians as Lord Elcho in 1861; Lord Robert Cecil, M.P., in 1862; Palmerston in 1864; Mr Horsman, M.P., in 1866, Cardwell in 1873 and by Lord Derby as late as 1882.[73] However, the assumption that the existence of the Volunteer Force had increased British prestige in Europe was, to say the least, questionable. Indeed, Palmerston had agreed with Sidney Herbert in November 1859 that to allow any 'raw shop-boys' to visit Paris in Volunteer uniform would destroy any impression in France that the Volunteers were a formidable element of national defence. Garibaldi considered that the Volunteers had rendered England 'impregnable' against invasion but it is clear, from his interview with James Walter in March 1860, that Napoleon III harboured no such illusions of a Force which he felt would be mismanaged by the military authorities.[74] Kaiser Wilhelm II watched a Volunteer review at Long Valley, Aldershot, on 7 August 1889, expressing the opinion that he now realised that the Volunteers were 'really effective soldiers' equal to the Landwehr. One journal considered that this was 'one of the truest and best compliments with which the English Volunteers have hitherto been honoured'. It had apparently been forgotten that the German Chief of Staff, von Moltke, had testified to the vulnerability of England to an invasion in May 1886, an opinion reported at the time in the *Daily Telegraph* and responsible for a fair degree of panic in the Cabinet.[75]

The growth of a military spirit in England as a result of the Volunteer Movement was a favourite theme of Wolseley who considered that the Volunteers had created a 'public opinion' on military matters. Thus the public had been sufficiently interested to both read and understand highly technical accounts of the Austro-Prussian War in 1866. Such a 'military bent' on the part of the public had, in his view, helped to popularise the Army 'and the soldier is now looked upon as one from whom much is to be learnt, as a model to be copied, rather than as a pariah to be despised, which he was before our citizen Army sprang into existence'.[76] In fact, although increasing attention has been paid to militarism in mid- and late-Victorian England, the role of the Auxiliary Forces as a whole has gone unremarked.

Clearly the Volunteer Movement did introduce military affairs to a large number of those, particularly middle class, elements of society previously uninterested in the Army. As noted in the second chapter, a total of 632,911 men had already passed through the ranks of the Volunteers by 1877. Similarly, between 1882 and 1904 a total of 472,924 men who did not subsequently enter the Regular Army passed through the Militia. In this both the Militia and especially the Volunteers were spreading military knowledge through the public at large. Volunteer reviews and parades were as much a public spectacle and pageant as a military exercise and these, too, projected military values to the public. In 1885, for example, when J.H.A. Macdonald conducted a spectacular night assembly of the Queen's Edinburgh Rifle Brigade, the exercise resulted in bringing in 500 new recruits. Similarly, the Volunteers played an important part in the origin of the Grand Military Tournament and Assault at Arms, first held at the Royal Agricultural Hall, Islington, in 1880 which survives as the annual Royal Tournament.[77]

It would be wrong to claim that the Volunteers played the major role in the growth of militarism in late Victorian England, but they can be said to have played an integral part in its development. The Volunteers were of course a product of the phenomenon of the invasion panic which characterised mid- and late-Victorian society. This in itself generated a considerable amount of popular literature and was reflected in the considerable amount of space devoted to military affairs in the serious periodicals.[78] The development of the ideal of the 'Christian Hero' and the popularisation of military values through commemorative pottery and popular literature owed far more to the Crimean War and the Indian Mutiny than to the Volunteers, but Christian militarism was undoubtedly a factor interwoven in the fabric of the Volunteer Movement. Professor Hanham, for example, has attributed the greater popularity of the Army by the end of the South African War to the role of the Boys' Brigades in undermining the traditionally civilian values of Nonconformism. Nonconformist militarism had its own roots in such international events as Garibaldi's struggle for the unification of Italy, but the Boys' Brigades, which numbered over 35,000 members by 1899, were essentially a product of the Volunteer Movement harnessing its patriotic and moral values to a primarily religious aim.[79] The moral aspects of the Volunteer Movement mirrored the cult of athleticism developing within both the public schools and contemporary literature which, together with vague notions of social Darwinism, culminated in the considerable concern with physical deterioration after the South African War. Baden-Powell was partly inspired to create the Boy Scout movement through his belief that the physical condition of the nation had declined, a situation investigated by an Inter-Departmental Committee in 1903. The National Service League founded in 1901 similarly advocated physical training and military drill in schools as well as conscription.[80] In one respect, however, the Volunteer Movement did have the effect of postponing consideration of military problems until after the South African War. This was the issue of conscription. Robert Home foresaw the Volunteers as a means of uniting people and Army and paving the way for conscription. But, as Lord Elcho realised, the very existence of the Volunteer Force was a further argument against the ballot rather than an additional factor in its favour.[81]

The qualified achievement of the Volunteers in imbuing England with a military spirit is perhaps best summarised in the words of one speaker at the Royal United Service Institution, who testified in 1898: 'If the Volunteers had never done anything else, we owe them a debt of gratitude for one thing, that they have brought military knowledge to the people much more that it was before they existed.'[82] This had the beneficial result of turning the thoughts of the Volunteers to military subjects, as Lord Elcho wrote to Lady Verney in September 1862: 'Volunteering has naturally given me a great interest in all that relates to the Army, and as I look upon the hard work of Volunteering and like work, I would gladly know something of Army matters and try to make myself useful in that field.' Regulars like Maurice and Henderson welcomed the Volunteers as an additional market for their military books and Wolseley, too, welcomed the turning of 'fresh, unprejudiced and unbiased minds' to military problems previously considered only by Regular officers shackled by military discipline or antagonistic to innovation. Volunteers were able to speak their minds freely and this fresh approach to military matters was, perhaps, their greatest contribution to the Army.[83]

The Volunteers were not only a fertile breeding ground for new ideas but an ideal field for economical experimentation but, unfortunately, their efforts were not always fully appreciated by the authorities. This is clearly illustrated in the cases of machine-guns and Mounted Infantry.

In June 1882 Col. Alt of the Central London Rangers purchased two Nordenfelt machine-guns but the regiment was not allowed to use them on parade although permission was granted to use them at Aldershot. The machine-gun was, in the view of Volunteers such as T. Sturmy Cave of the 1st V.B. Hants., a potential solution to the Volunteers' lack of artillery support. The attitude of the War Office was not encouraging and prompted the *Volunteer Service Gazette* to comment that presumably the Central London Rangers would not be invited to leave their guns at home in the event of an invasion. The possession of machine-guns by Volunteer battalions was, however, authorised in October 1883 and by 1893 there were some 19 guns distributed amongst the Volunteer Force. All these machine-guns were, of course, privately purchased, mostly, as in the case of the 1st V.B. Hants., as a result of public appeal.[84] Similarly, the War Office showed little interest in the concept of Volunteer Mounted Infantry, the value of which had been demonstrated in earlier years by the Light Horse corps of Sir Thomas Acland and Lt.-Col. John Bower. Volunteers such as Elcho and Robert Loyd-Lindsay were strongly in favour of Mounted Infantry and of converting the Yeomanry to Mounted Infantry as the mounted arm of the Volunteer Force. Mounted companies were authorised in the Victoria Rifles, the 1st Midlothian R.V. and in Plymouth in December 1882 and others followed in such battalions as the 1st V.B. South Staffs. and 1st V.B. Berks.[85] However, these companies were never given an adequate grant to cover the high cost of upkeep and most quickly disappeared. A great opportunity had been wasted and the British Army was to suffer from this neglect in the South African War.

Another new 'weapon' tested by the Volunteer Force was the bicycle. It was hoped that the employment of the bicycle in the Force would not only harness the growing number of keen cyclists to the Volunteer Force but compensate for the lack of cavalry support, in the same way in which machine-guns might compensate for the deficiency in artillery. The Volunteers and Regulars, such as Maurice, Evelyn Wood and Lt.-Col. Savile, Professor of Tactics at the Royal Military College, became rather carried away in their enthusiasm for the bicycle, 'a machine capable of great possibilities in the future of actual warfare'. The cyclist could perform all the functions of cavalry in rapid movement, reconnaisance and carrying messages; could act as 'saboteur' behind enemy lines and had the additional advantage over the cavalryman of not requiring forage and of being able to take his machine into the firing line. Indeed, there seemed no limit to the potential of the bicycle, although Eustace Balfour was careful to stress that the cyclist would really count 'in countries where roads exist'. *The Illustrated Naval and Military Magazine* suggested more unkindly that: 'a cyclist with perhaps two cavalrymen behind him in pursuit would, except on a good road, be surely hard pressed'.[86]

Cyclists first appeared in Volunteer uniform at Brighton in April 1885 as scouts with the 1st Sussex R.V. However, the real origin lay in the use of cyclists on a march from Canterbury to Dover on 9 April 1887 at which a motley collection of bicycles, tricycles, triplets and tandems was employed under the supervision of Lt.-Col. Savile and Lt.-Col. Stacey, O.C. 1st Battalion Scots Guards. A War Office Committee, chaired by Savile, was then set up in December 1887 to consider the specifications of a military bicycle, the clothing and equipment of cyclists, the conditions of efficiency and the training of cyclists. The safety cycle recommended by the Committee unfortunately incorporated a number of individual ideas and would have weighed 90 lbs! Nevertheless, a specialist cyclist battalion, designated the 26th Middlesex, was raised in 1888 from men who were, in the words of Sir Francis Vane, good cyclists but had 'a very hazy idea of what discipline means'. The new theories, largely inspired by Eustace Balfour (then only a Lieutenant in the London Scottish) were tested at Guildford just before Easter 1888. Some good work was accomplished but a projected attack on Salisbury bogged down at Farnham due to bad weather, bad roads, want of drill and the inequality in riding abilities. A special multi-cycle designed to carry a machine gun repeatedly broke down.[87] The bicycle was clearly not a major development in warfare and had obvious limitations, but the experiments do reveal the way in which the Volunteers could initiate and test new theories.

On a more practical level, the Volunteers played an important role in the development of the service rifle by their encouragement of marksmanship and by the participation in successive War Office Small Arms Committees of leading Volunteer experts, such as Elcho, Earl Spencer, Edward Ross, Sir Henry Halford, Bt., and, later, T.F. Fremantle.[88] Elcho himself also designed a sword bayonet, issued in limited numbers to men of the 23rd and 42nd Foot and the Rifle Brigade for the Ashanti campaign of 1873-74 and praised by Wolseley, but ultimately turned down by the War Office in favour of a 'Chicago pig-knife'. The Volunteer Force has sometimes been credited with the invention of the Moncrieff gun-carriage but, in fact, Moncrieff was a Militia officer.[89] The Volunteer Force also pioneered more sensible uniforms, similarly praised by Wolseley as a 'pattern that all sensible men adopt for themselves when going out shooting, or on a walking tour, or when about to embark on any wild expedition where the necessity for great exertion is to be expected . . .'. In fact, in March 1883, a War Office Colour Committee recommended the grey uniform of the 3rd Devon R.V. (formerly 1st Devon A.B.) as the pattern for the new service dress but, in the event, Indian Khaki was preferred. The 1st Bucks. Volunteers was one of the first units to change to the new khaki field service dress in August 1901.[90]

Other practical innovations came from the Volunteers such as the postal system of the 49th/24th Middlesex R.V.C. and the ration distribution system developed by the same regiment. It was, for example, at the Brighton/Lewes review in 1880 that the 16th Lancers operated a field telephone and experiments were conducted with a captive balloon.[91] Indeed, at a time when, in the words of George Melly of the 4th Lancs. Artillery Brigade, 'No General in the Army could take 10,000 men in and out of Hyde Park without confusion', and in the absence of large scale manoeuvres, the existence of Volunteers enabled Regular officers to handle large bodies of men in peacetime and, indeed, explore their own abilities. J.F.C. Fuller, the military theorist, was inspired to begin his studies by his service as Adjutant to the old 2nd South Middlesex R.V.C. in 1907 and the new 10th Middlesex Bn., Territorial Force.[92] By 1914 there were 12 Regulars of the rank of Major-General and above who had seen service as Adjutants with the Auxiliary Forces, including the C.-in-C., Sir John French; the former C.G.S., General Sir Charles Douglas; the C.G.S., Major-General Sir Archibald Murray; the A.G., Sir Nevil Macready and the G.O.C. 1st Division, Major-General Lomax. The percentage of Regulars with such experience increased accordingly in lower ranks and the lessons of handling amateur soldiers must surely have been of some value for those who were to command the New Armies of 1915-16 and the conscript Armies of 1917-18. One recent writer has pointed out that the Volunteer Movement, in common with other 'leisure' activities, could not have existed without the development of the railways but it can also be said that, by the necessity of frequent rail journeys, the Volunteers displayed a pioneering use of railways for military traffic in Britain, which the American Civil War would shortly prove to be of vital importance in modern warfare.[93]

Many Volunteers were also determined to reform the antiquated drill system which they were forced to utilise in 1859. Volunteers such as Elcho, Lt.-Col. Brewster of the Inns of Court R.V.C. and, notably, J.H.A. Macdonald, were highly critical of the 'stuck up wooden attitude, contrary to every natural articulation of the body, and hampering circulation'. In particular, they attacked the 'fetish' of 'front' by which 'it was apparently considered essential that for the purpose of drill the original front rank should always be in front, and the original rear rank always in rear, and that these ranks should never be changed'. Added to this was the necessity for 'locking up', which meant that rear ranks must be no more than 21 ins. from the rank in front thus courting disaster in the event of rough ground or obstacles. Macdonald struggled for thirty years to have his basic rules of simplicity, celerity and convenience as well as attention to the probable effects of modern fire power implemented in the Drill Book. His views, advocated in lectures and pamphlets such as *On the Best Detail Formation for the New Infantry Tactics* (1873) and *Commonsense on Parade, or Drill without Strings* (1886), were shared by many of his Regular correspondents and, indeed, Maurice adopted many of his ideas. But progress was slow, the 1886 Drill Book, for example, differing from that of 1877 in the words of Macdonald only in that it was printed on newer paper. Macdonald's mode of 'forming fours' was adopted in 1893, 'touch' abolished in 1896 and 'front' finally abandoned in 1902 following Macdonald's co-operation on a new Drill Book with Henderson.[94]

The mutual suspicion and ignorance on the part of both Volunteers and Regular soldiers hampered the progress of the Volunteer Force in the early years of its existence. In such circumstances the Volunteers had been allowed, to use the later words of Haldane, 'to go very much their own way, not because by this means they were likely to produce the best result, but because it did not matter what they did'.[95] However, closer co-operation and the realisation by many Regulars that the Volunteers might after all prove useful induced considerable progress from the late 1870's onwards. This was a two-way process in that each side had much to give the other and whilst the Volunteers became steadily more efficient, so the Regular Army benefited from the 'fresh' approach to military problems by Volunteers. In the process there is no doubt that a larger section of society became involved in military affairs than would have been possible before 1859. It could not be said that the Volunteers would not have done their best in the event of an invasion but whether they would have succeeded in any measure is extremely doubtful. Despite the progress made by the eve of the South African War, on balance it must be said that in 1899 the Volunteer Force was as unprepared for modern war as the rest of the Armed Forces.

[1] Brookfield, p 247.
[2] Wethered Mss, op cit, p 6.
[3] *BPP*. 1860 (441) VII, 1 evidence of Burgoyne, 2762-98, evidence of Cambridge, 4327-32; *VSG* 17.12.59, p 57, 62; 21.1.60; 4.2.60, p 116; 30.1.60, p 117; 25.2.60, p 203; Wrottesley, *Life*, II, p 396-7; *USM* 1859 Pt II, p 178-83 'A Few Observations on

the Formation of Volunteer Artillery and Rifle Corps'.

4 *BPP*. 1860 [2682] xxiii 431, p 7.

5 *VSG* 26.10.59, p 2; 18.5.78, p 466-7; Lady Wantage, p 272.

6 *INMM* II (March 1885) 'Experiences of a Volunteer Adjutant', p 164; Macdonald, p 12.

7 Cf order of 49th Middx., May 1870 *Guildhall Mss* 9408 No 120; order 23.4.61 Northumberland R.O. BMO/B 15.

8 Somerset R.O. DD/SAS/SY 2; Gwent R.O. LLCM+V 9/33 and D.766.54; Warburton to Vane Tempest, 28.3.62 Durham R.O. *Londonderry* D/Lo/C 235/37; Lincs. R.O. *Hill 12th Deposit* 12/1/1; Fisher, p 103-4; Rose, *LB*, p 47-66; *VSG* 29.3.73, p 343-4 'Appointment of Officers'; 18.10.73, p 805 'Appointment of Officers'; 25.3.76, p 326 'Discipline and Financial Meetings'; 29.9.83, p 802 'Selection of Officers'; 6.10.83, p 818 'Volunteer CO's'.

9 de Grey Memo 8.12.60 Dorset Military Museum, Misc.

10 G.L.R.O. (M) *Lieutenancy* L/C/70 and 72 and *Cruikshank Mss* Acc 534/5; Durham R.O. *Londonderry* D/Lo/C 235/1-10; *VSG* 12.12.74; p 79, 85-6; 4.9.69, p 629 'Subordination of Officers'; 21.10.71, p 741 'Discipline and Subordination'; Gilbey Mss, V, p 1.

11 Order 10.12.60 Order Book 36th Middx. *PRO* W.O. 70/7 p 26.

12 Wethered, p 3.

13 Wethered, p 6; Lamont, p 65-6; Macdonald, p 38-44.

14 Herbert to Cambridge, 21.2.60 quoted Verner, I, p 274.

15 Cave, p 115-120; Hants. R.O. *Lieutenancy* L.L.69; de Grey Memo 26.8.61 Quoted Northants. R.O. *Eunson* II, p 71; *VSG* 16.3.64, p 309; 20.8.64, p 598.

16 *VSG* 27.6.68, p 464-7; 4.7.68, p 485; 11.7.68, p 502, 520-2; 1.6.68, p 563; 15.8.68, p 581 Edit; 21.5.68, p 458.

17 Wethered, p 23.

18 Ibid, p 14-15; 'Notes on the Old Easter Monday Review' *LSRG* IV (Jan 1899), p 15-16; Lt.-Col. H. Jones and Gen. Erskine at Hamley's lecture *JRUSI*. XXIX (1885), p 657; *VSG* 18.4.66, p 309; 30.7.81, p 652.

19 Prince Consort to Ellenborough, 3.10.61 quoted Martin, V, p 401-3; Woodburne, p 101-3; Preston, *AQ* 89 (1964-5), p 57-74; Luvaas, *Military Legacy*, p 16-51, 100-118; *USM*. 1861 Pt III p 328-336, 430-2; 1865 Pt II, p 29-32; *VSG* 10.8.61; 14.11.67, p 21; 11.1.68, p 84; 11.2.71, p 165 'Public Feeling and the Volunteers'.

20 *VSG* 15.6.61, p 532-5; 21.3.63, p 345; 3.10.63, p 792 Edit; 18.8.66, p 596-7 'The Army and the Volunteers'; 15.5.69, p 372; 4.6.70, p 421-2 'Militia and Volunteers'; 15.10.81, p 831; 17.3.83, p 313 Edit. For the Finsbury dispute cf *VSG* 26.4.73, p 400; 7.8.75, p 623; 1.8.74, p 634; 20.12.79, p 117; Lubbock, 11.3.89 *AD* (1889) 60-1.

21 Memories of Earl Wemyss, *LSRG* I (July 1896), p 76; *VSG* 12.9.63, p 744 paper by Allhusen; 1.4.71, p 270; 22.4.71, p 325 Edit; 11.3.82, p 290-1 'Volunteer Field Artillery'; 11.3.82, p 294-5 Edit; 15.7.82, p 617; 5.7.77, p 422 'Lord Elcho's Letter'; 23.5.85, p 476-9.

22 *VSG* 19.4.62, p 409; 3.5.62, p 440 Edit; 2.8.64, p 581; 27.5.64, p 613; 7.7.66, p 501-2 'Our Recent Critics'; 5.1.67, p 85 Edit; Chaloner and Henderson, op cit, p 1-43.

23 Cf *VSG* 18.4.68, p 309 'A Military Critic'; 9.1.69, p 85 'Criticism and Advice'; 20.2.69, p 180-1 'More Counsel'; 12.11.70, p 789 Edit; 19.11.70, p 805-6 'Patronising'; 3.2.72, p 149-50 'Professional Testimony on the Easter Review'; *USM* 1861 Pt II, p 102-5; 1863 Pt II, p 118; 1865 Pt II, p 123; 1867 Pt II, p 111-2; Hope Grant to Cambridge, 11.4.71 quoted Verner, II, Appl 1, p 435-6.

24 *VSG* 22.5.69, p 388; 5.6.69, p 420-1; 26.6.69, p 470 Erskine to Elcho; 3.7.69, p 484-5 'Discipline and Organisation'; 11.6.70, p 437.

25 *VSG* 3.11.72, p 72-3; 29.3.73, p 343 'The Volunteers Place in National Defence'; p

344 Home 'On the Recent War, with reference to the Militia and Volunteers'; 5.4.73, p 355 Maurice 'On Connection between the Ordinary Work of Soldiers in Peacetime and Warlike Efficiency'; F Maurice, *Sir Frederick Maurice: A Record of His Work and Opinions* (London 1913), p 153-75.

[26] *VSG* 15.3.79, p 308-9; *BPP*. 1878-9 [c 2235] XV 181 App XXI.

[27] *VSG* 30.6.77, p 553-4; 27.10.77, p 833-6 'The Past Year'; Ian Hamilton, *Listening for the Drums* (London 1944), p 109; Col. R. Harrison, 'What can the Volunteers of England do to render themselves fit to take the field?' *JRUSI* XXIX (1885) No 132, p 1087ff; Captain W. Adye, 'The Drill and Training of Volunteer Infantry' *JRUSI* XXXIV (1890) No 135, p 567ff.

[28] C.E. Callwell, *Stray Recollections* (London 1923), II. p 8-9.

[29] Wethered, op cit, p 24.

[30] *VSG* 8.3.79, p 294.

[31] *VSG* 8.3.73, p 294-5 'The New Organisation'; 1.10.81, p 800 'Territorial Organisation'.

[32] *VSG* 10.3.77, p 293-4; 27.10.77, p 833 'The Past Year'; 16.11.78, p 37; 21.1.82, p 181-2; 28.4.83, p 416; 9.2.84, p 230 'A Good Understanding'.

[33] *VSG* 17.11.83, p 37; 29.3.84, p 341; *LSRG* III (Sept 1898), p 130-144 for report of march through Scotland; Gen. Sir George Higginson, *Seventy One Years of a Guardsman's Life* (London 1916), p 347-8.

[34] *VSG* 18.10.84, p 845; 8.8.85, p 697-8; Cave, op cit, p 321-36; *BPP* 1904 [Cd 2064] xxxi. 587. App CVII 'History of Volunteer Transport'.

[35] Luvaas, *Military Legacy*, p 170-202; Luvaas, *Education*, p 218.

[36] *VSG* 3.10.85, p 826-7; F.M. Sir Evelyn Wood, *From Midshipman to Field Marshal* (London 1906), II, p 215; Howard Vincent to H.O. Arnold-Forster, 6.5.1904 'The Auxiliary Forces and the War Office' in *BM* Add Mss 50313 Section 1.

[37] *VSG* 5.8.71, p 562; 30.12.71, p 70; 20.1.72, p 105; 24.1.80, p 195; 17.4.80, p 393-4 'The War Office 1874-80'; 9.2.84, p 230; Lady Wantage, p 211-3; War Office Council minutes June 1871-July 1872 *P.R.O.* W.O. 163/1; Macdonald, p 185; for an account of the manoeuvres of J.B. Collier, 2nd Hants.,'The Autumn Manoeuvres of 1872' in *JSAHR* L (1972) No 204, p 221-36.

[38] *VSG* 6.11.80, p 7 'Prospects'; 17.12.81, p 101 'General Higginson's Forecast'; 26.5.83, p 482 'Discipline'; 9.2.84, p 230 'A Good Understanding'; 1.11.84, p 8 'Twenty Five Years'; Wilkinson, op cit, p 24.

[39] Cf Hardy to Disraeli 19.10.76 *Hughenden* B/XX/Ha; Wolseley 'Preparing for War with Russia', W.O. Library *Wolseley Papers* Volume 22; *BPP* 1878-9 [c 2235] XV 181, App XXXIII; *P.R.O.* W.O. 32/5974 for Wolseley's letter with attached comments of Duke of Cambridge; W.O. Lib. *Wolseley Papers* Volume 38 for Wolseley's annotated copy of the letter; *VSG* 2.6.77, p 485-6 'Col. Fletcher's Scheme'; *JRUSI*. XXI (1877), p 635-58; XXII (1878), p 350-68. For a discussion of strategic options open to the Cabinet cf Preston, *Military Policy*, op cit, chapters 2-5.

[40] 'Committee to consider the formation of a Corps for the performance of postal duties with an Army in the field' Post Office R.O. 'Regimental Records of the Post Office Rifles' R7/1, 2(b), 2(c); *VSG* 29.7.82, p 647; 5.8.82, p 670 'Volunteer Postal Corps'; 9.9.82, p 749 'Volunteering for Active Service'; 28.10.82, p 855 'Return of the PO Detachment'.

[41] *VSG* 30.5.85, p 506 'Volunteers in the Field'; 31.10.85, p 890-4; R.H. Vetch, *The Life of General Sir Andrew Clarke* (London 1905), p 270.

[42] *VSG* 23.2.84, p 261; 22.3.84, p 325 Notes; Norfolk, *East Riding*, p 38-9; Vetch, p 241; speech of Sir Gerald Graham to Hants. A.V. 1.12.88, *Royal Engineers Journal* XVIII (1888) No 206, p 10.

[43] Wolseley to Parliamentary Under Secretary, 16.3.86 Hove Central Library,

Wolseley Papers W/MEM/2.4 'Volunteer Regt. Transport'.

44 These themes are developed in Preston (ed) *Wolseley's South African Diaries and Journals,* op cit, passim; Moon, op cit, esp chap 1; W.S. Hamer, *The British Army: Civil Military Relations 1885-1905* (Oxford 1970) esp chap 1-4. Relevant documents in *PRO.* Cab 37/21 Nos 6, 14, 15, 17, 18; 37/22 Nos 32, 37; 37/20 No 49.

45 Hamley, 'The Volunteers in Time of Need' *Nineteenth Century* XVII (1885), p 405-423; *JRUSI.* XXIX (1885) No 130, p 629ff; Shand, op cit, II, p 259-72; for Brackenbury memos of 23.9.86 (A58) and 1.12.86 (A67) *PRO* 30/40/13 *Ardagh Papers;* Stanhope estimates *AD* (1887), 312-5; *AD* (1888) 65-100.

46 Relevant papers are to be found in *PRO* 30/40/2, 13 and 14 Vol 1 No 12. See also Ardagh to Cmte on Volunteer Medical Organisation 18.10.88 *PRO* W.O. 33/48 A 116 and A 147 and Stanhope to deputation 9.5.88 W.O. 33/48 A 121; meetings of War Office Council *PRO* W.O. 163/4; Shand, op cit, II, p 251-9.

47 *PRO* W.O. 33/48 A 138; Grove to Ardagh 31.1.89, W.O. 33/49 A170; Fleetwood-Wilson to Ardagh 15.8.89, *PRO* 30/40/13.

48 Gerald Ellison 'From Here and There: Reminiscences' *Lancashire Lad* Pt XII (October 1934), p 6-7; D.M. Schurmann, *The Education of a Navy* (London 1965), esp chaps 2-3 for 'Blue Water' School; Moon, op cit, passim.

49 Memories of Earl Wemyss, Pt II *LSRG* I (March 1896), p 25.

50 *VSG* 21.11.85, p 37-8 'Lord Ranelagh', p 38-9 'Obituary'; Woodburne, op cit, p 94-6; Chaloner and Henderson, op cit, p 9-11.

51 Ibid; *VSG* 26.7.62, p 634-8; 7.2.63, p 250 'The Commanding Officers and Lord Ranelagh'; 25.1.68, p 116-7 Edit; 15.2.68, p 165 'Lord Ranelagh's Charges'; p 166 statement by Capt. Templer; p 166-7 speech of Lord Ranelagh; Woodburne, op cit, p 96; Verner, op cit, I, p 274.

52 *VSG* 5.9.74, p 709-10 'A Review of our Position'; 6.5.82, p 426-7; 30.12.82, p 133 Notes.

53 Sir Thomas Acland, *Volunteer Organisation* (London 1868), p xi-xii in West Sussex R.O. *Barttelot Papers* Add. Mss 324/1.

54 *VSG* 25.2.71, p 197 'Mr Cardwell's Bill and the Volunteers'; 22.4.71, p 318-22; 8.7.71, p 501-2 'The Mutiny Act'; 29.9.83, p 802; 24.1.85, p 198-9 'The Volunteers — How to make the most of them'.

55 *VSG* 21.4.77, p 389-90 'Mr Hoste's Lecture'; 14.7.77, p 590-1; 13.10.77, p 802 'A Mutiny Act for Volunteers'; 6.10.77, p 785 'Discipline or the Volunteer Force'; 14.9.78, p 757 'A Dangerous Suggestion'; 8.10.81, p 815-6; 17.12.81, p 101 Edit.

56 *VSG* 24.1.78, p 191-210; 15.2.79, p 247; 29.3.79, p 342; 29.11.79, p 70 'The Standard of Efficiency'; 20.9.84, p 781; *BPP* 1878-9 [c 2235] XV 181, paragraph 14 of report and App X.

57 *VSG* 26.7.73, p 609; 3.5.79, p 422 'Training and Supply'; 31.12.81, p 133-4 'The Education of Officers'.

58 *VSG* 31.12.81, p 133-4; Minute Book, Manchester Tactical Society W.O. Lib; Wilkinson, *Thirty Five Years,* op cit, p 20-9; Wilkinson, *Citizen Soldiers* (London 2nd Edition 1894), App ii, p 97-9; Wilkinson, *The Proposed Tactical Examination for Volunteer Officers* (Manchester 1881) in *Spenser Wilkinson Papers,* Ogilby Trust O.T.P. 13/44.

59 *VSG* 7.1.82, p 150 'The Examination in Tactics'; 3.6.82, p 493; 12.8.82, p 686 'The Tactical Examination'; 8.9.82, p 753; 22.3.84, p 325; 20.9.84, p 781; 29.8.85, p 745; Sir Beauchamp Walker *JRUSI* XXIX (1885) No 130, p 650.

60 *VSG* 23.6.83, Notes; 17.11.83, p 37; 15.3.84, p 310; 28.2.85, p 278; Macdonald, op cit, p 364; T. Sturmy Cave 'The Training of Volunteer Officers' *JRUSI* XXXVIII (1894), p 902-3; Lt.-Col. Mayhew, 'The Training of Volunteer Infantry' *JRUSI* XXXVIII (1894), p 1335ff; Eustace Balfour, 'The Tactical Training of Officers of

Volunteers' *JRUSI* XL (1896), p 25ff.
61 Wilkinson to Roberts, 24.8.92 NAM *Roberts Papers* 7101-23, 87/5; Wilkinson, *Citizen Soldiers* (2nd edit), esp preface and p 89-93; Luvaas, *Education* p 258.
62 *VSG* 21.11.67, p 37 'The Prospects of the Volunteer Force'; 5.11.70, p 773 Edit.
63 *VSG* 15.2.79, p 246; 16.7.81, p 617 'The Review of Last Saturday'; 4.9.80, p 746-7; 12.1.84, p 166 'Requirements of the Volunteers'; 8.10.81, p 816 speech by Mr Grant, M.P.
64 *VSG* 4.1.79, p 149-50; 4.9.80, p 746-7; 5.5.83, p 433; 5.1.84, p 150 'Next Monday's Meeting'; 7.6.84, p 510 'The Prospect of the Future'; 13.9.84, p 766 'A Pressing Want'.
65 *VSG* 26.8.71, p 613; 12.9.74, p 757; 17.9.81, p 183; 18.11.82, p 38; 9.8.84, p 686 Obituary; E.A. Pratt, *The Rise of Rail Power in War and Conquest 1833-1914* (London 1915) p 175-204.
66 Cantlie and Seaver, op cit, p 31-7, 41-7, 52-3; report of Volunteer Medical Organisation Committee 6.11.88 *PRO* W.O. 33/48 A 147; *VSG* 16.7.81, p 617; 21.1.82, p 183; 17.2.83, p 245 Notes; 28.3.85, p 341; 16.6.83, p 538; 5.5.83, p 435.
67 *VSG* 26.8.71, p 613; 4.9.80, p 746-7; 27.12.84, p 133-4; 28.2.85, p 278-9; 'Auxiliary Transport and Commissariat'; 8.8.85, p 697-8 Edit; 31.10.85, p 890-3; Cave, op cit, p 321-6; *PRO* W.O. 35/51 A 209; W.O. 33/56 A 416.
68 *VSG* 14.12.61, p 120 'Volunteering for War'; 29.10.70, p 757; 2.6.77, p 485-6; 19.3.81, p 309.
69 *VSG* 14.12.61, p 120; 10.9.70, p 642; 10.10.74, p 790 'Volunteers for Foreign Service'; 2.6.77, p 485-6 'Col. Fletcher's Scheme'; Lamont, p 50.
70 *VSG* 16.2.78, p 254 'Dangerous Counsel'; 2.3.78, p 286 'Volunteers and the Crisis'; 9.3.78, p 295; 4.5.78, p 438 'A British Legion'; 15.2.79, p 247; 5.7.79, p 585-6; *BPP* 1878-9 [c2235] XV 181 esp evidence paras 501-16, 756, 780, 855, 1370-2, 1486-91, 3044-6.
71 *VSG* 15.8.63, p 681; 28.2.80, p 278; 22.11.84 Notes; 28.3.85, p 337; 1.9.83, p 737; 5.8.82, p 669; Cave, op cit, p 213; Janet Fyfe, 'Scottish Volunteers with Garibaldi'; *SHR* 57 (1978), p 168-181.
72 *VSG* 2.8.73, p 627 letter of Loyd-Lindsay; 5.3.81, p 278; 26.3.81, p 325-6; 13.8.81, p 617-8; 27.8.81, p 719-20 'Loyd-Lindsay's Paper'; 9.9.82, p 750 'Volunteering for Active Service'; 16.9.82, p 765; 14.2.85, p 246-7 'The Crisis and the Auxiliaries'; 30.5.85, p 506 'Volunteers in the Field'; 18.7.85, p 640 'The Volunteers and the Nation'.
73 *VSG* 15.6.61, p 532-5; 1.11.62, p 29-30; 24.9.64, p 675; 4.1.66; 2.8.73, p 625-7; 4.2.82, p 214.
74 *VSG* 11.2.60, p 124; 11.9.80, p 761-2 'Napoleon III and the Volunteers'; Walter, op cit, p 135-42; Palmerston to Herbert, 8.11.59 quoted Stanmore II, op cit, p 392-3.
75 Lady Wantage, op cit, p 328-9; *INMM* III (1889), p 1418-21 'Volunteer Notes'; for the Moltke affair cf *Daily Telegraph* 23.5.88, p 7-8; *PRO* Cab 37/21 No 18; Moon, op cit, chap 2.
76 *VSG* 9.3.78, p 302 'The Nation and the Army' discussing Wolseley's article entitled 'England as a Military Power' in *Nineteenth Century*; 5.7.79, p 585-6; 12.2.81, p 230-1 Wolseley speech to 1st Derby R.V.C.; Lamont, op cit, p 104; Wolseley to Bury Dept. Cmte *BPP* 1878-9 [c 2235] XV 181 App XXXIII para 4; *PRO* W.O. 32/5974.
77 Memories of Earl Wemyss *LSRG* I (March 1896), p 25; IV (January 1899), 'Notes on the Old Easter Monday Review', p 15-16; Macdonald, op cit, p 273; Lt.-Col. P.L. Binns, *The Story of the Royal Tournament* (Aldershot 1952), passim; G.T. Hay, *An Epitomised History of the Militia* (London 1905) p 167.
78 John Gooch, 'Attitudes to War in Late Victorian and Edwardian England' in B. Bond and I. Roy (eds), *War and Society: A Yearbook of Military History* (London 1976), p 88-102.

[79] H.J. Hanham, 'Religion and Nationality in the Mid-Victorian Army' in M.R.D. Foot (ed) *War and Society* (London 1973), p 159-181; J.O. Springhall, *Youth, Empire and Society* (London 1977); Olive Anderson, 'The growth of Christian Militarism in Mid-Victorian Britain' *EHR* LXXXVI (1971), p 46-72; Anne Summers, 'Militarism in Britain before the Great War' *History Workshop* II (1976), p 104-23.

[80] G. Best, 'Militarism and the Victorian Public School' and J.A. Mangan, 'Athleticism' both in B. Simon and I. Bradley (eds), *The Victorian Public School* (London 1975), p 129-46, 147-67; M. Allison, 'The National Service Issue, 1899-1914' (Unpub PhD London 1975).

[81] *VSG* 29.3.73, p 344; Wemyss 3.8.1900 *AD* (1900) 627-30.

[82] Capt. W.H. Jones at RUSI 10.3.1898 quoted J.K. Dunlop, *The Development of the British Army* (London 1938), p 9.

[83] Lord Elcho to Lady Verney 19.9.62 *Verney/Calvert Papers*, Claydon House; Luvaas, *Education*, p 181, 244; *VSG* 25.9.69, p 677 'The Future of the Force'; 13.10.83, p 834-5 Edit; Memories of Earl Wemyss *LSRG* I (April 1896), p 41.

[84] *VSG* 3.6.82, p 493; 1.9.83, p 737; 13.10.83, p 834-5; 27.10.83, p 865; May, op cit, p 25; Cave, op cit, p 387-8; W.H. Goodenough and J.C. Dalton, *The Army Book of the British Empire* (London 1893), p 383.

[85] *VSG* 10.9.70, p 645; 10.6.71, p 437; 7.7.77, p 568-9; 19.8.82, p 701; 2.12.82, p 69; 13.10.83, p 834-5; 12.1.84, p 165; Lady Wantage, op cit, p 155-6, 272-3; Wemyss Memories *LSRG* I (July 1896), p 76.

[86] *INMM* IV (August 1890) p 631-2 'Volunteer Notes'; *Lancashire and Cheshire Volunteer* I (1895) 'The Advance and Influence of the Volunteer Movement'; Maurice, *Work and Opinions*, op cit, p 97-103; Eustace Balfour, 'The History of Military Cycling' Pt 1 *LSRG* II (February 1897), p 27; Vane, op cit, p 70-3.

[87] Vane, op cit, p 72-3; Balfour Pt II, IV and VI *LSRG* II (April 1897), p 58, (Aug) 141, III (December 1898) p 175; *PRO* W.O. 33/49 A 160.

[88] *VSG* 28.3.68, p 257-8; 26.2.70 Notes; 8.4.71, 'A Fact for the War Office'; Cottesloe, op cit, passim; Memories of Wemyss *LSRG* I (April 1896), p 41; for papers of Halford and Fremantle on various W.O. Small Arms Cmtes cf Bucks. R.O. *Fremantle* D/FR/165, 169, 170, 171.

[89] *VSG* 16.3.78, p 302; Wolseley to Bury Dept. Cmte, op cit, para 17; Wemyss Memories, op cit, April 1896, p 41.

[90] *VSG* 28.8.69, p 612; 31.3.83, p 350.

[91] *VSG* 20.3.80, p 325; 30.10.80, p 877-80 'The Past Year'; 16.9.82, p 765; Macdonald, op cit, p 293.

[92] *VSG* 30.10.80, p 877-80; Melly, *Recollections*, op cit, p 105; Wemyss Memories *LSRG* (March 1896), p 25; Thomas Hughes, 'The Volunteer Force — Prospects of the Force in its Fifth Year' *British Army and Navy Review* I (1864), p 81-7; J.F.C. Fuller, *Memoirs of an Unconventional Soldier* (London 1936), p 19-21.

[93] G. Best, *Mid-Victorian Britain, 1851-75* (London, paperback edition 1973), p 223.

[94] May, op cit, p 23-5; Macdonald, op cit, p 20, 308-9, 478-81; Luvaas, *Education*, op cit, p 212; Lamont, op cit, p 30-1; *VSG* 16.2.78, p 253 'On the Best Detail Formations for Infantry Attack'.

[95] Haldane to Cabinet 23.11.1906 *PRO* Cab 37/85 No 89 para 7.

CHAPTER VII

THE VOLUNTEERS AND THE SOUTH AFRICAN WAR
1899-1902

"In despatches from the seat of war you may not
  find their names,
But they did their work as well as those who won
  a wider fame;
If Fortune gave them not the chance to inscribe
  in these their part,
What matter? — they've their names inscribed deep
  down in Danetree's heart."

'The Danetree Khaki Boys'
1901.

$\mathbf{T}$ The South African war represented for the Volunteers that major crisis in which they had always predicted that their true value would at last be universally acknowledged by Army, politicians and public alike. Yet the dream fell short of reality and by the end of the War there were disturbing signs that the attitude of the War Office was once more hostile to the interests of the Volunteer Force. This chapter will examine the role and military performance of the Force during the South African War and the overall effects of the war on its relationship with both Government and Army.

Patriotism and necessity

The chief drawback to any Volunteer participation in the event of conflict in South Africa was, of course, that it was illegal unless the Volunteers were temporarily enlisted in the Regular Army. Nevertheless, as the situation in South Africa grew more tense during the summer of 1899, the Volunteers once more began to offer their services as they had done in 1878 and 1885. The first offer came from Lt.-Col. Eustace Balfour of the London Scottish. On 19 July 1899 he proposed to the Under-Secretary of State, George Wyndham, that a special service company be raised from the regiment and attached to the Gordon Highlanders in the event of war. This was followed in August by an offer from Howard Vincent of the Queen's Westminsters to raise eight companies of 132 men each. Although the Inspector-General of Auxiliary Forces and Recruiting, Major-General T. Kelly-Kenny, expressed the War Office's appreciation of the spirit behind the offers, they were declined. This led Balfour to criticise others who had 'rushed in where we delicately ventured to tread' and confused 'our quality and their quantity'.[1] *The Volunteer Service Gazette* was still opposed to Volunteers serving abroad as it had been on previous occasions, and the *Broad Arrow* calculated that 50 per cent of the Volunteers would be unfit and 80 per cent would not volunteer for service. Incensed by their attitude Balfour commented:

> Taunted for staying at home when our Regular comrades are fighting overseas, howled at when we offer ourselves for active service, expected to be fit for service while we are vigorously debarred from ever seeing any, though our Colonial brethren are freely accepted, we have need, indeed, of all the patience at our command, and can only wait for the time when the war may come nearer home, knowing that then, at least, the country will go down on its knees to us to help.[2]

Offers were renewed when war finally broke out on 11 October 1899

211

but Wyndham, in reply to Vincent on 26 October, emphasised the legal difficulties. Evelyn Wood, now Adjutant-General, indicated another reason for refusal when he declined Arthur Brookfield's offer to raise 1,000 men on the grounds that they would cost as much to transport as Regulars and would not be as efficient.[3]

What induced the Government to change its mind was the disastrous 'Black Week' of 9-15 December 1899 with the triple reverses of Magersfontein, Stormberg and Colenso. It would appear that Wolseley, now Commander-in-Chief, had already pressed Salisbury and his Secretary of State, Lord Lansdowne, to send Volunteers to South Africa, when, on 15 December, the Lord Mayor, Sir Alfred Newton, offered to raise the 1st City of London Imperial Volunteers based on a scheme of Col. C.G. Boxall, C.B. The participation of Colonial Volunteers had been discussed as early as June 1899 and Lansdowne was now prepared to accept the Volunteers; as he wrote to Salisbury on 15 December:

> It seems to me to be impossible to refuse altogether, and, apart from purely military considerations, I see some advantage in affording an outlet to public feeling, which is beginning to run very high.

As a result Wolseley gave unofficial permission to Newton to proceed on the 16 December. The formal offer to raise 1,000 men in twenty-one days with full transport was officially accepted on 20 December 1899.[4]

The raising of the City Imperial Volunteers, as the unit was renamed at the suggestion of Wolseley, was, in many ways, a remarkable piece of improvisation. The Court of Common Council voted £25,000 for the purpose; further large sums were donated by City banks and livery companies; City and West End firms assisted with clothing; Wellcome and Co., gave all medicines free and offers of ships were received, notably from C.H. Wilson, M.P., of Hull. All was arranged from the Mansion House by five committees — Finance, Organisation, Transport, Clothing and Equipment, Horses and Saddlery — set up by a meeting of Metropolitan C.O.'s on 22 December. Matters requiring War Office decision were settled on the spot by two officers seconded for the purpose — Major-General Alfred Turner and Major T.F. Fremantle of the Bucks. Volunteers, who was A.D.C. to Wolseley and had drafted the order of 20 December for Wolseley.[5] There were some differences of opinion with the War Office on transport arrangements and the actual command of the corps, but horses were arranged in South Africa through a contact of Newton and the command was given to the A.A.G., Home

District, Col. W.H. Mackinnon. Subordinate commands were given to Volunteers — Lt.-Col. Hugh Cholmondeley of the London Rifle Brigade in charge of the Mounted Infantry and Lt.-Col. the Earl of Albemarle of the 12th Middlesex, who took over the Infantry when Howard Vincent was pronounced unfit through a heart condition. The men were recruited on condition that they were fit, preferably bachelors, aged between 20 and 30 years and ready to embark at 15 days' notice. The C.I.V., enlisted for 1 year, comprised 1 infantry battalion, 2 mounted infantry companies and, at the insistence of the Earl of Denbigh, 1 battery drawn from the H.A.C. and armed with 4 Vickers-Maxim 12½ pdr. quick-firing guns. It was suitably attested, feted and granted the freedom of the City. It embarked for South Africa in 3 contingents on 13, 20 and 29 January 1900, with a further draft being dispatched in July 1900.[6]

Whilst the C.I.V. was being organised, the War Office by Special Army Order authorised the raising of 66 service companies of 116 men each on 2 January 1900. Those attested would be enlisted for 1 year or the duration and those joining the 66 'waiting' companies also authorised would be transferred to the Army Reserve. Service Company Volunteers must be aged 20-35, first class shots, physically fit, of good character, efficient for the last 2 years and preferably unmarried or childless widowers. A special grant of £9 was given to the Volunteer corps to equip any man and he would continue to earn the capitation grant as a supernumerary on the strength of the unit.[7] On active service the Volunteer would receive Army pay and get a special annuity of £5 on discharge in addition to any amount granted the Army as a whole. On 13 January Volunteer Engineers were invited to enlist in sections and, in March, members of the Volunteer Medical Staff Corps were offered a year's engagement in the Army Medical Staff Corps or six months in a home hospital. A further call was made for the service companies in January 1901 and, finally, in January 1902. At the same time, in response to Buller's call for 8,000 Mounted Infantry, an Imperial Yeomanry Committee was working at the War Office to raise that force, which sent two contingents abroad in 1900 and January 1901.[8] There was some discontent among Volunteers that men rejected medically for the Service companies were accepted by the Imperial Yeomanry, which was described by J.H.A. Macdonald as 'not a very creditable official episode'. There were also some unfortunate cases in which men had been attested before the medical and subsequently rejected after they had taken leave of their families and professions, which Lansdowne excused on the grounds that all had been done at short notice and under pressure. Similarly, there was some objection when the second contingent of Imperial Yeomanry raised in January 1901 was granted £5 a day whereas the Volunteers were still on the lower army pay as infantrymen.[9]

There is some confusion on precisely how many Volunteers served in South Africa. This was later the subject of sharp exchanges between Volunteers and H.O. Arnold-Forster, arising out of some disparaging remarks made by the latter in the Commons on 23 February 1905 on the number of the Volunteers who had come forward during the War. Arnold-Forster maintained that although the Volunteer Force had increased by 40,000 men at home, only about 11,000, or under 6 per cent had answered the first War Office call for the service companies in January 1900, only 5,300 in 1901 and a bare 2,588 men in 1902. These figures, as Howard Vincent pointed out, were somewhat inaccurate as Arnold-Forster had ignored the 5 to 6,000 Volunteers who had joined the Regular Army in 1899, helping to repair the 36 per cent deficit in men on mobilisation. He had also implied that the War Office accepted all who offered their service, whereas those accepted represented only a quarter of those who had applied. In fact, of some 20,929 men who came forward in January 1900, some 3,528 were rejected as medically unfit and a further 3,333 through failing to satisfy the efficiency standards. Between the 1 October 1899 and the 1 March 1900 alone the Volunteer Force increased by 19,279 men exclusive of the 11,389 Volunteers already serving in South Africa.[10]

The exact figures given for Volunteers serving in South Africa in the C.I.V., 132 service companies, 38 engineer sections and 1 artillery battery* between 1899 and 1902, vary slightly from 19,648 to 19,856 men or roughly 8.5 per cent of the enrolled strength of the Volunteer Force.[11] To these could be added an estimated 7,000 Volunteers who had joined the Regular Army during the war and about 700 who had joined the Imperial Yeomanry. The C.I.V. is generally taken to have supplied 1,739 men to the total though some small variations are found. Figures of losses are available for the C.I.V. and the first 64 service companies which served in South Africa in 1900. Of 15,721 men of the service companies, some 361 were killed, wounded or died of disease; a further 1,309 were invalided and discharged and other wastage amounted to 963 men, giving a total wastage of 2,633 or roughly 16 per cent. Of the 1,739 men of the C.I.V., some 1,323 returned to England in Ocotber 1900. Some 122 were dead or wounded; 155 had been invalided and 121 had been discharged or found Government employment in South Africa.[12]

What can be deduced from the pattern of Volunteer recruitment for

**This was the so-called 'Elswick' battery drawn from the old Armstrong works at Newcastle. Both Capt. J.C. Wedgwood of the Elswick battery and Maj. Gilbert McMicking of the C.I.V. battery were elected Liberal M.P.'s in 1906.

214

the South African war? Unfortunately, although figures are available for the contribution of various Volunteer battalions to individual service companies,[13] there is no detailed evidence on the class of men who volunteered for South Africa other than those in the C.I.V. Men from 53 Volunteer regiments and over 125 different professions and trades served in the C.I.V., of whom the largest single group was clerks. The lower middle class and artisan elements, based on the professions listed in the official report, both comprised roughly 40 per cent of the total.[14] Figures recently calculated for the Imperial Yeomanry, of whom 71 per cent had not previously served in the Volunteer Force, indicate a situation not unlike 1859, with an early preponderance of middle class elements declining and the working class element gradually increasing after 1900, possibly due to domestic unemployment. This is not, however, really applicable to the Volunteers who served in South Africa. Although the figures for the C.I.V. show a ratio of clerks to artisans somewhat higher than the national average, this may well be explained in terms of the co-operation of employers rather than a greater enthusiasm for the war among the middle class Volunteers. The evidence which does exist for the 1st Norfolk Service company and for the Liverpool Irish company shows a mixture of all classes and suggests that class was not particularly relevant to the service of Volunteers in South Africa. Michael Howard has further suggested that the lack of response from the Volunteers may be explained in terms of the maturity of the age group involved rather than a lack of public spirit.[15] Volunteers themselves were not surprised that enthusiasm declined after 1900, when it seemed the war was all but over, and especially after the increased efficiency requirements of the so-called 'Christmas Card' order of December 1901, the crucial effect of which on Volunteer recruitment will be discussed later.

There is little to suggest why men chose to serve in South Africa. There is no doubt that patriotism played a major part for many Volunteers and men such as Erskine Childers, a clerk of the House of Commons; his friend Basil Williams and Lord Salisbury's private secretary, the Hon. Schomberg MacDonnell, or the 35 members of the Lords and Commons who served with the Imperial Yeomanry or the Volunteers in South Africa.[16] J. Barclay Lloyd, who served as a cyclist with the C.I.V., considered the unit provided 'famous cover to draw for useful persons to assist in the civil and military administration of the newly conquered country' and, indeed, many Volunteers remained in South Africa. This virtually concealed emigration included Lionel Curtis, who became private secretary to Milner, and E. Belcher of D. Coy., C.I.V., who had not intended to stay but decided to find a berth in the Government Stationery Office. But whatever the reason, to quote from the *London Scottish Regimental Gazette:* 'If it was not for patriotism it was for adventure, and we can honour either, for these two qualities together have planted the British flag in every part of the world . . .'.[17]

The experience of actual warfare for the Volunteers was novel. Erskine Childers recalled the 'great and sudden' transition, both mental and physical, from civil to military life:

> There was no perspective left; no planning of the future, no questioning of the present; none of that free planning of mind and will with which we order our lives at home; instead abandonment to superior wills, one's only concern the present point of time and the moment's duty, whatever it might be.[18]

The Volunteers experienced discomfort: 'It is no great pleasure to be on duty at night alone half a mile from everywhere, in a tin shanty without a door, and ventilation all round . . .' They experienced privation: 'We have suffered most from want of tobacco, and I was reduced to scraping out the inside of my pocket and smoking the product and trying eucalyptus leaves . . .'. They experienced those long periods of boredom when the 'small things' like the day's meal were the details, in the words of J. Barclay Lloyd, 'that overshadow the importance of the progress of the war, the excitement of our first battle, and the greatness of the movement in which we were taking part'. And, of course, they went into battle for the first time when 'to men who were facing a standing enemy, for the first time, it sounded as if nothing could live in this inferno'. The London Scottish service company was hit by a shell near Lydenburg in September 1900: 'We saw the puff as the gun was fired, then about thirty seconds later heard the shell hissing through the air, then it burst, and nineteen of the Volunteer Company were lying on the ground, two killed . . .'. To Childers it was 'all very novel, laborious, exciting, hungry work . . .', and to Barclay Lloyd a 'businesslike realisation of a nasty job that has to be carried through, tempered by a pleasing sense of sport, but rendered unpleasant by the dangers of the situation, and saddened by the loss of a comrade or of a friend'. Childers considered that the personal experience of the war, of healthy exercise, patience, discipline and self-restraint had been of enormous value and given him a new admiration for that 'dusty khaki figure still plodding the distant veldt'.[19]

In terms of military achievement the contribution of the Volunteers to the actual conflict of operations could not be said to have been decisive. Indeed, by the time the first Service companies reached Cape

Town, in March 1900, Kimberley and Ladysmith had been relieved and Cronje had surrendered. The C.I.V., however, and many service companies did participate in the advance on Pretoria. Between 26 April and 23 August 1900, the C.I.V. marched 1,018 miles on 75 marching days at an average speed of 13½ miles per day and fought two major actions at Doornkop on 29 May and Diamond Hill on 11-12 June 1900. Their conduct under fire at Diamond Hill earned the praise of Major-General Horace Smith-Dorrien who told them that 'no regiment in the Army of South Africa has done more splendid work'. Lord Roberts, too, in taking his leave of the C.I.V. praised their intelligence and excellence. Lt.-Gen. Ian Hamilton remarked that 'they got better and better every day and at the end they were quite famous' although he later indicated that he felt the unit had got 'stale' by the end of their period in South Africa. Erskine Childers considered that the work of the C.I.V. battery had at last proved the worth of Volunteer artillery and, indeed, it was something of an achievement for men of so many different regiments to work so well together.[20] In many ways the service companies were far better off than the Militiamen, who were largely consigned to line of communications, in that most saw some sort of action with their Regular battalions. The Dorset Service company, for example, was in action at Alleman's Nek on 11 June 1900, winning two D.C.M.'s, but the Service company joining the 2nd Battalion Somerset Light Infantry in March 1900 saw more marching than fighting in attempts to catch de Wet. After the fall of Pretoria, however, the first Norfolk Service company spent long periods in garrison duty or road making and by 1902 most of the Service companies were being used in the blockhouses.[21] Nevertheless, the Service companies were generally held in higher esteem than the Imperial Yeomanry which, despite letters produced for the Cabinet in November 1901 in praise of their role, was poorly regarded.[22] The Duke of Bedford, a leading Militia officer, commented in June 1901 that the performance of under ten per cent of the Volunteer Force in South Africa was no criterion of the potential of the remainder. Lord Roberts too was anxious that a false impression of the abilities of the Auxiliaries should not emerge from the War. He warned against this in a memorandum to the Cabinet in March 1903 but, nonetheless, gave qualified praise to the Service companies thus:

> The Auxiliary Forces were no doubt of great use. They helped to guard the long lines of communication and intermingled with the Regulars rendered excellent service in the fighting line, notably the Volunteer Service Companies who were attached to the Regular units of their Line battalions. It is impossible to state that, until they

had gained some fighting experience, the Auxiliary Forces who worked independently of the Regulars were of anything like the same value.[23]

It is clear from his farewell speech to the C.I.V. on 2 October 1900 that Roberts saw the real value of a Volunteer presence in South Africa in the effect of their experience would have on the Volunteer Force at home[24] and it is the progress of the Force at home which can now be examined.

Public Concession

As George Wyndham admitted in the Commons on the 12 February 1900, in the absence of the bulk of the Regular Army abroad the Volunteer Force was now the main defence against the raids on the British coast, which were still considered possible from hostile European powers. This new situation brought, as will be discussed later, concessions from the Governmment on the one hand and, on the other, new public interest in the Volunteer Force. This latter interest was boosted considerably by the disasters of 'Black Week' and a renewed invasion panic in the press, to which Eustace Balfour contributed with some alarmist articles in the *Daily Express*.[25] On 21 December 1899 the Middlesex County Council resolved to form a Committee to encourage the expansion of the Volunteer Force as a mark of support to the Government and to fill the vacancies of men volunteering for South Africa. These resolutions were then conveyed to other County Councils on the following day by Richard Nicholson, the veteran campaigner for Clerks' allowances as long ago as 1863. Lt.-Col. Edis of the Artists Rifles, in fact, began recruiting to fill his vacancies before he had received official permission and on 12 February 1900, in response to such pressures, the Government authorised Volunteer battalions to expand to a strength of 1,000 men with a second battalion authorised if necessary.[26]

As was indicated earlier, the response was already enthusiastic throughout the country. In Dorset, for example, B. Edmund Freame had circularised former members of the Gillingham company: 'I hope that under the present circumstances you will consider whether you cannot rejoin the Company, and that you will make a serious effort to do so.' In March 1900 Eustace Balfour was able to write: 'In reference to numbers, the Boers have at least done this for us: for the first time since the establishment was increased from 8 to 10 companies we are up to full strength.' Following the lead of Middlesex, Bucks. County Council had established a Home Defence Committee which undertook to investigate range facilities in the county and to raise three new companies for the Bucks. Volunteers. It also pressed the Education authorities to instigate drill in schools and the War Office to give Bucks. back the county regiment it had lost in 1881.[27] Many varied funds appeared to equip the Volunteers and provide comforts for those going to South Africa. The London Scottish had a 'Shilling Fund' and the Central Telegraph Office, for example, raised £100 by an 'Absent Minded Beggars Concert' at Holborn Town Hall in April 1900. The 'War Fund for Middlesex Volunteers' raised £2,554.2s.0d, in 1900 with, for example, the Heston and Isleworth U.D.C. contributing £50 on 31 January 1900 to provide tobacco and warm clothing for the 2nd Battalion, Middlesex Regiment:

> It is hoped that every person who is in receipt of wages or of an income, will feel it a pleasure to contribute something towards this patriotic movement, however small the amount may be, and whatever can be given should be given quickly, as our Volunteer Forces ought to be at once enlarged.[28]

Concerts were a common feature of fund-raising activities and the Service Companies themselves were feted throughout the country. The Chichester contingent joining the Royal Sussex Regiment, for example, were given a farewell supper on 6 March 1900 and a lunch on their return on 11 June 1901. The contingent of the Liverpool Irish, which served with the King's Liverpool Regiment, was rewarded on its return in November 1900 with a week long celebration though the Chief Constable reported 'no violence, no disturbance and no exceptional indulgence'.[29]

At the same time as the Volunteers were increasing, the call for the formation of rifle clubs was raised, largely as a result of a speech by Lord Salisbury to the Primrose League on 9 May 1900. Many Volunteers were critical of any bodies which would openly compete with the Force, the *Volunteer Service Gazette* urging that they be placed under Volunteer control. The Bucks. County Rifle Association went as far as refusing to recognise any rifle clubs unless they excluded all men between the ages of 18 and 35 years who had not served in the Volunteer Force for at least five years.[30]

The authorisation to recruit above establishment was but one of many concessions to the Volunteer Force announced by Lansdowne and Wyndham on 12 February 1900. The 98 Volunteer artillery batteries were to be re-armed with the more modern 4.7 inch guns in position batteries with the 15 pdr. field-gun for the remainder; Mounted Infantry companies would now be encouraged; a limited number of Regular commissions would be offered to the Volunteers among others to fill the vacancies in the twelve new Regular battalions to be raised; regimental transport would be supported and Volunteers could enlist in the Reserve on a scheme proposed by Earl Wemyss. The Government also proposed to get all the Volunteer Force under canvas in summer emergency camps of exercise, lasting for one month in the case of infantry and three months in the case of artillery. This would fit the Volunteer Force for the defence of the country upon level with Regulars now that it must depended upon to supply garrisons and protect the coast against raids. Wyndham commented: 'We cannot compel the Volunteers — we do not wish to compel them — all that we say is that we are ready to give them all that they need in order to make themselves into an efficient force.'[31]

The irony of this sudden Government support for the Volunteer Force after the years of neglect was not lost on M.P.'s although Wyndham's proposals were welcomed by Volunteer M.P.'s and those not implacably hostile to the war. Several Volunteer M.P.'s, however, doubted the ability of the Force to go into camp for a month and Wyndham subsequently indicated that the Government was prepared to allow corps to earn the special camp grant provided at least 50 per cent of the unit camped for 14 days. The allowances, in addition to the normal capitation grant, were in fact attractive with two guineas per man, army pay and allowances and separation allowances for families. The Government was prepared to set an example by releasing its own employees, and Lansdowne announced in May 1900 that 179 of the 216 Volunteer battalions had already agreed to camp for 14 days. Other units such as J.H.A. Macdonald's Queen's Edinburgh Rifle Brigade were able to camp for the full 28 days and concentrate on progressive instruction in field duties and fire training. Wyndham further promised an additional £100,000 for ranges and T.F. Fremantle and another officer were sent to Switzerland to investigate the possibility of utilising shorter ranges.[32]

A new Military Lands Bill was introduced to extend to Urban District Councils those powers given County Councils and Borough Councils in the 1892 Act, and to give them powers of compulsory hire similar to those used for allotments under the 1892 Local Government Act. The measure was strongly supported by the new Counties Volunteer Development Association and the County Councils Association, for which Lord Northbrook was the chief spokesman, and the Bill received the Royal Assent without much opposition on 8 August 1900.[33] More controversial, however, was the Volunteer's Bill introduced in the Lords by Lansdowne on 18 May 1900. The Bill sought once more to change Volunteer law and enable Volunteers to be called out in cases of imminent national danger or great emergency. The Bill also allowed Volunteers to enter into agreements to serve anywhere in the world without the prior necessity of Royal proclamation, which would allow such as submarine miners to be utilised at once in an emergency and allow the Government to accept garrison offers and service companies. Lansdowne argued that the bill would enable the War Office to determine the Volunteer response in a crisis and would avoid the hasty improvisation of December 1899. In the Commons Wyndham insisted that the Bill was merely an extension of the concept of the Select Committee on Volunteer Acts of 1894 and was supported by the opinion of a conference of 16 Volunteer C.O.s which had met in April 1899. The Institute of C.O.s of Volunteers was, in fact, in favour of the Bill and Volunteer M.P.'s such as Howard Vincent and Lt.-Col. Pilkington spoke in its support, but the Bill encountered opposition. In the Lords, Lord Monkswell, the Earl of Kimberley and Earl Spencer had all argued that the Government was taking advantage of a 'hot fit' of patriotism and attempting to bind the Volunteers to agreements for the future which would be opposed by employers. The Earl of Kimberley also suggested that if the Bill was passed, 'great emergencies' might often occur, but Wyndham refuted this sort of argument by insisting that it was not a ploy to dispatch the Volunteers to Ceylon or the Mediterranean at the first indication of Imperial unrest. More opposition was encountered in the Commons from Campbell-Bannerman and Radicals such as Captain Norton, Captain Sinclair and John Burns and also Arnold-Forster, who feared the reaction of employers. Although the Bill passed both the Lords and Commons fairly comforably, the provisions were modified considerably in the Commons Committee stage so that Volunteers could undertake only to do garrison duty in specified places in Great Britain.[34] The Bill received the Royal Assent on 6 August 1900.

Yet, despite the new attention given to the Volunteer Force, it was becoming clear that some sections of the War Office maintained the almost traditional antipathy to the Force and, indeed, 1902 was to prove the worst year of Volunteer recruiting in the entire history of the Force. The development of this hostile attitude to the Volunteer Force and its consequences can now be examined.

Private Hostility

On 12 March 1900 Wyndham announced that the I.G.A.F. would be freed of the duties of Inspector General of Recruiting, which he had undertaken since 1894, and 2 D.A.A.G.'s would be appointed to recreate A.G.3 as a separate branch. The new D.A.A.G.'s were Major E.L. Engleheart for the Volunteers and Captain R.G. Merriman for the Militia in addition to Lt.-Col. H. Le Roy Lewis, who had been appointed in March 1901 to help organise the Imperial Yeomanry and who now remained with A.G.3. The new I.G.A.F. was Major-General Alfred Turner, who in the past had attended Volunteer wargames and exercises and who had been Lansdowne's liaison officer at the Mansion House in December 1899. Turner enjoyed the support of Lansdowne and Wolseley, but he discovered that his new department was much resented and constantly under attack: 'I must cordially admit that the energy displayed was great and worthy of a better cause.' In March 1901 the Adjutant-General, Evelyn Wood, called for the dismantling of A.G.3. but Lord Roberts, now C.-in-C., refused. In September 1901 Wood insisted that Turner was not entitled to carry out inspections and, on this point, Roberts agreed that it should rest with O.C.'s of Regimental Districts. Kelly-Kenny, who succeeded Wood as Adjutant-General, was no more friendly to Turner's branch and in December 1901, without reference to Turner, the War Office Council resolved to abolish the 2 D.A.A.G.'s. An attempt to reduce Turner once more to the status of D.A.G. was vetoed by the Secretary of State, Brodrick, in March 1902, but the 2 D.A.A.G.'s were abolished leaving only Le Roy Lewis as Turner's assistant. In line with the recommendations of the Dawkins Committee, the civilian clerks were removed and replaced by 2 retired officers and 7 pensioner clerks.[35] Eustace Balfour had warned his brother, Arthur, as early as June 1900 that although Turner would do his best there were other influences at work in the War Office 'which are universally believed to be inimical to Volunteers. It is not a good thing to propagate such a belief among a million intelligent voters!'.[36] Given the precarious nature of Turner's position and his lack of influence within the War Office, it was not surprising that the Volunteer Force began to suffer from new policies, the most notorious of which was the 'Christmas Card' order of December 1901.

The 'Christmas Card' order of 24 December 1901 originated in the following manner. In March 1901 Brodrick, who had succeeded Lansdowne as Secretary of State in the preceding October, unfolded his plans for 6 Army Corps to which the Volunteer Force would contribute 15 batteries and 25 battalions in the 4th, 5th and 6th Corps. The Volunteer 'Field Army' battalions would be required to fulfil special training liabilities, including 13 days' camp annually exclusive of travelling, whilst the remainder of the Force would also be subject to increased efficiency standards. Brodrick indicated that he was more concerned with efficiency than numbers in the Volunteer Force, and he was ready, as he wrote to Roberts in May 1901, to court unpopularity: 'I am quite prepared to push up the tests for efficiency till we reduce them.'[37] In August 1901 a committee on Volunteer Training chaired by the Under-Secretary of State, Lord Raglan, recommended compulsory annual camps of at least 6 days for all the Volunteer Force with no corps allowed to miss camping in 2 consecutive years; extra drills in lieu of camp and an increased musketry standard. These new efficiency regulations, approved by Order in Council on 4 November 1901, were then issued on 24 December 1901 but the order began with the provocative passage:

> For some years past the Volunteer Force has constantly claimed to be seriously accepted as a reliable and organised section of the Army for Home Defence. It is now determined that the responsibility claimed shall be realised.[38]

There was an immediate outcry not only at the new standards of efficiency but also with the offending passage, especially when it became clear that Turner had not been consulted on the wording of the order. Howard Vincent indicated in the Commons on 6 March 1902 that he had discovered the identity of the drafter of the order. He hinted at the author's identity again in an open letter to Arnold-Forster in May 1904; in the Commons in February 1905, and, finally, on 13 July 1905, he named Lt.-Col. Walter Adye as responsible for both the 1901 order and the equally notorious June circular of 1905, which will be discussed in the next chapter.[39] As noted previously, Adye had delivered a lecture highly critical of the Volunteers at the R.U.S.I. in 1890 and he had served as the representative of the A.G.'s Training Branch on Raglan's committee. He had also been involved in the disaster at Nicholson's Nek during the South African War but had been cleared by the inquiry and returned to duty. In a memorandum to Arnold-Forster, written in June 1904 in reply to Vincent's open letter, Adye denied that he was responsible, claiming that Roberts and Brodrick had approved the order, that Brodrick had actually drafted it and that Turner had only been by-passed in his absence because of the necessity to send out the order before Christmas.[40] The tone of the memorandum, however, with its strictures on the 'loud-mouthed section' of the Volunteers indicates that Adye was no friend of the Volunteers or of a separate Volunteer branch.

The outcry against the efficiency standards themselves was also considerable, although Eustace Balfour was inclined to be charitable and ignore the seemingly 'overwhelming' evidence that the War Office wished to destroy the Volunteer Force. Both the Under-Secretary of State, Lord Raglan and the Financial Secretary, Lord Stanley, believed, however, that the opposition in London was bogus and 'got up by a few malcontent Metropolitan Commanding Officers who would oppose any change'. Spenser Wilkinson similarly believed that the 'commanding officers of the London corps found it easy to ventilate their discontent, while the provincial Volunteers had no means of expressing their satisfaction and no reason for doing so'. Indeed, Wilkinson communicated the support of the Manchester Tactical Society for compulsory camps to Roberts on 30 December 1901, feeling that Roberts had received the impression that his efforts to improve the Volunteers had not met with the response they deserved.[41] In response to the pressure, Brodrick announced on 27 January that he was inviting five Volunteers — Col. Villiers, 1st Surrey; Col. Haworth, 3rd V.B. Lancs. Fusiliers; Col. Williamson, M.P., 1st V.B. Dorset; Lt.-Col. Sir R. Moncrieffe, 4th V.B. Black Watch, and Col. Allen, 4th West Riding A.V. — to join a new committee under Lord Raglan to consider the representations of difficulty on the new regulations.[42] Whilst the Committee was still sitting, Brodrick again stressed that he aimed at efficiency rather than numbers, while Howard Vincent blamed a loss of 18,000 men between October and January on the new regulations and Mr Wylie, M.P., calculated at least a 25 per cent reduction in the Force if not a 60 per cent reduction. Raglan's Committee, which interviewed some fifteen witnesses, including Howard Vincent and T. Sturmy Cave, recommended some minor concessions in drill requirements before camp but declined to alter the new camping regulations. The Committee did, however, recommend special consideration for those corps unable to attend and, bearing in mind the tendency to recruit inefficients for monetary purposes, recommended a full inquiry into grants which had remained basically unchanged since 1887. Brodrick and Roberts with the leading members of the Committee met a deputation from the Institute of C.O.'s of Volunteers and Scottish Institute of C.O.'s of Volunteers, led by Vincent, on 12 March 1902 and communicated the recommendations. There was still some disquiet at the effect which the regulations would have and Brodrick's idea of a Volunteer Reserve was rejected, but Col. Denny, M.P., of the 1st Dumbarton R.V., indicated that the Force would once more do its best to meet the new requirements as it had done with so many unpopular measures in the past. Under the revised conditions, Brodrick was now prepared to grant exemption from the camps in special circumstances provided additional drills were completed but no corps would be exempted for two consecutive years. The new conditions would, in certain circumstances, not come into force until 1 November 1904.[43]

Lesser indications of War Office antipathy to the Volunteers can also be detected in some of the decisions of the War Office Council at the end of 1901. In October 1901, for example, it was decided to reorganise the Volunteer Force into 51 brigades instead of 34 as before. This followed the recommendations of an Adjutant-General's Committee of August 1901 consisting of Percy Lake, Walter Adye and Engelheart, the D.A.A.G. of A.G.3. But Volunteers would only command 8 of the new brigads with the remainder under the O.C.'s of Regimental Districts. In the War Office Council, both the Adjutant-General, Wood, and the Inspector-General of Fortifications, General Sir Richard Harrison, had opposed even this limited number of Volunteer brigadiers. In a further meeting of the Council in November 1901, all but the I.G.A.F, Turner, opposed the principle of Volunteer field artillery and it was resolved to abandon all experiments.[44]

The year 1902 thus closed with considerable uncertainty for the Volunteer Force. It had lost nearly 20,000 men during the year and, of course, a loss of numbers meant a loss of income from the capitation grant, a situation which put a severe strain on many Commanding Officers. By March 1903 the Force was over 98,000 men short of establishment. In such a situation the Royal Commission into the Militia and Volunteers, proposed by the Government in March 1903, was seen as an attempt to muzzle discussion rather than cure the ills of the Force. Sir Gilbert Parker considered that the Royal Commission was 'designed to kill agitation in the healing springs of time' but Mr Renwick, M.P., remarked that if Brodrick intended it as a sleeping draught like the other 12 Royal Commissions appointed by the Government then he would 'find himself mistaken'.[45] On 6 October 1903, whilst the Commission was still at work, Eustace Balfour, retired but still actively interested in Volunteer affairs, wrote to his brother, now Prime Minister, that the decrease in numbers was still continuing by leaps and bounds. For this, there was but one reason: 'I find the reason to be a deep distrust of the War Office and its present chief in particular.' The same day H.O. Arnold-Forster was given permission by his doctor to take up the duties of Secretary of State and Brodrick went to the India Office. In Winston Churchill's picturesque words 'that fertile imagination which used to call forth Armies so easily was no condemned to exile in the frozen deserts of Tibet'.[46] If the Volunteers had once been neglected by successive governments, they were now about to receive more attention than they wished.

The South African War saw a tremendous upsurge in the popularity of both Army and Volunteers. In the crisis so long awaited, over 19,000 Volunteers had served abroad and proved themselves at least fairly useful auxiliaries to the Regular Army. More important, the Volunteer Force was virtually the only home defence left to the United Kingdom apart, of course, from the Navy and was recognised as such with major Government concessions. This did not mean to say that the Force did not need reform. Brodrick determined on efficiency rather than numbers in the Volunteer Force, which would have been hard enough to enforce without the tactless interventions of elements in the War Office clearly hostile to the Volunteers. Inevitably, distrust of the War Office grew amongst the Volunteers and numbers declined. In such circumstances, the worst enemy of the Volunteer Force was uncertainty and that, perhaps, would be ended with a newly appointed Royal Commission and a new Secretary of State.

[1] *LSRG* IV (August 1899), p 124 and IV (Nov. 1899), p 159-160. Jeyes and How, op. cit., p 307-11.

[2] *VSG* 23.9.99, p 305; 13.10.99, p 806; *LSRG* IV (Nov. 1899), p 163-4.

[3] Wyndham, 26.10.99 *AD* (1900), I, 305-6 Brookfield, op. cit., p 248.

[4] F. Maurice and Sir George Arthur, *The Life of Lord Wolseley*, (London 1924), p 332; Report by Col. Boxall in *Reports on the Raising, Organising, Equipping and Dispatching of the City Imperial Volunteers* (London June 1900), p 1-18; *Daily Graphic* Special CIV Number of 27.10.99 in NAM CIV Papers, 6505-71; G. St. J. Barclay, *The Empire is Marching* (London 1976) p 27-41; *Salisbury Papers*, Lansdowne to Salisbury, 15.12.99.

[5] Ibid., *Reports* by H.K. Newton, Equipment Committee, p 43-58 and by T.F. Fremantle, p 19; Turner, op cit., p 302-4; Bucks. R.O., *Fremantle* D/FR/176 Fremantle to Wife, 20.12.99.

[6] Guildhall Library *CIV Collection* Mss 10,197; 10,199 and 10,206; W.H. Mackinnon, *The Journal of the CIV in South Africa* (London 1901), p 1-2; G.H. Scott and G.L. McDonnell, *The Record of the Mounted Infantry of the CIV* (London 1901), p 1; Jeyes and How, op. cit., p 312-8.

[7] Dunlop, op. cit., p 99-103; Grierson, op. cit., p 92-5; NAM 6505-71 and 7203-13 Scrapbook of 1st Middx. V.B.

[8] Dunlop, op. cit., p 103-118.

[9] Lamont, op. cit., p 127; Macdonald, op. cit., p 485-6; Brownlow, 15.2.1900 *AD* (1900), I, 1358-60 and Seely, 4.2.1900 *AD* (1902), I, 587.

[10] Arnold Forster 23.2.05 AD (1905), 263; *Arnold-Forster Papers* Add Mss 50312 Section 45 and 47; H.O. Arnold-Forster, *The Army in 1906* (London 1906) App. IV., p 538-9; Wyndham, 16.3.1900 *AD* (1900), II, 687.

[11] Colomb, 15.6.04 AD (1904); Colomb, 23.2.05 *AD* (1905), 210-11; *LSRG* VII (July 1902), p 121.

[12] Mackinnon, op. cit., appendices H, I and K; *Reports* op. cit. p 20-42; *LSRG* VII (July 1902), p 121; *BPP* 1901[Cd 610]XL. 175; *NAM* 6505-71-50.

[13] *PRO* WO 108/5.

[14] *Reports* op. cit., p 20-42; Mackinnon, p 221-3; Guildhall Mss 10193 Misc. Correspondence.

[15] R. Price, *An Imperial War and the British Working Class* (London 1972), p 197-216, 257-8 from *PRO* WO 128/1-165; *BPP* 1904[Cd 2064]xxxi, 587 Pt. IV, p 190-275; Forbes, op. cit., p 11-12; H. Josling, *The Autobiography of a Military Greatcoat* (London 1907), p 19-20; M. Howard, op. cit. p 88.

[16] Erskine Childers, *In the Ranks of the CIV* (London 1900); *BPP* 1900 (67); H.W. Wilson, *With the Flag to Pretoria* (London 1900), p 230-4.

[17] J. Barclay Lloyd, *One Thousand Miles with the CIV* (London 1901), p 272; J. Barclay Lloyd and Lionel Curtis, *The CIV in South Africa* (London 1900); Letters of Private E. Blecher NAM 7302-7; *LSRG* V (Nov. 1900), p 141.

[18] Childers, op. cit., p 5.

[19] Metcalfe to Kemp, 16.1.1900 in *Khaki Letters* (Central Telegraph Office 1900-1) in Post Office R.O. R7/3; Guildhall Mss 10,205 Letters of Stuart Hills, 30.8.00 and Barclay Lloyd 8.5.00; Josling, op. cit. p 155-6; *LSRG* V (Nov. 1900), p 145 and V (Dec. 1900), 155-6; Childers, op. cit., p 103 and 301; Lloyd and Curtis op. cit., pt XX.

[20] *Arnold-Forster Papers* Add Mss 50312 section 45; Mackinnon, op. cit., p 202-3, 224-6; Scott and McDonnell, op. cit., p xiv and 223; Dunlop, op cit., p 99; Childers, op. cit. p 298; NAM 6505-71-50; *BPP* 1904 [Cd 2062] xxx 259 Minutes of evidence, I, 1145.

[21] *Western Gazette* 14.6.1901 in Dorset Military Museum DMM/3/220; Fisher, op. cit. p 123-7; Sainsbury, op. cit, p 52; Josling, op. cit. passim; Dunlop, op. cit., p 102-3.

[22] Brodrick to Cabinet 20.11.01 *PRO* Cab 37/59 No. 122.

[23] Bedford, 25.6.01 *AD* (1901), II, 876-880; Roberts to Cabinet 9.3.03 *PRO* Cab 37/64 No. 17.

[24] Mackinnon, op. cit., p 224-6.

[25] Wyndham, 12.2.1900 *AD* (1900), I, 1178-85; Moon, op. cit., I, p 161-2.

[26] Bucks. R.O. *Fremantle* D/FR/169 County Rifle Association Papers and circulars of Middlesex CC; Lansdowne and Dunraven 5.2.1900 *AD* (1900), I, 779-81, 783-4; Lansdowne, 12.2.1900 *AD* (1900), I, 1144-48.

[27] Gillingham Local History Society Museum *Freame Mss* L. Coy, Diaries, 29.12.99; *LSRG* V (Mar 1900), p 36; Bucks. R.O. *Fremantle* D/FR/169 Reports of Bucks. Home Defence Committee; W. Carlile, 29.3.1900 *AD* (1900), II, 854.

[28] *LSRG* IV (Dec. 1899), p 172; *Khaki Letters* No. 3, p 135; G.L.R.O. (M) *Lieutenancy* L/C/99 Papers of War Fund for Middx. Volunteers.

[29] West Sussex R.O. *MP* 17 nos. 15-17; Forde, op. cit. p 114-5.

[30] Cottesloe, op. cit. p 258; Lamont, op. cit. p 134; Brownlow, 28.5.1900 *AD* (1900), II, 1324-5; *VSG* 18.5.1900, p 456; Bucks. R.O. *Fremantle* D/FR/169 Meeting of Home Defence Committee 30.3.1900.

[31] Lansdowne, 2.2.1900 *AD* (1900), I, 1133-48; Wyndham, 12.2.1900, 1185-96; *PRO* Cab 37/52 No. 14 Lansdowne to Cabinet 8.2.1900; Grierson, op. cit., p 101; Lamont, op. cit. p 130.

[32] Cf. *AD* (1900), I, 1220-1; 1248-58; 1275-81; 1327-9; 1330-3; Wyndham, 12.3.1900 *AD* (1900) II, 434-40; Lansdowne, 22.5.1900 *AD* (1900), II, 1252-3; Macdonald, op. cit. p 486-94; Seely, 16.3.1900 *AD* (1900), II, 691.

[33] Lansdowne, 18.5.1900, *AD* (1900), 1232-4; Northbrook, 18.5.1900 *AD* (1900), II, 1235-6 and 28.5.1900, 1331.

[34] *PRO* Cab 37/52 No. 47 Lansdowne to Cabinet, 9.5.1900; Wyndham, 18.7.1900 *AD* (1900) III, 137-147, Lords debate *AD* (1900) II, 1317-30 and 1509-14; Wyndham 18.7.1900 *AD* (1900) III, 144, Commons debate 18.7.1900 *AD* (1900) III, 137-77, *LSRG* VII (Aug. 1902), p 148.

[35] Turner, op cit., p 304-7; *BPP* 1904 [Cd 2063] xxx I Mins of evidence, II, 21806-22048, 23708-23734; NAM *Roberts Papers* 7101-23-122/2 No. 136, p 157-9, Roberts to Wood, 21.9.01; Hamer, op. cit. p 174-200.

[36] *Balfour Papers* Add Mss 49831 Eustace Balfour to A.J. Balfour, 14.6.1900.

[37] Brodrick, 8.3.01 *AD* (1901), I, 1268-70; NAM *Roberts Papers*, 7101-23, 13/55 Brodrick to Roberts, 10.5.1901.

[38] *PRO* WO 33/206 A 698; *BPP* 1902(224) LVIII. 705; *LSRG* VII (Jan. 1902), p 9-17; Vincent, 6.3.1902 *AD* (1902) I, 1004-16.

[39] Vincent, 6.3.02 *AD* (1902), I, 1008-10; Vincent, 22.2.05 and 13.7.05 *AD* (1905), 91-4 and 1985-6; *Arnold-Forster Papers* Add Mss 50313 section 1 and Add Mss 50349 diary entries for 14, 15 and 19 July 1905.

[40] NAM *Roberts Papers* 7101-23-122/1 No. 34, p 111 Roberts Memo of 23.3.01; Add

227

Mss 50313 section 1.

[41] *LSRG* VII (Mar. 1902), p 50; *PRO* WO 163/5 War Office Council meeting of 16.12.01 and 20.1.02; Wilkinson, *Thirty Five Years*, op. cit., p 256-8; NAM *Roberts Papers* 7101-23-122/3 No. 305, p 41-2 Roberts to Wilkinson, 30.12.01; WO Library, Minutes of Manchester Tactical Society, p 145-154.

[42] Brodrick, 27.1.02 AD (1902), I, 374; PRO WO 163/5 Minutes of meeting of 27.1.02; WO 33/222 A 724 Committee on the New Volunteer Efficiency Regulations.

[43] Brodrick, 4.3.02 *AD* (1902), I, 901-6; *PRO* WO 33/222 A 724A; *LSRG* VII (Aug. 1902), p 142 and VIII (Jan. 1903), p 16.

[44] *PRO* WO 33/205 A 697 Report of Committee to consider the organisation of Volunteer and Militia Brigades; WO 163/5 War Office Council meetings of 31.10.01 and 11.11.01; Col. A.G. Hayward, 'Volunteer Artillery, past, present and future', *JRUSI* XLVI (1902), p 784ff.

[45] Lambton, Parker and Renwick, 9.3.03. *AD* (1903), I. 521-4, 530-1, 566-8.

[46] *Balfour Papers* Add Mss 49851 E. Balfour to A.J. Balfour, 6.10.03; *Arnold-Forster Papers* Add Mss 50335 diary entry for 4-6.10.03; Winston Churchill, 23.2.05. *AD* (1905), 276-7.

CHAPTER VIII

THE VOLUNTEERS AND ARMY REFORM
1902-1908

"For we as Volunteers, joined that British band
  When dread invasion's shadow crossed our land,
And with a love of home as deep as keen,
  Joined hearts and hands to guard our widowed Queen.
T'was but a shadow, and ere the phantom's flight
  A hundred thousand Volunteers had sprung to light".

'Prologue'
13th Surrey R.V.C. Dramatic Club

Although much has been written on the Army reform schemes of Brodrick, Arnold-Forster and Haldane, very little mention has been made of the role of the Volunteers in the years between 1902 and 1908. The central issues concerning the final years of the Volunteer Force from the appointment of the Norfolk Commission to the creation of the Territorial Force lie, firstly, in the reasons for the success of the Volunteers in resisting Arnold-Forster. Secondly, they concern the reasons why there was not similar success against Haldane.

Brodrick's plans for the Volunteers were not, strictly speaking, part of his larger six Army Corps scheme, and the scheme itself received little attention from Volunteer M.P.'s, who were far more concerned with the practical difficulties of the new camping regulations. There was, however, some difficulty with the Treasury and vociferous opposition to Brodrick from a small group of discontented young Conservatives, the central figures being Lord Hugh Cecil, Ernest Beckett, Winston Churchill, J.E.B. Seely, Sir John Dickson-Poynder and Ivor Guest. There was a feeling at the time that the group, four of whom were Yeomanry officers, was more concerned with self-assertion than army reform. Seely, indeed, later admitted that they had no coherent alternative policy to offer. Subsequently the group, all of whom were members of the 'Free Food League', found a more profitable issue in tariff reform and, as a result, all crossed the floor to the Liberals.[1] Their carefully planned assault on Brodrick's scheme began with the debate on the Address on 23 February 1903, when nearly twenty Conservatives voted against the Government. It is likely that the appointment of the Royal Commission on Militia and Volunteers, first proposed by Brodrick in the War Office Council on 2 March 1903, was partly influenced by the desire to avoid any additional agitation from Volunteer M.P.'s who were still far from happy with the new regulations. Volunteer M.P.'s, as was noted in the last chapter, certainly believed that it was an attempt to suspend discussion on grievances they were once more about to raise, and the Royal Commission did effectively end discussion of the Volunteer Force for twelve months. The difficulties encountered by the Royal Commission itself lent additional support to the suspicion that little importance was attached to its deliberations.

The Norfolk Commission

The War Office Council resolved that the Royal Commission should determine the minimum standard of efficiency required of Volunteers, a minimum term of service, a definite military scheme and that it should also consider problems such as Volunteer field artillery and transport. In order to give guidance the D.M.I., Lt.-Gen. Sir William Nicholson, was directed to produce a paper on the number of Auxiliaries required for Imperial defence. Nicholson, whose report was dated 30 March 1903, contrasted the interpretations on the likelihood of invasion by the Admiralty and the War Office. Whereas the Navy believed a raid of 5,000 men the maximum likely, the War Office required a field army of 100,000 men to meet a possible invasion of up to 50,000 troops. Nicholson naturally subscribed to the War Office view but, even so, considered that the Auxiliaries were not only too numerous for home defence but unreliable as reinforcements for the Regular Army abroad due to the legal difficulties. He recommended extended liability on the part of the Militia and some Volunteers and Imperial Yeomanry, with responsibility for home defence handed to a more efficiently organised Auxiliary Force stiffened by Regulars. As part of the more efficient organisation, he recommended a reduction of the Volunteer establishment by 70,000 to 278,000 men. Unfortunately, Nicholson's paper was considered too secret to be given to the Royal Commission, especially in view of the divergence of opinion it revealed between Admiralty and War Office. There was some discussion on extended liability, which Brodrick resisted on the grounds of increased cost, and it was decided to leave the whole problem to the Committee of Imperial Defence. A further paper by Nicholson, dated 7 May 1903, considered the exact number of Auxiliaries required for reinforcement of the Regular Army abroad. It was based on the assumption that two Militiamen or three Volunteers were equal to one Continental soldier. This was also deferred for possible discussion by the C.I.D.[2] with the result that the D.M.I. could give little assistance to the Royal Commission.

The Royal Commission, chaired by the Duke of Norfolk, began work on 19 May 1903 and at once attempted to define the actual function of the Militia and Volunteers. It received no help from the authorities. The D.M.I. gave the Commission a rough total of 264,000 Auxiliaries which he considered necessary, though the Commission was told not to regard this as the proper figure. The D.N.I., Prince Louis of Battenberg, declined on 20 May to attend at all.[3] The Duke of Norfolk requested the C.I.D. on 26 May to define the duties of the Auxiliaries, the scale of the invasion likely and the number of Regulars expected to be available to aid the defence, but on 22 June 1903 the C.I.D. replied that the Commission must work on the existing numbers of Auxiliaries. On 22 July 1903 the C.I.D. instructed the Royal Commission to confine its enquiry to maintaining the numbers and efficiency of the Auxiliary Forces and to calculate on the present mobilisation scheme. However, when the Duke of Norfolk requested details of the mobilisation scheme, the C.I.D. replied on 5 August 1903 that they could not reveal the mobilisation scheme. They suggested, however, that the Commission assume a limit of 200,000 Volunteers and 100,000 Militia though this was only a basis to work on and not a definite total.[4]

The C.I.D. set up by Balfour in 1902, had, in fact, been carrying out its own enquiries into the invasion problem and Balfour had come down on the side of the Admiralty in believing invasion impracticable and only raids likely. Balfour, himself, was far more concerned with the defence of India.[5] However, the C.I.D. did not see fit to reveal its decisions to the Norfolk Commission. Possibly, as one writer has suggested, this was because it regarded the Commissioners as the type of amateur body it was designed to eliminate or because it considered, as Lansdowne and Arnold-Forster later indicated, that the Commission was exceeding its terms of reference and 'poaching' on the domain of the C.I.D.[6]

In a memorandum to the Cabinet, dated 9 March 1903 and authorised by the War Office Council, Lord Roberts had stated his own belief and that of his leading Military advisers that the Auxiliary Forces could not be safely entrusted with the defence of the United Kingdom unaided due to the deficiencies in officers and training. In view of this memorandum, which at the suggestion of King Edward VII was not published to avoid offending the Auxiliaries, it is not surprising that the Regular witnesses to the Norfolk Commission all considered the Militia and Volunteers not sufficiently trained to face Continental troops. It was felt this would only be possible if the Auxiliaries had the advantage of superior numbers and a period of continuous training, which varied between witnesses from three months to one year. Even Howard Vincent admitted that the Force was not absolutely fit for the field.[7] Inevitably the Commission concluded that the Militia was unfit for the field and that, in view of deficiencies in equipment and training, the Volunteer Force was 'not qualified to take the field against a Regular Army'.

The Commissioners made detailed proposals for both the Militia and the Volunteers, those for the Volunteers largely inspired by Spenser Wilkinson, including; Regular commissions, training 'in situ', increased camping allowances, 14 day camps, state aid for ranges and transport, a Volunteer Staff and A.S.C., tactical schools and a separate Volunteer department at the War Office. However, the Commissioners and many witnesses were men who largely believed in the possibility of invasion, and many saw the best solution to the problem in terms of conscription, notably the Duke of Wellington and George Shee, who were called as representatives of the National

Service League formed in 1902. The Commission therefore concluded that the only means of defeating an invasion without Regular support would be by a Home Defence Army raised by conscription. Eight of the Commissioners signed the majority report, largely drafted by Wilkinson and Major-Gen. Sir Coleridge Grove, though Wilkinson saw no need for conscription if the other proposals were effected.[9]

The report, dated 20 May 1904, was welcomed by advocates of conscription such as Lord Newton, Lord Raglan and the Duke of Wellington, but many Volunteers such as Lt.-Col. Greig of the London Scottish and Lt.-Col. Alfred Gilbey of the 1st Bucks. found little comfort in its findings. T.F. Fremantle favoured a Home Defence Army but based on the existing auxiliaries, and he feared the discouragement the report might cause: 'They (the Volunteers) have no wish to continue their efforts if those efforts are not accepted as having a definite place in a definite scheme for home defence, such as has too long been lacking in this country.'[9] The Army Council was in favour of conscription but Arnold-Forster totally rejected the findings of the Commission:

> The Commission has gone altogether beyond the terms of reference, in reporting upon the desirability of conscription, a matter about which it was not asked for an opinion, and with regard to which it speaks without authority.

As far as he was concerned, the report was 'unimportant' and only showed that reform was needed. Arnold-Forster had written to Guy Fleetwood Wilson on 20 May that the Norfolk Commission was 'a tiresome thing which never ought to have been created'. Although he was prepared to accept some of the proposals, he announced in the Commons on 2 June that the report would not be acted upon. A.J. Balfour repeated the decision on 6 June. The press and others had emphasised the conscription proposals and as a result the whole was discarded, many useful proposals lost and nearly thirteen months' work wasted.[10] Nothing had been achieved, the Volunteer Force was still declining in numbers and it was now faced with the plans of H.O. Arnold-Forster. But, before examining Arnold-Forster's struggle with the Volunteer Force in detail, it is necessary to outline his overall military policies and to identify the many other sources of opposition besides the Volunteers to his plans.

The Fall of H.O. Arnold-Forster

Arnold-Forster was not Balfour's first choice for the War Office in October 1903 and, in all, nine men were considered of whom five refused, including the former Tory Whip, Akers-Douglas, and Lord Esher. Arnold-Forster himself had many apparent qualifications for the post, having studied military problems for many years and published such works as *Army Letters* in 1898 and *The War Office, the Army and the Empire* in 1900 as well as co-operating with Spenser Wilkinson, Sir Charles Dilke and Sir George Chesney on the celebrated joint letter on national defences in 1894.[11] Arnold-Forster had developed very definite ideas on what was required in Army reform, the origins of his policies being clearly indicated in his earlier books. He was not prepared to change these ideas, as Lord Roberts recognised when he wrote to Balfour in July 1904:

> perhaps the fact that he long ago formed very decided opinions as to the way in which it should be dealt with has lead him to formulate a scheme in accordance with these opinions, without his having sufficient knowledge of the Army to enable him to appreciate the consequences of the changes he proposes.[12]

Nor was Arnold-Forster's character conducive to good relationships with his colleagues and subordinates, and all who came into contact with him recorded their impressions of his dogmatism, irritability and tactlessness. Leo Amery recalled that his 'zeal' outran his patience in dealing with senior officers: 'They complained, not altogether without reason, that he was too apt to lecture them and too little inclined to listen . . .'. One story widely circulated at the time was that Arnold-Forster had summoned Grenfell from Ireland in January 1904 to give his opinion on the Army reform scheme but had then lectured him for forty-five minutes without Grenfell being able to express his views. Arnold-Forster's conduct of his affairs was often tactless, as when the previous heads of the War Office, including the C.-in-C., Lord Roberts, were informed by letter on a Sunday afternoon that the new Army Council, recommended by the Esher Committee, would commence its work the following day and that they were all dismissed. The I.G.A.F., Turner, escaped 'Black Monday' and was asked to remain at his post, but a few weeks later, without explanation, Arnold-Forster informed him that a successor had been appointed — Major-General W.H. Mackinnon.[13]

A.J. Balfour wrote to Lord Esher in July 1904 of Arnold-Forster's habits of regarding arguments against his scheme as personal attacks and of his conveying the impression that everyone to whom he had talked agreed with him: 'so that he is perpetually quoting eminent soldiers to me as being among his supporters, though I suspect they look with considerable coldness on many parts of his scheme'. However, to be fair to Arnold-Forster, he was the victim of considerable duplicity on the part of his colleagues, so much so that he wrote to Jack Sandars, Balfour's secretary, in January 1905 that the War Office was 'a perfect caravanserai, where everybody has turned in at any casual moment to talk with all my subordinates about what is my business'. Also Arnold-Forster was very much a 'sick man in a hurry' following a severe strain to his heart whilst out riding in 1903. He was well aware of his state of health: 'It is particularly trying to me after so many years of active life to have to give up almost all forms of exercise, to think twice before I do anything, and to know that the most important part of my machinery may play me false any day.' He was frequently ill and, on one occasion, Leo Amery was called in by Mary Arnold-Forster to assist in the preparation of a policy statement for the Commons on 14 July 1904, owing to her husband's collapse. Though they might disagree with his policies, all recognised his courage in face of his heart trouble: 'In feeble health and in frequent pain he never flunked. His devotion to his work and his dogged determination, notwithstanding his disability, commanded respect and admiration.'[14]

Arnold-Forster's scheme was influenced by three basic factors. Firstly, he wished to harness efficiency and economy. Secondly, there was the serious depletion in foreign drafts due to the introduction of three years' short service enlistment by Brodrick and the subsequent failure of men to extend their service. Lastly, Arnold-Forster was an adherent to the 'Blue Water' school and he accepted the decision of the C.I.D., re-emphasised in June 1904 and February 1905, which gave the defence of India the first priority.[15] He proposed to end the old Cardwell scheme of linked battalions and utilise large depots to supply drafts to groups of battalions. More important, he proposed to create two Armies — firstly, a Long Service Army, enlisted for nine years with the colours which would provide foreign garrisons and a striking force; secondly, a Home, or Short Service, Army enlisted for two years with the colours and providing drafts for the Long Service Army in war. The Militia, for which Arnold-Forster had no great regard, would contribute thirty battalions to the Short Service Army and a further twenty-four Militia battalions would be disbanded entirely. The Volunteer Force, would also be considerably reduced and divided into two classes of efficiency. He also proposed to reorganise the cavalry, to build improved barracks and to improve the employment prospects of ex-soldiers.[16]

The main sources of opposition to Arnold-Forster's scheme, other than the Volunteers, have frequently been identified, and it is sufficient here merely to indicate the political background against which the opposition of the Volunteers should be considered. In the Cabinet there was considerable opposition to the Militia plans led by two Militia officers, Lord Selborne, the First Lord of the Admiralty, and Lord Cranborne, the Lord Privy Seal. The Militia plans were also under attack from Lord Salisbury, Sir George Clarke, secretary of the C.I.D., and Balfour because, in Arnold-Forster's words, 'Jim Cranborne and Selborne are good fellows and good Militiamen and naturally stick up for a force which they have worked so hard to save from decay'.[17] The opposition was so successful that Arnold-Forster's Militia plans never reached the floor of the Commons. He was reduced to explaining his ideas to the Commons on 14 July 1904 and to a Militia deputation on 20 July merely as a personal opinion without Cabinet backing.[18] The Chancellor of the Exchequer, Austen Chamberlain, was also opposed to Arnold-Forster's plans on the grounds that they did not cut expenditure sufficiently, but Arnold-Forster continued to complain that he was receiving no co-operation from his colleagues: 'They bid me economise and reform. If I could do as I please I could accomplish this feat; but every man who says "Economise" cried "Hands Off" directly I touch his particular preserve.'[19] Thus the Foreign Office refused to allow troops to be withdrawn from Egypt; the Admiralty refused to take over more overseas responsibilities; the Colonial Office refused to pressure the Dominions into assuming more defence responsibilities and Lord Milner took exception to withdrawing troops from South Africa.

A further difficulty was the presence in the Cabinet of two former Secretaries of State — Brodrick and Lansdowne — whose work Arnold-Forster was reversing. The Army Council proved completely unco-operative with the exception of the Q.M.G., Major-General Plumer, and although giving initial support to the scheme, retracted when it became apparent that Arnold-Forster did not enjoy the confidence of the Cabinet. Arnold-Forster's diary is studded with criticism of the Army Council and of the C.G.S., Lyttelton, in particular. There was also friction between Lyttelton and the Adjutant-General, Douglas, which Lyttelton inadvertently admitted in a speech to the 1st V.B. Leicestershire Regiment in December 1904.[20]

But the most damaging obstructionism, not least because it was largely underhand, came from the triumvirate of Sir George Clarke, Arthur Balfour and Lord Esher, of whom it can best be said that he preferred power to responsibility. The extent of the intrigues of these three, and especially Esher, who enjoyed the confidence and close friendship of both Balfour and the King and their private secretaries (Sandars and Knollys), has been fully examined elsewhere and the details need not be repeated here.[21] It can be noted, however, that the intrigues resulted in a Sub-Committee of the C.I.D. undertaking an investigation of Arnold-Forster's plans in January and February 1905 which endorsed the entirely different plan, based on retention of the Militia, which had been proposed by Balfour. Arnold-Forster, who had originally welcomed the Sub-Committee, soon recognised that it was little more than a tribunal: 'I regret that I speak without accurate knowledge of what is going on; my subordinates know far more than I do, and I think that fact is a proof of the falseness of the situation.' In June 1905, under threat of Arnold-Forster's resignation, the Cabinet allowed him to proceed with short service recruiting for eight battalions despite the objections of the Army Council to such a course.[22] By June 1905, time was running out for the hard-pressed Unionist Government, and it was unlikely that any part of Arnold-Forster's scheme would come to fruition, especially as that part of it which had reached the Commons — the Volunteer plans — was vehemently opposed by Volunteer M.P.'s.

In fact, Arnold-Forster's plans for the Volunteer Force were the most judicious part of his entire scheme of reform. The Force was deficient in both training and equipment and had been allowed to evolve in the localities without any regard to a coherent plan. Finance in particular was a pressing problem for many commanding officers who, in many cases, had been forced to recruit non-efficients simply to earn a grant. There was, however, no more money available for the Volunteer Force without taking it from the Regular Army. Therefore, as Arnold-Forster told a Volunteer deputation in July 1904: 'The only condition on which you will be able to obtain money for the improvement of the Force is by the reduction in numbers, i.e. those that are not and never could be fit to meet a European Force in the field.' Thus he proposed to reduce the establishment of the Volunteer Force by a fourth from 364,000 to 200,000 which, not without justification, he considered would only anticipate reality. The C.I.D. had pronounced that invasion was improbable and thus the reduction in numbers would also be compatible with the size of Force required to defend the country against raids. The actual field strength of the Volunteer Force would be reduced to 180,000 men, of whom 60,000 would be on higher efficiency conditions and receive higher allowances, thus making a distinction not between 'good' and 'bad' men but between those who could afford to give their time and those who could not. Arnold-Forster calculated that there would be a saving of £380,000 which would then be ploughed back into the Force to provide such necessities as transport and provide £50,000 for the development of the rifle clubs. Precisely how the reduction was to be achieved was not clear and in December 1903 the Army Board considered schemes by Arnold-Forster; the I.G.A.F., Turner, and the Adjutant-General,

Kelly-Kenny, based on the new scales of grant and allowances. No decision was reached and on 1 January 1904 Arnold-Forster resolved to await the report of the Norfolk Royal Commission. The report of the Norfolk Commission was, as already described, rejected by Arnold-Forster, and in his Commons statement of 14 July 1904 he merely outlined his plans to reduce the Force without giving details of how it would be done.[23]

Meanwhile, in May and June 1904 Arnold-Forster had already clashed with the Volunteers over the old issue of a separate Volunteer department at the War Office. The Adjutant-General, Kelly-Kenny, was still bitterly opposed to Turner's separate department as Arnold-Forster noted in January 1904: 'I know that the A.G. wishes to see the Volunteers destroyed altogether, and has done his level best, by exasperating and neglecting them, to achieve his object.' Arnold-Forster directed on 17 February that the Auxiliary Forces department should remain separate at least until the report of the Norfolk Commission, but on 31 March the I.G.A.F.'s direct access to the new Army Council was cancelled and the department put firmly back under the Adjutant-General. Turner and Le Roy Lewis were dismissed on 5 April 1904 and the Auxiliary Forces Advisory Boards set up By Brodrick in February 1903 were abolished. The new D.A.F., Major-General Mackinnon, was reduced to responsibility for examining inspection reports, appointments, promotions and retirements, A.D.C.'s, honours and decorations, with the real work being done in new A.G.1, A.G.3, A.G.5, and A.G.8. The only access to the Army Council was now through the Adjutant-General and the new Adjutant-General, Charles Douglas, was as determined as his predecessor that there should be no separate branch.[24] There was considerable disquiet amongst the Volunteers at Turner's dismissal and Turner himself criticised the new arrangements in the press. On 20 April the Institute of C.O.'s of Volunteers passed a resolution calling for a separate department directly responsible to the Army Council through the Parliamentary Under-Secretary of State, one of the civilian members of the Council. Arnold-Forster's circular of the 17 February had meanwhile found its way, 'through the disloyalty of an individual', to the press. Howard Vincent led a demand from the Service Members Committee of the Commons that they be granted an interview with Balfour, and Vincent published his 'open letter' to Arnold-Forster on the need for a separate department. Arnold-Forster was particularly annoyed at former colleagues of the Service Members Committee making proposals on the basis 'of newspaper rumours, and of the half informed, wholly erroneous, stories of certain individuals'. The Secretary of State supplied Balfour with details of his views on a separate department and also his plans for the Volunteers, urging him to remind the deputation that the Regular Army 'is infinitely more important than even the Auxiliary Forces'. On 9 June 1904 Balfour informed the deputation, headed by Vincent, that the D.A.F. would be permitted to have access to the Secretary of State through the Adjutant-General, which had been agreed between Arnold-Forster, Douglas and the C.G.S., Lyttelton, on 8 June 1904.[25]

Balfour steered the deputation away from the planned reduction in the Volunteer Force, and the full extent of Arnold-Forster's proposals was not known until his Commons statement of 14 July. There were doubts on the part of many Volunteer M.P.'s but the main discussions centred on the Militia. Parliament was prorogued on 15 August without any major discussion of the Volunteer proposals which, in any case, were still rather vague. On 25 July Vincent and another Parliamentary deputation met Arnold-Forster at the Commons, and the Secretary of State again outlined his proposals and urged the Volunteers to consider the Army as a whole. The Volunteers themselves were extremely sceptical of dividing the Force into two classes but Arnold-Forster made it clear that there would be reductions. There was no more Parliamentary activity until the following year, but the Volunteers no longer regarded Arnold-Forster as the 'sympathetic' Secretary of State he had claimed to be in January 1904. In the words of Leo Amery, Arnold-Forster had 'raised a hornet's nest of indignant protest from the interests affected'.[26]

Arnold-Forster could hardly afford to incur the animosity of over forty Volunteer M.P.'s but he was, in fact, confident that he could sway the Volunteers to his own point of view. However, on 22 and 23 February 1905, almost as soon as Parliament had re-assembled, the Volunteers obstructed the debate on the address. Volunteer spokesmen such as Howard Vincent, Lt.-Col. Robert Williams, Sir Albert Rollit and the Scottish Liberal, Lt.-Col. McCrae and close allies such as A.C.M. Welby and J.E.B. Seely, strongly opposed reduction of any kind. Arnold-Forster commented, after five hours of obstruction on 22 February:

> A stranger coming into the House would never have realised that we have any Regular Army, that we live on an island, or that there is such a thing as the Royal Navy. The whole idea is there are so many existing Volunteers, and that these Volunteers must be paid to go on existing, simply to please themselves and to oblige their Commanding Officers.[27]

Arnold-Forster was able to allay some fears by announcing that he no longer intended to create two classes in the Force but his new proposals, evolved during the winter, would have much the same effect. Discussions on how to reduce the Volunteer Force had begun in September 1904 between Arnold-Forster, the Adjutant-General and Mackinnon. It had been decided to effect the reduction by means of a gradual raising of physical standards and by the amalgamation or abolition of inefficient units. Arnold-Forster now proposed to reduce the establishment by 5 per cent to 230,000, although this was still a larger Force than was considered necessary for home defence. It was hoped that this would allow 60,000 Volunteers to camp for 14 days at a new allowance of 4s. per man per day, which was 1s. less than had been earned by Brodrick's Field Army battalions. Other allowances would also be raised, notably travelling allowances. There would be new N.C.O. classes and an increased allocation of heavy artillery ammunition to the Volunteer Force; the capitation grant would remain at 35s. for campers but non-campers would only earn a capitation grant of £1. Finally Arnold-Forster proposed to increase Volunteer transport and create a divisional staff for one Volunteer division as an experiment. All this was, however, conditional upon a reduction in numbers providing the necessary money and little could be done in 1905.[28]

These Estimates were introduced by Arnold-Forster on 28 March 1905 but the debate 'degenerated, as usual, into the ordinary drivel about Volunteers . . . etc.'. Arnold-Forster was increasingly critical of Volunteers 'who take not the slightest interest or concern in the Army as a whole, and seem to regard the Regular Army rather as a necessary evil than as the principal land defence of the Empire', an opinion in which he was supported by Sir John Colomb. Balfour refused to allow Howard Vincent to discuss the Volunteer proposals outside the Estimates but the Volunteers then disrupted the Pay Vote on 4, 5 and 6 April 1905 to press their points. The crux of the Volunteer argument, again principally in the hands of Vincent and McCrae, was that a large Volunteer Force was still vital to home defence. Much to Arnold-Forster's annoyance, Balfour replied that the C.I.D. had considered invasion unlikely under existing conditions, one of which was the existence of the Volunteer Force. Thus the necessity of the Volunteers and the improbability of invasion were not mutually contradictory truths. The issue of invasion had rarely been raised by Volunteers in the past and the arguments now employed against Arnold-Forster's plans were something of a new departure in Volunteer Parliamentary tactics. But, although the Volunteers were prepared to delay the Government time-table, they were not as yet prepared to vote against their own party, and McCrae's motion to reduce the Pay Vote was defeated by 218 to 187 votes.[29]

Arnold-Forster still claimed that nine-tenths of Volunteer officers in the country supported him but this appeared somewhat optimistic. On 11 April 1905, J.H.A. Macdonald, speaking at the R.U.S.I., attacked the disastrous effect of Arnold-Forster's policies on the Volunteer Force. He revealed that the London Scottish, Artists, London Irish and Queen's Westminsters had lost 2,872 men between them since the announcement of the plans for reduction:

> Thus they excuse the squeezing out of the Volunteer Service of one-fifth of its present strength, while they ask that it be assumed that attenuated numbers must bring about greater efficiency in those that are left, without there being the slightest ground for so believing, and in direct contradiction of the advice of those who are in the most intimate touch with the Volunteer, as the denizens of Pall Mall have never been . . .[30]

Similarly, the Institute of C.O.'s of Volunteers was also opposed to Arnold-Forster and it was reported that Volunteers might well vote against the Government in any election, leading the *Standard* to comment:

> Of course, it will be from every point of view deplorable if the Volunteer vote becomes an engine of political warfare; but, under the circumstances, we can hardly blame individual Volunteers for resorting to what seems to be almost their last alternative, if they are to continue to exist as a military body.[31]

The true attitude of the Volunteer Force as a whole, rather than that expressed by Volunteer M.P.s or newspapers like the *Standard* opposed to Arnold-Forster, was, however, soon to be tested by the 'June Circular'.

There is, in some ways, a certain similarity between the circumstances surrounding the circular and the 'Christmas Card' order of 1901, although Walter Adye was not, as Howard Vincent implied, responsible for the June circular. At the Army Council meeting on 13 April 1905 it had been decided that little could be done to reduce the Volunteers in the current year, with the exception of obtaining reports from G.O.C.'s with recommendations on units which might be disbanded or amalgamated on the grounds of inefficiency or lack of numbers. It was also decided to ask G.O.C.'s for information on the number of Volunteers fit to serve abroad but nothing would be done until after the annual inspections. A circular to G.O.C.'s was accordingly drawn up after consultations between Mackinnon, Douglas and the D.A.D.G. of Army Medical Services on the exact medical requirements for Volunteers serving abroad. Arnold-Forster approved the circular on the 6 June and it was issued on 20 June 1905 by the Secretary of the Army Council, Edward Ward. Unfortunately, the wording was ambiguous, and when the contents were revealed in the press on 4 July it appeared that the Government was introducing a severe medical requirement designed to reduce the Volunteer Force. The Under-Secretary of State, the Earl of Donoughmore, insisted that the Government merely required to know how many men were fit for active service and that no action was contemplated. Earl Spencer expressed himself satisfied that the press had misled the public, but on 5 July J.E.B. Seely attempted to move an adjournment debate on the circular which he considered was the basis for further action. There was, in fact, only one day left for discussing Supply and, at the instigation of Campbell-Bannerman, Balfour agreed to allot this day — 13 July — to the Volunteers.[32]

Although many provincial newspapers such as the *Nottingham Daily Guardian, Nottingham Express, Birmingham Daily Post* and *Lincolnshire Echo* and some nationals such as *The Globe* and *Morning Advertiser* supported the idea of the circular, there was considerable criticism of Arnold-Forster, notably in the *Standard*.[33] As a result of the press and Parliamentary opposition both Douglas and Mackinnon attempted to dissociate themselves from the circular. Mackinnon threatened to resign when Arnold-Forster implied he had drafted the circular. He appealed to Lord Roberts, claiming that he had told Douglas that he disapproved, that he had only drafted an Army Council resolution and that he did not have sufficient access to the Secretary of State.[34] Douglas also claimed that he had disapproved of the circular, but Arnold-Forster replied that he had no record of dissent from Mackinnon and that he could not accept that Douglas was not responsible:

> Every member of the Army Council is responsible for all its decisions. I see the A.G.'s initials on the minutes of the proceedings of the 13 April. We all know perfectly well that the reasonable precautions we are now taking are necessary. I have heard no word of this disapproval till now.[35]

A new circular was issued on 11 July clearly setting out the purpose of the medical enquiry but the Commons debate went ahead on 13 July and Arnold-Forster was bitterly attacked by McCrae, Vincent, J.M. Denny, C.R. Spencer, Charles Hobhouse, Seely and other Volunteers and sympathisers. The Secretary of State defended himself against the charge that he was aiming at reduction by stealth, and Volunteers such as Denny and Vincent were sufficiently impressed by his speech to vote with the Government.[36] As a result, McCrae's motion was narrowly defeated by 232 to 206 votes but the debate was by no means over in the country.

Arnold-Forster claimed on 13 July that there was considerably less criticism of the circulars in the country than in Parliament, and it would appear that he was correct in his assumption. Most C.O.'s naturally considered that the best means of asserting the fitness of their men in accordance with the G.O.C.'s enquiries would be by a proper medical examination, which the circulars had not actually ordered. There was encouragement in the press, notably in the *Standard*, to refuse the medical examination and, indeed, there were isolated cases where this occurred such as at a camp of Dorset Artillery Volunteers at Portland and in the 2nd London E.V. The Deputy-Judge-Advocate-General ruled that these men could not be held guilty of disobedience since the examination was based on foreign service requirements, which were no part of a Volunteer's duty and therefore no Volunteer could legally be compelled to undergo an examination. All the military members of the Army Council, with the exception of Plumer, now wanted to withdraw the circulars but Arnold-Forster considered that 'few corps will care to write themselves down as manifestly unfit, which they certainly would do if they deliberately declined to supply the information asked for'. A large number of Commanding Officers openly supported medical examination in the press, including Col. Ludlow of Birmingham, Alfred Gilbey of Bucks., Col. Mitchell, late C.O. 2nd V.B. East Lancs., Lt.-Col. H.T. Crook and Col. J.B. Pollitt of Manchester and Col. J.W. Read of 3rd Middlesex R.G.A.V. By November 1905, out of a possible 239,543 men in units examined, some 187,880 had agreed to be examined and of these 84 per cent declared fit. The main reason reported for non-examination was that medical officers had not had the time to examine men and only in the Midlands and Wales was it reported that men had refused to come forward because of incitement by the press.[37] Arnold-Forster believed his claim had been justified:

> Despite the most frantic appeals in newspapers, whose Editors forgot that politics and soldiering have nothing to do with each other; despite deliberate incitement to insubordination, and invitations to officers and men to behave in an unsoldierly and disgraceful fashion, the Volunteers have, with exceptions so few as to be quite unimportant, behaved admirably.[38]

In the Commons, however, the Volunteers had taken up nine days allotted to Supply and obstructed the proceedings throughout. The debate on 13 July 1905 was the last day on which any of Arnold-

Forster's plans were debated in the Commons.

Although the session had ended, Arnold-Forster still hoped to effect some reforms in the Volunteers. On 28 July 1905 he had met forty-two Volunteer Commanding Officers at the Commons to hear their views on a wide range of problems such as new camping arrangements, extra drills for non campers, transport, Regular commissions, brigades and divisions, allowances and terms of enlistment. He considered that he had cleared up some misapprehensions at the meeting and those participating such as Sir Robert Cranston, Lord Provost of Edinburgh and Lt.-Col. of the Queen's Edinburgh Rifle Brigade, and Lt.-Col. Hughes of the 1st V.B. York and Lancaster, were quick to deny claims in the *Standard* that the meeting had discussed the circulars.[39] Arnold-Forster believed that progress on the Volunteers could now be made, but on 26 September 1905 Douglas advised that the policy of reduction must be abandoned: 'I fear that any attempt to reduce numbers or capitation grant would in the present temper of the Volunteers, be doomed to failure; it would increase the unrest, it would have a bad effect on the Country, and would further weaken the position of the Army Council.' It is more than likely that Douglas' decision was influenced by a speech which went a considerable way towards undermining Arnold-Forster's reduction policy. On 9 September 1905 Balfour, speaking at North Berwick, maintained that the Regular Army could only be sent abroad 'so long as the patriotism of this country will provide us with a sufficiency of trained Volunteers, to deal with any emergency that may arise'. This was followed by a speech at Liverpool on 29 September in which Sir George White called for four times as many Volunteers and by a speech by the King to Scottish Volunteers in Edinburgh in October in which he urged more men to enlist in the Volunteers. Arnold-Forster was also made aware by the Government Whips of the likely reaction in the Commons to a continued policy of reduction: 'I cannot conceal from myself, that in the opinion of our Whips, the policy of reduction is exceedingly unpopular and likely to be resented.'[40]

In the circumstances he saw little alternative but to accept the suggestions of Douglas, Fleetwood Wilson, the Director of Finance, the Financial Secretary, Bromley-Davenport, and the rest of the Army Council, that Parliament must be asked for more money for the Volunteers. Douglas, Bromley-Davenport and Mackinnon drew up proposals, and these were agreed by the Army Council on 6 November 1905 and submitted to the Cabinet on 11 November. It was now proposed to alter the capitation grant giving 2 guineas to those camping for 15 days, £1.18s.6d. for 8 days and £1 for non-campers.

Allowances were also altered accordingly and each man would now complete 30 drills to earn the grant, camping days counting towards this total. It was also proposed to reorganise the Volunteer Force into about 40 brigades and create an experimental division. Cyclists' allowances were reduced and Mounted Infantry companies were to be disbanded. It was calculated that the new grants would add £170,000 to the Estimates. The C.G.S., Lyttelton, the M.G.O., Wolfe-Murray, and Douglas then attempted to cancel their own proposals on 25 November because they did not want the Volunteer Force to be given preference to the Militia, but the proposals were already in the hands of the Cabinet and had been approved.[41] On 23 November 1905 Arnold-Forster also secured the reluctant agreement of the Army Council to a field artillery experiment utilising the 6th West York. R.G.A. Volunteers and the 1st Lanark A.V., which were to be re-armed with Ehrhardt quick-firing guns. But on 11 December 1905 the new Liberal Government took office. It was decided at the first meeting of the Army Council under Haldane's chairmanship to continue with the reorganisation of brigades and the other policies for the time being as a temporary expedient but, in January 1906, Mackinnon and the D.M.T., F.W. Stopford, agreed to suspend the experimental division. At the next meeting of the Army Council, the field artillery experiment was also abandoned.[42]

In twenty-six months of office, Arnold-Forster had conspicuously failed to implement his Volunteer policies due to the intransigence of Volunteer M.P.'s, the Army Council and his own colleagues. The Volunteer plans had been virtually the only ones accepted by the Cabinet but there is a strong suspicion that Balfour knew their likely fate in the Commons. The Volunteer Force as a whole was by no means entirely opposed to Arnold-Forster's policies which were, in many ways, a sensible solution to Volunteer financial problems. Arnold-Forster was also justified to a large extent in believing that Vincent and his fellow M.P'.s were unrepresentative of the Force as a whole. However, Volunteer M.P.'s consistently refused to accept reductions of any kind and destroyed the policies by their obstruction. Some Volunteers welcomed the defeat of Arnold-Forster but Arnold-Forster himself noted after meeting with his successor, Haldane:

> The 'talkin' Volunteers, who are always silly, are already rejoicing because they think they are going to squeeze more money out of him (Haldane), in return for less work. My impression is they may have a rude awakening.[43]

The 'rude awakening' of the Volunteers and their failure to succeed against Haldane, as they had done against Arnold-Forster, can now be examined.

Towards an Hegelian Army

Several of Haldane's contemporaries sought the credit, in later years, for the concept of the Territorial Force. Amery, for example, believed that he had been the first to suggest County Associations. Spenser Wilkinson, who had sent some of his Volunter publications to Haldane, saw in the Territorial Force the embodiment of the Volunteer Army proposed to the Norfolk Commission by the Manchester Tactical Society. Many of the claims were exaggerated although it must also be said that, for many years, Haldane's alleged originality was given undue prominence by his own autobiography in much the same way that Cardwell's reputation was enhanced by the writings of his supporters like Sir Robert Biddulph.[44] There were in fact many schemes being expounded in 1906. Sir George Clarke, for example, saw no need for a large Volunteer field army in view of the improbability of invasion, and in March 1905 he had proposed to Balfour that the Force be reduced to small coastal brigades. The function of this emasculated Volunteer Force would be to defend the country against raids, which he considered equally unlikely; to act as garrisons for fixed port defences and to prevent sabotage and civil disorder in wartime. Clarke's ideas were submitted to the C.I.D. in December 1905 and again in January and April 1906. His concept of the function of the Volunteer Force was identical to that proposed for the Territorial Force by Esher in a memorandum to the Territorial Force Committee (or 'Duma') in May 1906.[45] A major influence on the Territorial Scheme was Haldane's military secretary, Gerald Ellison, who had tutored Haldane on military affairs throughout the election campaign. Ellison had evolved a plan for a new Volunteer organisation in 1905 whilst A.A.G. in A.G.1. and this now became a basis for discussion on the proposed Territorial Force. Ellison's earlier book on home defence, published in 1898, and which advocated a Swiss style militia in Britain, may also have formed some basis for discussion. Both Wilkinson and Clarke certainly believed Ellison mainly responsible for the evolution of the concept of County Associations, which represented the one clear departure from existing ideas of a new structure for the Volunteer Force. However, Ellison himself gave credit for this to Haldane and the Territorial Force bore a closer similarity to German practise than it did to that of the Swiss.[46]

The Territorial Scheme, which was slowly evolved through 1906, was in many ways little more than the fulfilment of old Volunteer and Regular ideas as to the ultimate development of the Volunteer Force.

The Territorial Force would consist of 42 brigades (already being formed), organised into 14 divisions with the Imperial Yeomanry, organised into 14 cavalry brigades, incorporated as the mounted arm of the Territorial Force. The Force would have full supporting services and field artillery armed with 15 pdr. field-guns. All these in addition to the bonus of jury exemption were old Volunteer aims. From, as it were, the Regulars and 'Advanced School' traditions came elements of compulsion — a definite term of four years' enlistment terminable on three months' notice on penalty of a fine; fifteen days' annual camp with pay and the entire Force permanently under military law. The County Associations were designed to relieve Commanding Officers of crippling financial burdens, but they also represented a further encroachment on Volunteer independence by the War Office. The County Associations, headed by Lords Lieutenant and including local worthies and employers, would be responsible for the raising, supply, pay and administration of the Territorial Force providing such necessities as ranges, training grounds, uniforms and equipment. The War Office would now be placed firmly in control of training and command although it was hoped to place Territorial officers in command of divisions in due course and, by way of concession, all papers on the Territorial Force would be referred to the new Director-General of the Territorial Force before decision and the Force would be represented on the Army Council by the Parliamentary Under-Secretary of State. The County Associations, and more especially the creation of the new Officers Training Corps from the former university, school and cadet units, also fell in with Haldane's essentially Germanic concept of a 'nation in arms'. The Territorial Scheme was thus not quite as original as Haldane later implied. As Spenser Wilkinson recorded, 'He spoke and wrote in his memoirs as though he had created a new Army. All that he had done was to rechristen the Volunteers.'[47]

The Territorial Force, although its precise purpose was at first 'shrouded in mystery', was to be given a definite role of second line, providing both support for the first line and the means of wartime expansion. The Force would provide garrisons for naval ports, replace Regular garrisons on mobilisation and defend the United Kingdom against raids, although these were considered unlikely. After six months' continuous training on mobilisation, the Territorial Force would be available for foreign service. The six months' continuous training implied that the Territorial Force would be required to reinforce the Expeditionary Force in India. Indeed, the six divisions of the new B.E.F. were based on Indian divisional scales despite the secret staff conversations begun with France during the election campaign and the conclusion of the C.I.D. that the weakness of Russia after the Russo-Japanese War precluded any threat to India for ten years.[48] The B.E.F. itself was determined simply by what troops were available in Great Britain. Some eight surplus Regular battalions together with some colonial garrisons and the London fortifications erected by Stanhope were ruthlessly swept away as a sop to Liberal prejudices. It was also demonstrated that the Territorial Force would cost only an estimated £2,886,408 per annum whereas the Auxiliary estimates for 1906-7 were £4,431,210. By such apparent concession, through Haldane's very vagueness in outlining his proposals, and through the support of Campbell-Bannerman, who was convinced of Haldane's adherence to Cardwellian principles, Haldane disarmed opposition to his proposals in his own party.[49]

There was, however, opposition from many other quarters. There are, for example, indications that the Army Council was by no means behind Haldane, and at one stage it was not consulted once in seven months. The C.I.D. Sub-Committee on Haldane's plans, set up in November 1906, gave only qualified support to the scheme since it was not authorised to propose alternatives. Among other criticisms it cast doubt on the ability of the Territorial Force to expand sufficiently in war. Most Regulars still favoured conscription. Additional weight had been given to the conscription lobby by the resignation of Lord Roberts from the C.I.D. in November 1905 on the issue of universal service and his assumption of the Presidency of the National Service League. The National Service League considered a Territorial Force which required six months' continuous training on mobilisation as little better than an 'armed crowd', and in November 1907 Roberts, with Lord Lovat, Sir Samuel Scott and *The Times* correspondent, Repington, was able to force another invasion enquiry by the C.I.D.[50]

The Militia, which was little more than a draft-finding body for the Regular Army, opposed absorption into either the Regular Army or the Territorial Force. In the summer and autumn of 1906 Haldane made three attempts to reach agreement with the Militia Colonels at the Militia conference at the War Office in June; in the 'Duma' which broke up in July 1906 and, finally at a meeting arranged by Lord Derby at Knowsley. All failed and Haldane resolved to abolish the Militia and creat a Special Reserve. The Militia was strongly represented in the Lords and, under the leadership of the Duke of Bedford, would prove something of a problem when the Territorial and Reserve Forces Bill reached Parliament. The King was not inclined to support Haldane at first, due to Haldane's proposal to reduce two battalions of Guards and because of the membership of the Territorial Forces Committee, or 'Duma', set up in May 1906. The

Duma consisted of forty-five rather ill-assorted men such as Regulars like Stopford and Mackinnon; Militia representatives such as the Duke of Bedford; Yeomanry representatives like Freeman-Thomas; conscriptionists like Roberts; Volunteers such as Vincent and Fremantle and others such as J.E.B. Seely. Arnold-Forster was particularly critical of 'A crowd of cranks, critics and amateurs' and 'stupid people' like Vincent and Seely. The King had to be reassured by Esher that the Committee would maintain the authority of the Crown over the Armed Forces and not recommend 'anything in the shape of what is generally understood by the term 'citizen army'. . . . .'.[51]

Opposition was also expected from the Volunteer Force in the House of Commons in view of the destruction of Arnold-Forster's scheme. It is clear that both Sir George Clarke and Esher viewed Volunteer influence in the Commons as potentially dangerous. Clarke wrote to Balfour in August 1905 that 'their political influence is becoming a public danger, and military debates in the House tend to be monopolised by Volunteer grievances'. Esher, as was noted in an earlier chapter, wrote to the King in 1906 of the political dangers of Volunteer 'trade unionism' in the Commons and of his hope that County Associations might break up the Force into regional groups of conflicting interests and competing aims. In December 1906 Esher considered that 'great strength of character will be required to push the scheme through the House of Commons, where the Volunteers command large interests', and Arnold-Forster commented in March 1907 that 'the Volunteers are quite capable, I may say too capable, of looking after themselves in the House of Commons'. Balfour, as Esher informed the King in March 1907, felt that Haldane had underrated the opposition to the Bill 'now being organised by the Duke of Bedford, Colonel Howard Vincent, and Mr Harry Lawson, and it may become more formidable than Mr Haldane supposes'.[52] But, in fact, the opposition of the Volunteers in the House of Commons was negligible due to the success of Haldane outside the Commons and the paucity of Volunteer M.P.'s remaining after the Unionist electoral disaster of 1906.

Haldane, with his high-pitched voice and rapid delivery, was by no means an impressive speaker. Leo Amery recalled that 'his exposition of his Army Scheme, in which he explained at terrific speed, but with great suavity, that the more battalions and batteries he scrapped the stronger he made the Army, always reminded me a little of a conjurer's patter'. Others, too, commented that Haldane was 'over conscious of his own ability' or 'better pleased with himself than anyone I had known'.[53] However, Haldane, unlike Arnold-Forster, was not only a good listener and a good host but exuded charm; for example, one Colonel remarked to Amery after a dinner with Haldane that: 'he felt exactly like a calf well licked over by a boa-constrictor as a preliminery to deglutition'. Haldane's charm was a vital factor in undermining Volunteer opposition as he energetically campaigned throughout the country at dinners, speeches and meetings. His letters to his mother reveal that between August 1906 and March 1907 there was not one week when he did not visit or dine somewhere to explain his scheme. It would also seem that, as in the past, the majority of the Volunteer Force was prepared to continue its duties as best it could, a policy which Lt.-Col. J.W. Greig of the London Scottish considered the safest, soundest and most useful to adopt. Nevertheless, representatives of the Volunteers rejected the idea of County Associations at a War Office meeting on 4 September 1906 and this, coupled with considerable pressure being applied to M.P.'s by Volunteer Commanding Officers, led Haldane to seriously contemplate removing financial and other powers from County Associations. Esher convinced Haldane in October 1906 of the need to press ahead although the County Associations as they finally emerged in the Territorial Bill were undoubtedly weakened by a compromise which abandoned an elective element on the Associations from local borough and county councils.[54] The disquiet, especially at the additional compulsion implied in the Territorial Scheme, was to see the Volunteer Force decline to only 224,217 men by 1 April 1908 when it officially ceased to exist — its lowest strength since 1891.

There remained opposition from Volunteer M.P.'s in the House of Commons but it would appear that Clarke, Esher and Balfour simply overlooked the fact that the Volunteer pressure group had been severely reduced at the election. There were now only 28 Volunteer M.P.'s and of these 14 were Liberals. Of these, 9 Liberals and 4 Tories were newly elected in 1906 and of the old Tory pressure group there were just 10 members, although these included Sir Henry Fletcher, Sir John Kennaway, Robert Williams, Sir Gilbert Parker and Howard Vincent, all of whom had by now retired from active service in the Force. In the debates of the Territorial and Reserve Force Bill it became clear that McCrae and Seely, who succeeded Haldane as Secretary of State in 1912, supported the Bill. McCrae welcomed a better scheme than that of Brodrick or Arnold-Forster, despite some doubts on County Associations. One new Tory Volunteer, G.L. Courthope, also expressed support, leaving the Volunteer opposition principally in the hands of Vincent, Lord Balcarres, Sir Gilbert Parker and a new Tory M.P., W.W. Ashley.[55]

Vincent and his fellow Volunteers were chiefly opposed to the six

251

months' liability on the grounds of difficulties with employers and the County Associations, which, it was felt, deprived Volunteer Commanding Officers of their authority. Vincent also opposed the transfer of debts on Volunteer drill halls from the Public Works Loan Commissioners to the War Office. The result, with the overwhelming Liberal majority in the House, was never really in doubt especially as Balfour tacitly supported the Bill and Arnold-Forster also recognised that the Unionists would be put in a false position by opposing the separation of the 'wheat from the chaff'.[56] Amendments were moved on 28 May 1907 to exclude both the Militia and Yeomanry from the Bill but these were lost by 260 - 80 and 291 - 89 votes respectively and the same fate met an amendment of Vincent on 3 June to create a separate Territorial Forces Department at the War Office by 295 to 113 votes. In the final vote on the third reading on 19 June 1907 Vincent, Col. W.H. Walker and W.W. Ashley found themselves sharing the lobby with Sir Charles Dilke and an assorted group of Labour and Irish M.P.'s. The Bill was passed by 286 to 63 votes[57] and went to the Lords, where the Government was defeated on a number of occasions but the opposition of the Volunteers was at an end. Appropriately, as some thought, the Territorial Force came into existence on 1 April 1908.*

Order books show that activities in the Territorial Force continued much the same as they had done in the Volunteer Force.[58] Indeed, the problems facing the Territorial Force in terms of manpower, the criticisms of Regular Army officers on its effectiveness and the continuing invasion debate do not seem all that different either. And at the last, in 1914, the whole Territorial scheme was ignored by Kitchener in favour of a new manifestation of the amateur military spirit which the Volunteers had done so much to preserve — the New Armies.

The years from 1903 to 1908 represented rather a sad dénouement for the Volunteer Force after the enthusiastic heights of the South African War, when it had appeared that the Force had at last in some measure justified its continuing existence. It was clear, however, that the Force was unfit to take the field against Continental troops and that reform was necessary. Conflicting schemes of reform and the decision by the C.I.D. that invasion, the original *raison d'etre* of the Volunteer Force, was improbable, led to uncertainty and declining numbers. If many at the time felt that in opposing successive Secretaries of State, the Volunteers were not concerned with the

*The Territorial and Reserve Forces Bill did not, in fact, remove the Volunteer Act from the Statute book and Volunteers were raised under its provisions in the 1914-18 war.

interests of the Army as a whole, then it could be argued that long years of neglect and continuing antipathy on the part of the War Office had only encouraged the Volunteer Force to place its own interests first. Thus, although there was some support for Arnold-Forster's schemes in the Volunteer Force, Volunteer M.P.'s destroyed his policies on the floor of the Commons. But against the overwhelming Liberal majority in the House after 1906 resistance was impossible and the Volunteer Force could only accept its fate as it had accepted so many unpopular Government policies in the past, for it depended upon the State for its finances. There was, however, considerable continuity between the old Volunteer Force and the new Territorial Force. In September 1914 the first Territorial Infantry battalion in France was the 14th The County of London Battalion — the old 15th Middlesex (London Scottish) R.V.C. The first Territorial Victoria Cross was won on Hill 60 in 1915 by 2nd Lt. G.H. Woolley of the 9th The County of London Battalion — the former 1st Middlesex (Queen Victoria's Rifles) and the direct descendant of the Duke of Cumberland's Sharpshooters, which alone had survived the reductions at the close of the Napoleonic Wars. The traditions of the Volunteer Movement lived on.

[1] Midleton, op cit, p 126, 139-42; Griffith-Boscawen, op cit, p 197-8, 252-5, 274-5; Leo Amery, *My Political Life: England before the Storm, 1896-1914* (London 1953), I, p 195-201; Randolph S. Churchill, *Winston Churchill* (London 1967), II, p 17-21, 38, 63; J.E.B. Seely, *Adventure* (London 1930), p 96-111; Winston S. Churchill, *Mr Brodrick's Army* (London 1903). For a discussion of the role of the Treasury see John Gooch, *The Origin and Development of the British and Imperial General Staffs to 1916* (Unpub Ph.D London 1969), p 42-5. For Brodrick's reforms generally see L.J. Satre 'St John Brodrick and Army Reform 1901-3' *JBS* 15 (1976) No 2, p 117-139.
[2] *PRO* WO 163/6 Meetings of 16.3.03. 23.3.03, 30.3.03, 27.4.03 and 11.5.03 and precis no 97 'The Auxiliaries and the Defence of the Empire' and no 97A.
[3] *BPP* 1904 [Cd 2061] xxx, 175 Introduction, p 1-5.
[4] *PRO* Cab 38/2 No 39; 38/3 Nos 48, 62 and 65.
[5] J.P. Mackintosh, 'The Role of the CID before 1914' *EHR* LXXVII (1962), p 490-503; N. d'Ombrain, *War Machinery and High Policy* (Oxford 1973); M. Howard, *The Continental Commitment* (London 1972) chapter 1 passim; G. Monger, *The End of Isolation* (London 1963), p 95; Moon, op cit, chapter IV; F.A. Johnson, *Defence by Committee* (Oxford 1960); J. Ehrman, *Cabinet Government and War* (Cambridge 1958).
[6] Moon, op cit, p 197; Lansdowne, 27.6.04 *AD* (1904), 1137-8; Arnold-Forster to Cabinet, 30.5.04 *PRO* Cab. 37/71 No 73.
[7] *PRO* WO 163/6 minutes of meeting of 2.3.03; *PRO* Cab 37/64 No 17; *BPP* 1904 [Cd 2062] xxx 259 Minutes of Evidence Volume 1. *BPP* 1904 [Cd 2063] xxxi 1 Minutes of Evidence Volume 2. See also 'Military Opinion on the Volunteers' *Glasgow Herald* 30.9.1905 in Add Mss 50312 section 2.
[8] *BPP* 1904 [Cd 2061] xxx 175, p 7; Wilkinson, *Thirty Five Years*, op cit, p 263-6; Luvaas, *Education*, p 258; Moon, op cit, p 198. For the conscription debate see T. Ropp, 'Conscription in Great Britain, 1900-1914: A Failure in Civil Military

Communication' *Military Affairs* (Summer 1956), p 71-6 and M. Allison, *The National Service Issue, 1899-1914* (Unpub PhD London 1975).

[9] House of Lords 27.6.04 *AD* (1904), 1101-39; *LSRG* IX (June 1904), p 105; Bucks. R.O. *T.A. Coll* Box 15 Gilbey Mss, chap x, p 3; and *Fremantle Mss* D/FR/169.

[10] Arnold-Forster to Cabinet 30.5.04 *PRO* Cab 37/71 No 73; Arnold-Forster diary for 30.5.04 and 5.8.04, Add Mss 50338 and 50339; Arnold-Forster to Fleetwood Wilson, 20.5.04, Add Mss 50338; Arnold-Forster to Adjutant General, 2.6.04, Add Mss 50303 section 4; Arnold-Forster 2.6.04 *AD* (1904), 995; Balfour 6.6.04 *AD* (1904), 1001; Turner, op cit, p 308.

[11] Viscount Chilston, *Chief Whip* (London 1961), p 313-20; Dunlop, op cit, p 162; A.V. Tucker, 'The Issue of Army Reform in the Unionist Government' *HJ* IX, I (1966), p 90-100; Mary Arnold-Forster, *The Rt. Hon. H.O. Arnold-Forster: A Memoir by his Wife* (London 1910), p 68-85, 145-7, 195-9; Wilkinson, *Thirty Five Years*, op cit, p 180-3; Amery, op cit, p 208-9; S. Gwynn and G.M. Tuckwell, *The Life of the Rt. Hon-Sir Charles Dilke* (London 1918), II, p 413-26, 451-57. Papers on the joint letter are to be found in Ogilby Trust *Wilkinson Papers*, O.T.P. 13/9. See also Ian Beckett, 'Arnold-Forster and the Volunteers' in I. Beckett and J. Gooch (eds), *Politicians and Defence* (Manchester 1981), p 47-68.

[12] Roberts to Balfour, 11.7.04 *Balfour Papers*, Add Mss 49725.

[13] Amery, op cit, p 209; Grenfell, op cit, p 171-2; Austen Chamberlain, *Politics from the Inside* (London 1936). p 60-1; Gen. Sir Neville Lyttelton, *Eighty Years Soldiering, Politics and Games* (London 1927), p 273; Turner, op cit, p 309-11. For the Esher Committee and Arnold-Forster's part in establishing the General Staff see John Gooch, *The Plans of War* (London 1974), p 62-97.

[14] Balfour to Esher, 30.7.04 Add Mss 49718; Arnold-Forster to Sandars, 24.1.05, Add Mss 49723; Mary Arnold-Forster, op cit, p 223-5; Amery, op cit, p 210-11; Sir Guy Fleetwood Wilson, *Letters to Somebody: A Retrospect* (London 1922), p 135.

[15] CID deliberations on the 'Military Requirements of the Empire' can be traced in *PRO* Cab 38/6 Nos 122, 123 and 124 and Cab 38/8 Nos 14 and 18.

[16] H.O. Arnold-Forster, *Army in 1906*, op cit, passim; *PRO* Cab 37/68 Nos 5 and 19; 37/69 Nos 30 and 49 and 37/70 Nos 55 and 66.

[17] Arnold-Forster diary entries for 12.7.04, 22.4.04, 11.7.04, 29.6.04 in Add Mss 50337, 50338 and 50339; Salisbury to Cabinet, 14.6.04 *PRO* Cab 37/71 No 80; Clarke to Balfour, 18.6.04, 27.6.04 and 28.12.04 in Add Mss 49700; Brett, op cit, II, p 58; Lord Sydenham, *My Working Life* (London 1927), I, p 176-188, 192-3.

[18] Mary Arnold-Forster, op cit, p 263; Tucker, op cit, p 96-7; *PRO* Cab 37/71 No 107; Peter Fraser, *Lord Esher: A Political Biography* (London 1973), p 119-120.

[19] Chamberlain Memos *PRO* Cab 37/70 No 61 and 37/74 No 21; Arnold-Forster's diary for 1.5.04, 3.6.04, 13.6.04, 3.11.05 in Add Mss 50338, 50342 and 50352; Mary Arnold-Forster, op cit, p 254-5.

[20] *PRO* Cab 37/70 No 63; 37/74 No 12; 37/69 No 27, 59; 37/76 No 85; Fleetwood Wilson op cit, p 136; Gen. Sir Charles Harrington, *Plumer of Messines* (London 1935), p 56-9; Mary Arnold-Forster, op cit, p 11-3; Hamer, op cit, p 255-60. Cf Arnold-Forster's diary for 13.7.04, 6.8.04 and 12.12.04 in Add Mss 50339 and 50342.

[21] Fraser, op cit, p 108-148; John Gooch, 'Sir George Clarke's Career at the CID, 1904-7' *HJ* XVIII, 3 (1975), p 555-69. Brodrick had suspected Esher of undue influence when he was secretary of state, see Midleton, op cit, p 147-59. Similarly Mary Arnold-Forster identified Esher as the 'villain' in a letter to her husband's military secretary, Raymond Marker, in 1906 — *Kitchener/Marker Papers* Add Mss 522276 B f 21.

[22] Balfour/Arnold-Forster correspondence in *PRO* Cab 37/74 No 10; also Arnold-Forster to Cabinet of 9.6.05 Cab 37/78 No 106; diary, 22.6.05 Add Mss 50348; Roberts

to Balfour, 5.4.05 NAM *Roberts Papers* 7101-23-122/8 No 768, p 236; Lyttleton to Cabinet, 10.6.05 Cab 37/78 No 107; Roberts to Balfour, 5.4.05 *Balfour Papers* Add Mss 49725.

[23] *Arnold-Forster Papers* Add Mss 50303; *PRO* Cab 37/70 No 55; Arnold-Forster, *Army in 1906*, op cit, p 211-24; Arnold-Forster, 14.7.04 *AD* (1904), 1337-50.

[24] Arnold-Forster's diary for 5.1.04 Add Mss 50336; Howard Vincent, 'The Auxiliary Forces and the War Office: an open letter to H.O. Arnold-Forster' 6.5.04 in Add Mss 50313; Douglas to DAF, 25.4.04 in Add Mss 50303 section 3 and Add Mss 49722.

[25] Diary, 19.4.04 Add Mss 50337; Arnold-Forster to Balfour, 5.5.04 Add Mss 50303; Diary 10.5.04 and 9.6.04 Add Mss 50338; Arnold-Forster to AG and CGS, 31.5.04 Add Mss 50303 section 2; *PRO* 32/6457 Duties of DAF.

[26] Arnold-Forster to deputation, 25.7.04 Add Mss 50303 and diary, Add Mss 50339; Amery, op cit, p 209.

[27] Diary, 30.9.04 Add Mss 50340 and 22.2.05 Add Mss 50344.

[28] Diary entries 12.10.04, 17.1.05, Add Mss 50340 and 50343; Arnold-Forster to AG, 23.12.04 Add Mss 50312 section 30; Arnold-Forster to Balfour, 15.9.04 Add Mss 49722; *PRO* Cab 37/74 No 7; Arnold-Forster, 10.3.05 *AD* (1905).

[29] Diary, 28.3.05 and 14.4.05 Add Mss 50345 and 50346; Colomb, 29.3.05 *AD* (1905), 784-50; Balfour, 3.4.05 *AD* (1905), 898; Vincent, 6.4.05 *AD* (1905), 1017-1024 and McCrae, 1066-71; Balfour, 5.4.05 *AD* (1905), 1076-8; diary 5.4.05 and 6.4.05 Add Mss 50346. There had already been 23 divisions on the Estimates.

[30] Arnold-Forster, 28.3.05 *AD* (1904), 693-4; J.H.A. Macdonald, 'The Volunteers in 1905' *JRUSI* XLIX (1905), p 910-33.

[31] Add Mss 50312 section 20 'Misrepresentation of the Press'.

[32] 'Papers relating to the origin of the circulars' in *Arnold-Forster's Papers* Add Mss 50312 section 23; diary 13.4.05 Add Mss 50346; minutes of W O Council meeting of 13.4.05 *PRO* WO 163/10; *BPP* 1905 [Cd 2437] XLVI, 905; Dounoughmore, and Spencer 4.7.05 *AD* (1905) 821-3; Seely, 5.7.05 *AD* (1905), 1873-5; Major J.E.B. Seely, 'Our Saturday Talk No XXXVIII' in *Westminster Gazette* 8.7.05; Campbell-Bannerman, 6.7.05 *AD* (1905), 1886.

[33] Add Mss 50312 section 54.

[34] Correspondence between Roberts, Mackinnon and Arnold-Forster can be found in NAM *Roberts Papers* 7101-23 R4/61-7. See also diary 11-12.7.05, 21.7.05, 2.8.05, 29.9.05 in Add Mss 50349 and 50350.

[35] Correspondence between Arnold-Forster and Douglas can be found in Add Mss 50312 sections 23 and 50. See also diary for 28-29.9.05 in Add Mss 50350.

[36] *BPP* 1905 [Cd 2439] XLVI 909; Commons debate *AD* (1905), 1975-2038; diary for 13.7.05 Add Mss 50349.

[37] Reaction to the circulars can be traced in *Arnold-Forster Papers* Add Mss 50312 section 23 and 54; results of the examinations can be found in Add Mss 50312 sections 27 and 28. See also diary entries for 31.7.05, Add Mss 50349; Arnold-Forster, 13.7.05 *AD* (1905), 2030-1.

[38] Arnold-Forster to Col. W.H. Walker, MP, 30.10.05 Add Mss 50312 section 51.

[39] 'Report of the Volunteer Conference', 28.7.05 Add Mss 50312 section 19 and 'Misrepresentation of the Press', section 21. The editor of the *Standard*, H.A. Gwynne, believed Arnold-Forster was ruining the defensive power of the country — see his letters to Marker in Add Mss 52278.

[40] 'Correspondence with AG' Add Mss 50312 section 50; diary for 11.9.05, 19.10.05, 30.9.05 in Add Mss 50350 and 50351; *PRO* Cab 37/80 No 170.

[41] Diary entries for 30.9.05, 10.10.05. 2.11.05, 6.11.05, 11.11.05 and 23.11.05 in Add Mss 50350, 50351, 50352; *PRO* Cab 37/80 No 172; *Arnold-Forster Papers* Add Mss 50312 sections 10 and 11 and 17 for artillery correspondence; Arnold-Forster, *Army in*

1906, op cit, p 540-8.

[42] *PRO* WO 32/6378 'Reorganisation of Volunteer Infantry Brigades'; WO 162/11 meetings of 19.12.05 and 22.2.06.

[43] Diary, 16.12.05 Add Mss 50353.

[44] Amery, op cit, p 124; Haldane to Wilkinson of 27.12.05 and 6.1.06 in Ogilby Trust *Wilkinson Papers* O.T.P. 13/32/2 and 4; Wilkinson, op cit, p 306-7; R.B. Haldane, *An Autobiography* (London 1929), p 173-95; R.B. Haldane, *Before the War* (London 1920); Sir R. Biddulph, *Cardwell at the War Office* (London 1904), op cit, passim. The Haldane reforms have now been fully re-assessed in Edward Spiers, *Haldane: An Army Reformer* (Edinburgh 1980).

[45] Clarke to Balfour, 25.3.05 and 9.8.05, and Clarke to Sandars, 5.6.05 in Add Mss 49701 and 49702; Clarke memoranda to CID in *PRO* Cab 38/10 No 9, 38/11 Nos 3 and 16; Esher to Balfour, 9.1.07 *Balfour Papers* Add Mss 49719.

[46] G. Ellison, 'Reminiscences', Pt XVII *Lancashire Lad* (Feb 1936), p 7-9; Wilkinson, op cit, p 305; Sydenham, op cit, p 191; Spiers, op cit, p 96-97.

[47] B.J. Bond, 'Haldane at the War Office, 1905-12' *AQ* 86 (1963), p 33-43; Maj.-Gen. Sir F. Maurice, *Haldane* (London n.d.), p 304-34; Howard, op cit, p 86-98; *PRO* Cab 37/85 Nos 89 and 102, and Cab 37/86 No 12 'The Territorial and Reserve Forces Bill'; *PRO* WO 163/12 minutes of Army Council; Wilkinson, op cit, p 308.

[48] J.E. Tyler, *The British Army and the Continent, 1904-1914* (London 1938); S. Williamson, *The Politics of Grand Strategy* (Harvard 1969); N. Summerton, *British Military Preparations for a War Against Germany* (Unpub PhD London 1969); *PRO* Cab 38/11 No 11. See also John Gooch, 'Haldane and the National Army', in Beckett and Gooch, op cit, p 69-86.

[49] A.J.A. Morris, 'Haldane's Army Reforms, 1906-8: The Deception of the Radicals' *History* (Feb 1971), p 17-34; A.J.A. Morris, *Radicalism Against War, 1906-14* (London 1972), p 77-96; *PRO* Cab 37/86 No 86.

[50] Allison, op cit; D. James, *The Life of Lord Roberts* (London 1954), p 411-63; correspondence of Balfour and Roberts of November 1905 in *PRO* Cab 38/10 No 82; CID inquiry papers Cab 38/13 No 27, 38/14 Nos 10 and 11; WO 105/44; Charles A'Court Repington, *The Foundation of Reform* (London 1908); C. Repington, *Vestigia: Reminiscences of Peace and War* (London 1919), p 312-40.

[51] Col. the Duke of Bedford, *The Destruction of the Militia* (London 1907); Col. the Duke of Bedford, *The Extinction of the Militia* (London 1908); Ellison Reminiscences, op cit, Pt XVIII *LL* (May 1936), p 53-5; Maj.-Gen. E.K.G. Sixsmith, 'Reserve and Auxiliary Forces: Some Former Controversies' *AQ* (1966), p 71-7; Seely, op cit, p 126-7; Arnold-Forster to Marker, 14.5.06 in *Kitchener/Marker Papers* Add Mss 52277 f 20(3); Brett, op cit, II, p 169.

[52] Clarke to Balfour, 9.8.05 *Balfour Papers* Add Mss 49702; Brett, op cit, II, p 167-9, 205, 227-9; Arnold-Forster to Balfour, 19.3.07 in Add Mss 49723.

[53] Amery, op cit, p 227; Midleton op cit, p 279; Wilkinson, op cit, p 305.

[54] Amery, op cit, p 212; *LSRG* XI (1906), Jan, p 11 and Aug p 173; XII (1907), Apl p 78 and Nov, p 220; Haldane's letters to his mother are in National Library of Scotland *Haldane Papers* Ms 5901-6109 esp 5907 and 5977. Gooch, 'Haldane and the National Army', op cit, p 79-80; Spiers, op cit, p 102-105.

[55] McCrae, 9.4.07 *AD* (1907), 819-23 and Courthope, 27.2.07 *AD* (1907), 189-195.

[56] Cf Vincent, 25.2.07 and 4.3.07 and Balcarres, 4.3.07 *AD* (1907), 116-20, 349, 357-9; Arnold-Forster to Balfour, 19.3.07 Add Mss 49723. The County Associations were a major source of objection, see Eustace Balfour to Arthur Balfour, 10.4.07 *Balfour Papers* Add Mss 49831.

[57] F.E. Smith, 28.5.07 *AD* (1907), 1271-1313, Viscount Valentia, 1313-42; Vincent, 3.6.07, 1526-36; third reading 19.6.07 *AD* (1907), 227-86.

⁵⁸ Cf Order Books of 36/18th Middx. R.V.C. (later 10th County of London Bn.) *PRO* WO 70/17-19; Minute Book of G Coy, London Rifle Brigade, Guildhall Mss 9387; *Oxford University OTC Papers, 1908-25* Bodleian Library G.A. Oxon. c 121; Sir John Dunlop, 'The Territorial Army: The Early Years' *AQ* (April 1967), p 153-9. For a full discussion of the manifold problems of the new Territorial Force after 1908 see Spiers, op cit, p 161-186. For Kitchener's failure to utilise the Territorials in 1914 see Peter Simkins, 'Kitchener and the Expansion of the British Army' in Beckett and Gooch, op cit, p 87-109.

CONCLUSION

In 1859 there was no reason to suppose that the spontaneous national response, in the shape of the Volunteer Movement, to the latest of a series of invasion 'panics' in mid-Victorian Britain would not prove to be the temporary phenomenon which the Government of the day expected. Yet despite the often open hostility of the Regular Army, the neglect of successive Governments and the apathy of the general public, which made a period of international peace a threat to the very existence of the Movement, the Volunteer Force survived until 1908. This, of course, is not to say that the Volunteer Force of 1859 resembled that of 1908.

The broad cross section of the national community which had embraced the Movement in 1859, largely from purely patriotic motives, changed significantly as the crucial factors of time, increasing expense and the absence of visible social reward came to bear upon the professional and other upper middle class elements of the Volunteer Force. In such circumstances the Volunteer Force came to rely upon the artisan classes of Victorian England as the backbone of the ranks with the lower middle class elements, which had formed the backbone in 1859, steadily decreasing in numbers. With the change in social composition so there was a change in the essential upper middle class concept of independent and self-sufficient Volunteer corps. Increasing expense shattered the illusion of self-sufficiency and necessitated state aid, the price of which was more state control. In this manner the Volunteer Force illustrates that gradual process by which the *laissez faire* attitudes of mid-Victorianism were translated into the increasing state control of the twentieth century.

In terms of numbers, the Volunteer Force never enjoyed the support of more than a small percentage of the population, though it was far more representative of society as a whole than either the Regular Army or Militia, and it still numbered in real terms upwards of half a million men for most of its existence. The Volunteer Movement was clearly not a passport to social eminence but it did unite widely differing social groups in a common experience, and it was largely recognised that the moral assumptions underlying the Movement were of considerable benefit to society in that it was inclined to promote both greater self-discipline and better health amongst its members. For this reason the Volunteers enjoyed the early support of employers although increasing Government requirements led to greater opposition on the part of employers. Above all, in

259

the social field, the Volunteer Movement opened up previously unknown recreational opportunities to the lower middle and artisan classes of Victorian England, and this not only enabled the Volunteer Force to survive in periods of international calm but seems to have had the additional effect of encouraging the growth of organised sport.

That the Volunteer Movement embraced all classes and persuasions, and tended to be a cohesive factor in society, is best indicated in the way in which the Force as a whole studiously avoided party political issues and the potentially explosive political and social issues involved in their possible use in aid of the civil power. This attitude prevented the development of an effective Volunteer Parliamentary pressure group until the 1880's, but thereafter Volunteer M.P.'s strongly resisted the encroachment of the state on their interests. The Volunteers had some measure of success in this role, but long years of Government neglect resulted in the rather selfish attitude on the part of the Volunteers towards the interests of the Army as a whole, which was evident in their opposition to army reform after the South African War. Successive Governments had, in fact, been too inclined to ignore the special problems of recruitment which faced the Volunteer Force, and a similar failure to comprehend Volunteer problems was a feature of the attitude of the Regular Army to the Volunteer Force.

The mutual suspicion of Regulars and Volunteers was only gradually overcome with the closer co-operation desired by the more progressive Volunteers and necessitated by increasing state intervention and by increasing official need for the additional manpower which the Volunteer Force represented. The Volunteer Force could never be said to have been fit enough to face Continental troops and its *raison d'etre* — invasion — was largely hypothetical. Nevertheless, the Volunteer Force proved itself a useful auxiliary to the Regular Army in the South African War. More important, although hostility to the Volunteers remained in some circles, the Regular Army benefited enormously from the fresh approach of the Volunteers to military affairs in terms of both technical and tactical innovation.

But the most important contribution of the Volunteer Movement to Victorian and Edwardian England was to project military values to the public at large and to introduce military affairs to a large number of those previously uninterested in the Army. In the process there is no doubt that a larger section of society became involved in military affairs than would have been possible before 1859. In short, the Volunteer Movement kept alive the amateur military tradition and in no small way prepared the country for its great test in 1914. Indeed, by preserving that amateur tradition, the Volunteers long averted the solution to Britain's problem which eventually had to be enforced in

1916 — conscription. The Movement is not perhaps as important as Wolseley predicted in 1881 but this uniquely English phenomenon, so much a product of its time and so long forgotten, is nonetheless interesting for all that and its role as part of the structure of Victorian England deserves to be recorded.

APPENDICES

APPENDIX I — A VOLUNTEER ANTHOLOGY

The Volunteer Movement inspired the growth of a large ancillary literature in terms of poetry and song and although much of it has little merit it is interesting in that it gives insight into the philosophy of the Volunteers.

The agitation for the formation of Volunteers in the 1840's and 1850's was frequently stirred by patriotic verse of the type produced by Martin Tupper and Lord Tennyson which conjured up alarming visions of the results of French invasion. For example here are some verses from Tupper's famous poem 'Arm' published in 1852:

> Think of the rapine the flames and the slaughter
>   If the fierce Algerine-Frenchman here stood
> Think if you dare of your wife and your daughter
>   Think of your little ones choked in their blood!
> What? — is the wolf so squeamish and tender
>   As to be stopp'd by a peacemonger's tear?
> No! — if it find not a stalwarth defender
>   Every man's home is a Golgotha here!
>
> Up then and Arm! it is wisdom and duty
>   We are too tempting a prize to be weak.
> Lo what a pillage of riches and beauty
>   Glories to gain and revenges to wreak
> Run for your rifles and stand to your drilling
>   Let not the wolf have his will as he might
> If in the midst of their trading and tilling
>   Englishmen cannot — or care not to-fight![1]

The theme was repeated by Tennyson in that most celebrated of all Volunteer poems 'The War' published in *The Times* on 9 May 1859 with its appeal to lay aside domestic political differences:

> There is a sound of thunder afar
>   Storm in the South that darkens the day
> Storm of battle and thunder of war!
>   Well, if it do not roll away,
> Storm, Storm, Riflemen form!
>   Ready, be ready, against the storm!
> Riflemen, riflemen, riflemen form!
>
> Let your reforms for a moment go!
>   Look to your butts and take good aims!
> Better a rotten borough or so,
>   Than a rotten flesh and a city in flames!

Storm, storm, riflemen form!
    Ready, be ready, against the storm!
Riflemen, riflemen, riflemen, form![2]

The poems which appeared in 1859 and 1860 after the formation of the first Volunteer corps echoed both the fear of invasion emphasised by Tupper and Tennyson and the theme of the Volunteers in 1859 that it was necessary to 'arm for peace'. An example of the 'fear of invasion' is 'The Furness Rifle Volunteers' written by Thomas Town of Ulverston in 1860:

Could we bear to see these valleys trampled by invading feet?
Could we hear the drum of victory o'er our native mountain beat?
Nay, the men of beauteous Furness are more worthy of their sires,
For the very thought of conquest every loyal soul inspires;
And away from sea washed Walney, to the shores of farthest meres,
Patriotic spirits muster to the rifle Volunteers.[3]

An example of the 'arm for peace' theme is found in 'The British Volunteers or England's Iron Rails' published in the *Volunteer Service Gazette* in April 1860:

By no ambition cruel led,
Britannia calls her sons to arms;
The crimson fields of human dead
For her possess no charms.
A nobler impulse fires the land,
which scorns to live in constant fear,
Which dares for Freedom boldly stand,
And holds o'en life less dear.[4]

A poem written by Alfred Richards 'Our Volunteers' repeats the theme and also shows Richards own interest in promoting social harmony by uniting all classes in the Volunteers:

We are not armed to carry war
    To near or distant land,
To steep the smiling globe with gore
    or prowl with hostile band.
But we are trained with trust above
    To guard our native coast,
Our Queen, our fame — the home we love,
    And those we love the most.

For this, the noble and the brave
    Of gentle birth and name
Ay, and the manhood nature gave
    Stand proudly armed the same.

The courtier with the peasant blunt,
　　Who thinks not 'neath his stave,
And looks as boldly to the front,
　　And working men are there.[5]

A poem written by a private in the band of the Liverpool Borough Guard reveals the class encouraged to join that particular unit:

Then join us tradesmen, oh! join us soon,
And learn the Bullet's Whistling Tune,
The Chaplet — Victory shall award,
To the Liverpool Patriot Borough Guard.[6]

The Althorp Volunteers, on the other hand, had a song to the tune of the 'British Grenadiers' which emphasised the more personal approach:

Now every man of sense, Sir.
Should welcome with three cheers
And rally round Lord Spencer
And the Althorp Volunteers.[7]

Another theme of Volunteer poetry was their own prowess with the rifle and the additional strength given to England. Private Henry Feist of the 13th Surrey R.V.C. composed this prologue for the unit's Dramatic Club in 1861:

Skilled at the butts, with well directed aim,
Our modern marksmen uphold our ancient fame,
Our Queen and Country eulogise our will
And England's foremost among nations still.
Forfend! Great Power! That warfare's fearful blast.
Should rouse the English in their strength at last.
Let meek-eyed Peace with all her radiance smile,
Still make her home in this our favoured isle,
Still let the sword be sheathed, the banner furled,
And friendship's link encircle the world![8]

In such circumstances Volunteers were hardly likely to take notice of the criticisms of the Regular Army as Captain W.G. Hartley stressed in his poem of January 1860:

Ye Champions of our hearths and homes,
　　Your duties now fulfil;
Above all things, be steady in
　　Your practise and your drill.
Heed not the martinets whom age

265

And prejudice enthral.
Or any bogies, which old fogies
    Fright themselves withal.
Your native foe shall quickly know
    We are still a match for Gaul.[9]

The first of the Volunteer issue rifles was, of course, the Enfield and when a changeover to the Snider was mooted, the poem 'The Enfield's Goodbye' appeared in the *Volunteer Service Gazette* in 1865:

We the Enfield's attention engage —
    The rage
We became and just suited the age
    The Commons, the Peers,
    The troops, Volunteers,
Lord Elcho, and Captain Flood-Page.[10]

After the first few years there was an apparent dearth of Volunteer poetry although, in 1876, Lt.-Col. Buck of the 16th Kent R.V.C. produced the 'Volunteer National Song' dedicated to the late I.G.A.F., Major-General Sir Garnet Wolseley, and largely echoing old themes:

The Volunteer Defenders
    of Britain's Isle are we,
To Heaven sworn to hold it
    From all Invaders free.
Let foemen, at the threshold,
    To seek but entrance dare,
And, ready we shall greet him,
    With foemen's welcome, there.[11]

However, the South African War saw the revival of Volunteer literature as much as that produced in 1859 and 1860. One example is a poem published in the *Daventry Express* to celebrate the return of the Daventry contingent of the active service company attached to the Northants Regiment, 'The Danetree Khaki Boys':

They faced the weary marches 'neath the burning, broiling sun,
And the cold and freezing midnight when the long day's march was done;
And never unprepared to fight when the guns the echoes woke;
And 'Fighting Mac* was ready — when he'd had his little smoke;
Then cheer! Men of Danetree town!

*Major-General Hector MacDonald

266

Welcome home the gallant boys who've fought for England's
Crown;
Who've helped to keep the Union Jack respected, great and free;
Then greet the Danetree Khaki Boys with three times three![12]

There is more than a trace of Victorian sentiment in many of these
later poems, as in the case of one written by W.H.F. Webb of the Post
Office Rifles in memory of a colleague who died of disease in South
Africa in March 1900:

Little we thought as we said Good bye!
Returning to clasp your hand —
That you went for the sake of the old flag, to die,
Away in the unknown land;
You went with the light-hearted soldier host.
That answered the War-God's call —
You yielded the hopes that you valued most,
And gave to your country — all!
But the hand of the War-God smote you not —
No victim of shot or shell —
Though you died — and death is the soldier's lot —
At the stroke of disease you fell.
And hence, from the Homeland by wide rolling wave,
Go thoughts from old friends to your distant grave.[13]

[1] 'Arm!' Bucks R.O. *TA Coll* Box 14 Lee Papers.
[2] *The Times* 9.5.59, p 10.
[3] Fell, op cit, p 257-8.
[4] *VSG* 7.4.60, p 11.
[5] *VSG*, 9.2.67, p 168.
[6] Rose, *Liverpool Bulletin*, op cit, p 59.
[7] Eunson, II, p 2.
[8] Ellis, *The Keep*, op cit, p 6.
[9] *VSG*, 28.1.60, p 109.
[10] *VSG*, 1.4.65, p 272.
[11] *VSG*, 15.4.76, p 371.
[12] Northants R.O. *Daventry Volunteer Papers* Box X 4232.
[13] *Khaki Letters* No 3 Post Office RO, R7/3.

APPENDIX II — THE AUXILIARY FORCES BRANCH AT THE WAR OFFICE 1860/1908

Date	Branch	Title of Head	Head of Branch
1860	V	Inspector-General of Volunteers	Col. W.M.S. McMurdo, C.B.
1865	"	"	Col G Erskine
1868	R.F.	Inspector-General of Reserve Forces	Maj.-Gen. Hon. James Lindsay.
1870	"	"	Lt.-Gen. Hon. Sir James Lindsay, K.C.M.G.
1872	A.F.	Inspector-General of Auxiliary Forces	"
1874	"	"	Maj.-Gen. Sir Garnet Wolseley, G.C.M.G.
1875	"	" (Acting)	Maj.-Gen. F.C.A. Stephenson, C.B.
1876	"	"	Lt.-Gen. J.W. Armstrong
1879	"	Deputy-Adjutant-General acting as Inspector-General of Auxiliary Forces	"
1880	"	"	Maj.-Gen. J.H.F. Elkington, C.B.
1885	"	"	Maj.-Gen. Hon. J.C. Dormer, C.B.
1886	"	"	Maj.-Gen. A.J. Lyon-Fremantle, C.B.
1888	A.G.3	"	"
1891	"	Deputy-Adjutant-General for Militia, Yeomanry and Volunteers	Lt.-Gen. A.J. Lyon-Fremantle, C.B.
1891	"	"	Lt.-Gen. Sir R. Gipps, K.C.B.
1892	"	" (Acting)	Lt.-Gen. A.J. Lyon-Fremantle, C.B.
1892	"	"	Maj.-Gen. Sir Francis Grenfell, K.C.B.
1894	"	Inspector-General of Auxiliary Forces and Recruiting	"
1897	"	"	Maj.-Gen. T. Kelly-Kenny, C.B.
1899	"	"	Maj.-Gen. H.C. Borrett
1900	"	Inspector-General of Auxiliary Forces	Maj.-Gen. A.E. Turner, C.B.
1904	"	Director of Auxiliary Forces	Maj.-Gen. W.H. Mackinnon
1908	"	Director-General of The Territorial Force	"

APPENDIX III — THE EFFECTIVE VOLUNTEER INTEREST IN THE HOUSE OF COMMONS, 1862-74

MP	PARTY	CONSTITUENCY
*W.P. Adam	Liberal	Clackmannon 1859-80
Edward Akroyd	Liberal	Huddersfield 1857-9
		Halifax 1865-8
George Anderson	Liberal	Glasgow 1868-85
R.S. Aytoun	Liberal	Kirkcaldy 1862-74
*M.A. Bass	Liberal	East Staffs 1868-85
		Burton 1885-6
Walter Barttelot	Conservative	West Sussex 1860-85
		NW Sussex 1885-92
*†H.F. Beaumont**	Liberal/	West Riding South 1865-74
	Liberal Unionist	Colne 1885-6, 1886-92
Sir Percy Burrell	Conservative	Shoreham 1862-76
Viscount Bury	Liberal	Norwich 1859-60
		Wick 1860-5
		Berwick 1868-74
Charles Buxton	Liberal	Newport 1857-9
		Maidstone 1859-65
		East Surrey 1865-71
Sir Thomas Fowell Buxton	Liberal	Lynn Regis 1865-8
*†W.T. Charley	Conservative	Salford 1868-80
*†S.S. Dickinson	Liberal	Stroud 1868-74
Lewis Dillwyn	Liberal	Swansea 1855-92
Hon. A.F. Egerton	Conservative	South Lancs 1859-68
		SE Lancs 1868-80
		Wigan 1882-5
Lord Elcho	Liberal/	E Gloucester 1841-6
	Conservative	Haddingtonshire 1847-83
*Viscount Enfield	Liberal	Middlesex 1857-74
W.D. Fordyce	Liberal	Aberdeenshire 1866-75
*W.E. Forster	Liberal	Bradford 1861-86
Samuel Graves	Conservative	Liverpool 1865-73
William Gray	Conservative	Bolton 1857-74
Earl Grosvenor	Liberal	Chester 1847-69
E.T. Gourley	Liberal	Sunderland 1868-1900
Francis Hastings-Russell	Liberal	Beds 1859-72
Hon. J. Henniker-Major	Conservative	East Suffolk 1866-70
*Thomas Hughes	Liberal	Lambeth 1865-8
		Frome 1868-74
Charles Lindsay	Conservative	Abingdon 1865-74
Robert Loyd-Lindsay	Conservative	Berks 1865-85
R.A. Macfie	Liberal	Leith 1868-74
Walter Morrison	Liberal	Plymouth 1861-74
		Skipton 1886-92, 1895-1900
A Orr-Ewing	Conservative	Dumbarton 1868-92
*W.S. Roden	Liberal	Stoke 1868-74
*Sir John Shelley	Liberal	Westminster 1852-65

Sir Henry H. Vivian	Liberal	Glamorgan 1857-85
		Swansea 1885-93
*†John Whitwell	Liberal	Kendal 1868-80
Sir Henry Wilmot	Conservative	South Derbyshire 1869-85
C.I. Wright	Conservative	Nottingham 1868-70

*indicates those included primarily by virtue of 'vocal' activity in the House.
†indicates those included by virtue of 'vocal' activity alone.
**Beaumont is the only one of the above who had no serving rank being solely an Honorary Colonel. Several others became Honorary Colonels of their respective regiments on retiring from command.

APPENDIX IV — THE EFFECTIVE VOLUNTEER INTEREST IN THE HOUSE OF COMMONS, 1886-95

MP	PARTY	CONSTITUENCY
Arthur Brookfield	Conservative	East Sussex 1885-1903
*T.H. Bolton	Liberal	St. Pancras 1885-6, 1890-5
T.W. Boord	Conservative	Greenwich 1873-95
H.F. Bowles	Conservative	Enfield 1889-1906
A.H. Brown	Liberal	Wenlock 1868-85
	Liberal Unionist	Mid Salop 1885-1906
W. Cornwallis-West	Liberal Unionist	West Denbigh 1885-92
E.T.D. Cotton-Jodrell	Conservative	Wirrel 1885-1900
Henry Eyre	Conservative	Gainsborough 1886-92
Sir Henry Fletcher	Conservative	Horsham 1880-5
		Mid Sussex 1885-1906
Lord George Hamilton	Conservative	Middlesex 1868-85
		Ealing 1885-1900
Edward Hill	Conservative	South Bristol 1886-1900
Edwin Hughes	Conservative	Woolwich 1885-1902
W.L. Jackson	Conservative	North Leeds 1885-1902
*E.H. Kennard	Conservative	Beverley 1868-9
		Lymington 1874-85
R.P. Laurie	Conservative	Bath 1886-92
E.H. Llewellyn	Conservative	North Somerset 1885-92
		1895-1906
		North Leeds 1885-1902
Sir Richard Paget	Conservative	East Somerset 1865-8
		Mid-Somerset 1868-85
		Wells 1885-95
Sir Albert Rollit	Conservative	Islington South 1886-1906
*Sir Mark Stewart	Conservative	Kirkcudbrightshire 1885-1906,
		1910
Howard Vincent	Conservative	Central Sheffield 1885-1913
Sir William Walrond	Conservative	East Devon 1880-5
		North East Devon 1885-1906

*indicates those included primarily by virtue of 'vocal' activity in the House.

APPENDIX V — ADDITIONAL VOLUNTEER PRESSURE GROUPS

Although the principal economic, social and military grievances of the Volunteers were represented in the House of Commons by the main Volunteer 'Interest', there were at various times a number of peripheral Volunteer interest groups deserving mention who sought to obtain the support of the majority of Volunteer M.P.s for their own specific aims. At least four such small groups can be detected as operating within the shadows of the Volunteer interest of which one — the 'Old Adjutants' has already been described in Chapter IV.

The second of the groups can be detected in the opposition by some Radical and other M.P.s to the Volunteer Bill of 1863. In particular, both Sir R.J. Clifton, Liberal Conservative M.P. for Nottingham, and Mr W. Cox, Liberal M.P. for Finsbury, attempted to strip Volunteer Commanding Officers of their only real disciplinary power, that of dismissal. Curiously enough even a Regular officer such as Lt.-Col. Luard, the Assistant-Inspector of Volunteers, believed that this was a power 'greater than is awarded to any officer in the Army and one not to be in the hands of the Commanding Officer of any Volunteer Corps'.[1] In reality, the power of dismissal for disobedience, neglect and misconduct and the power of arrest on duty were little more effective than the minor fines which were the only other means of instilling discipline. The opposition in the House of Commons stemmed from some controversial dismissal cases notably one in the 2nd Middlesex R.V.C. which had resulted in Lord Ranelagh being accused by his political opponents of wishing to introduce flogging to the Volunteer Force. Cox was suspected of involvement with a shadowy 'Volunteer Defence Association' campaigning against the power of dismissal, and on 20 June 1863 Earl de Grey received a deputation from a so-called 'Metropolitan Committee on the Volunteer Bill' seeking the same object.[2] However, the Radical motion was defeated by 108 votes to 21 on 4 June 1863 and again by 100 votes to 29 on the 14 June when it was alleged that the earlier vote had been influenced by the absence of members at the Ascot Gold Cup. A final attempt to get the bill recommitted was defeated by 138 votes to 31 and it went to the Lords where the Duke of Richmond and the Earl of Derby succeeded in removing the powers of compulsory purchase of land for ranges although it was argued that large landowners had nothing to fear. Hartington expressed disappointment on behalf of the Government and accepted the amendments.[3]

The third interest group was the Clerks of Lieutenancy in the Counties seeking to retain their remunerative allowances and fees from Volunteer administration. The Clerks were frequently in correspondence with one another in 1859 concerning their relative scales of fees on commission. In May 1863 Richard Nicholson, the long serving Clerk in Middlesex, circularised his colleagues and requested them to pressure their Lords Lieutenant and local M.P.'s to secure adequate Militia scales of allowances in the forthcoming Volunteer Bill.[4] There were frequent complaints after 1871 by Volunteer M.P.'s that these allowances were still borne on the Volunteer Vote, and in August 1887 Brodrick, as Financial Secretary at the War Office, was moved to institute an inquiry into the amount of Volunteer work still undertaken by the Clerks. As a result Nicholson once more mobilised his colleagues and organised a meeting in London in October 1887 to resist attempts to cut their emoluments.[5]

The fourth interest group involved with the Volunteers was the Irish M.P.'s. The Irish problem touched on the Volunteer Movement in several ways and, indeed, it was the Fenian threat in 1867 which had led to the codification of the Volunteer's role in aid of the civil power. It was also as a result of the Fenian troubles that the 49th Middlesex (Post Office) R.V.C. was formed in 1867 from Special Constables recruited within the Post Office during that period. The 64th Lancs. (Liverpool Irish) R.V.C. was constantly suspected of Republican leanings and Lt.-Col. Bidwell, the Liberal Catholic corn importer and opponent of Home Rule who commanded the unit, had twenty unenviable years trying to alleviate the suspicions.[6] Sectarian differences, too, were frequently at the root of clashes between Volunteers and the public. In September 1883, for example, fighting broke out between men of the 2nd Lancs. Engineers, on a route march from St. Helens to Knotty Ash, and an Irish mob inflamed by the tune deliberately being played by the Volunteer band.[7] Palmerston made it quite clear in 1859 that Volunteer corps would not be authorised in Ireland where arms might easily fall into the hands of bodies 'whose intentions might not be what they professed'. This policy was reiterated in 1860 when leave to introduce a bill upon the matter was defeated by 86 votes to 30. It was again repeated by both Palmerston and Hartington during the debates upon the Volunteer Bill in 1863. Both denied the Irish claim that the Volunteer Force was to be financed by Irish taxes and the Irish motion was defeated by 156 votes to 45.[8] The issue was again raised by the Chevalier O'Clery, Nationalist M.P. for Wexford, in 1877 and 1878 and Irish M.P.'s disrupted the Volunteer Vote forcing divisions on the matter in 1878, 1881, 1884, 1886 and 1897. Each motion was overwhelmingly defeated.[9] O'Clery introduced a Volunteer Corps (Ireland) Bill in 1879 to which the Conservative ministry was prepared to give qualified assent provided adequate safeguards were incorporated at the committee stage. However, it was feared that the security of arms was a serious problem and the Bill was thrown out in the Lords by 39 votes to 16 largely at the instigation of the Liberal Irish peer, Lord Waveney, who argued that the internal state of the country had not materially changed from that of 1863. O'Clery reintroduced the Bill in the following year but the Government had now reconsidered the situation and had determined that the Bill was unwise. It was defeated by 81 votes to 12 on its second reading in the Commons.[10] The attempts to extend the Volunteer Movement to Ireland were also accompanied by some extra-Parliamentary pressure such as a memorial to the Queen in April 1878 but other developments such as an inflammatory speech by Parnell in the United States in 1880 and an illegal attempt to drill Irishmen in the Flint Volunteers tended to alienate support amongst Volunteer M.P.'s.[11]

[1] Berry, op cit, p 167.
[2] *VSG* 25.4.63, p 425 case of Meyrick and Pignett versus Ranelagh; 6.6.63, p 514-17; 27.6.63, p 566.
[3] *VSG* 13.6.63, p 537; 26.6.63, p 548; 27.6.63, p 565; 18.7.63, p 617.
[4] Oxon R.O. L/M I/ix/1 Nicholson to Davenport, 28.5.63 and 18.5.63.
[5] Arthur O'Connor 6.9.86 *AD* (1886), 615; Kent R.O. *Cinque Ports Mss* RP/2 Brodrick memo of 29.8.87 and circulars by Nicholson of 17.9.87 and 19.10.87.
[6] *VSG* 15.9.66, p 659; 18.12.69, p 36; 11.12.69, p 19; 5.4.73, p 357; 3.5.73, p 421; 7.7.83, p 598; Forde, op cit, p 106-23.
[7] *VSG* 15.9.83, p 769.
[8] Add Mss 48581, 96 (f 57) Palmerston to Herbert, 19.12.59 and 84 (f 51) Palmerston to Cardwell 1.12.59; *Hansard* CLX, 428-40; *VSG* 6.6.63, p 514-5.
[9] *VSG* 3.2.77, p 214; 19.1.78, p 175; 22.6.78, p. 548-50; 29.6.78, p 577; 13.8.81, p 687; 10.5.84, p 440; *AD* (1886), 615-35; *AD* (1897), 375-85.
[10] *VSG* 10.5.79, p 437; 19.7.79, p 622 'Irish Volunteers'; 16.8.79, p 690-1; 9.8.79, p 673-4 'The Irish Volunteers Bill'; 6.3.80, p 291
[11] *VSG* 20.4.78, p 401; 24.1.80, p 198; 16.12.82, p 101; 10.3.83, p 293.

APPENDIX VI — VOLUNTEER BIOGRAPHIES

Acland, Sir Thomas Dyke, Bt. (1809-98). Conservative MP for North Devon, 1837-57 and Liberal M.P. for North Devon, 1865-86. Commanded 1st Devon Administrative Battalion, 1860-81 and also raised five companies of Mounted Rifle Volunteers. Author of several Volunteer pamphlets. His son, Sir Charles T.D. Acland (1842-1920), took command of the 1st Devon Mounted Rifles in 1862.

Bousfield, Nathaniel (1820-83). Liverpool cotton broker and Conservative MP for Bath, 1874-1880. First commissioned officer of the Volunteer Force having been a leading Volunteer advocate in the 1850's. Reached rank of Major in 1st Lancs. R.V.C. There is a tablet to Bousfield in Coniston Lake Church.

Busk, Hans (1815-1882). Claimed to have been the originator of the Volunteer Force. Served as High Sheriff of Radnor in 1847. Barrister. Instrumental in reviving the moribund Victoria Rifles in 1858. Author of *The Rifle and How to Use It* (1853), *Navies of the World* (1859) and *Rifle Volunteers: How to Organise and Drill Them* (1859).

Brookfield, Arthur Montagu (1853-1940). Militia Lieutenant 1871. Commissioned in 13th Hussars 1873 resigning in 1881. Conservative M.P. for Rye, 1885-1903. Lt.-Col. 1st Cinque Ports Volunteers 1884-1903. Commanded 14th Battalion Imperial Yeomanry in South African War. British Consul at Dansig, 1903-1910 and at Savannah, U.S.A.

Charteris, Hon. Francis, Lord Elcho, Earl Wemyss (1818-1914). Conservative M.P. for East Gloucester 1841-6, Liberal Conservative M.P. for Haddingtonshire, 1847-83. Lord of Treasury under Aberdeen, 1852-5. Leading Adullamite. Sponsored the reform of the Master and Servant Act, 1866 and sat on the Royal Commission on Trade Unions, 1867-9. Founder member of the Liberty and Property Defence League, 1882. Commanded 15th Middx. (London Scottish) R.V.C., 1859-1878. Honorary Colonel 1878-1900 when resigned on grounds that existence of the Volunteers was prejudicial to the reintroduction of the ballot. Succeeded to peerage as Earl Wemyss 1883.

Childers, Robert Erskine (1870-1922). Clerk of the House of Commons, 1895-1910. Author of the celebrated *Riddle of the Sands* (1903) and of serious military works such as the fifth volume of the *Times History of the South African War* and *War and the Arme Blanche* (1900). Served in the C.I.V. in South Africa and in the R.N.A.S.

1914-19. His later involvement with Irish nationalism led to his execution by the Free State in 1922.

Fletcher, Col. Henry (1833-79). Designated Brigadier of the Metropolitan Volunteer Brigade in his capacity as C.O. 2nd Battalion, Scots Guards. Official observer of the American Civil War and military secretary to Lord Dufferin in Canada, 1871-5. President of the Martini Henry Committee, member of the National Rifle Association Council and of the R.U.S.I. Council. Chairman of the 1878 R.U.S.I. Conference on the Volunteer Force. Firm friend of the Volunteers and advocate of their use on foreign service.

Grosvenor, Hugh Lupus, Earl Grosvenor, Duke of Westminster (1825-99). Liberal M.P. for Chester 1847-69. Earl Grosvenor 1845; 3rd Marquis of Westminster, 1869; Duke of Westminster, 1874. Owner of extensive London and Cheshire properties; philanthropist and patron of the Turf. Lt.-Col. of the 22nd Middx. (Queen's Westminsters) R.V.C. 1859-1881. Honorary Colonel, 1881-1899. Lord Lieutenant of Cheshire 1883. An unpretentious backbencher save for a brief flirtation with the Adullamites.

Halford, Sir Henry St. John, Bt. (1828-97). Lt.-Col. 1st Leicester Administrative Battalion, 1862-8 and 1870-91. Shot for England twenty times 1862-91 and captain of the British Team in the United States of America in 1877 and 1882. High Sheriff of Leicestershire 1872 and Chairman of Leicestershire County Council, 1889-93. Member of several War Office Small Arms Committees.

Hamley, General Sir Edward (1824-93). Military theorist best known for *Operations of War* (1866). Commandant of the Staff College, 1870-7. Resigned from the Army after his quarrel with Wolseley in Egyptian campaign of 1882. Conservative M.P. for Birkenhead, 1885-92. Honorary Colonel 2nd Middx. Artillery, 1887.

Hughes, Thomas (1822-96). Author of *Tom Brown's Schooldays* (1858). Commanded 19th Middx. R.V.C. drawn from the Working Men's College in Bloomsbury where he was a lecturer and Principal from 1872-83. Coadjutor and deputy editor of the *Volunteer Service Gazette*. Liberal M.P. for Lambeth, 1865-8 and for Frome, 1868-74. Sat on the Royal Commission on Trade Unions, 1867-9. County Court Judge 1882. Later a Liberal Unionist.

Jones, Sir Thomas Heron, 7th Viscount Ranelagh (1812-85). Served in 1st Life Guards and 7th Royal Fusiliers. Soldier of fortune in various European affrays ending in Spain, 1835-7. Lt.-Col. of 2nd South Middx. R.V.C., 1859-85. Made C.B. for services to the Volunteers, 1881. Enjoyed the reputation of a roue and in later years

276

was frequently seen in the company of two young girls variously described as 'daughters' (he never married) or members of the corps de ballet at Covent Garden.

Keppel, William Coutts, Viscount Bury, 7th Earl Albemarle (1832-94). Served in Scots Fusilier Guards and then in Canada, 1854-6 as Civil Secretary and Superintendent General of Indian Affairs, marrying the daughter of the Canadian premier. Former private secretary to Lord John Russell. Liberal M.P. for Norwich, 1859-60, Wick, 1960-5 and for Berwick, 1868-74. Stood as Conservative candidate for Stroud in 1875 being dissatisfied with the abolition of purchase by Royal Warrant. Elevated to the Lords in 1875 as Lord Ashford and Under-Secretary of State for War Office 1878-80 and 1885-6. Excellent marksman who represented England three times in the Elcho Shield at Wimbledon. Succeeded as 7th Earl Albemarle in 1891.

Loyd-Lindsay, Robert, Lord Wantage (1832-1902). Served with Scots Fusilier Guards 1850-9 and won the Victoria Cross in the Crimea. Conservative M.P. for Berkshire, 1865-85. Financial Secretary to the War Office, 1877-8. Founder of the British Red Cross having served as Red Cross observer during the Serbo-Turkish War of 1876-7. C.O. 1st Berkshire Volunteers and also raised 1st Northants L.H.V. Awarded K.C.B. for services to the Volunteers in 1881 and created Lord Wantage 1885.

McMurdo, General Sir William Montague Scott (1819-1894). Son-in-law of Sir Charles Napier and A.Q.M.G. to Napier in India. Director-General of the Land Transport Corps in the Crimea. Inspector-General of Volunteers, 1860-5. Brigade Commander in Dublin 1866-70, district Commander in Bengal, 1870-3. K.C.B., 1881. Honorary Colonel Inns of Court R.V.C. and Engineer and Railway Volunteer Staff Corps.

Macdonald, John Hay Athol, Lord Kingsburgh (1836-1919). Conservative M.P. for Edinburgh and St Andrews Universities 1885-8. Conservative Solicitor General for Scotland, 1876-80 and Lord Advocate of Scotland, 1885-6 and 1886-8. Took judicial title of Lord Kingsburgh, 1888 and made K.C.B., 1900. Lt.-Col. of the Queen's Edinburgh Rifle Brigade, 1864-82, Lt.-Col. Commanding, 1882-92. Honorary Colonel 1901. Leading Volunteer advocate of drill reform. Author of *On the Best Detail Formation for the New Infantry Tactics* (1873) and *Commonsense on Parade or Drill without Strings* (1886).

Richards, Alfred Bate (1820-76). Editor of *Mirror of the Times*, 1850-1; *British Army Despatches*, 1851-3; *The Daily Telegraph and Courier*,

1855-7; and the *Morning Advertiser*, 1870-6. Secretary of the National and Constitutional Defence Association, 1855-9. Playwright and poet. Defeated as Liberal candidate for Ripon, 1859. Commanded 3rd City of London R.V.C., 1861-67.

Vincent, Sir Charles Edward Howard (1849-1908). Served in Royal Welch Fusiliers. Called to the Bar, 1876. War Correspondent for the *Daily Telegraph*, 1876. Lt.-Col. 40th Middx. (Central London Rangers), 1875-8. Director of Criminal Investigation at Scotland Yard, 1878-84. Lt.-Col. Queen's Westminsters, 1884-1908. Conservative M.P. for Central Sheffield 1885-1908. Organised R.U.S.I. Volunteer Conference, 1878 and led Volunteer Interest in the Commons, 1878-1908. President of Working Men's Association for the Defence of British Industry and founder of the United Empire Trade League.

Wilkinson, Henry Spenser (1853-1937). Journalist with the *Manchester Guardian*, 1882-92 and the *Morning Post*, 1895-1914. Author of *The Brain of an Army* (1890) and *Citizen Soldiers* (1883). Captain in the 2nd Manchester R.V.C. Founder of the Manchester Tactical Society, 1881. Served on the Norfolk Commission, 1904-5. First Chichele Professor of the History of War at the University of Oxford, 1909-23.

APPENDIX VII — NOMINAL LIST OF RIFLE VOLUNTEER CORPS

The following lists are based on the Jacques Steeple Mss in the collection of the Ogilby Trust. The date shown is that of the commission of the first officer in the Corps and therefore does not indicate the actual date of offer of services to the Lord Lieutenant or the actual date of acceptance of those services. In each case this would have been a little earlier than the date shown.

Aberdeen

1st (Aberdeen Rifles)		Renumbered 2nd, 1860
2nd (Aberdeen)		
3rd (Cluny)	16.4.59	
4th (Alford)	12.3.60	
5th —		
6th (City of Aberdeen)	19.11.59	To 1st, 1860
7th (City of Aberdeen)	19.11.59	To 1st, 1860
8th (City of Aberdeen)	26.11.59	To 1st, 1860 (merchants)
9th (City of Aberdeen)	23.12.59	To 1st, 1860 (merchants)
10th (City of Aberdeen)	1859	To 1st, 1860 (Sir Wm. Forbes Co.)
11th (City of Aberdeen)	13.1.60	To 6th, 1860 (N.E. Railway)
12th (City of Aberdeen)	27.1.60	To 6th, 1860 (2nd N.E. Railway)
13th (City of Aberdeen)	21.1.60	To 6th, 1860 (3rd N.E. Railway)
14th (City of Aberdeen)	—	To 6th, 1860 (artisans)
15th —	—	To 6th, 1860
16th —	—	To 6th, 1860
17th —	12.4.60	Renumbered 5th, 1860
18th (Ellon)	18.4.60	Renumbered 6th, 1860
19th (Huntly)	6.3.60	Renumbered 7th, 1860
20th (Echt)	9.9.60	Renumbered 8th, 1860
21st (Peterhead)	4.4.60	Renumbered 9th, 1860
22nd (Inverurie)	10.4.60	Renumbered 10th, 1860
23rd (Inverurie)	20.6.60	Renumbered 11th, 1860
12th (Old Aberdeen)	21.7.60	Disbanded 1863
13th (Turriff)	8.8.60	
14th (Tarland)	29.10.60	
15th (Fyvie)	1.10.60	
16th (Meldrum)	2.10.60	
17th (Old Deer)	29.10.60	
18th (Tarves)	11.6.67	
19th (New Deer)	30.6.61	
20th (Longside)	30.7.61	
21st (Marquis of Huntly's Highlanders)	22.11.61	
22nd (Auchmull)	18.6.62	
23rd (Lumphanan)	29.3.62	

24th (Fergus)	23.12.67	
6th (Glenkindie)	7.60	To 11th, 1860
19th (Insch)	1867	
25th (New Pitsligo)	14.4.68	
26th (Cruden)	25.9.72	
12th (Udny)	1864	
24th (Fraserburgh)	1875	

Anglesey

1st (Anglesey)	6.11.60	Disbanded
2nd (Anglesey)	5.11.60	Disbanded
3rd (Anglesey)	2.11.60	Disbanded

Argyll

1st (Argyll)		
2nd (Inveraray)	4.5.60	
3rd (Campbeltown)	16.4.60	
4th — not formed		
5th (Mull)	6.12.60	Disbanded 1862
6th (Melfort)	22.4.60	Disbanded 1864
7th (Dunoon)	28.3.60	
8th (Cowal)	4.6.60	
9th (Glenorchy)	12.4.60	Disbanded 1870
10th (Tayvollick)	4.6.60	Disbanded 1869
11th (Oban)	7.7.60	Disbanded 1865
12th (Bridgend)	7.6.61	Disbanded 1865
13th (Ballachulish)	31.8.67	
14th (Kilmartin)	15.1.68	

Ayrshire

1st (Kilmarnock)	14.7.60	
2nd (Irvine)	27.12.60	
3rd (Ayr)	19.1.60	
4th (Largs)	27.2.60	
5th (Maybole)	27.2.60	
6th (Beith)	15.2.60	
7th (Saltcoats)	28.2.60	
8th (Colmonell)	25.5.60	Disbanded 1875
9th (2nd Kilmarnock)	19.5.60	To 1st, 1875
10th (Girvan)	22.10.60	
11th (Dalry)	4.12.60	
12th (Cumnock)	14.1.61	
13th (Sorn)	18.3.61	
14th (2nd Ayr)	14.4.62	
15th (Darvel)	24.12.73	
16th (Newmilns)	24.12.73	
17th (Galston)	10.10.74	

Banffshire

1st (Macduff)		Disbanded 1860
2nd (Banff)	18.4.60	Renumbered 1st
3rd (Aberlour)	29.9.60	Renumbered 2nd

4th (South Banffshire)	2.11.60	Renumbered 3rd
5th (Buckie)	12.3.63	
6th (Glenlivet)	19.4.67	
7th (Dufftown)	1.5.68	

Bedfordshire

1st (Bedford)	27.2.60	
2nd (Toddington)	1.3.60	
3rd (Leighton Buzzard)	1860	Disbanded 1860
4th (Dunstable)	24.4.60	
5th (Ampthill)	26.4.60	
6th (Luton)	16.5.60	
7th (Shefford)	11.9.60	
8th (Woburn)	18.9.60	
9th (2nd Bedford)	16.5.64	Disbanded

Berkshire

1st (Reading)	10.9.59	
2nd (Windsor)	2.1.60	
3rd (Newbury)	29.5.60	
4th (Abingdon)	23.2.60	
5th (Maidenhead)	24.2.60	
6th (Forest Rifles)	14.5.60	Disbanded 1865
7th (Sandhurst)	25.8.60	
8th (Faringdon)	21.9.60	
9th (Wantage)	24.10.60	
10th (Forest Rifles)	12.3.61	Later to Bracknell
11th (Wallingford)	13.2.61	
12th (Windsor Great Park)	22.8.66	
13th (Windsor)	1860	Later to 12th

Berwickshire

1st (Duns)	16.12.59	
2nd (Coldstream)	30.3.60	
3rd (Ayton)	11.5.60	
4th (Greenlaw)	24.2.60	
5th (Lauderdale)	10.4.60	
6th (Duns)	5.6.63	
7th (Chirnside)	7.7.63	

Berwick on Tweed

1st —	28.3.60	Later divided between 1st Newcastle A.V. and 1st A.B. Northumberland.

Brecknockshire

1st (Brecknock)	21.8.59	
2nd (Brynmawr)	13.2.60	
3rd (Crickhowell)	30.8.60	
4th (Hay)	7.4.60	
5th (Builth)	4.6.60	
6th (Talgarth)	14.2.61	
7th (Cefn)	1878	

281

Buckinghamshire
1st (Marlow)	8.12.59	
2nd (Wycombe)	2.60	
3rd (Buckingham)	1860	
4th (Aylesbury)	25.3.60	
5th (Slough)	3.60	
6th (Newport Pagnell)	1860	Disbanded 1864
7th (Princes Risborough)	1860	Disbanded 1860
8th (Eton College)	22.1.60	

Buteshire
1st (Rothesay)	19.1.60	

Caernarvonshire
1st (Caernarvon)	1.3.60	Disbanded
2nd (Caernarvon)	1.3.60	Disbanded
3rd (Caernarvon)	2.6.60	
4th (Tremadoc)	1.3.60	
5th (Pwllheli)	1.3.60	
6th (Bangor)	3.3.60	Disbanded 1860
7th (Conway)	4.4.60	Disbanded 1860

Caithness
1st (Thurso)	10.4.60	
2nd (Wick)	16.2.61	
3rd (Halkirk)	11.4.61	
4th (Watten)	25.9.67	

Cambridgeshire
1st (Cambs Town)	16.1.60	
2nd (Wisbech)	19.1.60	
3rd (Cambs. University)	10.1.60	
4th (Whittlesey)	17.1.60	
5th (March)	21.8.60	
6th (Ely)	11.7.60	
7th (Upwell)	7.9.60	Disbanded 1893
8th (Cambs. Town)	6.11.60	To 1st, 1863
9th (Newmarket)	1860	To 20th Suffolk
10th (Soham)		

Cardiganshire
1st (Aberystwyth)	12.3.60	Disbanded 1863
2nd (Aberystwyth)	12.3.60	Renumbered 1st, 1873
3rd (Aberbank)	12.3.60	Disbanded 1861
4th (Cardigan)	6.5.60	Renumbered 3rd, 1861

Carmarthenshire
1st (Llandilo)	28.2.60	
2nd (Carmarthen)	20.2.60	
3rd (Llandovery)	4.5.60	Disbanded 1875
4th (Llansawel)	29.5.60	Disbanded 1869
5th (Llanelly)	8.5.61	
6th (2nd Carmarthen)	29.7.62	

Cheshire

1st (Wirral Rifles)	25.8.59	
2nd (Oxton)	30.8.59	
3rd (Wallasey)	5.9.59	
4th (Bebbington)	10.9.59	
5th (Congleton)	15.9.59	
6th (Earl of Chester's)	25.2.60	
7th (Runcorn)	30.11.59	
8th (Macclesfield)	5.1.60	
9th (Mottram)	10.2.60	Disbanded
10th — not formed		
11th (Neston)	28.2.60	
12th (Altrincham)	1.3.60	
13th (Dukinfield)	5.11.60	
14th (Hooton)	3.3.60	
15th (Knutsford)	5.3.60	
16th (Sandbach)	7.3.60	
17th (Stockport)	20.8.60	
18th (Stockport)	12.3.60	
19th (Stockport)	15.3.60	
20th (Stockport)	20.3.60	
21st (Stockport)	22.3.60	
22nd (Northwich)	26.3.60	
23rd (Weaverham)	28.3.60	
24th (Frodsham)	30.3.60	
25th (Timperley)	2.4.60	
26th (Northenden)	15.12.60	
27th (Wilmslow)	5.4.60	
28th (Sale Moor)	7.4.60	
29th (Stockport)	10.4.60	
30th (1st Tranmere)	30.4.60	
31st (Hyde)	15.8.60	
32nd (Lymm)	10.9.60	
33rd (Nantwich)	5.11.60	
34th (Upton		Struck off 1864
35th (2nd Tranmere)	25.2.63	
36th (Crewe)	20.1.65	Disbanded 1880

Cinque Ports

1st (Hastings)	17.12.59	
2nd (Ramsgate)	18.9.59	
3rd (ex-2nd Rye)	4.1.60	
4th (Hythe)	13.2.60	
5th (Folkestone)	30.3.60	Disbanded 1878
6th (Deal and Walmer)	20.4.60	Disbanded 1863
7th (Margate)	22.3.60	
8th (Dover)	30.7.60	
9th (Tenterden)	12.12.64	
10th (New Romney)	22.12.64	
11th (Etchingham)		
12th (Eastbourne)		
13th (Winchelsea)		

Clackmannon

1st (Alloa Rifles)	2.6.60	
2nd (Tillicoultry)	10.3.60	

Cornwall

1st (Duke of Cornwall's Rifles)	10.9.59	
2nd (Camborne)	17.10.59	
3rd (Falmouth)	28.10.59	
4th (Liskeard)	13.12.59	
5th (Collingham)	3.1.60	
6th (Launceston)	10.1.60	
7th (Helston)	25.1.60	
8th (Penryn)	1860	To 21st
9th (St. Austell)	14.2.60	
10th (Bodmin)	6.3.60	
11th (Truro)	11.5.60	
12th (Truro)	12.4.60	
13th (Wadebridge)	7.4.60	
14th (Calstock)	1860	To 7th
15th (Copperhouse Rifles)	2.5.60	
16th (St. Columb)	2.4.60	
17th (Redruth)	2.6.60	
18th (Meneage)	7.4.60	
19th (Camelford)	26.7.60	
20th (St. Just)	14.8.60	
21st (Penryn)	1.12.60	
22nd (Saltash)	23.2.65	

Cumberland

1st (Carlisle)	15.2.60	
2nd (Whitehaven)	14.2.60	
3rd (Skiddaw Greys)	10.3.60	
4th (Belted Will Rifle Club)	4.4.60	
5th (Inglewood Rangers)	19.7.60	
6th (Alston Mountaineer Rifles)	2.3.60	
7th (Solway Marksmen)	12.4.60	
8th (Cockermouth)	24.3.60	
9th (2nd Whitehaven)	21.5.60	
10th (Egremont)	3.7.60	
11th (Wigton)	18.7.60	

Denbighshire

1st (Wrexham)	30.1.60	
2nd (Ruabon)	12.4.60	
3rd (Denbigh and Ruthin)	21.7.60	
4th (Vale of Gresford)	10.9.60	
5th (Gwersyllt)	1860	
6th (Ruthin)	20.2.61	
7th (Chirk)	6.4.64	
8th (Llanrwst)	25.10.61	Disbanded 1861
9th (Llangollen)	6.6.68	

Derbyshire

1st (Derby)	23.7.59	
2nd (Sudbury)	28.2.60	
3rd (Chesterfield)	7.1.60	
4th (2nd Derby)	31.12.59	
5th (Derby Artisan)	18.1.60	
6th (High Peak Rifles)	16.2.60	
7th (High Peak Rifles)	1.2.60	
8th (Dove Valley)	1.2.60	
9th (High Peak)	28.2.60	
10th (Wirlesworth)	10.3.60	
11th (Matlock)	17.3.60	
12th (Butterley)	3.4.60	
13th (Belper)	14.3.60	
14th — not formed		
15th (Chaddesdon)	22.8.60	
16th (Erewash Valley Rifle Club)	7.9.60	Disbanded
17th (Clay Cross)	26.1.61	
18th (Whaley Bridge)	16.3.66	
19th (Elvaston)	5.2.70	
20th (Trent)	31.7.71	
21st (Harbington)	21.7.75	
22nd (Staveley)	23.9.74	
23rd (Glossop)	2.2.76	

Devon

1st (Exeter and South Devon)	26.3.52	The premier Volunteer unit
2nd Devon (Plymouth)	7.12.59	
3rd (Devonport Dockyard)	7.12.59	
4th (Ilfracombe)	3.3.60	
5th (Upper Cullompton)	22.3.60	
6th (Barnstaple)	15.9.60	
7th — Not formed		
8th (Buckerell)	8.2.60	
9th (Ashburton)	23.2.60	
10th (Newton Abbott)	27.3.60	
11th (Bampton)	28.2.60	
12th — Not formed		
13th (East Devon and Honiton)	20.2.60	
14th (Tiverton)	1.3.60	
15th — Not formed		
16th (Stonehouse)	29.2.60	Absorbed 1874
17th (Totnes)	3.3.60	
18th (Hatherleigh)	15.9.60	
19th (Okehampton)	3.3.60	
20th (Broadhembury)	3.3.60	Disbanded 1875
21st (Bideford)	6.3.60	
22nd (Tavistock)	27.3.60	
23rd (Chudleigh)	27.3.60	

24th (Budleigh Salterton)		Disbanded
25th (Ottery St. Mary)	4.4.60	
26th (Kingsbridge)	5.7.60	
27th (Colyton)	7.12.60	
28th (Lynton)	13.4.61	
28th (South Molton)		Merged

Dorset

1st (Bridport)	22.8.59	
2nd (Wareham and Corfe Castle)	28.1.60	
3rd (Dorchester)	14.2.60	
4th (Poole)	13.2.60	
5th (Weymouth)	14.5.60	
6th (Wimborne)	14.3.60	
7th (Sherborne)	29.3.60	
8th (Blandford)	9.5.60	
9th (Shaftesbury)	10.3.60	
10th (Sturminster Newton)	10.7.60	
11th (Gillingham)	7.7.60	
12th (Stalbridge)	10.7.60	Disbanded

10th/11th/12th usually known as Vale of Blackmore Forces

Dumbartonshire

1st (Row)	18.2.60	
2nd (East Kilpatrick)	18.2.60	
3rd (Bonhill)	8.2.60	
4th (Jamestown)	8.2.60	
5th (Alexandria)	8.2.60	
6th (Burgh of Dumbarton)	8.2.60	
7th (Cardross)	11.11.59	
8th (Gareloch)	16.2.60	To 1st, 1865
9th (Luss and Arrochar)	8.2.60	Highlanders
10th (Kirkintilloch)	5.3.60	
11th (Cumbernauld)	13.6.60	
12th (Tarbert and Arrochar)	7.3.61	Disbanded 1869
13th (Milngavie)	9.8.67	
14th (Clydebank)	18.5.73	

Dumfries

1st (Dumfries)	25.2.60
2nd (Thornhill)	28.2.60
3rd (Sanquhar)	28.2.60
4th (Penpont)	29.2.60
5th (Annan)	14.6.60
6th (Upper Annandale)	20.6.60
7th (Langholm)	1.6.60
8th (Lockerbie)	20.6.60
9th (Lochmaben)	18.2.61

Durham

1st (Stockton)	27.2.60

2nd — Not formed		
3rd (Sunderland Rifles)	6.3.60	
4th (Teesdale)	24.5.60	
5th (West Rainbow)		Disbanded 1869
6th (Tyne Docks)	20.3.60	
7th (Durham City 'Black Watch')	24.3.60	
8th (Gateshead)	14.3.60	
9th (Tyne and Derwent Rifles)	3.5.60	
10th (Beamish)	12.5.60	
11th (Chester le Street, Pelton Colliery)	5.6.60	
12th (Middleton, London Lead Co.)	14.7.60	
13th (Birtley, Perkins and Co.)	17.8.60	
14th (Felling)	31.10.60	
15th (Darlington)	6.10.60	
16th (Castle Eden)	14.12.60	
17th (Wolsingham)	24.11.60	Disbanded 1866
18th (Stanhope)	1.12.60	Disbanded 1865
19th (Hartlepool)	26.1.61	Became 1st Durham A.V. 1872
20th (Stanhope)	19.2.62	
21st (Barnard Castle)	26.12.63	

City of Edinburgh

1st (City of Edinburgh)	31.8.59	Queen's City of Edinburgh Rifle Vol. Brigade 1865
2nd (City of Edinburgh)	3.5.62	To 1st, (artisans)
3rd (City of Edinburgh)	27.5.67	To 1st, 1867 (total abstainers)

Elgin

1st (Forres)	11.1.60	
2nd (Elgin)	31.1.60	
3rd (Elgin)	20.2.60	
4th (Rothes)	28.5.60	
5th (Fochabers)	10.4.61	
6th (Carrbridge)	26.8.61	
7th (The Duff)	15.4.63	
8th (Garmouth)	2.12.67	
9th (Grantown)	9.1.71	

Essex

1st (Romford)	25.3.59	
2nd (Ilford)	12.8.59	
3rd (Brentwood)	1859	Disbanded
3rd (ex 4th, Chelmsford)	12.10.59	
4th (Brentwood)	8.11.59	Combined with 3rd Chelmsford
4th (Brentwood)	8.11.59	

5th (Plaistow and Victoria Docks)	8.11.59	Mainly Docks
6th (Colchester)	8.9.59	
7th (Rochford)	6.3.60	
8th (Eastern Counties Railway)	6.3.60	
9th (Silvertown)	25.2.60	
10th (Witham)	10.7.60	
11th (Dunmore)	21.3.60	Struck off 14.8.63
12th (Braintree)	18.8.60	
13th (Stow Valley)	8.3.60	Disbanded 1870
14th (Manningtree)	17.5.60	Disbanded
15th (Hornchurch)	11.6.60	Renumbered 14th
16th (Gt. Bentley-Tendring Hundred Rifles)	10.9.60	
17th (Saffron Walden)	23.10.60	
18th (Chipping Ongar)	4.12.60	
19th (Epping)	22.9.60	Disbanded 1873
20th (Haverhill)	27.12.60	Disbanded 1871
21st (2nd Brentwood)	24.9.60	To 3rd, 1870
22nd (Waltham Abbey-West Essex Rifles)	27.11.60	
23rd (Maldon)	13.11.60	
24th (Essex Forest)	10.4.61	Disbanded 1873

Fife

1st (Dunfermline)	25.2.60
2nd (Cupar)	6.3.60
3rd (Kilconquhar)	25.4.60
4th (Colinsburgh)	20.4.60
5th (St. Andrews)	23.4.60
6th (Strathleven)	25.8.60
7th (Kirkcaldy Vols.)	23.4.60
8th (Auchterderran)	20.4.60
9th (Dysart)	28.7.60

Flintshire

1st (Mold)	27.3.60
2nd (Hawarden)	30.4.60
3rd (Vale of Clwyd)	1860
4th (Holywell)	29.6.60
5th (Flint)	13.4.64
6th (Caergwrle)	16.12.74

Forfar

1st (Dundee)	10.5.59	
2nd (Forfar)	15.11.59	
3rd (Arbroath)	15.11.59	
4th (Arbroath)	15.11.59	To 3rd, 1860
5th (Montrose)	15.11.59	
6th —		Disbanded 1861
7th (Brechin)	26.3.60	

8th (The Warncliffe)	4.4.60	
9th (Glamis)	8.5.60	
10th (Dundee Highland Rifles)	10.4.60	To 1st, 1861
11th (Tannadice)	8.10.60	Disbanded 1861
12th (Kirriemuir)	17.9.60	
13th (Friockheim)	4.6.61	
14th (Dundee Highland)	14.6.61	To 1st, 1861. To 10th 1868
15th (Cortachy)	16.3.65	Disbanded 1872

Glamorganshire

1st (Margam)	12.10.59	
2nd (Dowlais)	12.10.59	
3rd (Swansea)	12.10.59	
4th (Taibach)	12.10.59	To Swansea
5th (Penllergare)	12.10.59	Disbanded
6th (Swansea Kilvey Rifles)	10.12.59	Disbanded
7th (Taibach)	3.1.60	
8th (Aberdare)	12.3.60	
9th (Baglan)	5.5.60	
10th (Cardiff)	13.1.60	
11th (Bridgend)	14.2.60	
12th (Merthyr Tydfil)	7.2.60	
13th (Llandaff)	7.2.60	
14th (Aberdare)	14.2.60	
15th (Neath)	14.2.60	
16th (Bute)	18.1.60	
17th (Vale of Neath Brewery R.V.)	2.6.60	Disbanded
18th (Cowbridge)	25.6.60	
19th (Pontypridd)	23.5.61	
20th (Hirwain)		

Gloucestershire

1st (Bristol Rifles)	12.9.59	
2nd (Gloucester Docks Coy.)	21.10.59	
3rd (Gloucester City)	21.10.59	
4th (Stroud)	5.9.59	Disbanded
5th (Stroud)	6.9.59	
6th (Stroud)	7.9.59	Disbanded
7th (Cheltenham)	20.9.59	Disbanded 1864
8th (Tewkesbury)	6.12.60	Disbanded 1876
9th (Cirencester)	13.2.60	
10th (Cotswold Rifles)	1.3.60	
11th (Dursley)	9.3.60	
12th (Forest of Dean)	21.4.60	
13th (Oddfellows-Cheltenham)	23.3.60	To 7th, 1860
14th (Cheltenham)	3.7.60	To 7th, 1860
15th (Stow on the Wold)	3.12.60	
16th (North Cotswold Rifles)	23.11.60	
14th (City of Gloucester Rifles)	1874/5	To 7th

Haddington

1st (East Lothian Rifles)	19.1.60	
2nd (Gifford)	20.1.60	Disbanded 1874
3rd (Haddington)	21.1.60	
4th (Aberlady)	17.3.60	
5th (East Linton)	7.4.60	
6th (Dunglass)	27.8.61	
7th (North Berwick)	25.11.69	

Hampshire

1st (Winchester)	18.10.59	
2nd (Southampton)	18.5.60	
3rd (Lymington)	30.12.59	
4th (Havant)	3.2.60	
5th (Portsmouth)	14.4.60	
6th (Gosport)	17.4.60	
7th (Fareham)	2.6.60	
8th (Bitterne)	14.5.60	
9th —		Disbanded
10th (Christchurch)	9.3.60	
11th (Romsey)	7.4.60	
12th (Petersfield)	28.4.60	
13th (Andover)	25.5.60	
14th (Lyndhurst)	6.7.60	
15th (Yateley)	5.6.60	
16th (Alresford)	7.6.60	
17th (Titchfield)	29.8.60	Disbanded 1874
18th (Basingstoke)	6.8.60	Disbanded 1864, after Guildford review
19th (Bournemouth)	18.8.60	
20th (Wickham)	22.7.60	Disbanded 1874
21st (Alton)	5.9.60	
22nd (Bishops Waltham)	13.9.60	
23rd (Cosham)	29.11.60	
24th (Winchester)	24.2.75	
25th (Basingstoke)	9.6.75	

Haverfordwest

1st (Haverfordwest)	4.2.60	
2nd —		To 1st
3rd —		To 1st

Herefordshire

1st (Hereford City)	10.4.60	
2nd (Ross)	27.3.60	
3rd (Ledbury)	27.3.60	
4th (Bromyard)	15.5.60	
5th (South Archenfield Forest Border Rifles)	15.5.60	Disbanded 1874
6th (Leominster)	15.5.60	
7th (Kington)	18.5.60	
8th (Oddfellows)	27.9.60	

9th (1st Radnor)
10th (2nd Radnor)
11th (3rd Radnor)   Disbanded 1874

Hertfordshire
1st (Hertford)   25.10.59
2nd (Watford)   5.1.60
3rd (St. Albans)   12.5.60
4th (Ashridge)   12.4.60
5th (Hemel Hempstead)   3.12.60
6th (Bishops Stortford)   2.4.60
7th (Berkhamsted)   20.2.60
8th (Tring)   23.4.60
9th (Ware)   3.7.60
10th (Royston)   25.6.60
11th (Cheshunt)   25.8.60   Disbanded 1870
12th (Hitchin)   15.9.60   Disbanded 1870
13th (Walton)   8.9.64   Struck off 1868
14th (Welwyn)   1875

Huntingdon
1st (Hunts)   18.4.60

Inverness
1st (Inverness Rifles)   15.10.59
2nd (Lochaber)   9.4.60
3rd (2nd Inverness)   26.3.60   merchants
4th (3rd Inverness   3.5.60
    Clachnacuddin)
5th (4th Inverness Celtic)   16.7.60
6th (Badenoch Highland)   3.6.61
7th (Beauly)   1.7.61
8th (Skye)   20.7.67
9th (Ardersier)   12.11.67
10th (Roy Bridge)   11.2.69

Isle of Man
1st (Castletown and Foxdale)   10.10.60 Disbanded 1870
2nd (Douglas)   5.7.61
3rd (Ramsey Rifles)   23.7.61
4th (Crosby)   1868 Disbanded 1870

Isle of Wight
1st (Ryde)   25.1.60
2nd (Newport)   27.8.60
3rd (2nd Ryde)   7.12.60 Disbanded
4th (Nunwell)   17.7.60
5th (Ventnor)   22.10.60
6th (Sandown)   31.3.60   Disbanded 1862
7th (Cowes and Osborne)   27.4.60
8th (Freshwater)   6.7.60   Disbanded 1869

Kent

1st (Maidstone Rifles)	25.8.59	
2nd (Ramsgate)	18.9.59	
3rd (Blackheath)	7.11.59	
4th (Woolwich Town)	21.12.59	To 26th, 1880
5th (East Kent — Tradesmen)	1.12.59	
6th (East Kent — Artisan)	6.12.59	
7th (Kidbrooke)	21.12.59	Disbanded 1869
8th (Sydenham)	22.12.59	Disbanded 1871
9th (Chatham)	31.12.59	Disbanded 1860
10th (Sittingbourne)		Disbanded 1860
11th (Farnborough)	24.1.60	Disbanded 1862
12th (Dartford)	22.2.60	
13th (Greenwich)	11.11.59	
14th (Tonbridge)	2.12.59	Disbanded 1870
15th (West Kent)	15.2.60	Disbanded 1874
16th (Sittingbourne and Milton)	13.2.60	
17th (Tunbridge Wells)	20.2.60	
18th (Bromley Rifle Club)	13.7.60	Disbanded
19th (Rochester City)	20.2.60	Disbanded 1874
20th (Northfleet)	11.4.60	Disbanded 1868
21st (Lewisham)	15.2.60	Disbanded 1861
22nd (Sheerness and Sheppey)	13.4.60	Disbanded 1870
23rd (Penshurst)	28.2.60	Disbanded 1869
24th (Ash)	29.2.60	Disbanded 1868
25th (Blackheath Artisans)	18.2.60	
26th (Royal Arsenal)	20.2.60	To 4th
27th (Deptford Dockyard)	28.2.60	
28th (Charlton)	18.2.60	
29th (Ashford — S.E. Railway)	15.3.60	
30th —		Disbanded 1860
31st (Leeds Castle)	23.3.60	
32nd (Eltham)	22.3.60	Disbanded 1875
33rd (Sevenoaks)	23.3.60	
34th (Deptford Town Artisans)	23.3.60	
35th (Westerham)	7.5.60	
36th (Wingham)	18.5.60	
37th (Weald)	6.6.60	
38th (Sheerness, later Hawkhurst)	12.6.61	
39th (West Malling)	26.6.60	Disbanded 1865
40th (Staplehurst)	6.6.60	
41st (Weald)	5.12.61	
42nd (Weald)	4.5.63	
43rd (Weald)	6.6.60	
44th (Weald)	4.7.61	To 42nd, 1863
45th (City of Rochester)	21.2.70	Disbanded 1875

Kincardineshire

1st (Fetteresso)	10.1.60	Disbanded 1870
2nd (Banchory)	28.1.60	
3rd (Laurencekirk)	2.60	To 5th, 1873
4th (Fettercairn)	13.3.60	Disbanded 1871
5th (Auchinblae)	6.60	
6th (Netherley)	7.5.60	
7th (Durris)	13.2.61	
8th (Maryculter and Peterculter)	21.10.69	

Kinross

1st —	31.10.60	

Kircudbrightshire or East Galloway

1st (Galloway)	2.3.60	
2nd (Castle Douglas)	2.3.60	
3rd (New Galloway)	28.3.60	
4th (Gatehouse)	19.5.60	Disbanded 1866
5th (Maxwelltown)	1.6.60	
6th (Dalbeattie)	23.6.69	

Lanarkshire

1st (Western Rifles)	24.9.59	
2nd (University of Glasgow)	24.9.59	To 1st, 1860
3rd (1st Southern)	9.9.59	
4th (1st Northern Glasgow)	10.10.59	
5th (1st Eastern)	24.9.59	To 31st, 1873
6th (Glasgow 2nd Northern)	10.10.59	To 4th, 1859, artisans
7th (Glasgow 3rd Northern)	10.10.59	To 4th, 1859, artisans
8th (Glasgow 4th Northern)	10.10.59	To 4th, 1859, artisans
9th (Glasgow 1st Bankers)	10.10.59	To 1st, 1860
10th (Glasgow 2nd Southern)	19.10.59	To 3rd, 1860
11th (2nd Western)	4.11.59	To 1st, 1860
12th (North Eastern)	5.12.59	To 4th, 1859, tenants
13th (St. Rollox — 5th Northern)	5.12.59	To 4th, 1859, artisans
14th (South Western — 2nd Western)	5.12.59	To 3rd, 1860, engineers and ironfounders
15th (Procurators)	5.12.59	To 1st, 1860
16th (No. 1 Coy. Hamilton)	24.2.60	
17th (Stockbrokers and Accountants)	5.12.59	To 1st, 1860
18th —	5.12.59	To 1st, 1860
19th (Glasgow 2nd Northern)	5.12.59	Bn. 1860
20th — Not completed		
21st (Parkhead Artisans)	5.12.59	To 5th, 1860
22nd (Artisans)	5.12.59	To 3rd, 1860
23rd (Warehousemen)	5.12.59	To 19th, 1860
24th (North Western)	6.12.59	To 19th, 1860
25th (Clyde Artisans)	14.12.59	
26th (Clyde Artisans)	14.12.59	To 25th, 1861

293

27th (Clyde Artisans)	14.12.59	To 25th, 1861
28th (Railway)	22.12.59	To 19th, 1860
29th (Coatbridge)	13.2.60	
30th (1st Central)	28.12.59	Disbanded 1865
31st (Central Blythswood)	21.12.59	
32nd (Summerlee)	10.1.60	artisans
33rd (1st Partick)	22.12.59	To 1st, 1860
34th (1st Rifle Rangers)	27.12.59	To 5th, 1860
35th (2nd Rifle Rangers)	27.12.59	To 5th, 1860
36th (Port Dundas Artisans)	28.12.59	To 19th, 1860
37th (Lesmahagow)	3.2.60	
38th (Rifle Rangers)	29.12.59	To 31st, 1865 artisans
39th —	29.12.59	To 1st, 1860
40th (Clyde Artisans)	29.12.59	To 25th, 1861
41st (North Western Artisans)	31.12.59	To 19th, 1860
42nd (Uddington)	31.1.60	
43rd (Gartsherrie)	10.1.60	artisans
44th (Blantyre)	10.2.60	
45th (Grocers)	10.1.60	To 31st, 1865
46th (Grocers)	10.1.60	To 31st, 1865
47th (Grocers)	10.1.60	To 31st, 1865
48th (Airdrie)	11.2.60	
49th (Lambhill)	3.5.60	Disbanded 1862
50th (1st Press)	10.1.60	To 1st, 1860 Disbanded 1863
51st (2nd Press)	11.1.60	To 19th, 1860
52nd (Hamilton No. 2 Coy.)	24.2.60	
53rd —	30.1.60	To 1st, 1860
54th (Total Abstainers)	30.1.60	To 3rd, 1860
55th (Lanark)	23.2.60	
56th (Bothwell)	23.2.60	
57th (Wishaw)	7.3.60	
58th (1st Eastern Artisans)	10.2.60	To 5th, 1860
59th (2nd Eastern Artisans)	21.2.60	To 5th, 1860
60th (1st Highland)	18.2.60	To 4th, 1861
61st (2nd Highland)	18.2.60	To 4th, 1861 artisans
62nd (Biggar)	22.2.60	
63rd —	15.2.60	To 1st, 1860
64th (1st Rutherglen)	18.2.60	To 5th, 1860
65th (2nd Rutherglen)	18.2.60	To 5th, 1860
66th (Eastern Rifle Rangers)	17.2.60	To 5th, 1860
67th (Artisans)	17.2.60	To 19th, 1860
68th (Clyde Artisans)	17.2.60	To 25th, 1861
69th (Clyde Artisans)	17.2.60	To 25th, 1861
70th (Clyde Artisans)	17.2.60	To 25th, 1861
71st (Clyde Artisans)	17.2.60	To 25th, 1861
72nd (Fine Arts)	26.2.60	To 1st, 1860
73rd (Carluke)	12.3.60	
74th (Grenadiers)	20.2.60	To 19th, 1860
75th (2nd Coy. Leather and Boot Trade)	29.2.60	To 31st, 1865
76th (Port Dundas)	26.3.60	To 1st, 1860

77th (City Rifle Guard or 2nd Univ)	8.3.60	To 1st, 1860
78th (The Old Guard of Glasgow)	29.3.60	To 3rd
79th (3rd Western)	29.3.60	To 1st, 1860
80th (Artisans)	29.3.60	To 19th, 1860
81st (Northern Artisans)	2.4.60	To 19th, 1860
82nd (Total Abstainers)	11.4.60	To 3rd, 1860 artisans
83rd (Northern Artisans)	24.4.60	To 19th, 1860
84th —	24.4.60	To 31st, 1860
85th (2nd North Eastern)	7.5.60	To 19th, 1860
86th (Tailors)	7.5.60	To 31st, 1860
87th (Busby Artisans)	18.5.60	To 3rd, 1860
88th (Fleshers)	9.5.60	Disbanded 1864
89th (Manufacturers)	9.5.60	To 19th, 1860
90th (Whitevale)	24.5.60	To 5th, 1860
91st (3rd Abstainers)		To 19th, 1860 artisans
92nd (Uddingston)		Not accepted
93rd (3rd Highlanders or Glasgow Highland Rifle Rangers)	8.8.60	To 4th, 1861
94th (Douglas)	21.9.60	
95th (Bailliestown)	16.10.60	To Coatbridge 1875
96th —	29.11.60	To 31st, 1865
97th (Glasgow Guards)	30.7.61	To 1st Lanarkshire Engineers 1863
97th (Woodhead)	11.2.65	To Coatbridge 1871
98th (Gartness)	12.5.65	To Waterstown 1869
100th (Clarkston)	27.7.65	
101st (Calderbank)	8.7.65	To Caldercruix 1866
102nd (Motherwell)	14.2.67	
103rd (East Kilbride)	6.6.67	
104th —	18.4.68	
105th (Glasgow Highlanders)	21.7.68	
106th (Strathearn)	10.73	
107th (Leadhills)	5.75	

Lancashire

1st (Liverpool-Bousfields)	9.6.59	
2nd (Blackburn)	4.10.59	
3rd (Blackburn)	4.10.59	To 2nd 1860
4th (Rossendale)	4.7.59	
5th (Liverpool Rifle Vol. Brig.)	19.8.59	
6th (Manchester)	25.8.59	
7th (Accrington)	20.9.59	
8th (Bury)	22.9.59	
9th (Warrington)	16.9.59	
10th (Lancaster)	20.9.59	
11th (1st Preston)	4.10.59	
12th (2nd Preston)	7.10.59	To 11th, 1860
13th (1st Southport)	6.12.59	

14th (2nd Southport)	16.2.60	To 13th, 1862
15th (Liverpool-Everton/ Seaforth)	10.1.60	
16th — Not formed		
17th (Burnley)	26.2.60	
18th — Not formed		
19th (Liverpool Lowland Scottish)	18.1.60	
20th — Not formed		
21st (Wigan)	31.1.60	
22nd (Liverpool Exchange)	27.3.60	To 1st, 1863
23rd (Ashton)	17.11.60	
24th (Rochdale)	24.2.60	
25th (Liverpool)	9.1.60	To 8th Lancs A.V.
26th (Haigh)	9.2.60	Disbanded 1864
27th (Bolton)	25.2.60	
28th (2nd Manchester)	21.2.60	To 33rd, 1864
29th (Lytham)	28.1.60	
30th — Not formed		
31st (Oldham)	1.2.60	
32nd (Liverpool)	28.1.60	To 5th, 1862
33rd (1st Ardwick)	28.1.60	
34th — Not formed		
35th — Not formed		
36th (Accrington)	7.2.60	To 7th, 1861
37th (Lonsdale)	28.2.60	
37th (b) 37th (c)		
38th (Liverpool)	20.1.60	To 1st, 1861/2
39th (Liverpool Welsh)	9.2.60	To 5th, 1862
40th (3rd Manchester)	29.2.60	Warehousemen and clerks
41st (Liverpool)	16.2.60	Disbanded 1864
42nd (Childwall Rifles)	3.2.60	Disbanded 1870
43rd (Fallowfield)	11.2.60	To 6th, 1861
44th (Langton)	2.3.60	To 11th, 1866
45th —	27.2.60	To 1st, 1862
46th (Swinton)	24.2.60	
47th (St. Helens)	29.2.60	
48th (Prescott)	15.3.60	To 47th, 1880
49th (Newton)	3.3.60	To 9th, 1863
50th — Not formed		
51st (Liverpool)	3.3.60	Disbanded 1865
52nd (Dalton-in-Furness)	7.3.60	To 37th, 1871
53rd (Cartmel)	7.3.60	
54th (Ormskirk)	15.3.60	
55th (Leigh)	3.3.60	
56th (Salford)	5.3.60	
57th (Tittington)	26.3.60	
58th — Not formed		
59th (Leyland)	29.2.60	
60th (Atherton)	6.3.60	
61st (Chorley)	6.3.60	To 11th, 1869
62nd (Clitheroe)	27.3.60	

63rd (Toxteth)	9.4.60	To 5th, 1861
64th (Liverpool Irish)	25.4.60	
65th (Rossall)	27.4.60	
66th (Liverpool Borough Guard)	27.4.60	To 1st, 1862
67th (Worsley)	7.5.60	
68th (Liverpool)	31.5.60	To 5th, 1862
69th (Liverpool)	31.5.60	To 1st, 1862
70th (Droylsden)	5.5.70	To 28th, 1862
71st (Liverpool Highlanders)	24.5.60	To 5th, 1862
72nd (Liverpool)	8.6.60	To 5th, 1862
73rd (Newton-le-Willows)	9.6.60	To 80th, 1864
74th (St. Annes)	2.7.60	To 1st, 1864
75th (Broughton and Kirby)	28.8.60	Disbanded 1863
76th (Farnworth)	3.7.60	
77th (Widnes)	1.10.60	To 47th, 1863
78th (4th Manchester)	2.11.60	To 33rd, 1862
79th (Liverpool)	16.2.61	To 5th, 1862
80th (Liverpool Press Guard)	8.1.61	
81st (Withnell)	20.2.61	Disbanded 1877
82nd (Hindley)	14.6.61	To 27th, 1877
83rd (Knowsley)	11.2.61	Disbanded 1872
84th (Padiham)	18.2.61	
85th — Not formed		
86th (Liverpool)	18.5.61	To 5th, 1862
87th (Nelson)	7.2.62	Disbanded 1865
88th (Haslingden)	6.4.63	
89th —		Struck off 1868
90th (Fleetwood)	3.6.68	
91st (Flixton)	14.8.72	

Leicestershire

1st (1st Leic. Town Rifles)	31.8.59
2nd (Duke of Rutland's Belvoir Rifles)	13.2.60
3rd (Melton Coy.)	2.3.60
4th (2nd Leic. Town)	20.7.60
5th (3rd Leic. Town)	3.3.60
6th (Loughborough)	7.7.60
7th (Lutterworth)	6.10.60
8th (Ashby de la Z.)	16.9.60
9th (Leic. Town)	1860
10th (Hinckley)	27.11.60

Lincolnshire

1st (Lincoln Rifles)	26.10.59
2nd (Lough Rifles)	21.11.59
3rd (Grantham)	28.2.60
4th (Boston)	9.2.60
5th (Stamford)	14.2.60
6th (Grimsby Rifles)	20.3.60
7th (Spilsby)	17.3.60

8th (Sleaford)	23.2.60	
9th (Horncastle)	22.3.60	
10th — Not formed		
11th (Alford)	23.2.60	
12th (Barton)	12.1.60	
13th (Spalding)	28.2.60	
14th (Swineshead)	6.3.60	Disbanded 1865
15th (Bourne)	23.4.60	Disbanded 1873
16th (South Holland)	20.3.60	Disbanded 1871
17th (Gosberton)	17.3.60	
18th (Billingbourne)	13.3.61	
19th (Gainsborough)	10.7.60	
20th (Market Raisen)	16.7.60	

Linlithgowshire
1st (Linlithgow)	19.3.60	
2nd (Bowness)	19.3.60	
3rd (Bathgate)	25.4.60	
4th (Bathgate)	9.8.62	Young's Chemical Works
5th (Uphall)	18.3.72	
6th (West Calder)	17.4.78	

City of London
1st (City of London Rifle Vol. Brigade Bn.)	14.12.59	
2nd (Printers)	16.5.60	Eyre and Spottiswoode/Harmsworth
3rd (Working mens)	26.4.61	
4th (Foresters)	1861	Disbanded 1865
5th (London Temperance)	1861	Disbanded 1861
5th (London Welsh)	1861	

Merioneth
1st (Penllyn)	11.11.59	Disbanded 1864
2nd (Cader Idris)	15.5.60	To 1st
3rd (Ardwdwy)	3.11.60	To 1st

Middlesex
1st (Victoria Rifle Club)	4.8.55	
2nd (South Middx.)	14.10.59	
3rd (Hampstead)	6.12.59	
4th (N. London)	15.10.59	
5th (N. London)	27.12.59	To 4th, 1859
6th (N. London)	27.12.59	To 4th, 1859
7th (N. London)	26.11.59	To 4th, 1859
8th (N. London)	26.11.59	To 4th, 1859
9th (Marylebone and West Middx.)	14.10.59	
10th (Marylebone)	14.10.59	Disbanded 1861
11th (St. George's)	14.10.59	
12th (Barnet Garibaldeans)	20.10.59	
13th (Hornsey)	10.12.59	

14th (Highgate)	2.11.59	
15th (London Scottish)	2.11.59	
16th (Hounslow)	6.1.60	
17th — Not formed		
18th (Harrow Rifles)	30.12.59	
19th (Workingmen's Coll.-Bloomsbury)	13.12.59	
20th (Railway Rifles)	13.12.59	
21st (Civil Service Rifles)	2.1.60	
22nd (Pimlico)	1.60	
23rd (Inns of Court)	3.2.60	
24th (Uxbridge)	14.2.60	
25th (St. Martin in the Fields)		To 22nd, 1860
26th (Customs and Excise)	9.2.60	
27th (Inland Revenue)	10.2.60	
28th (London Irish)	28.2.60	
29th (North Middx.)	28.2.60	
30th (Ealing)	29.2.60	
31st (Whitehall)	25.2.60	To 21st
32nd (Volunteer Guards)	14.2.60	To 11th. Disbanded
33rd (Tottenham and Edmonton)	16.2.60	
34th (Admiralty)	29.2.60	To 21st, 6/1860.
35th (Enfield)	29.2.60	To 41st, 26.4.61
36th (Paddington Rifles)	29.2.60	
37th (St. Giles and St. George)	19.6.60	
38th (United Artists Rifles)	25.5.60	
39th (Clerkenwell)	6.3.60	
40th (Central London Rangers)	30.4.60	
41st (Royal Small Arms Factory)	11.6.60	To 35th
42nd (St. Catherine's Docks)	19.6.60	To 26th, 1866
43rd (Hampton)	25.9.60	
44th (Staines)	7.12.60	
45th (Sunbury)		To 43rd
46th (London and Westminster)	16.4.61	
47th (Stanmore)		To 18th, 1866
48th (Havelock's, Temperance Vols.)	27.2.62	To 2nd London 1872
49th (Post Office Vols.)	2.3.68	
50th (Somerset House)	1.2.75	
50th (Bank of E. Metropolitan Rifles)		To 20th, 12/1860

Midlothian

1st (Midlothian)	6.12.59	
2nd (Dalkeith Rifles)	22.5.60	
3rd (Penicuik)	22.5.60	
4th (Corstorphine)	26.11.60	To 1st, 1863
5th (Musselburgh)	19.4.61	
6th (Cloanhead)	29.4.76	

Monmouth
1st (Chepstow)	9.9.59	
2nd (1st Pontypool)	8.12.59	
3rd (1st Newport)	3.3.60	
4th (Tredegar)	17.2.60	
5th (2nd Pontypool — Hanbury)	27.9.60	
6th (Monmouth)	29.2.60	
7th (Newport Borough)	1.3.60	
8th (Usk)	14.6.60	
9th (Abergavenny)	11.8.60	
10th (Risca)	19.11.60	Disbanded 1875
11th (Tredegar)	1876	

Montgomeryshire
1st (Newtown)	19.2.60	Disbanded 1873
2nd (Welshpool)	26.3.60	Disbanded 1876
3rd (2nd Welshpool)	14.5.60	Disbanded 1873
4th (Machnynlleth)	9.4.61	Disbanded 1876
5th (Llanidloes)	1861	Renumbered 4th, 1864

Nairn
1st —	14.4.60	Disbanded 1862

Newcastle
1st (Newcastle)	22.2.60	

Norfolk
1st (City of Norwich)	31.8.59	
2nd (Norwich)	2.9.59	To 1st, 1859
3rd (East Dereham)		
4th (Great Yarmouth)	5.9.59	Renumbered 2nd
5th (Kings Lynn)	5.9.59	
6th — Not formed		
7th (Aylsham)	7.8.60	Renumbered 6th Disbanded
8th (Harleston)	30.9.59	Renumbered 7th Disbanded
9th (Diss)	7.10.59	Renumbered 8th
10th (Loddon)	8.10.59	Renumbered 9th Disbanded
11th (Fakenham)	21.10.59	Renumbered 10th
12th (Holkham)	21.10.59	Renumbered 11th Disbanded
12th (Reepham)	3.5.60	
13th (Cromer)	16.4.60	
14th (Stalham)	18.4.60	
15th (East Dereham)	27.4.60	
16th (Swaffham)	9.8.60	
17th (Snettisham)	27.8.60	
18th (Blofield)	16.8.60	
19th (Holt)	1.3.61	
20th (Attleburgh)	6.10.60	
21st (Wymondham Vols.)	11.10.60	
22nd (Thetford)	13.12.60	
23rd (Downham Market)	8.8.61	
24th (North Walsham)	13.1.62	

Northamptonshire
1st (Althorp)	28.8.59
2nd (Towcester)	19.10.59
3rd (Overstone)	3.3.60
4th (Northampton)	15.2.60
5th (Northampton)	3.3.60
6th (Peterborough)	3.3.60
7th (Wellingborough)	20.9.60
8th (Daventry)	23.11.60
9th (Kettering)	22.4.67

Northumberland
1st (Northumberland Rifles)	16.8.59	Disbanded 1862
2nd (Hexham)	1.5.60	
3rd (Morpeth)	12.3.60	
4th (Glendale)	23.4.60	
5th (Alnwick)	27.3.60	
6th (Tynedale)	23.4.60	
7th (Allendale)	11.9.60	
8th (Walker on Tyne)	10.4.60	
9th (Crumlington)		Disbanded 1864
10th (Lowick)	7.1.64	
11th (Sandhoe)	25.4.68	
12th (Haltwhistle)	1878	

Nottinghamshire
1st (Robin Hood Rifles)	15.11.59
2nd (East Retford)	3.3.60
3rd (Newark)	3.3.60
4th (Mansfield or Sherwood Rifles)	9.3.60
5th (Forest)	9.3.60
6th (Collingham)	9.3.60
7th (Worksop)	28.4.60
8th (Southwell)	7.7.60

Orkney
1st (Orkney and Shetland/1st Zetland)	24.4.60

Oxfordshire
1st (Oxford University)	8.8.59
2nd (Oxford City Rifles)	1.5.60
3rd (Banbury)	13.2.60
4th (Henley)	24.12.60
5th (Woodstock and Witney)	26.5.60
6th (Deddington)	25.4.60
7th (Bicester)	12.5.60
8th (Thame)	27.11.60
9th (Woodstock)	26.5.60

Peebleshire

1st (Peebles)	31.8.60	
2nd (Broughton)	31.8.60	Disbanded 1873
3rd (Inverleithen)	31.8.60	
4th (Linton)	16.10.60	Disbanded 1862

Pembrokeshire

1st (Milford)	23.6.59	
2nd (Pembroke Dock)	26.9.60	Converted to Artill 6.5.64
3rd (Pembroke)	26.9.60	

Perthshire

1st (Perth Vols. 'Citizens')	13.12.59	
2nd (Perth 'Artisans')	13.12.59	To 1st, 1860
3rd (Breadalbane)	27.2.60	Highlanders
4th (Breadalbane)	1860	Highlanders
5th (Blairgowrie)	16.3.60	
6th (Dunblane)	24.9.60	
7th (Coupar Angus)	5.5.60	
8th (Crieff)	1860	
9th (Alyth)	26.5.60	
10th (Strath Tay)	19.3.60	Disbanded 1874 Highlanders
11th (Doune)	26.5.60	
12th (Callander)	26.5.60	Disbanded 1865
13th (St. Martins)		Highlanders
14th (Birnam)		Highlanders
15th (Auchterarder)	4.12.60	
16th (Stanley)	22.1.60	Disbanded 1863/4
17th (Bridge of Earn)	4.63	Disbanded 1863
18th (Perth)	8.5.63	Highlanders
19th (Crieff)	7.12.68	To 8th, 1878 Disbanded — Highlanders
20th (Atholl Highland)	27.5.69	
21st (Comrie)	7.75	Disbanded 1876

Radnor

1st (Presteigne)	8.3.60	
2nd (Knighton)	25.4.60	Disbanded 1868
3rd (New Radnor)	6.8.60	Disbanded 1874

Renfrew

1st (Greenock)	10.9.59
2nd (2nd Greenock)	20.9.59
3rd (Paisley)	22.9.59
4th (Pollockshaws)	22.9.59
5th (Port Glasgow)	15.11.59
6th (Paisley)	23.11.59
7th (1st Barrhead)	15.2.60
8th (Neilston)	6.3.60
9th (Johnstone)	6.2.60
10th (Highlanders)	3.2.60
11th (Highlanders)	3.2.60

12th (Greenock)	3.2.60	Disbanded 1860
13th (Greenock)	24.1.60	To 1st, 1860
14th (Paisley)	8.2.60	
15th (Kilbarchan)	20.1.60	
16th (Thornliebank)	15.2.60	
17th (Lochwinnoch)	20.1.60	
18th (Greenock)	6.2.60	To 1st, 1860
19th (Nitshill)	6.3.60	
20th (Renfrew)	1.3.60	
21st (2nd Barrhead)	12.3.60	
22nd (Gourock)	6.4.60	
23rd (Cathcart)	6.4.60	
24th (Paisley)	10.4.60	
25th (Thornliebank)	15.2.62	

Ross

1st (Ross Rifles)	15.2.60	
2nd (Eastern Ross)	15.2.60	
3rd (Avoch)	17.2.60	
4th (Knockbain)	22.3.60	
5th (Alness and Ullapool)	20.5.61	Disbanded 1864
6th (Celtic)	21.5.61	
7th (Evanton)	12.5.66	
8th (Brahan)	11.8.66	
9th (Gairloch)	23.2.67	

Roxburghshire

1st (Jedburgh)	15.9.59	
2nd (Kelso)	29.3.60	
3rd (Melrose)	15.7.60	
4th (Hawick — Upper Teviotdale)	11.6.60	
5th (Hawick)	15.1.61	Disbanded 1867

Selkirkshire

1st (Border Rifles or Gala Forest Rifles)	27.3.60	
2nd (Border Rifles or Ettrick Forest Rifles)	15.6.60	

Shropshire

1st (Shrewsbury)	14.12.59	
2nd (Market Drayton)	15.2.60	
3rd (Whitchurch)	13.2.60	
4th (Bridgnorth)	13.2.60	
5th (Condover)	5.3.60	
6th (Ironbridge)	13.2.60	
7th (Wellington)	27.2.60	
8th (Hodnet)	2.3.60	
9th (2nd Shrewsbury)	2.3.60	To 1st Salop Artill. Vols. 1860
10th (Ludlow)	2.3.60	
11th (Cleobury Mortimer)	4.5.60	
12th (Wem)	3.5.60	

13th (Ellesmere)	2.6.60	Disbanded 1879
14th (Shifnal)	21.4.60	
15th (Oswestry)	28.4.60	
16th (Munslow)	24.5.60	Not completed — disbanded 1860
17th (3rd Shrewsbury)	8.1.61	
18th (Newport)	17.1.62	

Somerset

1st (Bath)	20.10.59	
2nd (Bathwick)	21.10.59	
3rd (Taunton)	22.10.59	
4th (Burnham)	12.1.60	
5th (Bridgewater)	14.1.60	
6th (Weston-super-Mare)	11.2.60	
7th (Keynsham)	25.2.60	
8th (Wellington)	28.2.60	
9th (Williton)	22.2.60	
10th (Wells)	14.2.60	
11th (Stogursey)	21.2.60	Disbanded 1873
12th (Wiveliscombe)	29.2.60	
13th (Frome Vols.)	9.3.60	
14th (Avon Vols.)	5.3.60	
15th (Shepton Mallet)	24.3.60	
16th (Yeovil)	4.4.60	
17th (Lyncombe)	2.3.60	
18th (Walcot)	3.3.60	
19th (Glastonbury)	17.3.60	
20th (Crewkerne)	25.4.60	
21st (Langport)	12.4.60	
22nd (East Mendip)	10.9.60	
23rd (Wincanton)	30.6.60	
24th (Somerton)	20.7.60	Disbanded 1871
25th (Keinton)	14.1.61	
26th (Bristol and Exeter Railway)	5.2.61	
27th (Vale of Wington)	23.7.61	
28th (South Petherton)	1876	

Staffordshire

1st (Handsworth)	15.8.59	
2nd (Langton)	30.9.59	
3rd (1st Hanley)	27.9.59	
4th (Walsall)	4.11.59	
5th (Wolverhampton)	24.7.60	
6th (North Potteries)	28.12.59	
7th (1st Burton)	18.2.60	
8th (2nd Burton)	10.2.60	Bass Brewery
9th (Tunstall)	4.1.60	
10th (Stoke on Trent)	19.1.60	
11th (Tipton)	11.1.60	
12th (Bilston)	26.1.60	

13th (Kidsgrove)	26.2.60	
14th (Bloxwich)	10.12.59	
15th (Brierley)	1.8.60	
16th (Newcastle under Lyme)	24.2.60	
17th (Seisdon)	21.2.60	Disbanded 1874
18th (Kingswinford)	21.2.60	
19th (Tamworth)	21.2.60	
20th (West Bromwich)	1.8.60	
21st (Rugeley Rangers)	4.4.60	
22nd (Brownhills)	24.2.60	
23rd (2nd Wolverhampton)	1.3.60	
24th (Lichfield)	1.8.60	
25th (1st/2nd Stafford)	26.9.60	
26th (Willenhall)	27.2.60	To 5th, 1875
27th (Patshull)	1.8.60	
28th (Leek)	26.4.60	
29th (Sedgley)	9.4.60	
30th (Tettenhall)	11.7.60	
31st (Smethwick)	19.4.60	
32nd (3rd Wolverhampton)	1860	
33rd (Cannock)	14.7.60	
34th (Wednesbury)	18.5.60	
35th (Kinver)	3.7.60	Disbanded 1865
36th (2nd Hanley)	18.6.60	
37th (Cheadle)	30.8.60	Disbanded 1872
38th (Eccleshall)	17.9.60	Disbanded 1870
39th (3rd Burton)	27.9.60	
40th (Stone)	1.12.60	

Stirlingshire

1st (Stirling Rifles)	14.10.59	citizens
2nd (Stirling)	3.2.60	artisans
3rd (Falkirk)	27.3.60	
4th (Lennoxtown)	6.3.60	
5th (Balfron)	1.5.60	Disbanded 1879
6th (Denny)	11.4.60	
7th (Lennox Mill)	11.5.60	
8th (Strathblane)	25.5.60	Disbanded 1864
9th (Bannockburn)	21.5.60	
10th (Highland)	10.11.60	Disbanded 1864
11th (Highland)	6.12.60	
12th (Carron Company)	10.2.62	
13th (Kilsyth)	19.7.66	
14th (Clackmannon)	17.10.68	

Suffolk

1st (Suffolk Rifles)	11.10.59	
2nd (Framlingham)	20.7.60	
3rd (Woodbridge)	20.7.60	
4th (Bungay)	20.7.60	
5th (Wickham Market)	13.2.60	Disbanded 1876
6th (Stowmarket)	13.2.60	

7th (Blything Hundred)	28.2.60	
8th (Saxmundham)	29.2.60	
9th (Aldeburgh)	9.3.60	
10th (Eye Rifles — Bumpkin Corps)	26.5.60	
11th (Sudbury)	14.4.60	
12th (Bosmere)	1.6.60	
13th (Bury St. Edmunds)	30.7.60	
14th (Beccles)	1.5.60	
15th (Wrentham)	9.6.60	
16th (Hadleigh)	2.7.60	
17th (Lowestoft)	11.9.60	
18th (Wickham Brook)	22.10.60	Disbanded 1870
19th — Not formed		
20th (Newmarket)	7.7.61	Ex 9th Cambs.

Surrey

1st (South London Rifles)	14.6.59	
2nd (Croydon)	16.6.59	
3rd (Camberwell)	26.8.59	To 1st, 1860
4th (Brixton)	10.9.59	
5th (Reigate)	12.9.59	
6th (Esher)	29.10.59	
7th (Southwark)	30.11.59	
8th (Epsom)	21.12.59	
9th (Richmond)	24.12.59	
10th (Bermondsey)	7.2.60	
11th (Wimbledon)	11.2.60	
12th (Kingston)	16.2.60	
13th (Guildford)	18.2.60	
14th (Dorking)	9.9.59	Disbanded 1876
15th (Chertsey)	25.2.60	
16th (Egham)	2.3.60	Disbanded 1868
17th (Godstone)	23.12.60	
18th (Farnham)	6.3.60	
19th (Lambeth)	13.3.60	
20th (Norwood)	27.4.60	To 4th, 1863
21st (Battersea)	3.5.60	Disbanded 1866
22nd (Albury)	16.1.61	Disbanded 1875
23rd (Rotherhithe)	1.2.61	
24th (Havelocks Own)	9.3.61	Disbanded 1862
25th (Guildford)	31.1.62	Renumbered 24th
26th (Epsom)	1.3.62	Renumbered 25th
27th (Shaftesbury Park)	28.4.75	To 7th, 1880

Sussex

1st (Brighton)	4.4.60	
2nd (Cuckfield)	2.12.59	
3rd — Not formed		
4th (Lewes)	25.1.60	
5th (East Grinstead)	9.2.60	
6th (Petworth)	15.2.60	

7th (Horsham)	2.4.60	
8th (Storrington)	16.2.60	Disbanded 1873
9th (Arundel)	24.11.60	
10th (West Sussex)	26.4.60	
11th (Worthing)	10.3.60	
12th (Westbourne)	8.12.60	
13th (Hurstpierpoint)	14.3.60	
14th (Crawley)	14.3.60	Disbanded 1863
15th (Bognor)	9.4.60	Disbanded 1865
16th (Battle)	4.6.60	Disbanded
17th (Etchingham)	4.6.60	To 37th Kent
18th (Henfield)	14.6.60	
19th (Eastbourne)	6.10.60	Disbanded
20th (Billingshurst)	27.10.70	To Uckfield 1874 Disbanded 1875

Sutherland

1st (Golspie Rifles)	2.12.59	
2nd (Dornoch)	2.12.59	
3rd (Brora)	3.1.60	
4th (Duchess Harriet's Coy. Rogart Rifles)	1.61	
5th (Bonar Bridge)	6.8.68	

Tower Hamlets

1st (Tower Hamlets Rifle Vol. Brigade)	1860	
2nd (Hackney)	6.4.60	To 4th, 1868
3rd (Truman, Hanbury, Buxton)	4.5.60	Brewers
4th (Shoreditch)	14.6.60	To 6th, 1867
5th (Dalston)	8.8.60	Disbanded 1862
6th (N.E. London)	25.9.60	To 1st, 1873
7th (Mile End)	13.9.60	
8th (West India Docks)	7.11.60	To 26th Middx. 1860
9th (London Docks)	23.11.60	To 26th Middx. 1865
10th (Finsbury)	13.12.60	
11th (East Metropolitan)	1861	To 6th, Disbanded 1864
12th (Stoke Newington)	24.4.61	To 1st London

Warwickshire

1st (Birmingham Rifles)	20.10.59	
2nd (Coventry)	8.11.59	
3rd (Birmingham)		Ex 5th Disbanded 1860
3rd (Rugby)	14.5.60	Ex 4th
4th (Warwick)	13.2.60	Ex 5th
5th (Stratford)	9.2.60	Ex 7th
6th (Coventry)	15.6.60	Ex 8th To 2nd, 1862
7th (Coventry)	31.10.60	Ex 9th To 2nd, 1862
8th (Nuneaton)	1.12.60	Ex 10th
9th (Saltley)	20.6.61	Ex 11th
10th (Leamington)	13.2.60	

11th (Leamington)	3.4.62	
12th (Rugby)	7.68	To 3rd

Westmorland

1st (Lunesdale)	28.2.60	
2nd (Appleby)	1860	Revived 1878
3rd (Kendal)	28.2.60	
4th (Windermere)	1.5.60	
5th (Ambleside)	28.2.60	
6th (Grasmere Rifles)	16.5.60	

Wigtown

1st (Wigtown)	24.2.60	
2nd (Stranraer)	16.3.60	
3rd (Newton Stewart)	21.3.60	
4th (Whithorn)	11.4.60	Disbanded 1874
5th (Dunmore)	23.11.60	Disbanded 1866

Wiltshire

1st (Salisbury)	10.8.59	
2nd (Trowbridge)	16.2.60	
3rd (Malmesbury)	28.1.60	
4th (Chippenham)	16.5.60	
5th (Devizes)	3.3.60	
6th (Maiden Bradley)	2.4.60	Disbanded 1874
7th (Market Lavington)	2.3.60	
8th (Mere)	1.5.60	Disbanded 1875
9th (Bradford)	17.5.60	
10th (Warminster)	5.3.60	
11th (New Swindon)	31.3.60	
12th (Melksham)	1.3.60	
13th (Westbury)	12.3.60	
14th (Wootton Bassett)	18.6.60	
16th (Old Swindon)	17.7.60	Great Western Railway
17th (Marlborough)	27.7.60	
18th (Highworth)	24.11.60	

Worcestershire

1st (Worcs. Rifles)	4.5.59	
2nd (Tenbury)	18.11.59	
3rd (Kidderminster)	17.1.60	
4th (2nd Kidderminster)	24.1.60	
5th (Bewdley)	2.3.60	
6th (Halesowen)	8.6.60	
7th (Dudley)	2.3.60	
8th (Stourport)	2.3.60	
9th (Stourbridge)	2.3.60	
10th (Pershore)	28.9.60	
11th (Malvern Hill)	6.11.60	
12th (Evesham)	6.11.60	
13th (No. 1 Worc. City)	10.4.60	
14th (No. 2 Worc. City)	13.4.60	

15th (Ombersley)	13.4.60	Disbanded
16th (Oldbury)	13.4.60	
17th (Redditch)	4.5.60	
18th (Droitwich)	15.6.60	
19th (Upton-on-Severn)	6.11.60	
20th (Kidderminster)	16.11.60	
21st (Bromsgrove)	20.8.61	

Yorks — East Riding

1st (Hull Rifles)	24.11.59	
2nd (Hull)		To 1st, 1860
3rd (Howdenshire)	9.6.60	
4th (Hull)		To 1st, 1860
5th (Bridlington)	19.1.60	
6th (Beverley)	28.2.60	
7th (Hedon)		Ex 10th To 1st, 1860
		Disbanded 1860
8th (Driffield)	11.5.60	
9th (Market Weighton)	12.5.60	
10th (Hedon)	8.11.60	Disbanded 1860
10th (Hull)	1860	To 1st, 1860
11th (Hull)	1860	To 1st, 1860
11th (Pocklington)	6.8.68	

Yorks — North Riding

1st (North Riding of York Vols.)	18.2.60	
2nd (Swaledale)	18.2.60	Disbanded 1863
3rd (Havingham)	10.2.60	
4th (Leyburn)	29.2.60	
5th (Forcett)	27.2.60	Disbanded 1875
6th (Scarborough)	26.6.60	
7th (Teesdale Vols.)	29.2.60	Renumbered 21st Durham
8th (Bedale)	19.3.60	
9th (Stokesley)	6.3.60	
10th (Helmsley Rifles)	9.3.60	
11th (Masham)	17.3.60	Disbanded
12th (Wensleydale)	10.3.60	Disbanded 1875
13th (Thirsk)	27.3.60	Disbanded
14th (Catterick)	19.4.60	
15th (Richmond)	23.10.60	
16th (Pickering)	6.11.60	
17th (Stainton)	28.4.60	To 16th
18th (Skelton)	30.5.60	
19th (Northallerton)	21.9.60	
20th (Whitby)	3.2.63	
21st (Middlesbrough)	1877	

Yorks — West Riding

1st (West Riding Vols.)	9.9.59	
2nd (Hallamshire)	30.9.59	
3rd (Sheffield)	30.9.59	To 2nd, 1859

4th (Sheffield)	30.9.59	To 2nd, 1859
5th (Bradford)	28.9.59	
6th (Bradford)	27.9.59	To 5th, 1859
4th (Halifax)	13.10.59	Ex 7th/8th
5th (Wakefield)	13.8.60	Ex 9th
6th (York)		To 1st, Disbanded 1860
6th (Huddersfield)	24.2.60	Ex 10th
7th/8th to 4th Halifax		
11th (Leeds Rifles)	17.11.59	
12th (Skipton)	7.9.60	
13th/14th		To 17th, 1860
15th (North Craven Rifles)	17.11.59	
16th (Harrogate)	21.2.60	
17th (Claro Rifles)	27.2.60	
18th (Pontefract)	2.3.60	
19th (Rotherham)	29.2.60	
20th (Doncaster — Gt. North Railway)	5.2.60	
21st (Doncaster Burgesses)	5.2.60	
22nd (Leeds)	1860	To 11th, 5.60
23rd (Wharfedale)	21.2.60	
24th (Eccleshill)		Disbanded 1860
25th (Guiseley Township Corps)	5.3.60	
26th (Ingleton)	21.1.60	Disbanded 1874
27th (Ripon)	13.4.60	
28th (Goole)	2.5.60	
29th (Dewsbury)	3.5.60	
30th (Birstal)	1.9.60	Disbanded 1861
31st (Tadcaster)	1860	
32nd (Holmfirth)	2.6.60	
33rd (Wetherby)	1860	Struck off 1863
34th (Saddleworth)	10.9.60	
35th (Airedale)	20.10.60	
36th (Rotherham)	19.10.60	
37th (Barnsley)	21.11.60	
38th (Selby)	1.1.61	
39th (Bingley)	6.4.61	Disbanded 1875
40th (Wath-upon-Dearne)	3.63	
41st (Mirfield)	15.3.69	
42nd (Haworth)	19.5.75	
43rd (Batley)	16.10.67	
44th (Meltham)	29.8.68	Disbanded 1875
45th (Bingley)	7.6.76	

APPENDIX VIII — NOMINAL ROLL OF ARTILLERY VOLUNTEER CORPS

Honourable Artillery
Company   1537

Aberdeen
1st (Peterhead)   13.3.60
2nd (Peterhead)   3.60   Disbanded 1864
3rd (Aberdeen)   2.5.60 Artisans
4th (Town of Aberdeen)   14.4.60
5th (Fraserburgh)   15.2.60
6th (Aberdeen)   9.2.60 Blaikie Bros (Artisans)
7th (Aberdeen)   23.9.61

Anglesey
1st (Holyhead)   14.12.60 Disbanded 1873
2nd (Holyhead)   14.12.60 Disbanded 1868
3rd (Beaumaris)   14.12.60 Disbanded 1868

Argyllshire
1st (Easdale)   7.3.60
2nd (Tarbert)   12.4.60 Disbanded 1862
3rd (Oban)   2.3.60
4th (West Tarbert)   12.4.60 Disbanded 1874
5th (Ardgour)   16.1.60 Disbanded 1865
6th (Campbeltown)   11.2.61
7th (Islay)   3.7.61
8th (South Hall)   10.9.61
9th (Mull)   15.5.63
10th (Lochgilphead)   15.5.63
11th (Tarbert)   13.2.66
12th (Inveraray)   2.4.67 Furnace Quarries

Ayrshire
1st (Irvine)   9.11.59
2nd (Ayr)   31.1.60
3rd (Largs)   1.3.60
4th (Ardrossan)   3.3.60
5th (Kilmarnock)   12.7.60

Banffshire
1st (Macduff)   27.3.60
2nd (Banff)   5.4.60 Disbanded 1876
3rd (Banff)   5.4.60 To 2nd. Disbanded 1864
4th (Portsoy)   8.10.60
5th (Cullen)   18.1.60
3rd (Gardenstown)   13.11.75

Berwickshire
1st (Eyemouth)   6.4.60 To 1st City of Edinburgh
                                        A.V., 1864

2nd (Coldingham)	1861	To 1st, 1861

Berwick on Tweed
1st (Berwick)	2.60	

Bute
1st (Rothesay)	20.3.62	
2nd (Cumbrae)	5.10.67	

Caernarvonshire
1st (Caernarvon)	12.3.62	
2nd (Bangor)	7.3.67	

Caithness
1st (Wick)	6.3.60	
2nd (Thurso)	24.4.60	
3rd (Lybster)	30.9.61	Disbanded 1873
4th (Moy)	1.12.66	
5th (Castletown)	1.12.66	
6th (Thrumster)	4.5.67	Disbanded 1878

Cheshire
1st (Birkenhead)	30.12.59	The Canada Works
2nd (Earl of Chester's)	8.2.60	
3rd (Seacombe)	10.2.60	
4th (New Brighton)	15.2.60	
5th (Laird's Iron Works)	1.3.60	Disbanded 1869

Cinque Ports
1st A (Dover)	6.1.60	Renumbered 1st
1st B (Folkestone)	7.11.59	Renumbered 2nd
1st C (Ramsgate)	2.1.60	Renumbered 3rd
2nd (Sandwich)	13.2.60	Renumbered 4th
3rd (Deal and Walmer)	6.2.60	Renumbered 5th
4th (Hastings)	20.2.60	Renumbered 6th
5th (Hythe)	17.12.59	Renumbered 7th. Disbanded 1867
6th (Margate)	26.6.61	Renumbered 8th
7th (Ninfield and Pevensey)	3.66	Renumbered 9th
7th (St Leonards)	9.67	Renumbered 5th

Cornwall
1st (Padstow)	27.9.59	
2nd (Looe)	25.11.59	
3rd (Fowey)	17.10.59	
4th (Charlestown)	30.10.59	
5th (Par)	23.12.59	Consuls Mine
6th (Par Harbour)	4.2.60	Disbanded 1860
7th (Polruan)	27.2.60	
8th (Hayle Foundry)	2.4.60	
9th (West Fowey Consoles Mine)	2.4.60	Disbanded 1860

10th (St Buryan)	5.11.60	
11th (St Ives)	8.11.60	Disbanded 1878
12th (Marazion)		
13th (St Just)		

Cromarty
1st (Cromarty)	8.6.60	

Cumberland
1st (Whitehaven)	7.5.60	
2nd (Carlisle Artillery)	15.2.60	
3rd (Maryport)	28.4.60	
4th (Workington)	5.3.60	Disbanded
5th (Harrington)	11.5.60	Disbanded 1875

Devon
1st (United Woodbury and Topsham 'Royal')	18.8.59	
2nd (Sidmouth)	4.9.59	Disbanded 1873
3rd (Teignmouth)	15.11.59	
4th (Torquay)	15.2.60	
5th (Exeter)	8.2.60	
6th (Dartmouth)	25.1.60	
7th (Exmouth)	11.3.60	
8th (Topsham)	21.3.60	
9th (Paignton)	2.6.60	
10th (Salcombe)	7.7.60	
11th (Brixham)	20.7.60	
12th (Devonport Dockyard)	20.12.60	
13th (Keyham Steam Yard)	7.12.60	
14th (Ilfracombe)	1874	

Dorset
1st (Lyme Regis)	29.12.59	
2nd (Portland)	14.2.60	Disbanded 1861
3rd (Bridport)	8.2.60	Disbanded 1876
4th (Portland)	20.11.60	
5th (Charmouth)		Disbanded
6th (Swanage)		

Dumbartonshire
1st (Helensburgh)	9.2.60	
2nd (Rosneath)	5.3.60	Disbanded 1871
3rd (Dumbarton)	24.12.60	

Durham
1st (Sunderland)	14.3.60	To 1st Northumberland, 1864
2nd (Seaham)	14.3.60	
3rd (South Shields)	14.3.60	
4th (Hartlepool)	14.3.60	To 19th Durham R.V.C., 1872

City of Edinburgh
  1st (City of Edinburgh)   4.11.59

Elgin
  1st (Lossiemouth)   16.3.60
  2nd (Frockholm)   Disbanded 6.60
  3rd (Burghead)   16.10.72

Essex
  1st (Harwich)   11.59   To 1st Norfolk, 1860
  2nd (Grays)   18.2.60 Renumbered 1st, 1860
  3rd (Barking)   13.9.60 Renumbered 2nd, 1860
  3rd (Stratford)   26.6.61

Fife
  1st (Tayport)   26.1.60
  2nd (Newport)   13.4.60
  3rd (St Andrews)   6.3.60
  4th (Inverkeithing)   3.3.60
  5th (Kirkcaldy)   22.3.60
  6th (Burntisland)   20.2.60
  7th (Anstruther)   8.3.60
  8th (Leven)   21.7.60
  9th (Dysart)   19.9.60
  10th (Wemyss)   16.1.62
  11th (Kinghorn)   30.4.63

Forfarshire
  1st (Arbroath)   31.10.59
  2nd (Montrose)   31.10.59
  3rd (Broughty Ferry)   5.12.59
  4th (Broughty Ferry)   5.12.59 To 3rd, 1862
  5th (Dundee)   16.1.60 Renumbered 4th, 1862
  6th (Dundee)   24.4.60 To 4th, 1862
  7th (Dundee)   30.4.60 To 4th, 1862

Glamorgan
  1st (Swansea)   10.12.59
  2nd (Briton Ferry)   2.6.60
  3rd (Cardiff)   13.6.60 Artisans
  4th (Cardiff)   13.6.60 To 3rd, 1861. Struck off,
                                         1864.

Gloucestershire
  1st (Bristol)   21.12.59
  2nd (Newnham)   1.3.60
  3rd (Gloucester)   26.7.60
  4th (Forest of Dean)   1861

Haddingtonshire
  1st (Dunbar)   18.1.60
  2nd (North Berwick)   3.60 Disbanded 7.60

Hampshire
1st (Southampton)	25.4.60	
2nd (Southsea)	5.60	Disbanded 1860
3rd (Portsmouth Dockyard)	9.5.60	Renumbered 2nd, 1860
4th (Bournemouth)		
5th (Dockyard)	18.8.60	Disbanded

Inverness
1st (Inverness)	4.2.60	
2nd (Inverness)	6.60	To 1st, 1860

Isle of Man
1st (Douglas)	15.2.61	Disbanded 1875
2nd (Laxey)	29.6.64	Disbanded 1872

Kent
1st (Gravesend)	20.10.59	
2nd (Faversham)	15.11.59	
3rd (Folkestone)	7.11.59	Renumbered 1st Cinque Ports, 1860
4th (Sheerness Dockyard)	9.1.60	To 18th Kent R.V.C., 1869
5th (Blackheath)	28.2.60	
6th (Greenwich)		
7th (Greenwich)		
8th —		
9th (Plumstead)	13.2.60	To 10th, 1873
10th (Woolwich Arsenal)	28.2.60	
11th (Sandgate)	25.2.60	
12th (Gillingham)	6.3.60	
13th (Sheerness Dockyard)	1.3.60	
14th (Royal Dockyard)	29.3.60	Disbanded 1870

Kincardineshire
1st (Stonehaven)	10.1.60	Disbanded 1880
2nd (Johnshaven)	14.8.60	
3rd (St Cyrus)	30.7.60	
4th (Bervie)	29.10.60	
5th (Cowie)	29.1.61	Disbanded 1875

Kirkcudbrightshire
1st (Kirkcudbright)	2.2.60	

Lanarkshire
1st (Glasgow)	30.12.59	
2nd (Glasgow)	30.12.59	
3rd (Glasgow)	30.12.59	
4th (1st Northern)	6.12.59	
5th (2nd Northern)	27.11.59	
6th (3rd Northern)	27.11.59	
7th (1st Eastern)	10.1.60	
8th (Glasgow)	10.1.60	Ironmongers
9th (2nd Eastern)	30.1.60	

10th (Calton Artisans)	16.2.60	
11th (Maryhill Artisans)	5.3.60	
12th (Western)	12.5.60	
13th (Hillhead)	24.7.60	
14th —	26.7.60	
15th (Partick)	2.11.60	
16th —	13.12.65	
17th —	1868	

Lancashire

1st (Liverpool)	16.11.59	
2nd (Crosby)	12.12.59	To 1st, 1860. Struck off, 1864
3rd (Kirkdale)	5.12.59	Disbanded 1860
4th (Liverpool)	5.12.59	'The 4th Brigade'
5th (Blackburn)	9.1.60	Disbanded 1869
6th (Windsor Iron Works)	20.12.59	To 1st, 1860
7th (Liverpool)	21.12.59	To 1st, 1860
8th (Liverpool)	9.1.60	
9th (Kirkdale)	19.2.60	Disbanded 1863
10th (Kirkham)	15.3.60	
11th (Cunard Company)	19.2.60	Disbanded 1867
12th (Liverpool)	19.2.60	To 9th, 1863
13th (Everton)	28.2.60	To 1st, 1860
14th (Liverpool)	28.2.60	To 1st, 1860
15th (Garston and Hale)	2.4.60	
16th — Not formed		
17th (Liverpool)	3.8.60	
18th (Bolton)	29.5.60	
19th (Manchester)	17.8.60	
20th (Liverpool)	8.8.60	To 6th, 1861
21st (Preston)	20.9.60	
22nd (Church)	23.10.60	To 5th, 1869
23rd (Chorley)	20.11.60	
24th (Lancaster)	1861	Struck off 1863
25th (Blackpool)	6.7.65	
26th (Southport)	28.10.71	
27th (Fleetwood)	3.6.68	Disbanded 1875

Lincolnshire

1st (Boston)	12.1.60	
2nd (Grimsby)	27.1.60	
3rd (Louth)	12.11.60	

City of London

1st (London Artillery Brigade)	15.4.63	

Middlesex

1st (Hanover Square)	16.7.60	Disbanded 1873
2nd (The Customs)	26.4.61	To 26th Middx R.V.C.
3rd (Metropolitan Artillery Volunteers)	9.10.61	'Truro's Tigers'

4th (The Authors)	4.12.65	'The Authors' Volunteer Horse Artillery. To 3rd 1870. Disbanded

Midlothian
1st (Midlothian Coast Artillery)	16.9.59
2nd (Leith Artillery)	28.2.60
3rd (Portobello)	17.12.59
4th (Musselburgh)	28.2.60

Monmouthshire
1st (Newport)	4.10.60

Nairn
1st (Nairn)	10.4.60

Newcastle upon Tyne
1st (Newcastle)	2.6.60
2nd (Newcastle)	24.7.60

Norfolk
1st (Yarmouth)	29.5.59
2nd (Norwich)	1869

Northumberland
1st (Tynemouth)	2.8.59	To 2nd, 1860. Disbanded 1883
2nd (Tynemouth)	16.8.59	Renumbered 1st, 1860
3rd (The Percy Artillery)	22.3.60	Renumbered 2nd, 1860
4th (Newcastle)	23.11.60	To 1st, 1883

Orkney
1st (Kirkwall)	1.5.60	
2nd (Sanday)	23.6.63	
3rd (Shapinsay)	10.7.63	
4th (Stromness)	23.6.63	
5th (Stronsay)	17.8.65	
6th (Holm)	28.11.66	
7th (Firth)	31.10.68	Disbanded 1877
8th (Evie)	25.6.70	
9th (Rousay)	13.12.74	
10th (Birsay)	2.3.78	

Pembrokeshire
1st (Tenby)	6.1.60	Disbanded 1871
2nd (Pembroke Dock)	6.5.64	

Renfrew
1st (Greenock)	30.1.60	
2nd (Greenock)	30.1.60	To 1st, 1864
3rd (Greenock)	30.1.60	To 1st, 1864

Ross
1st (Stornoway)	16.2.60	
2nd (Lochcarron)	21.8.66	

Shropshire
1st (Shrewsbury)	23.7.60	Formerly 10th Shropshire R.V.C.

Somerset
1st (Clevedon)	18.6.60	
2nd (Weston-super-mare)	20.7.60	Disbanded 1864
3rd (Weston-super-mare)	1860	To 2nd, 1860

Staffordshire
1st (Etruria)	18.12.60	

Stirlingshire
1st (Grangemouth)	27.3.60	
2nd (Stirling)	30.5.60	

Suffolk
1st (Lowestoft)	10.7.60	
2nd (Walton)	15.10.60	Disbanded 1872
3rd (Aldeburgh)	9.3.60	
4th (Beccles)	14.7.68	

Surrey
1st —	12.10.60	Struck off 1864
2nd (Brixton)	10.11.60	Renumbered 1st, 1864

Sussex
1st (Brighton)	19.11.59	
2nd (Fairlight)	13.3.60	
3rd (Hailsham)	15.5.60	
4th (Shoreham)	23.12.60	

Sutherland
1st (Helmsdale)	26.4.60	
2nd (Golspie)	1862	

Tower Hamlets
1st (Poplar)	26.9.60	Disbanded 1873

Wigtown
1st (Stranraer)	20.2.60	
2nd (Portpatrick)	22.2.60	
3rd (Sandhead)	4.5.67	

Worcestershire
1st (Worcester)	6.6.65	

Yorkshire — East Riding

1st (Bridlington)	9.12.59	Disbanded
2nd (Filey)	9.2.60	
3rd (Hull)	28.3.60	Disbanded 1860
4th (Hull)	12.5.60	
5th (Hornsea)	17.3.65	Disbanded 1875
6th (Bridlington)	6.3.69	
7th (Flamborough)	28.6.69	
3rd (Hornsea)	1866	

Yorkshire — North Riding

1st (Grimsborough)	27.1.60
2nd (Whitby)	27.3.60
3rd (Scarborough)	20.5.61

Yorkshire — West Riding

1st (Leeds)	2.8.60	
2nd (Bradford)	10.10.60	
3rd (York)	9.2.61	
4th (Sheffield)	6.2.61	
5th (Bewling)	1.3.64	Formerly part of 2nd. To 2nd, 1874
6th (Heckmondwike)	24.5.67	Formerly part of 2nd. To 2nd, 1874
7th (Halifax)	19.5.71	
8th (Halifax)	19.5.71	
7th (Batley)	1867	Formerly part of 5th. Disbanded 1876

APPENDIX IX — NOMINAL ROLL OF ENGINEER VOLUNTEER CORPS

1st Aberdeen (Aberdeen)	22.4.78	
1st Cheshire (Birkenhead)	10.5.61	
1st Cumberland (Cockermouth)	17.9.62	Disbanded 1864
1st Denbigh (Wrexham)	15.2.62	Disbanded 1864
1st Devon (Torquay)	28.1.62	
1st Durham (Jarrow)	22.4.68	To 1st Northumberland, 1873
1st City of Edinburgh	30.3.60	Disbanded 1865
1st Essex (Heybridge)	24.12.61	Disbanded 1871
1st Flint (Buckley)	6.6.65	
1st Glamorgan (Dowlais)	31.12.61	Disbanded 1871
1st Gloucester (Gloucester)	28.1.61	
2nd Gloucester (Bristol)	11.4.61	Bristol and Eastern Railway Co
1st Hampshire (Southampton)	25.1.62	
1st Lanark (Glasgow)	11.2.60	
2nd Lanark (Glasgow)	16.5.60	To 1st, 1863
3rd Lanark (Glasgow)	28.4.62	To 1st, 1863
1st Lancashire (Liverpool)	1.10.60	
2nd Lancashire (Liverpool)	1.10.60	To 1st, 1875
3rd Lancashire (St. Helens)	29.12.60	Renumbered 2nd, 1876
1st City of London (Islington)	19.3.62	'Old Jewry'
1st Middlesex (South Kensington Museum)	6.1.60	
1st Newcastle	11.9.60	
1st Northumberland	11.11.67	
1st Somerset (Weston-super-mare)	5.9.68	
1st Surrey	6.4.62	Disbanded 1863
1st Tower Hamlets	20.6.61	Disbanded 1868
2nd Tower Hamlets (East London)	3.10.68	
1st West Riding (Sheffield)	8.11.60	Sheffield School of Art
2nd West Riding (Leeds)	21.5.61	
Engineer and Railway Volunteer Staff Corps (Westminster)	21.1.65	
Volunteer Medical Staff Corps (Charing Cross Hospital)	1877	

Note: The majority of surviving Engineer Volunteer units were incorporated into nine new Submarine Mining Engineer Corps in 1888.

APPENDIX X — NOMINAL ROLL OF LIGHT HORSE
AND MOUNTED RIFLE VOLUNTEER UNITS

1st Cambridge (Newmarket) M.R.V.   1860   Disbanded 1865

2nd Cambridge (Cambridge) M.R.V.   12.5.60   To 1st Hunts, 1863

1st Derbyshire (Derby) M.R.V.   22.6.60   Disbanded 1873

1st Devon (Broadclyst) M.R.V.   23.2.60   Disbanded 1877

2nd Devon (Exminster) M.R.V.   5.3.60   Disbanded 1861

3rd Devon (Upottery) M.R.V.   10.4.60   To 1st, 1872

4th Devon (Modbury) M.R.V.   20.4.60   Renumbered 3rd Devon L.H.V., 1865. Disbanded 1875

5th Devon (Berry) M.R.V.   24.5.60   Renumbered 1st Devon L.H.V., 1861. Disbanded 1875

6th Devon (South Molton) M.R.V.   12.7.60   Disbanded 1875

7th Devon (Yealmpton) M.R.V.   14.6.60   Renumbered 2nd Devon L.H.V., 1865. Disbanded 1874

1st Essex (Latchingdon) M.R.V.   11.1860   Disbanded 1862

1st Dumfries (Lockerbie) M.R.V.   25.11.74   Disbanded 1880

1st Elgin (Elgin) M.R.V.   3.7.68   Disbanded 1871

1st Fife (Cupar) L.H.V.   11.7.60   L.H., 1870. Fife and Forfar L.H.V., 1876. Fife and Forfar Imperial Yeomanry, 1901

2nd Fife (St Andrews) L.H.V.   11.7.60   To 1st

3rd Fife (Kirkcaldy) L.H.V.   11.7.60   To 1st

4th Fife (Dunfermline) L.H.V.   11.7.60   To 1st

1st Forfar (Dundee) L.H.V.   28.6.76   To 1st Fife, 1876

1st Glamorgan (Cardiff) L.H.V.   15.2.61   Disbanded 1873

1st Gloucester (Stroud) L.H.V.   19.5.60   Disbanded 1866

1st Hampshire (Droxford) M.R.V.   25.4.60   L.H.V., 1863. Disbanded 1878

2nd Hampshire (Southampton) M.R.V.   28.2.61   L.H.V., 1861. Disbanded 1865

1st Hertfordshire (Bishop's Stortford) L.H.V.   19.11.62   Disbanded 1879

1st Huntingdon (Kimbolton) M.R.V.   14.4.60   1st Hunts 'Duke of Manchester's Own' L.H.V., 1861. Disbanded 1879

2nd Huntingdon M.R.V.   13.8.60   Disbanded 1882

1st Lancashire (Manchester) M.R.V.   22.3.60   L.H.V., 1861. Disbanded 1873

2nd Lancashire (Liverpool) L.H.V.   11.7.61   Disbanded 1871

1st Lincolnshire (Spalding) L.H.V.	1860	'Earl of Yarborough's'. Disbanded 1887
2nd Lincolnshire L.H.V.	Not formed	
1st Middlesex (Regent Street) L.H.V.	18.1.61	Disbanded 1867
2nd Middlesex (St James' Place) L.H.V.	14.2.61	To 1st, 1861
1st Norfolk (Norwich) M.R.V.	25.3.61	L.H.V., 1862. Disbanded 1867
1st Northamptonshire (Overstone) M.R.V.	3.3.60	Disbanded 1869
1st Oxfordshire (Banbury) L.H.V.	12.1.64	Disbanded 1869
1st Roxburgh (St Boswells) M.R.V.	13.2.72	'Border Mounted Rifles', 1880. Disbanded 1892
1st Surrey (Clapham) M.R.V.	2.4.60	L.H.V., 1860. Disbanded 1868
1st Sussex (Brighton) L.H.V.	1.8.71	Disbanded 1875
1st Wiltshire (Maiden Bradley) M.R.V.	13.3.60	Attached to 6th Wilts R.V.C. Disbanded 1861

BIBLIOGRAPHY

UNPUBLISHED OFFICIAL PAPERS

Public Record Office

Cab 37	Cabinet Office, Photographic Copies of Cabinet Papers, 1880-1916.
Cab 38	Papers of the Committee of Imperial Defence, Photographic Copies, 1902-1914.
HO 45	Home Office Registered Files.
WO 32	War Office Registered Papers, General Series, 1855-1925.
WO 33	War Office Reports and Miscellaneous Papers, 1853-1911.
WO 70	Order Books of the 36th Middlesex (Paddington) R.V.C., 1860-1912.
WO 108	South African War Papers.
WO 163	Minutes of the War Office and Army Councils, 1870-1908.

UNPUBLISHED PRIVATE PAPERS

Public Record Office

WO 105	Roberts Papers.
WO 110	W.H. Smith Papers.
PRO 30/40	Ardagh Papers.
PRO 30/64	Sir Charles Napier Papers.
PRO 30/67	Midleton (St John Brodrick) Papers.

British Library

Add Mss 49700-2, 49718-26, 49831	A.J. Balfour Papers.
Add Mss 50303, 50312-3, 50335-53	H.O. Arnold-Forster Papers.
Add Mss 43893	Dilke Papers.
Add Mss 52776-8	Kitchener/Marker Papers.
Add Mss 48581-3	Palmerston Letter Books.
Add Mss 50835/6	Sydenham (Sir George Clarke) Papers.

National Army Museum
7101-23   Roberts Papers.

Christ Church, Oxford
Papers of the 3rd Marquess of Salisbury.

National Trust (Hughenden Manor)
Hughenden Papers.

Claydon House, Bucks.
Verney/Calvert Papers.

War Office Library
Wolseley Papers.
Minutes of the Manchester Tactical Society, 1888-1924.

East Sussex County Library (Hove)
Wolseley Papers.

Army Museums Ogilby Trust
Spenser Wilkinson Papers.
Jacques Steeple Mss.

UNPUBLISHED LOCAL COLLECTIONS

National Army Museum
6505-71   Miscellaneous City Imperial Volunteers Papers.
7203-13   Scrapbook of 1st Middlesex R.V.C., 1898-1900.
7302-7   Letters of Private E. Belcher, D Coy, C.I.V.

Guildhall Library
Mss 9386-9410   Regimental Archives of the London Rifle
                 Brigade.
Mss 10, 193-206 Regimental Archives of the City Imperial
                 Volunteers.

Post Office Record Office
R7   Regimental Records of the Post Office Rifles.

Bedfordshire Record Office
LCV 1-5   Lieutenancy Records.
CRT 190/141   Wade-Gery Papers.
X25/38   Booklet of 1st Duke of Manchester's Light
                 Horse, 1866.

X67/524-50   Papers of the Beds. Rifle Association.
X95/215-6   Papers of the 7th Earl Cowper.

Berkshire Record Office
D/EH Z/1-11   Papers of the 11th Berks. R.V.C., 1861-1903 and
              Berks. Rifle Association, 1865-1903.

Buckinghamshire Record Office
Box 14-15   Territorial Army Collection.
D/FR/135, 165, Fremantle Papers.
168-171, 177
D/RA Uncat.   Correspondence of 12th Duke of Somerset.
AR/41/62
Box 28   Carrington Mss.

Cornwall Record Office
22M/BO/34/28 Vyvyan Mss.

Cumbria Record Office
D/Cu/1/44-6   Curwen Family Papers.

Devon Record Office
1392 M/Box 18 Seymour of Berry Pomeroy Mss.
B 961/M/51   Kennaway Mss.
1148 M/18/4   Acland of Broadclyst Mss.
825 W/V 1-202 Papers of 1st Exeter and South Devon R.V.C.

Dorset Record Office
JC 1   Muster Roll, 5th Dorset R.V.C.
D264/1   Muster Roll, Dorchester R.V.C.

Dorset Military Museum
Assorted pamphlets.

Gillingham Local History Society Museum
Freame Mss.

Durham Record Office
D/Lo/F 494;   Londonderry Mss.
D/Lo/C 235;
D/Lo/F 509,
541

Essex Record Office
D/DOp F4;   Miscellaneous Papers.
D/DG g 14;
D/DV f 44
D/DTu (Acc   Papers of 1st Essex A.B.
4723)

Greater London Record Office (Middlesex)
L/C/40-99   Lieutenancy Papers.
Acc 534/1-12   Cruikshank Papers.
Acc 602   Papers of Middlesex Volunteer Development
             Fund, 1900-1906.

Gwent Record Office
LLCM+V   Lieutenancy Papers.
D.766.54   Minute Book of 8th Monmouth R.V.C.
Usk Gleaner and Monmouthshire Record, 1878.

Hampshire Record Office
L.L. 51-80   Lieutenancy Papers.

Kent Record Office
KAO U120 07   Muster Roll of 15th Kent R.V.C.
CPW/RP 1-5   Cinque Ports Mss.

Lewisham Public Libraries
A 58/6/1-10   Sydenham R.V.C. Papers.

Philip Haynes Esq., Hollingbourne
Papers relating to 1st Kent R.V.C.

Regimental Museum of Queen's Royal West Kent Regiment
Copies of the *Queen's Own Gazette*.

Lancashire Record Office
L.A. 10-11   Lieutenancy Papers.
L.C. 19   Papers of Counties Volunteer Development
             Association, 1900-1901.
L.N. 14, 22   Nominal rolls and annual returns.
Lancashire and Cheshire Volunteer, 1895-6.

Manchester Central Library
M53/1/4   Diary of Thomas Harrison Kirkham, 6th Lancs.
             R.V.C.

D/1/A/26   Muster Roll, 1st Manchester R.V.C., 1859-1860.
MS 356-14   Volunteer notes from the *Guardian*.
M25/5/5/6   Grand Military Bazaar programme, 1884.

Lincolnshire Record Office
Hill 12th Deposit 12/1, 1, 2, 3, 4.

Northamptonshire Record Office
Box X 319-320 Miscellaneous Volunteer Papers.
Box X 299   Muster Rolls.
Box X 4230-2   Daventry Volunteer Papers.
YZ 1228, 3512 Miscellaneous Printed Notices.
Eunson MSS

Northumberland Record Office
BMO/B 15-20   Papers of 3rd Northumberland R.V.C.

Oxfordshire Record Office
L/M I-XI   Lieutenancy Papers.

Bodleian Library
G.A. Oxon c 75 Papers of University Volunteers.
No 385; G.A.
Oxon c 281
(f56); G.A.
Oxon c 92;
G.A. Oxon c
121; G.A. Oxon
80 187

Somerset Record Office
DD/FS Box 60, Foster Mss.
77
DD/SAS/SY 2,   Papers of 3rd Somerset R.V.C.
9
DD/DN 386   Dickinson Family Papers.
DD/LW 25, 26 Lewis Papers.

Staffordshire Record Office
D79719   Muster Roll of Moorland R.V.C., 1859.
FAC 132   Muster Roll of 23rd Staffs. R.V.C., 1860.

Surrey Record Office
Acc 1011 Box 24   Mole, Metters and Forster Deposit.
Acc 257/14   Notice, 1860.

Guildford Muniment Room
122/4   Papers of 13th Surrey R.V.C.
The Keep (by permission of G.H. Underwood, Esq.).

Guildford Museum
LG 259   Notice, 1864.
LG 648, 649, 650   Papers of Dramatic Club of 13th Surrey R.V.C.

Surrey Archaeological Society
PF/GFD/87   Extract from *Surrey Gazette*, 1864.

West Sussex Record Office
Mss 81   Lavington Archives.
Mss 773   Petworth House.
Mss 324   Barttelot Papers.

Warwickshire Record Office
AC/CR 33   Muster Roll of Coventry Volunteers, 1859-63.

Wiltshire Record Office
W.R.O. 865/491 Troyte Bullock of Zeals House Collection.

Wiltshire Regimental Museum
File 216   Misc. papers including sermon to 2nd Wilts.
64/32-3   Order books of 1st Wilts. R.V.C., 1859-89.

1859 [2553 Sess 2] ix. l.
Report of the Royal Commission on the Militia of the United Kingdom.
1860 (441) VII.1.
Report of Select Committee on Military Organisation.
1860 [2682] xxiii. 431
Report of the Royal Commission on National Defences.
1860 (82) 1.633
Bill to prevent members of Benefit Societies from forfeiting their interest therein on being enrolled in the Yeomanry or Volunteers.
1860 (263) v 651
Bill for facilitating acquisition by Rifle Volunteer Corps of grounds for rifle practise.
1861 (67) 110 iv 611. 615
Bill to exempt Volunteers from tolls.
1862 (118) xxxii 833
Return of Address for copies of memorials received from Volunteer corps.
1862 [3053] XXVII 89
Report of Royal Commission on the condition of the Volunteer Force.
1862 (134) v 43
Bill to amend Rifle Volunteer Grounds Act of 1860.
1863 (108) v 327
The Volunteer Bill.
1867 (153) XLI 819
Memorandum on aid to the civil power.
1867 (184) XLI 813
Report of the Committee of Volunteer Officers.
1867 (364) XLI 821
Memorandum on aid to the civil power.
1868-9 (142) XXXVI 593
The memorial of Peers and M.P.'s to Cardwell.
1878 [c.2235] XV 181
Report of the Bury Departmental Committee.
1887 [c.4951] XVI 271
Report of the Volunteer Capitation Committee.
1890-1 (223) XVI 701
Report of the Select Committee on Rifle Ranges.
1892 (131) x. 555
Bill for jury exemption.
1893-4 (141) VIII. 531
Bill for exemption of efficient Volunteers from juries.

1894 (224) XV 631
Report of the Select Committee on Volunteer Acts.
1895 (281 Sess 1) VI 473
Bill to amend calling out of the Volunteer Force.
1900 (67)
Return of Lords and M.P.'s serving in South Africa.
1901 [Cd 610] L 175
Strength of Volunteer Service Companies and Drafts for South Africa from those embarked in 1900.
1902 (224) LVIII 705
Draft Efficiency Scheme as authorised by Order-in-Council of 4 November 1901.
1904 [Cd 2061] xxx 175
Report of the Royal Commission on the Militia and Volunteers.
1904 [Cd 2062] xxx 259
Minutes of Evidence of above, Vol. I.
1904 [Cd 2063] xxxi 1.
Minutes of Evidence, Vol. II.
1904 [Cd 2064] xxxi 587
Appendices of Royal Commission.
1905 [Cd 2437] XLVI 905
First circular of Arnold-Forster, June 1905.
1905 [Cd 2439] XLVI 909
Second circular, July 1905.
1906 (314) LXVII 561
Distribution of Volunteer Brigades and the services of Brigadiers.

UNPUBLISHED THESES

M. Allison, *The National Service Issue, 1899-1914* (Unpub. Ph. D., London 1975).

I.F.W. Beckett, *The English Rifle Volunteer Movement, 1859-1908* (Unpub. Ph.D. London 1974).

J. Gooch, *The Origin and Development of the British and Imperial General Staffs to 1916* (Unpub. Ph.D. London 1969).

H. Moon, *The Invasion of the United Kingdom: Public Controversy and Official Planning, 1888-1918* (Unpub. Ph.D., London 1968) 2 volumes.

A. Preston, *British Military Policy and the Defence of India: A Study of British Military Policy, Plans and Preparations during the Russian Crisis, 1875-1880* (Unpub. Ph.D., London 1966).

M.J. Salevouris, *Rifleman Form: The War Scare of 1859-60 in England* (Unpub. Ph.D. Minnesota 1971).

N. Summerton, *British Military Preparations for a War Against Germany* (Unpub. Ph.D., London 1969).

MEMOIRS AND BIOGRAPHIES

AMERY, Leo: *My Political Life: England before the Storm* (London 1953).

ARNOLD-FORSTER, Mary: *The Rt. Hon. H.O. Arnold-Forster: A Memoir by his Wife* (London 1910).

ASH, Bernard: *The Lost Dictator* (London 1968).

BARCLAY LLOYD, J.: *One Thousand Miles with the C.I.V.* (London 1901).

BARCLAY LLOYD, J. and CURTIS, Lionel: *The C.I.V. in South Africa* (London 1900).

BIDDULPH, Sir Ralph: *Lord Cardwell at the War Office* (London 1904).

BENSON, A.C. and ESHER, Viscount (ed.): *The Letters of Queen Victoria* (London 1907-8) 3 volumes.

BLAKE, Lord: *Disraeli* (London 1966).

BRETT, Maurice (ed.): *Journals and Letters of Reginald, Viscount Esher* (London 1934), 2 volumes.

BROOKFIELD, Arthur: *Annals of a Chequered Life* (London 1930).

BRUCE, H.A., M.P.: *The Life of General Sir William Napier* (London 1864) 2 volumes.

CALLWELL, C.E.: *Stray Recollections* (London 1923) 2 volumes.

CALLWELL, C.E.: *Field Marshal Sir Henry Wilson* (London 1927) 2 volumes.

CANTLIE, N. and SEAVER, G.: *Sir James Cantlie* (London 1939).

CHALONER, W.H. and HENDERSON, W.O. (ed.): *Engels as Military Critic* (Manchester 1959).

CHAMBERLAIN, Austen: *Down the Years* (London 1935).

CHAMBERLAIN, Austen: *Politics from Inside* (London 1936).

CHILDERS, Erskine: *In the Ranks of the C.I.V.* (London 1900).

CHILDERS, Lt.-Col. Spencer: *The Life and Correspondence of the Rt. Hon. H.C.E. Childers* (London 1901) 2 volumes.

CHILSTON, Viscount: *W.H. Smith* (London 1965).

CHILSTON, Viscount: *Chief Whip* (London 1961).

CHURCHILL, Randolph S.: *Winston S. Churchill* (London 1966) 2 volumes.

DALLING, Lord and ASHLEY, E.: *The Life of Henry John Temple, Viscount Palmerston* (London 1870-4) 5 volumes.

DOUGLAS, Sir G. and RAMSAY, Sir G.D.: *The Panmure Papers* (London 1908) 2 volumes.

331

FLEETWOOD WILSON, Sir Guy: *Letters to Somebody: A Retrospect* (London 1922).

FOWLER, J.K.: *Recollections of Old Country Life* (London 1894).

FRASER, Peter: *Lord Esher: A Political Biography* (London 1973).

FULLER, J.F.C.: *Memoirs of an Unconventional Soldier* (London 1936).

GARVIN, J.L.: *The Life of Joseph Chamberlain* (London 1932) 5 volumes.

GIBBON, F.P.: *Wm. A. Smith of the Boys' Brigades* (London and Glasgow 1934).

GOOCH, G.P.: *The Later Correspondence of Lord John Russell* (London 1925) 2 volumes.

GRENFELL, Field Marshal Lord: *Memoirs* (London 1925).

GRIFFITH-BOSCAWEN, A.S.T.: *Fourteen Years in Parliament* (London 1907).

GWYNN, S. and TUCKWELL, G.M.: *The Life of the Rt. Hon. Sir Charles Dilke* (London 1918) 2 volumes.

HALDANE, R.B.: *Before the War* (London 1920).

HALDANE, R.B.: *An Autobiography* (London 1929).

HAMILTON, Sir Ian: *Listening for the Drums* (London 1944).

HAMILTON, Ian: *The Happy Warrior: A Life of General Sir Ian Hamilton by his nephew* (London 1966).

HARRINGTON, General Sir Charles: *Plumer of Messines* (London 1935).

HIGGINSON, General Sir George: *Seventy One Years of a Guardsman's Life* (London 1916).

HOLLAND, Bernard: *The Life of the Duke of Devonshire* (London 1911) 2 volumes.

HUDSON, Derek: *Martin Tupper: His Rise and Fall* (London 1949).

HUXLEY, Gervas: *Victorian Duke: Hugh Lupus Grosvenor, 1st Duke of Westminster* (Oxford 1967).

JAMES, David: *The Life of Lord Roberts* (London 1954).

JEYES, S.H. and HOW, F.D.: *The Life of Sir Howard Vincent* (London 1912).

JOSLING, Harold: *The Autobiography of a Military Great Coat* (London 1907).

LAMONT, Colonel William: *Volunteer Memories* (Greenock 1911).

LYTTLETON, General Sir Neville: *Eighty Years Soldiering, Politics and Games* (London 1927).

MACDONALD, J.H.A.: *Fifty Years of It: The Experiences and Struggles of a Volunteer of 1859* (London and Edinburgh 1909).

MACKAIL, J.W. and WYNDHAM, G.: *Life and Letters of George Wyndham* (London n.d.) 2 volumes.

MACKINNON, Major General W.H.: *The Journal of the C.I.V. in South Africa* (London 1901).

MARTIN, Sir Theodore: *The Life of the Prince Consort* (London 1876-1880) 6 volumes.

MARTIN, Sir Theodore: *The Life of Lord Lyndhurst* (London 1883).

MAURICE, Lt. Col. F.: *Sir Frederick Maurice: A Record of His Work and Opinions* (London 1913).

MAURICE Major-General Sir F.: *Lord Haldane of Cloan* (London n.d.).

MAURICE, Major-General Sir F. and ARTHUR, Sir George: *The Life of Lord Wolseley* (London 1924).

MAXWELL, Sir H.: *The Life and Letters of 4th Earl of Clarendon* (London 1913) 2 volumes.

MAY, Colonel H.A.R.: *Memories of the Artists Rifles* (London 1929).

MELLY, George: *Recollections of Sixty Years* (Coventry 1893).

MIDLETON, The Earl of (Brodrick): *Records and Reactions, 1856-1939* (London 1939).

O'BRIEN, D.P.: *The Correspondence of Lord Overstone* (Cambridge 1971) 3 volumes.

PARKER, C.S.: *Sir Robert Peel* (London 1899).

PARKER, C.S.: *The Life and Letters of Sir James Graham* (London 1907).

PRESTON, A. (ed.): *The South African Diaries of Sir Garnet Wolseley, 1875* (Cape Town 1971).

PRESTON A. (ed.): *Sir Garnet Wolseley's South African Journal 1879-1880* (Cape Town 1973).

REPINGTON, Charles A.: *Vestigia: Reminiscences of Peace and War* (London 1919).

RHODES-JAMES, Robert: *Rosebery* (London 1963).

RIDLEY, J.: *Lord Palmerston* (London 1970).

ROBERTSON, Field Marshal Sir William: *From Private to Field Marshal* (London 1921).

SCOTT, G.H.G. and MCDONNELL, G.L.: *The Record of the Mounted Infantry of the C.I.V.* (London 1902).

SEELY, J.E.B.: *Adventure* (London 1930).

SHAND, A.I.: *The Life of General Sir Edward Bruce Hamley* (London and Edinburgh 1895), 2 volumes.

SPENDER, J.A.: *The Life of Sir Henry Campbell-Bannerman* (London 1923) 2 volumes.

SPIERS, E.M.: *Haldane: An Army Reformer* (Edinburgh 1980).

STANMORE, Lord: *Sidney Herbert: A Memoir* (London 1906) 2 volumes.

SYDENHAM, Colonel Lord (Sir George Clarke): *My Working Life* (London 1927).

TERRAINE, John: *Haig: The Educated Soldier* (London 1963).

TURNER, Sir Alfred: *Sixty Years of a Soldier's Life* (London 1912).

VANE, Sir Francis Fletcher: *Agin the Governments* (London 1928).

VERNER, Colonel Willoughby: *The Military Life of H.R.H. George Duke of Cambridge* (London 1905) 2 volumes.

VETCH, Colonel R.H.: *The Life of General Sir Andrew Clarke* (London 1905).

WALPOLE, Spencer: *The Life of Lord John Russell* (London 1889) 2 volumes.

WANTAGE, Lady: *Lord Wantage: A Memoir by his Wife* (London 1908).

WILKINSON, Henry Spenser: *Thirty-Five Years, 1874-1909* (London 1933).

WILSON, John: *The Life of Sir H. Campbell-Bannerman* (London 1973).

WOLF, L: *Life of 1st Marquis of Ripon* (London 1921) 2 volumes.

WOLSELEY, Field Marshal Viscount: *The Story of a Soldier's Life* (London 1903). 2 volumes.

WOOD, Field Marshal Sir Evelyn: *From Midshipman to Field Marshal* (London 1906) 2 volumes.

WROTTESLEY, Capt, the Hon. George: *The Military Opinions of General Sir John Fox Burgoyne Bt.* (London 1859).

WROTTESLEY, The Hon. G.: *The Life and Correspondence of Field Marshal Sir John Fox Burgoyne* (London 1873) 2 volumes.

YOUNG, Kenneth: *Arthur James Balfour* (London 1963).

CONTEMPORARY WORKS AND PAMPHLETS

ACLAND, T.D.: *Mounted Rifles* (London 1860).

ACLAND, T.D.: *Principles and Practise of Volunteer Discipline* (London 1868).

ACLAND, T.D.: *Volunteer Organisation* (London 1868).

ARNOLD-FORSTER, H.O.: *The Army in 1906* (London 1906).

BARRETT, Richard: *Reasons Against the Proposed Enrolment of the Militia* (London 1852).

BARRETT, Richard: *The Volunteer Movement* (London 1860).

BARRETT, Richard: *The Invasion Panic Once More* (London 1860).

BAXTER, R.D.: *The Volunteer Movement: Its Progress and Wants* (London 1860).

BEDFORD, Duke of: *The Destruction of the Militia* (London 1907).

BEDFORD, Duke of: *The Extinction of the Militia* (London 1908).

BLANCH, W.H.: *The Volunteers Book of Facts: An Annual Record* (London and Liverpool 1862).

BURRITT, Elihu: *Aggressive War* (London 1852).

BUSK, Hans: *The Rifle and How to Use It* (London 1853).

CHURCHILL, Winston S.: *Mr Brodrick's Army* (London 1903).

CLODE, C.M.: *Military Forces of the Crown* (London 1869) 2 volumes.

COBDEN, Richard: *The Three Panics* (London 1862).

CRUIKSHANK, George: *A Pop Gun fired off by George Cruikshank in defence of the British Volunteers of 1803* (London 1860).

ELCHO, Lord: *Letters on Military Organisation* (London 1871).

'F.G.': *The True History of the Origins of our Volunteer Army* (London 1867).

GOODENOUGH, W.H. and DALTON, J.C.: *The Army Book of the British Empire* (London 1893).

MACDOUGALL, Colonel Sir Duncan: *History of the Volunteer Movement: Its Promoters up to 16 April 1859* (London 1861).

NAPIER, Sir Charles: *A Letter on the Defence of England by Corps of Volunteers and Militia* (London 1852).

NEWTON, Sir Alfred, Bt. Lord Mayor — By Order of: *Reports on the Raising, Organising, Equipping and Dispatching of the C.I.V. to South Africa* (London June 1900).

PALLISER, Captain E. and NANGLE, Captain: *Volunteers in the Field* (London 1861).

PAYNE, J.B.: *Roots in support of Lt. Col. Richards' Claim of Chief Promoter of the Volunteer Movement of 1859* (London 1876).

PERRY, O.L.: *Rank and Badges of Her Majesty's Army and Navy and Auxiliary Forces* (London 1887).

PHIPPS, R.W.: *Our Sham Army* (Exeter 1868).

REPINGTON, Charles À. Court: *The Foundations of Reform* (London 1908).

'SENEX': *Are you prepared to resist Invasion?* (London 1859).

TUPPER, Martin: *Some Verses and Prose about National Rifle Clubs* (London 1859).

WILKINSON, Henry Spenser: *Citizen Soldiers* (London 1883).

WILKINSON, Henry Spenser: *Volunteers and the National Defence* (London 1896).

SECONDARY WORKS

Volunteer Histories

BERRY, Robert Potter: *A History of the Formation and Development of Volunteer Infantry* (London and Huddersfield 1903).

CUNNINGHAM, Hugh: *The Volunteer Force* (London 1975).

GRIERSON, Major-General Sir James: *Records of the Scottish Volunteer Force, 1859-1908* (London 1909).

MONTEFIORE, Cecil Sebag: *A History of the Volunteer Force: From Earliest Times to the Year 1860* (London 1908).

WALTER, James: *The Volunteer Force: History and Manual* (London 1881).

WOODBURNE, G.B.L.: *The Story of Our Volunteers* (London 1881).

Regimental Histories

For a full list of Volunteer regimental histories see A.S. White, *A Bibliography of Regimental Histories of the British Army* (S.A.H.R. 1965). However, the following were particularly useful:

STURMY CAVE, Colonel T.: *A History of the 1st V.B. Hampshire Regiment, 1859-1889* (London and Winchester 1905).

CHRISTIE-MILLER, John: *A Record of the Stockport Volunteers and their Armoury* (Stockport 1969).

FELL, Alfred: *A Furness Military Chronicle* (Ulverston 1937).

FISHER, W.G.: *The History of Somerset Yeomanry, Volunteer and Territorial Units* (Taunton 1924).

GAMM, T.H. : *The History of the 1st Warwick Bn. of Rifle Volunteers* (Birmingham 1876).

HART, C.J.: *The History of the 1st VB, The Royal Warwickshire Regiment* (Birmingham 1906).

HICKS, J.G.: *The Percy Artillery* (London 1899).

IGGLESDEN, C: *History of the East Kent Volunteers* (Ashford and London 1899).

KEESON, Major C.A.C.: *The History and Records of Queen Victoria's Rifles, 1792-1921* (London 1923).

KENRICK, N.C.E.: *The Wiltshire Regiment* (Aldershot 1963).

MERRICK, E.: *A History of the Civil Service Rifle Volunteers* (London 1891).

MORGAN, E.T.: *A Brief History of the Bristol Volunteers* (Bristol 1908).

NORFOLK, R.W.S.: *Militia, Yeomanry and Volunteer Forces of the East Riding, 1689-1908* (E. Yorks Local History Society 1965).

ORR, Captain James: *History of the 7th Lanark Rifle Volunteers* (Glasgow 1884).

SAINSBURY, J.D.: *Hertfordshire Soldiers* (Hitchin 1969).

SIMPSON, F.: *The Chester Volunteers* (Chester 1920).

TAMPLIN, J.M.A.: *The Surrey Rifle Volunteers* (Typescript 1959).

TAMPLIN, J.M.A.: *The Lambeth and Southwark Volunteers* (Regimental Historical Fund 1965).

General

ALDERMAN, G.: *The Railway Interest* (Leicester 1973).

ALLEN, E., CLARKE, J.F., McCORD, N. and ROWE, D.J.: *The North-East Engineers' Strikes of 1871* ((Newcastle 1971).

ANDERSON, G: *Victorian Clerks* (Manchester 1976).

ANDERSON, Olive: *A Liberal State at War* (Oxford 1967).

BARCLAY, G. St. J.: *The Empire is Marching* (London 1976).

BAYNES, John: *Morale* ((London 1967).

BAXTER, J.P.: *The Introduction of the Ironclad Warship* (Harvard 1933).

BECKETT, I.F.W. and GOOCH, J. (eds.): *Politicians and Defence* (Manchester 1981).

BEST, Geoffrey: *Mid Victorian Britain 1851-75* (London 1971).

BINNS, Lt.-Col. P.: *The Story of the Royal Tournament* (Aldershot 1952).

BOND, Brian (ed.): *Victorian Military Campaigns* (London 1967).

BOND, Brian: *The Victorian Army and the Staff College* (London 1972).

BOND, Brian and ROY, Ian (eds.): *War and Society: A Yearbook of Military History* (London 1976).

BOYNTON, L.: *The Elizabethan Militia, 1558-1638* (London 1967).

BRIGGS, A.: *Victorian People* (London 1954).

BROWN, K.D. (ed.): *Essays in Anti-Labour History* (London 1974).

BUTT, J. and CLARKE, I.F. (eds.): *The Victorians and Social Protest* (Newton Abbot 1973).

CLARKE, I.F.: *Voices Prophesying War, 1763-1984* (Oxford 1966).

CONACHER, J.B.: *The Peelites and the Party System* (Newton Abbot 1972).

COTTESLOE, Lord (T.F. Fremantle): *The Englishman and the Rifle* (London 1946).

COWLING, M.: *Disraeli, Gladstone and Revolution* (London 1967).

CUNLIFFE, Marcus: *Soldiers and Civilians: The Martial Spirit in America, 1775-1865* (London 1969).

DUNLOP, J.K.: *The Development of the British Army, 1899-1914* (London 1938).

EHRMAN, J.: *Cabinet Government and War* (Cambridge 1958).

ELDRIDGE, C.C.: *England's Mission* (London 1973).

ELLISON, M.: *Support for Secession: Lancashire and the U.S. Civil War* (Chicago 1972).

ERNLE, Lord: *English Farming Past and Present* (6th edition London 1961).

FOOT, M.R.D. (ed.): *War and Society* (London 1973).

GOOCH, John: *The Plans of War* (London 1974).

GRAY, R.Q.: *The Labour Aristocracy in Victorian Edinburgh* (Oxford 1976).

HAMER, W.S.: *The British Army: Civil Military Relations, 1885-1905* (Oxford 1970).

HARRIES JENKINS, G.: *The Army in Victorian Society* (London 1977).

HENDERSON, Col. G.F.R. and MALCOLM, Capt. N. (ed.): *The Science of War* (London 1908).

HENNOCK, E.P.: *Fit and Proper Persons* (London 1973).

HIRST, F.W.: *The Six Panics and Other Essays* (London 1913).

HORN, Pamela: *Labouring Life in the Victorian Countryside* (Dublin 1976).

HOWARD, Michael: *Studies in War and Peace* (London 1970).

HOWARD, Michael: *The Continental Commitment* (London 1972).

JOHNSON, F.A.: *Defence by Committee* (Oxford 1960).

JONES, Andrew: *The Politics of Reform 1884* (London 1972).

JONES, G.W.: *Borough Politics* (London 1969).

KING, C. Cooper: *The Story of the British Army* (London 1897).

KOSS, S.: *The Pro-Boers* (Chicago 1973).

LUVAAS, Jay: *The Education of an Army* (London 1965).

LUVAAS, Jay: *The Military Legacy of the Civil War: The European Inheritance* (Chicago 1959).

MATHER, H.C.G.: *The Liberal Imperialists* (Oxford 1973).

MONGER, G: *The End of Isolation* (London 1963).

MORRIS, A.J.A.: *Radicalism against War, 1906-14* (London 1972).

NOWELL-SMITH, S. (ed.): *Edwardian England* (Oxford 1964).

d'OMBRAIN, N.: *War Machinery and High Policy* (Oxford 1973).

ORMOND, J.S.: *Parliament and the Army, 1642-1904* (Cambridge 1933).

PELLING, Henry: *Social Geography of British Elections 1885-1910* (London 1967).

PERKIN, Harold: *The Origins of Modern English Society, 1780-1880* (London 1969).

PRICE, R.: *An Imperial War and the British Working Class* (London 1972).

QUINAULT, R. and STEVENSON, J. (eds.): *Popular Protest and Public Order* (London 1974).

READER, W.J.: *Professional Men: The Rise of Professional Classes in Nineteenth Century England* (London 1966).

REMPEL, R.A.: *Unionists Divided* (Newton Abbot 1972).

ROBSON, R. (ed.): *Ideas and Institutions of Victorian Britain* (London 1967).

SCHURMANN, D.M.: *The Education of a Navy* (London 1965).

SCOTT, J.D.: *Vickers: A History* (London 1962).

SIMON, B., and BRADLEY, I. (eds.): *The Victorian Public School* (London 1975).

SKELLEY, G. Ramsay: *The Victorian Army at Home* (London 1977).

SPRINGHALL, J.O.: *Youth, Empire and Society* (London 1977).

STACEY, C.P.: *Canada and the British Army, 1846-71* (London 1936).

STANLEY, G.F.G.: *Canada's Soldiers: The Military History of an Unmilitary People* (Toronto 1954).

TANSIG, W.J.: *Confederate Military Land Units* (London and New York 1967).

THOMAS, J.A.: *The House of Commons, 1832-1901* (Cardiff 1939).

THOMPSON, F.M.L.: *English Landed Society in the Nineteenth Century* (London 1963).

THORNTON, A.P.: *The Imperial Idea and its Enemies* (London 1959).

TYLER, J.E.: *The British Army and the Continent, 1904-1914* (London 1938).

VINCENT, J.R.: *The Formation of the British Liberal Party, 1857-1868* (London 1966).

VINCENT, J. and COOKE, A.B.: *The Governing Passion* (London 1974).

WARREN, J.G.H.: *A Century of Locomotive Building by Robert Stephenson and Co., 1823-1923* (London 1923).

WESTERN, J.R.: *The English Militia in the Eighteenth Century: The Story of a Political Issue, 1660-1802* (London 1965).

WILLIAMSON, S.: *The Politics of Grand Strategy* (Harvard 1969).

WILSON, H.W.: *With the Flag to Pretoria* (London 1900) 2 volumes.

WOOTTON, G.: *Pressure Groups in Britain, 1720-1970* (London 1975).

ZELDIN, T.: *The Political System of Napoleon III* (London 1958).

ARTICLES

Olive Anderson, 'The Growth of Christian Militarism in mid-Victorian Britain' *EHR* 86 no 338 (1971), p 46-72.

W.H.G. Armytage, 'The Railway Rates Question and the fall of the Third Gladstone Ministry' *EHR* LXV (1950), p 18-51.

W.O. Aydelotte, 'The House of Commons in the 1840's' *History* XXXIX (1954), p 249-62.

W.O. Aydelotte, 'The Conservative and Radical Interpretations of Early Victorian Social Legislation' *VS* XI (1967), p 225-36.

P.S. Bagwell, 'The Railway Interest: Its Organisation and Influence, 1839-1914' *J. Trans. Hist.* VII (1965-6), p 65-86.

Leslie Barlow, 'The History and Uniforms of the Mounted Rifle and Light Horse Volunteers', *Tradition* Nos. 52, 53, 54.

D.E.D. Beales, 'Parliamentary Parties and the Independent Member, 1810-60', in R. Robson (ed) *Ideas and Institutions of Victorian Britain* (London 1967), p 1-19.

I.F.W. Beckett, 'The 1st Bucks Volunteers, 1893', *Tradition* No. 58, p 24-27.

I.F.W. Beckett, 'The Problems of Military Discipline in the Volunteer Force, 1859-99' *JSAHR* LVI No. 226 (1978) p 66-78.

I.F,W. Beckett, 'The RUSI and the Volunteers' *JRUSI* 122 No. 1 (1977), p 58-63.

I.F.W. Beckett, 'The Amateur Military Tradition: New Tasks for the Locals Historian', *The Local Historian*, XIII, 8 (1979), p 475-481.

H. Berrington, 'Partisanship and Dissidence in the Nineteenth Century House of Commons' *Parliamentary Affairs* XXI (1967-8), p 338-74.

G. Best, 'Militarism and the Victorian Public School' in B. Simon and I. Bradley (eds.) *The Victorian Public School* (London 1975), p 129-146.

Brian Bond, 'The Effect of the Cardwell Reforms, 1874-1904', *JRUSI* CV (Nov. 1960), p 515-524.

Brian Bond, 'The Prelude to the Cardwell Reforms,' *JRUSI* CVI (May 1961), p 229-236.

Brian Bond, 'The Late Victorian Army', *History Today* (Sept. 1961) p 616-624.

Brian Bond, 'Recruiting the Victorian Army, 1870-1892', *Victorian Studies* V (1962), p 331-338.

Brian Bond, 'R.B. Haldane at the War Office, 1905-1912', *Army Quarterly* 86 (1963), p 33-43.

K.H. Bourne, 'British Preparations for a War with the North, 1861-2', *English Historical Review* LXXVI (1961), p 600-632.

G. Brennan, 'The Light Horse and Mounted Rifle Volunteer Corps', *JSAHR* XXI (Spring 1942) No. 81, p 3-16.

J.B. Collier, 'The Autumn Manoeuvres of 1872', *JSAHR*, L (1972) No. 204, p 221-236.

J. Cornford, 'The Transformation of Conservatism in the Late Nineteenth Century', *VS* VII (1963-4), p 36-8.

B.L. Crapster, 'A.B. Richards, 1820-1876: Journalist in Defence of Britain', *JSAHR* XLI (1963) No. 166, p 94-97.

Valerie Cromwell, 'The Losing of the Initiative by the House of Commons, 1780-1914' *TRHS* (1968), p 1-24.

G. Crossick, 'The Labour Aristocracy and Its Values: A Study of Mid-Victorian Kentish London' *VS* XX (1976), p 301-28.

Sir J.K. Dunlop, 'The Territorial Army: The Early Years', *Army Quarterly* (1967) April, p 153-159.

Lt.-Gen. Sir Gerald Ellison, 'From Here and There: Reminiscences', *Lancashire Lad*, in thirty parts from October 1931 to August 1939.

E.C. Ellis, 'The Dramatic Club of the Old 13th Surrey Volunteers', *The Keep* (Oct. 1915), p 6-7.

Frank Forde, 'The Liverpool Irish Volunteers', *The Irish Sword*, X (Winter 1971) No. 39, p 106-123.

P. Fraser, 'The Growth of Ministerial Control in Nineteenth Century House of Commons' *EHR* LXXV (1960), p 444-663.

Janet Fyfe, 'Scottish Volunteers with Garibaldi' *Scottish Historical Review*, 57 (1978) p 168-181.

S. Gilley, 'The Garibaldi Riots of 1862', *Historical Journal* (1973), p 697-732.

J. Gooch, 'The Creation of the British General Staff, 1904-1914', *JRUSI* (June 1971), p 50-53.

J. Gooch, 'Attitudes to War in Late Victorian and Edwardian England' in Brian Bond and Ian Roy (eds.), *War and Society: A Yearbook of Military History* (London 1976), p 88-102.

J. Gooch, 'Sir George Clarke's Career at the Committee of Imperial Defence, 1904-7' *HJ* XVIII, 3 (1975), p 555-69.

H.J. Hanham, 'Religion and Nationality in the Mid-Victorian Army' in M.R.D. Foot (ed.), *War and Society* (London 1973), p 159-181.

Capt. A.G. Harfield, 'The Great Volunteer Review at Salisbury, 29 May 1867', *JSAHR* (Autumn 1967), p 149-168.

Michael Howard, 'Lord Haldane and the Territorial Army' in M. Howard, *Studies in War and Peace* (London 1970), p 86-98.

C.J. Kauffman, 'Lord Elcho, Trade Unionism and Democracy' in K.D. Brown (ed.), *Essays in Anti-Labour History* (London 1974), p 183-207.

A.L. Lowell, 'The Influence of Party Upon Legislation in England and America', in *Annual Report of American Historical Assocation* (Washington 1902), I, p 319-542.

J.P Mackintosh, 'The Role of the CID before 1914', *English Historical Review*, LXXVII (1962), p 490-503.

A.J.A. Morris, 'Haldane's Army Reforms 1906-1908: The Deception of the Radicals', *History* (Feb. 1971), p 17-34.

H.J. Perkin, 'Land Reform and Class Conflict in Victorian Britain' in J. Butt and I.F. Clarke (eds.) *The Victorians and Social Protest* (Newton Abbot 1973), p 177-217.

A. Preston, 'British Military Thought, 1856-1890', *Army Quarterly* 89 (1965), p 57-74.

P.E. Razzell, 'Social Origins of Officers in the Indian and British Home Armies' *Brit. Journal of Sociology* XIV (1963), p 248-60.

Joanna Richardson, 'Tennyson: Most English of Englishmen', *History Today*, XXIII (1973), No. 11, p 776-784.

T. Ropp, 'Conscription in Great Britain, 1900-1914: A Failure in Civil Military Communication', *Military Affairs* (Summer 1956), p 71-76.

R.B. Rose 'Liverpool Volunteers of 1859' *Liverpool Bulletin*, VI (1954), p 47-66.

R.B. Rose, 'The Volunteers of 1859', *JSAHR* XXXVII (1959), p 97-110.

J.D. Sainsbury, 'The History of the 1st Herts. L.H.V.', *Herts. Countryside* 18, (1963), No. 69. p 12-13.

L.J. Satre, 'St. John Brodrick and Army Reform, 1901-3' *JBS* 15 (1976), No. 2 p. 117-139.

Maj.-Gen. E.K.G. Sixsmith, 'Reserve and Auxiliary Forces: Some Former Controversies', *Army Quarterly* (1966), p 71-77.

N. Soldon, 'Laissez Faire as Dogma: The Liberty and Property Defence League' in K.D. Brown (ed.) *Essays in Anti-Labour History* (London 1974), p 208-33.

Anne Summers, 'Militarism in Britain before the Great War' *History Workshop* 2 (1976), p 104-123.

A.V. Tucker, 'Army and Society in England, 1870-1900: A Reassessment of the Cardwell Reforms', *Journal of British Studies*, II (May 1963), p 110-141.

A.V. Tucker, 'The Issue of Army Reform in the Unionist Government, 1903-1905', *Historical Journal*, IX, I (1966), p. 90-100.

P.M. Williams, 'Public Opinion and the Railway Rates Question of 1886', *EHR* LXVII (1952), p 37-73.

PRINCIPAL NEWSPAPERS, MAGAZINES AND PERIODICALS CONSULTED

Army Debates
Dod's Parliamentary Companion
Hansard

Newspapers:
The Standard
The Times

Magazines:
The Pall Mall Gazette
Nineteenth Century
Punch

Military Periodicals:
The Army and Navy Gazette
The British Army and Navy Review
The Broad Arrow
Colborn's United Service Magazine
The Illustrated Naval and Military Magazine, 1884-1888
The Illustrated Naval and Military Magazine, New Series, 1889-1890
The Naval and Military Magazine, 1897-1899
The Royal Engineers Journal
The Journal of the Royal United Services Institution. Contains many valuable articles and accounts of debates.
The Queen's Own Gazette. Regimental Journal of the Royal West Kent Regiment.
The United Services Gazette

Volunteer Journals:
The Lancashire and Cheshire Volunteer, 1895-96, (Lancs. R.O.)
The London Scottish Regimental Gazette, 1896-1908. A useful source including the memoirs of Earl Wemyss. (London Scottish Regimental Library.)
The Volunteer Service Gazette, 1859-1908. An invaluable source of information on all aspects of the Volunteer Force including articles from other journals and newspapers and Volunteer debates in Parliament. (War Office Library.)

GENERAL INDEX

Bower, Major, 109
Bowles, H.F., 271
Boxall, Col. C.G., 212
Boy Scouts, 199
Boyle, Archibald, 33
Boys Brigades, 109, 110, 198, 199
Brackenbury, Maj. Gen. C.B., 179, 191
Brackenbury, Sir Henry, 183, 185, 186
Bradford, 70, 192
Brand, H.R., 156
Brassey, Thomas, 195
Brewster, Lt.-Col., 202
Bridges, Sir B.W., 93
Bridport, 15, 24, 33
Bright, John, 10, 31
Brighton reviews, 177; of 1861, 188; of 1862, 189; of 1863, 98; of 1865, 179; of 1871, 105, 179; of 1885, 201
Bristol, 19, 98
Britannia, 99
Brittania Works (Banbury), 58
Brittania Works (Bedford), 58
British Army Despatches, 14, 277
British Expeditionary Force (BEF), 248
Broad Arrow, 105, 211
Broadwood & Sons, Messrs, 45, 67
Brodrick, William St. John, 79, 137, 165, 166, 167, 222, 223, 224, 225, 226, 231, 236, 237, 239, 241, 251
Bromley-Davenport, W., 245
Brooke, Rajah James, 33
Brookfield, Arthur, 78n, 164, 165, 173, 271, 275
Brougham, Lord, 25
Browett, Frederick, 63
Brown, A.H., 161, 271
Brown, Captain, 148
Brunnell, Captain, 94
Brussels, 114
Buchanan, Robert, 61
Buck, Lt. Col., 171, 266
Buckingham, 79
Buckingham and Chandos, 3rd Duke of, 78, 145
Buckinghamshire, 27, 29, 51, 56, 72, 77, 114, 132, 133, 145, 174, 244

Buckinghamshire County Council, 218
Bucknill, Sir John, 16
Bull Run (1861), battle of, 178
Buller, Sir George, 179
Buller, Sir Redvers, 213
Bulwer, Col. E.K., 131
Burgess, William, 58
Burgoyne, Field Marshal Sir John Fox, 8, 9, 10, 11, 12, 18, 20, 173
Burlington House, 60
Burne-Jones, E.C., 60
Burnham, George, 56
Burnley, 149
Burns, John, 221
Burrell, Sir Percy, 269
Burritt, Elihu, 12
Bury, Viscount, 48, 94, 114, 132, 154, 156, 158, 161, 188, 195, 196, 269, 277
Bury Departmental Committee (1878), 75, 132, 133, 161, 180, 185, 190, 191, 193, 195
Bushby, Lt. Colonel, 195
Bushey Park, 97
Busk, Hans, 14, 16, 275
Butler, Lady, 116
Buxton, Charles, 154, 269
Buxton, Sir Thomas Fowell, 154, 156, 157, 269

Cabinet, The, 17, 21, 163, 197, 217, 233, 236, 237, 238, 245, 246
Cadet Corps, 109, 110
Callwell, Charles, 181
Cambridge, 59, 72
Cambridge, Duke of, 11, 12, 13, 17, 18, 21, 41, 97, 146, 155, 166, 173, 176, 177, 183, 184n, 185, 189
Cambridgeshire, 46, 72
Cameron, Maj. Gen. W., 182
Campaign of Fredericksburg, 182
Campbell-Bannerman, Henry, 136, 137, 162, 163, 166, 221, 243, 249
Camps, Volunteer, 113, 114, 196, 220, 222, 223, 224, 241, 245
Canada, 11, 14, 33, 76, 103, 104, 114, 177, 192, 195
Canada Building, 157
Canada Works, 74
Candlish, John, 62
Canterbury, 54, 201

Grant, Sir James Hope, 105, 177, 179

Graphic, The, 196

Graves, Samuel, 269

Gray, William, 269

Green, John, 52

'Green Book', 24, 176

Greenwich, 110

Greig, Lt. Col. J.W., 234, 251

Grenfell, Sir Francis, 136, 187, 193, 235, 268

Grey, Sir George, 15

Grey de Wilton, Viscount, 59

Grierson, Maj. Gen. Sir James, 2, 70

Griffith, C.D., 154

Grosvenor, Earl, 33, 45, 48, 49, 101, 144, 148, 154, 158, 276

Grosvenor Square, 60, 269

Grove, Maj. Gen. Sir Coleridge, 234

Grove, Mr Justice, 100

Guernsey, 11

Guest, Ivor, 231

Guildford review (1864), 98, 177

Gun Tax, 100

Haldane, Richard Burdon, 106, 143, 203, 231, 246-251

Half Holiday Movement, 101, 102, 147

Halford, Sir Henry, 114, 201, 276

Halsbury, Lord, 163

Hambleton, G.W., 195

Hamilton, Lord George, 271

Hamilton, Sir Ian, 181, 217

Hamley, Sir Edward Bruce, 161, 163, 164, 185, 276

Hampshire, 45, 53, 58, 70, 71

Hampton Wick, 97

Hanbury Tinplate Company, 62

Hanover Square, 60, 116

Hardinge, Lord, 74

Hardwicke, Lord, 46

Hardy, Gathorne, 132

Harman, C., 56

Harman, J., 56

Harris, Lord, 134

Harris Departmental Committee (1887), 100, 134, 135, 162

Harrison, Colonel, 181

Harrison, Gen. Sir Richard, 225

Hartington, Marquis of, 53, 134, 147, 194, 273

Hartlepool, West, 70

Hartley, Captain W.G., 265

Harvey, Robert Bateson, 145

Harvey, R.J., 25

Hastings, 78n

Hatherton, Lord, 25

Havelock-Allan, Sir Henry, 163

Haworth, Col., 224

Hay, Maj. General, 18

Hayle Foundry, 58

Haynes, William, 63

Hayter, Sir Arthur, 164, 195

Hayter, Lt. Colonel, 75

Head, Sir Francis, 9

Headcorn, 54

Helston, 52, 54

Hemptern Factory, 59

Henderson, G.F.R., 182, 199, 203

Henley, 55

Henniker-Major, Hon. J., 269

Herbert, Sidney, 12, 23, 24, 32, 42 45, 46, 125, 145, 146, 176, 197

Heston & Isleworth Urban District Council, 129

Heybridge, 58

Hibbert, Leicester, 30, 31

Hicks, Montague, 24, 33, 60

Higginson, Maj. Gen. Sir George, 182

High Wycombe, 29, 177, 179

Hill, Edward, 271

Hill, Octavia, 110

Hill & Co, Messrs T.G., 70

Hill 60, 253

Hobhouse, Charles, 243

Hockliffe, 99

Holborn, 219

Hollingworth, John. 63

Holt, J., 30

Home, Robert, 180, 199

Home Defence Committee (1858), 17, 18

Home Office, 97, 163

Honorary Colonels, 95, 152

Honorary Members, 24, 41, 49, 67

Honours and awards, 100, 134

Horse Guards, 126, 182, 188, 189

Horsley, Lieutenant, 192

Horsman, Mr, 25, 197

Hoste, George, 190

Howard, Frederick, 58

Howard, James, 58

361

and Haldane, 250-252
members of, 269-271
other interest groups, 272-274
Volunteer Journal for Lancashire and Cheshire, 33, 179
Volunteer Long Service Medal, 100, 137
Volunteer Prince Imperial Memorial Fund, 146
Volunteer Regulations, 2, 125
Volunteer Service Club, 194
Volunteer Service Companies, 211, 213, 214, 215, 216, 217, 219
Volunteer Service Gazette, 1, 2, 13, 14, 33, 49, 96, 97, 98, 102, 103, 104, 105, 106, 107, 109, 144, 147, 152, 155, 157, 158, 189, 192, 195, 200, 211, 219, 264, 266, 276
Volunteer Times, 33
Volunteer Training Ground and Rifle Range Company, 193
Volunteer Transport Committee (1891), 194 and (1896), 194
Volunteer Vote, 138, 152, 161, 273
Volunteers, Inspector General of, 127, 180
Volunteers,
origins of, 10-19
formation of, 19-24, 29-31
motivations of, 24-27, 107-112
opposition to formation, 27-29, 50, 51
growth of, 31-34, 59
urban, 48, 58-70
rural, 47, 50, 51, 52, 53-58
leadership of, 45, 46, 52, 53, 56, 61, 62, 63-67
ages of, 64, 67, 76, 77, 81, 82
military experience of, 64, 68, 174
change in original social composition of, 73-81
length of service of, 76, 77, 79, 81, 82
strength in proportion to population of, 84, 85
and local authorities, 97, 98
lack of respect for, 96, 97, 99
strength of, 103-107, 214, 242, 251
and growth of 'military spirit', 107, 197-199, 260

moral purpose of, 108, 109, 110, 199, 259
and social control, 109-112
and labour aristocracy, 110, 111
social harmony of, 111, 112
administration of, 125-138
and Cardwell reforms, 129-132, 151, 152, 174, 181, 182
liability for foreign service of, 135, 137, 163, 183, 184, 195, 196, 211-218, 220, 221
and domestic political issues, 144-147
and foreign policy issues, 114, 147
opinion of Regulars, 176, 181, 188, 189
on their own military role, 188, 195, 196
efforts to become efficient, 191-194
foreign views of, 197
performance of in South Africa, 211-216, 218
experiences of in South Africa, 216, 217
concessions to, 218-221

War Office hostility to after South Africa, 221-225
and Brodrick, 222-226, 231
and Arnold-Forster, 234-247
and Haldane, 247-253
poetry of, 263-267
See also Allowances, Artillery, Artisans, Bands, Capitation Grant, Clerks, Consolidation, Craftsmen, Cyclists, Drill, Discipline, Election of Officers, Elections, Aid to Civil Power, Enrolment Fees, Farmers, Finance, Fines, Honorary Members, Honours and awards, Inspections, Invasion, Jury exemption, Labourers, Landed Class, Metropolitan Commanding Officers, Middle Classes, Mounted Rifle Volunteers, Noncommissioned Officers, Officers, Professional Men, Public and Volunteers, Reform, Regular Army, Rifle shooting,

Index of Units (excluding Appendices VII to X). ★★

Royal Sussex Regt, 219
Royal Victoria Rifle Club, 14
Royal Welsh Fusiliers, 278
2nd VB Royal West Kent Regt, 194
3rd VB Royal West Kent Regt, 194
Scots Fusilier Guards, 148, 182, 277
1st Batt, Scots Guards, 201
2nd Batt, Scots Guards, 276
2nd Somerset AV, 175
3rd Somerset RVC, 56, 117, 175
7th Somerset RVC, 53
10th Somerset RVC, 54
13th Somerset RVC, 27, 49, 54, 56, 93
17th Somerset RVC, 175
18th Somerset RVC, 175
24th Somerset RVC, 53
2nd Batt, Somerset Light Infantry, 217
1st VB South Staffs, 200
2nd VB South Staffs, 109
37th Staffs RVC, 70, 82
1st Surrey LHV, 72, 116
1st Surrey RVC, 16, 60, 112, 117
5th Surrey RVC, 23, 54, 56, 82, 196
7th Surrey RVC, 109
13th Surrey RVC, 49, 96, 116, 117, 229, 265
18th Surrey RVC, 56, 82
19th Surrey RVC, 33, 69
24th Surrey RVC, 29, 45
1st Surrey RV, 224
1st Sussex AB, 75
3rd Sussex AV, 74, 178
7th Sussex RVC, 74

13th Sussex RVC, 53
1st Sussex RV, 201
Temple Rifle Club, 14
1st Tower Hamlets EV, 61
2nd Tower Hamlets RVC, 97
3rd Tower Hamlets RVC, 70
Volunteer Ambulance Department, 194
Volunteer Medical Association, 194
Volunteer Medical Staff Corps, 134, 135, 194, 213
Volunteer Reserve, 196, 224
Volunteer Transport and Commissariat Department, 194
1st Warwicks RVC, 59, 148
2nd Warwicks RVC, 63, 82
4th West Yorks AV, 224
6th West Yorks RGA, 246
6th West Yorks RVC, 2
8th West Yorks RVC, 195
10th West Yorks RVC, 70
11th West Yorks RVC, 151, 196
23rd West Yorks RVC, 70
1st Wilts RVC, 54
2nd Wilts RVC, 27, 48
6th Wilts RVC, 52, 95
8th Wilts RVC, 53
10th Wilts RVC, 53
1st Worcs AB, 74, 75
2nd Worcs AB, 75
1st Worcs AV, 145
'Workmen's Volunteer Brigade', 45
1st VB York and Lancaster Regt, 245

** AB=Administrative Battalion; AV=Artillery Volunteers; EV=Engineer Volunteers; LHV=Light Horse Volunteers; MRV=Mounted Rifle Volunteers; RV=Rifle Volunteers (A consolidated battalion); RVC=Rifle Volunteer Corps (prior to consolidation); TF=Territorial Force; VB=Volunteer Battalion (after territorialisation); RGAV=Royal Garrison Artillery Volunteers.